Automatic Religion

Automatic Religion

NEARHUMAN AGENTS OF
BRAZIL AND FRANCE

Paul Christopher Johnson

The University of Chicago Press   CHICAGO AND LONDON

The University of Chicago Press, Chicago 60637
The University of Chicago Press, Ltd., London
© 2021 by The University of Chicago
All rights reserved. No part of this book may be used or reproduced in any
manner whatsoever without written permission, except in the case of brief
quotations in critical articles and reviews. For more information, contact the
University of Chicago Press, 1427 E. 60th St., Chicago, IL 60637.
Published 2021

29 28 27 26 25 24 23 22 21 20   1 2 3 4 5

ISBN-13: 978-0-226-74969-3 (cloth)
ISBN-13: 978-0-226-74972-3 (paper)
ISBN-13: 978-0-226-74986-0 (e-book)
DOI: https://doi.org/10.7208/chicago/9780226749860.001.0001

Library of Congress Cataloging-in-Publication Data

Names: Johnson, Paul C. (Paul Christopher), 1964– author.
Title: Automatic religion : nearhuman agents of Brazil and France / Paul
   Christopher Johnson.
Description: Chicago : University of Chicago Press, 2020. | Includes
   bibliographical references and index.
Identifiers: LCCN 2020026470 | ISBN 9780226749693 (cloth) |
   ISBN 9780226749723 (paperback) | ISBN 9780226749860 (ebook)
Subjects: LCSH: Philosophical anthropology. | Human beings. | Agent
   (Philosophy) | Act (Philosophy) | Free will and determinism. | Religion—
   Philosophy. | Automatism. | Brazil—Religion—19th century—Case
   studies.
Classification: LCC BD450 .J57 2020 | DDC 128/.4—dc23
LC record available at https://lccn.loc.gov/2020026470y1

For Soren Wysockey-Johnson (2004–20), who shined so bright. We stay the watch.

Contents

Acknowledgments

Where do ideas come from? How are we inspired? This book, like all books, is a crossroads and a confluence, even sometimes a chorus. Let me mention a few of its voices.

Célia Anselme at the Núcleo de Memória do Instituto de Psiquiatria was extraordinarily helpful to me in reading nineteenth-century patient logs written in nearly illegible longhand. Thank you also to Daniele Ribeiro at the Centro de Documentação e Memória, Instituto Municipal Nise da Silveira, for direction and bibliographic tips. Ricardo Passos, director of the Museu do Negro and member of the Brotherhood of Our Lady of the Rosary, was a constant help and facilitator. The staff at the Museu Bispo do Rosário took the time to show me Bispo's undisplayed work and allowed me to sit in his now-overgrown cell. Thank you to Brigitte Laude for help with the Archives Charcot in Paris. Jean Hébrard pointed me to the psychiatric archives at the Fonds Lacassagne in Lyon. An earlier version of chapter 2 would never have been written without Sally Promey, who guided the working groups where parts of this book took shape. Stefania Capone also gave important advice on chapter 2 and has been a constant friend and colleague in both Paris and Rio de Janeiro. I am grateful to Winnifred Fallers Sullivan for feedback on earlier drafts of chapter 5 and to Courtney Bender, Kathryn Lofton, and Sarah Townsend, who each in different venues and at different junctures offered valuable input on chapter 4. Katerina Kerestetzi was generous and wise in helping me rework an earlier version of chapter 3. My students Roxana Maria-Aras and Richard Reinhardt also each gave careful feedback on chapter 3. Daniel Barbu beautifully translated a much earlier fragment of the introduction into French. Emily Floyd contributed a wonderful photograph that appears in the conclusion. Conversations with Webb Keane over mussels and martinis have sustained me over the years and helped launch some of the ideas presented here. Joseph Brown was meticulous and precise in his copyediting. The very resourceful Isabella Buzynski helped edit the notes and bring the bibliography into form. Two anonymous reviewers gave both encouragement and not a few challenges that made the work better. My editor, Priya Nelson, expertly steered this project along and gave key input on the manuscript as a whole.

Most important of all were three people who read the entire manuscript with care, each contributing in significant ways to the ultimate shape and argument of the book. John F. Collins pushed me to clarify the stakes. Matthew Hull and Henry Cowles each gave feedback on multiple drafts of every chapter. To quote the wit of my departed teacher and friend Martin Riesebrodt: "They are responsible for all of the errors and weaknesses in the work; the good insights came from me." You are heroes and pulled me from the wreckage too many times to count.

Books also depend on material support. I am grateful for help from the John Simon Guggenheim Fellowship, the Institute for the Humanities at the University of Michigan, and the Eisenberg Institute for Historical Studies at the University of Michigan.

All the chapters in this book have been presented in multiple venues, including the Graduate Institute, Geneva; the École des Hautes Études in Paris; the Society of Fellows at Columbia; the Eisenberg Historical Institute at the University of Michigan; the Department of Anthropology at the Universidade Federal da Bahia; the Center for the Study of Material and Visual Cultures of Religion at Yale; the Divinity School of the University of Chicago; the University of Virginia Centro de las Ámericas/Americas Center; the Center for Engaged Research and Collaborative Learning at Rice University; and the Doctoral Program in Anthropology and History at the University of Michigan. Those events were also part of the chorus that made this text. The difficult questions mattered.

An earlier and different version of chapter 2 appeared in *Sensational Religion: Sensory Cultures in Material Practice*, ed. Sally M. Promey (New Haven, CT: Yale University Press, 2014). An earlier and different version of chapter 3 appeared in the *Journal de la société des américanistes* 104, no. 1 (2018): 27–73. Cheers to those venues for allowing me to reuse parts of those earlier works.

Love to Anaïs Zubrzycki-Johnson for putting up with my arcane lectures, digressions, useless trivia, and only modestly funny jokes. And also just because. You always teach me new things and make me want to relearn what I thought I knew. Finally, thank you to Geneviève Zubrzycki for her very sound judgment and even better company and for reining me in whenever my arguments get too big for their empirical britches. You keep me honest.

Introduction
Religion-Like Situations

The best thing to do is to loosen my grip on my pen and let it go wandering about until it finds an entrance.

MACHADO DE ASSIS, "Those Cousins from Sapucaia!"
("Primas de Sapucaia"), 1883

Brazil's most famous outsider artist, Arthur Bispo do Rosário, spent fifty years in an asylum on the edge of Rio de Janeiro, diagnosed with schizophrenia. On the walls of his studio-cell as well as on objects therein, he created scores of works, many of them now displayed in museums. When, late in life, he gained public recognition, it caused him misgivings: "I'm not an artist. I'm directed by voices to create." He explained, "I hear a voice. . . . If it were up to me, I wouldn't do any of this." Further: "They say that what I make is art. They don't know anything. This is not art; this is my salvation on earth."[1] What he was doing, he felt, was less creating and more working automatically, recording everything he saw in a catalog presentable to God.

Not unlike Bispo do Rosário, the Swedish artist Hilma af Klint painted automatically in response to her spirit guides, a kind of visual dictation. Of her paintings she said: "I had no idea what they were supposed to depict. I worked swiftly and surely, without changing a single stroke."[2] When in 1908 Rudolf Steiner told her to forget her otherworldly masters and follow her own intuition, to rely only on her *individual self*, she lost the ability to paint for the next four years. His recommended self was elusive, vast, and overwhelming. It left her paralyzed, hemming the freedom that automaticity had provided. Only a more ambiguous agency, built on an automatic interface, could propel her work.[3]

Together, Bispo do Rosário's and af Klint's stories suggest how the capacity to craft and use agent ambiguity is part of our available human equipment. To be human is to be able to imagine and model non- and nearhumanness, to play at becoming or relying on an invisible other. At the same time, it is also to take up the project of lasting identity—to recognize and narrate an "I" from yesterday and to perform and project that same being toward tomorrow. The two skills—the craft of enacting scenes of agent ambiguity and the ability to perform a lasting self with a durable individual identity—stand in tension with one another, but they also pose a relation. Scenes and situations of moving *between* these modes are even constitutive of the events often gathered under the figure *religion*. Religion twists and jerks in a tug-of-war between *automatism* and *agency*. For that reason, those are the two terms that bookend this study. The introduction dwells on the automatic, the conclusion on agency. The intervening chapters are, along with their nearhuman protagonists, suspended betwixt and between.

Automatic artists like Bispo do Rosário and af Klint fascinate. They draw us in. Yet the fact that they resisted individual agency or discovered their own creative powers only in spirit-mediated kinds is also why they suffered. Bispo do Rosário was black, Afro-Brazilian, and a ward of the asylum. Hilma af Klint was an eccentric single woman who followed the directions of her spirits. That they found creative freedom only in the frame of the automatic is an issue worth pondering. Among other things, it indexes how, unlike agentive action, automatic was and is conceptualized in gendered and racialized ways. In fact, those judged incapable of rational agency—as automaton bodies possessed of motion but lacking genuine will—were mostly women and persons of color. Though they were seen as deficient, an exceptional few, like Bispo do Rosário and af Klint, found ways to create exactly in and through the terms of the automatic. They became heroes, even saints. This book considers a series of persons and nearhuman things coded as automatons without will who nevertheless became agents. Through their very automatism, they remade the terms of social life that surrounded them.

Consider: Two of the capacities most commonly taken to distinguish humanness from animal or machine life—religion and free will—are in significant ways opposed. Free will has long been figured in relation to qualities like spontaneity, authorship, and the conscious weighing of alternatives.[4] Religious acts mostly seem to contravene such classic formulations. In place of autonomous individuals, the religious are hybrid agents composed of selves and metahuman others.[5] To the Apostle Paul is attributed: "I live; yet not I, but Christ liveth in me" (Gal. 2:20 [AV]). The word *Islam* is commonly translated as *submission to the will of Allah*. An initiate into Afro-Brazilian Candomblé joins human destiny to that of a god (*orixá*) "seated" (*assentado*) in her head, the coauthor of all future action. Such hybrids of human and divine agency convey at once a limited and mediated individual will and the possibility of prosthetically extended selves equipped with metahuman reach. If agency is restricted in terms of individual volition, however, it may also be supercharged in scope and intensity: "Ye shall say unto this mountain, Remove hence to yonder place; and it shall remove; and nothing shall be impossible unto you" (Matt. 17:20 [AV]). In either case, religion is a regulator of agency and automaticity, working variously as brake, throttle, refinery, and mesh.

This book unwinds tensile bands linking agentive and automatic action in religion-like situations. It builds a perspective on religion-like scenes as the performance of suspended, deferred, or nonautonomous agency and as the craft of recoding human acts as automatic. Religion-like scenes and situations plot action between the spokes of agency and automatism, even as religious speech often decodes and declares who or what acts in any given agent-ambiguous event. Here, I reanimate the trope of the automaton to explore the uncertainty of human figures being acted through and the attraction to such figures. The idea is not just to see how automatons can take on unexpectedly humanish lives when animated. It is also—and this is the main point—to show how certain groups are made less than human, viewed as able to act only automatically but to act nevertheless in and through the terms of automatism. Diagnoses of free and automatic actors helped build a great anthropological divide. The book tells a story of humanish machines, but it is also—even especially—about humans condemned to the status of animals or machines—nearhumans—in their making and in their allure. I say *nearhuman* because the figures I describe share not only automatism but also the quality of being nearly but not quite human. The simultaneous proximity to and difference from real humans made them objects of ritual attraction, sites of revelation, and mediators of extraordinary power.

Automatic action is a constitutive part of the human practices grouped as religion because of the concealed agency it suggests. The prospect of human automaticity is, one might say, the discursive and phenomenological field on which religion is played. What kind of agency or doing is transpiring, acting in people, in a given situation? Religious events are explorations of the question of how individual wills are calibrated to extrahuman powers. Ritual events serve as laboratories of agency and automatism. They provide a venue and a language for seeing and speaking about agent ambiguity. They compose an experience of the human body being acted on or acted through by a transforming order. The craft of building situations and scenarios of agent ambiguity, of human bodies being enacted or acted through, requires learning and skill. Skillfully executed agent-ambiguous events cause something new to appear.[6] They produce a way of seeing in which human action is but one participant among or a spectator to other forces at work. From this vantage, religion is less a quest after agency as usually construed than a series of contexts and situations designed to be at least temporarily relieved of it. Paradoxically, that may make it the most radical kind of agency of all.[7] Radical because, not unlike science, it effaces the traces of human agency to create transcendental orders of nature that extend into domains beyond the initial act.[8] An encounter with a god in a human body changes the interpretation of the human in other sites, expanding outward to inflect arenas like death, healing, gender, diet, law, justice, and equality.

It is not only religions proper that generate attractions of agent ambiguity. Mostly such situations occur somewhere between religion and other parts of life, somewhere along a continuum. For that reason, instead of *religion* or *sacred*, I often use the phrase *religion-like situation*, adapted from Alfred Gell's *art-like situation*. Gell characterized art-like situations as involving a material index that permits an abduction of agency.[9] Art-like situations cause us to infer things about the person, animal, or thing depicted as well as to infer a humanish maker. We can think of religion-like situations as also motivating abduction—inference making—but about *near* and *meta*human agency and agents. They motivate inferences about agency because the agent taken to be acting is uncertain. The opacity or ambiguity about who or what is acting is even constitutive of the domain *religion*.

Religion-like situations present a recurring shape. They take on a familiar form and build, emphasizing divisions between inside and outside: soul and body; inner sanctum and public arena; closed compartment and unknown mechanisms; possessed body and the god within. Ritually used objects across multiple traditions share hidden inner compartments as a recurring feature: Catholic saints with doors, Indian gods with a flap opening to the heart, the Jewish Ark of the Covenant surrounded by curtains, a Sinhalese Buddha statue whose inner life is activated by the priest-artist, the third eye painted on the forehead that points to divine presence in the body, even the architecture of a Middle Ages church itself, which to be consecrated required the insertion of relics to activate the space. The forms are animated and gain in spiritual force via what Gell called, following Lucretius, the *duplication of skins*.[10] We can add more examples from the Atlantic world. An *inquice* (*nkisi*) sculpture of Angolan Candomblé in Brazil is animated by the unseen substances that reside within. A Haitian *wanga* is a bottle containing a spirit of the dead, bound tight. The Candomblé initiate in Brazil whose covered incision in her head hides but also publicizes her newborn hybrid agency, composed of her orixá and "herself."

The chapters of this book explore objects that exert a pull on their observers in part by virtue of a secret, unknown interior. They include a psychiatric patient's visions, a photograph that seems to have powers of its own, a drawing that becomes a saint, an automaton perched astride a closed cabinet with an obvious door, a spirit writer who describes his body as a mere shell, a mechanism and medium of the dead, and a drawing that somehow accrues and then carries the trace of a corpse displayed next to it. More than just having a secret interior, however, the shapes and structures deployed in religion-like situations announce and *advertise* a secret place inside. They feature or foreground the external door, lid, entrance, or passage that might or might not give access to a hidden wonder or horror. Our perception of these persons or things and their entrances and exits causes us to imagine an agent that occupies the visually suggested but hidden place. This is less a choice than simply how our minds work. Without evidence of other agency, we plot a humanish figure in the empty slot.

And it is not just that religion-like icons, altars, or buildings take this form but that taking this form renders anything and any place potentially religious. A human body becomes sacred when seen as possessed by a special agent. Objects, including self-conscious ones like our own bodies, morph into religion-like situations when the visible announcement of hidden chambers calls interior agents and the disjuncture between an external body and an inner agent to the mind of a perceiver.[11] In all these cases, what is shaped is a body within a body, an exterior that may or may not correspond to an interior character. The doubled form calls to mind the question of agency and the automatic; the attraction to and risk of being spoken through. That is, I suggest, a crucial religion-like trope: the figuration of unseen agency acting within an external body. What, then, are religion-like things like? Or, if you prefer, what sort of things lend themselves to religion-like situations and scenes? Objects that announce and even advertise doubleness through visible layers, obvious concealments, evident compartments, and passages to another, better place. Religious people are adept users of such doubled things, people who work to bring themselves into alignment and alliance with such things or who even recast themselves as or in the mold of doubled things.

I set this journey in the closing decades of the nineteenth century, when ideas and figures related to automatism (*automatic, automaton, automatism*) lurched into motion on multiple tracks and, not coincidentally, religion as a topic of study was born. The cluster joined previously separate domains, from questions of personal identity to machinery, and from psychiatry to animal behavior. Descriptions of slaves, psychiatric patients, animals, revival leaders, automata, and industrial laborers formed an assemblage that produced enduring social divisions between putatively automatic and free actors.[12] The former were depicted as lacking agency, yet they shared an uncanny attraction. Automatic bodies, or humans represented as automatons, generated not only pity or disdain, but also reverence, ecstasy, and vertigo. The fuzziness of their agency only fed their fame. The discussion in the following chapters is based on archival and ethnographic research in Brazil and France and includes encounters with a monkey, a psychiatric patient, a mechanical chess player, a drawing of a slave, a photograph of a possession priest, a corpse, and an automatic writer. Each is nearhuman in a distinct way, and each possesses a different vector of proximity: speech (sounds human), time (was once human or may be a future human), iconic likeness (looks human), synecdoche (has part of a human), and quality (is a captive or diminished human). What is at stake in this unlikely series of episodes is the question of the opaque quantity *agency* as constituted on the edges of humanness.

Brazil stars in these stories to show how distinct versions of automatism became linked and sedimented across the Atlantic in a particularly forceful way but one not yet adequately documented. These narratives present an Atlantic different from the usual Anglophone cast. This Atlantic is gauged between France and Brazil. Brazil was the nearest site of what Europeans and Euro-Americans too often, too naively, and too imperially saw as raw nature, a laboratory of the human.[13] Brazil offered a rare intensity of nearhuman encounters and comparisons. It was a site of convergences, a workshop of the human and of the automatic. There, psychiatric patients, spirit-possession priests, slaves, religious dissidents, crowds, checker-playing machines, and monkeys all were gathered under the moniker *automaton*. The discursive convergence sheds light on how ideas of automatic action crossed domains and had political consequences in ways completely unlike those in which these figures worked in Europe.

In Brazil, these categories were assembled under political duress, in a moment of radical change. The emancipation of slaves in 1888, the exile of the emperor to France in 1889, the birth of the republic in 1890—demanding a new constitution separating church and state and requiring for the first time a decision about what the term *religion* included and excluded—all these events transpired at the same time as the terms of psychiatry, religion, and the automatic were under construction. The nation saw an aggressive investment of technologies in order—in the then-fashionable terms of social Darwinism—to catch up with Europe and North America and the emergence of a school of psychiatry heavily influenced by the academies of Paris. Brazil was unusually receptive to European and especially French influence.

In Rio de Janeiro, Brazil's capital, the elites imagined themselves far more as spiritual descendants of Paris than of Lisbon. In the mid-nineteenth century, the poet Junqueira Freire wrote: "We are forced to follow some guiding principle, and let that principle be France. For she is the lighthouse that illuminates the entire civilized world."[14] Elites' bookshelves were lined with French classics and the travelogues of French observers of Brazil. Even a century later, as the North American anthropologist Ruth Landes recorded: "Brazilians said that their spiritual life was nourished only from France, and they were scornful, yet also admiring, of our mammoth automobile and film industries."[15] Yet Paris and Rio also rubbed each other wrong, not unlike the Parisians Inès and Estelle, antagonistic roommates of the Brazilian Joseph Garcín in Sartre's *No Exit* (1944). In the play, the trio embarks on an eternal war over the terms of their respective guilt, individual responsibility, and will.

Categories of automatism versus authentic will were created in Europe in relation to the Americas—both its peoples and its animals. In turn, those very categories and ways of parsing the world acquired new uses in the Americas. Brazil became a hothouse of vines in which previously separate shoots were spliced and rooted in new soil. The French ambassador to Brazil, Arthur de Gobineau, called its people *monkeys*; its slaves were called *automatons*; Afro-Brazilian spirit-possession priests were classed in the terms of French psychiatry's newly minted terms *dissociation* and *hysteria*. In fact, I first embarked on this historical tour by noticing how 1890s criminal psychiatrists in Brazil wrote about Afro-Brazilian patients and religions in terms directly imported from Paris: *dissociation, hysteria, dédoublement.* Raimundo Nina Rodrigues, writing in 1896, described Afro-Brazilian spirit possession as the "tam-tam da Salpêtrière," linking drumming to the class of hysteria drawn from the famed Paris asylum.[16] Nina Rodrigues could read Afro-Brazilian religious practices in Brazil only in the terms of French women's psychiatric diagnoses. That single transfer launched me on the journey that became this book. Why were Afro-Brazilian spirit-possession practices in Brazil being read through the prism of the Salpêtrière hospital in Paris? That question—and discovering how the two were linked as versions of automatism—motivated a dozen years of work in Brazil and France.

The issues this book sets out do not need to be set in Brazil, but they are usefully, even best set there. Brazil is an ideal exemplar and model for reasons of how the *animal*, the *human*, and the *nearhuman* were pulled into adjacency in compressed, intensive ways. In the chapters to come, I unpack how these terms became layered and tangled. I hope they inspire comparison with other visions of the divisions of humans, nonhumans, and nearhumans. To note two visions of the divisions with wide comparative potential, automatons and the automatic were both racialized and gendered. The role of gender in specific historical renderings of automatism is explored especially in chapters 1 and 3. Women were often drawn in the shape of automatons, from the Salpêtrière to the first psychiatric asylum in Latin America, the Hospício Pedro II in Rio, where female patients and, for that matter, nurses, alongside Afro-Brazilian "spiritists," were routinely described as lacking will and able to act only automatically. The intersections of gender and race in this story open out to a broader issue, namely, the historical *making* of agents and nonagents. Unlike categories like *nonhuman* or *metahuman*, which can have a static quality, *nearhuman* emphasizes the fluid historicity of the terms of agency. Agency and the automatic mark out shifting meters of power and classification. To oversimplify, automatism is attributed to some in order to expand the power of agents elsewhere. That is why eighteenth-century automatons included everything but white men, as Michael Taussig noted.[17] There are "negroes" in top hats, monkeys on drums, dancing Hottentots, defecating ducks, birds in cages, and women—lots of women. Occasionally, women were authors of their own automatons, but all too rarely: Even Mary Shelley's *Frankenstein* suffered the relentless tinkering of Mary's husband. We will meet Shelley's creature again in chapter 4.

Meanwhile, let us now turn to the three key terms that guide this work: *agency, automatic*, and *nearhuman*.

Ambiguous Agency

Agency once named a problem more than a solution. The agency problem in Hobbes, for example, expressed the misrecognition of natural causes for acts of "some Power, or Agent invisible."[18] Adam Smith named a different kind of gap—the lag between, on the one hand, the will of owners and, on the other hand, the managers enacting contracts on the ground—the agents. Owners knew little about how things work; agents had no skin in the game, no stakes in the company's success. That is the agency problem.[19] But, as the term emerged in twentieth-century social science, that notion of agency as a gap mostly disappeared, replaced by the idea of something one either has or does not have.[20] *Agency* came to denote the acts of an autonomous individual making choices within constraints.[21]

In the work of Judith Butler, for example, agency is the escape from sheer repetition or automatic mimesis: the "hiatus in iterability."[22] For Gayatri Spivak, it "relates to accountable reason . . . that one acts with responsibility, possibility of intention, freedom of subjectivity."[23] William H. Sewell described it as "the efficacy of human action" or, more precisely, "the capacity to transpose and extend schemas to new contexts . . . to be capable of exerting some degree of control over the social relations in which one is enmeshed" or, yet again, the capacity "for desiring, for forming intentions, and for acting creatively."[24] Across all these versions, agency was fitted out with terms like *capacity, control, transformation, intent,* and *freedom.* As such, it did important work in giving voice to those erased in earlier histories. But it also got heavy and encumbered. Walter Johnson accused it of smuggling a universal ideal of liberal selfhood. Talal Asad asked, Though it can be said that only agents make history, who says that everyone wants to make history? Bruno Latour, Constantin Fasolt, and Dipesh Chakrabarty each worry that historians' deployments of *agency* bracket out most things actual people in history see as acting: gods, spirits, and things.[25] And, in fact, people who want to critique the term *agency* often do so by bringing up religion.

One reason is that religious actors themselves are suspicious of direct links between subjectivity and agency. The self is hybrid, and agency is always mediated by gods and other actors. The religious often value disciplined submission or collective solidarity over individual agency. Simply enduring, maintaining a tradition, is also acting. In that sense, Saba Mahmood described how women in the 1990s Cairo Muslim piety movement did not want to be free in the standard terms of autonomy or Western feminism.[26] Religious acts often seem to contravene individual interests, giving the lie to any rational actor theory of the agent. That is why both Pierre Bourdieu and Judith Butler invoke suicide as a useful limit case of agency, with which the history of religions is flush.[27] Another reason is because religions often use notions of distributed agency in which things or special places are animated as transmitters or foci of power or even as themselves having soul. Religious differences can be seen as fundamentally differences in classifications of what is and is not an agent.[28]

To be sure, classic texts by Mauss, Foucault, and Weber argued—all in different ways—that religion—or at least Christian religion—was central in the production of the modern individual. Mostly, however, religious people complicate ideas of individual personhood. "What about the fact," asks Veena Das, "that in many cases [religious] techniques of the body are about our bodies being able to give expression to *other* bodies, such as bodies of animals?"[29] Or, we might add, the bodies of machines, or other humans. Ritual acts offer space to be acted on or through—or for hybrid kinds of authorship and will—rather than having to act as a lone, "buffered self."[30] Agency is, in that sense, thoroughly social. Here is Sewell again: "The transpositions of schemas and remobilizations of resources that constitute agency are always acts of communication with others. Agency entails an ability to coordinate one's actions with others and against others, to form collective projects, to persuade, to coerce, and to monitor the simultaneous effects of one's own and others' activities. Moreover, the extent of the agency exercised by individual persons depends profoundly on their positions in collective organizations."[31] This line of thinking calls to mind a trio in which agency is situated, one that restores the idea of the agency problem: not just agency versus structure but agency, collectives, and mediated action. Crafting situations for mediating nonagentive action and causing it to appear takes work. William James described the dialectic between voluntary effort and involuntary experience in 1902: "Mystical states may be facilitated by . . . voluntary operations, as by fixing the attention, or going through certain bodily performances."[32] He pointed to the tension between will and its abeyance, the work of "renounced agency,"[33] which turns the body into an instrument of other transmissions.

As Sewell mapped the issue, it is also social work. Religion entails, among other things, the communal craft of assembling scenes of agent ambiguity or, to take Lucy Suchman's phrase, "agency interfaces."[34] Religion recodes work performed by persons into work done "by itself" to activate a sensibility of automatism, of things being done to us from outside.[35] We can then also invert the statement. Agent ambiguity and the sensibility of automatism are productive of religious scenes and situations. Crafting scenes and scenarios of agent ambiguity—doing religion—discloses truth in the form of expanded repertoires of agents and capacities. It gives the lie to the great North Atlantic fiction of the freely acting autonomous individual. It cuts against the familiar Occidental grain and cast of the term *agency*, offering alternate modes of working in the world.

Agentive ambiguity is not only sought and made, however; it is also attributed, often by force. Some people get coded as or converted into agent-ambiguous nearhumans, clustered and classified in relation to the animal, the slave, the machine-man, the possessed, the automatic, the hysteric. Others are cast as history-making agents on the move. The stacking of categories of agency and automatism makes the terms dangerous and durable. Walter Benjamin called attention to this violence, the infilling of the human organism with the stuff of metal and machinery as the basic impulse of sadism, an issue that returns in chapter 3.[36] In social science terms of durability, attributions of agency and its lack produce "structures," long-lasting and consequential categories of the human. But take note. Agency and automatism seem opposed but are always shifting in relation to each other. Agency entails the selective activation of automatisms, even as automatism cites agency, the mechanical repetition of a once-agentive act. Then, too, agency and automatism never appear in pure form. For that reason, they are better configured as points on a continuum of action kinds in any event. We should think of agency and automatism as constituting a spectrum between tendencies or "attractor positions"[37] variously foregrounded or concealed in specific ritual scenes. Situations of agent ambiguity—religion-like situations—come into being through the performative tension and alternation between agency and automatism. The movement between agency and the automatic offers pleasure, intrigue, and truth, redoubled in the gaps between.

What is more, agency and automatism are not by necessity contrary forces, though they are in tension. One can, in theory, act in the world with causal effects or transforming power, as an agent, but without will or conscious intent.[38] For example, you might be startled by a strange face in a window and knock a hot cup of coffee off the table and onto a conversation partner, badly burning her knee.[39] You act as an agent, the direct cause of an injury to another, but without ill will. Or you might flick on the lights to find your glasses and in so doing scare off a raccoon or a burglar. That too is agency: changing the course of events and acting on others, but without intent, or at least not without intending what in fact occurred. We could say, then, that agency often involves conscious intent and choice, but not always or by necessity. *Religion* could even be defined as the human project of gaining agency exactly through relinquished or ambiguous will and intent. In this book, however, I approach agency and automatism as related frames for interpreting action. What is most important, for my purposes, is to say that religion is significantly *about* the distinctions between these frames, the making and narrating of them, and the experience of moving between them.[40]

Dizzying vistas open out from this line of ascent. What is gained in the suspension or deferral of agency in favor of being acted through, via automatic action? What is the attraction of the automatic? How is humanness differently made when viewed in relation to automatic agency rather than that of the autonomous individual? What did the comparative categories of automaton, automatism, and automatic actors do to fleshly humans when applied to them? Religion must be part of these inquiries, but mostly it has not been. This book places religion-like situations center stage. I present automatism as a distinctively religious form of agency, even a standard move in the repertory of religious practice. I think the study of religion will be advanced by analyzing a series of nearhuman figures related to but outside religion as usually construed. The path in this work leads to scenes and situations of agent ambiguity and automatic action, the ways they were linked together, the role of power in dividing agents from automatons, and the forms of fascination the supposed lack of agency inspired. I show how the terms *agency*, *nearhumanness*, and *the automatic* were jointed together as three legs of a wobbly stool, religion.

Automatic

In the late nineteenth century, will or conscious intent was defined in relation to automatic action. To be sure, today the term *automatic* is everywhere, part of the very air we breathe and how it moves. It is even too familiar. Automatic devices click on and off in every room. The humanish algorithms Siri and Alexa are hovering intimates, always ready at hand. If Shoshana Zuboff is right, in the present age of surveillance capitalism, automaticity is the new nature of individual, agentive expression; "anticipatory conformity" structures even our individual choices. We participate in social media and emit data in order to act in society, yet those avenues of action supposed to offer agency are prerouted through pulsing mass data algorithms, all calculated and commercially predicted.[41] Agency *is* automatic, from this algorithmic view. You are not as autonomous as you think. Mass data algorithms already know your next move and how to make it profitable. Lauren Berlant's phrase *lateral agency* describes the acts of sheer maintenance, survival, and "practical sovereignty" in this era of soul-killing dullness perpetrated in the name of the cutting edge.[42] In the digital world, the automatic has lost some of its brilliant strangeness. It seems too near. Still, our very humanness is defined in relation to it. We all imagine ourselves as choosing or selecting from possible courses of action in ways different from how Siri and Alexa calculate responses, and we treasure the difference. In this book, I show how the prospect of the automatic arrived so near as to raise alarm, working in turn toward the equally obsidian phrase *automatic religion*. I consider in turn the idea of the automaton, the automatic late nineteenth century, "around-the-world" travel narratives that indexed a privileged mobility compared with those trapped in place, and then, finally, automatic religion.

AUTOMATON

The most vivid image of automatic action is the automaton. The trope of the automaton as an entity performing action without will harks back to but departs from the first uses of *automaton*. The late nineteenth-century automaton was unlike earlier editions of automatons. What were those early models like? Aristotle's *Physics* announced "automaton" as consequential luck or chance that befalls humans with power but without intent. Automaton was the rock that fell on a man and altered the course of his life just when he passed in its way. Hobbes used the automaton or "Artificiall Man" as a descriptor of the state, with the sovereign as the automaton's artificial soul:

For seeing life is but a motion of limbs, the beginning whereof is in some principle part within, why may we not say, that all *Automata* (Engines that move themselves by springs and wheeles as doth a watch) have an artificiall life? For what is the *Heart* but a *Spring*; and the *Nerves*, but so many *Strings*; and the *Joynts*, but so many *Wheeles*, giving motion to the whole Body, such as was intended by the Artificer? *Art* goes yet further.... For by Art is created that great Leviathan called a COMMON-WEALTH, or STATE, (in latine, CIVITAS) which is but an Artificiall Man; though of greater stature and strength than the Naturall, for whose protection and defense it was intended; and in which the *Soveraignty* is an Artificiall *Soul*, as giving life and motion to the whole body.[43]

Hobbes pointed to the idea of the automaton as a (social) body directed or acted through by a separate, unseen agent, not unlike the soul, imagined as a body within a body, a kind of homunculus hunkered down at the levers of a human and directing its outward expressions and acts.

Descartes pushed the idea of automaton toward more familiar present-day uses. Automatons were human-like machines that presented an appearance of autonomy but might well lack it: "But what do I see apart from hats and coats, under which it may be the case that there are automatons hidden?"[44] Descartes described the prospect of machines that look human but also gestured toward the inverse, the person who resembles a machine—a self-acting organism that moves through the world without outside influence.[45] Spinoza, influenced by Descartes, described the "spiritual automaton" in related terms, as a mind that runs according to its own laws, a self-directed mechanism.[46] Pascal, among others, found this dubious and applied *automaton* to the force of custom on our habits. "We are as much automatic as intellectual," he wrote. "Custom is the source of our strongest and most believed proofs. It inclines the automaton."[47] No doubt he would not have been surprised by the events that allegedly befell Descartes, whose mechanical doll, Francine, served as his travel partner after the tragic death of his daughter of the same name. When the doll was discovered aboard the ship carrying Descartes to Queen Christina of Sweden in 1649, the captain saw it as nearhuman black magic. Because it was responsible for the deadly gale his ship was facing, he had it thrown into the sea.[48]

Aristotle emphasized the question of chance and nonhuman agency as it impinges on human life. Descartes, Spinoza, and Pascal were concerned with the question of individual will and sovereign personhood. Hobbes asked after the problem of individual will within a collective body, the state, governed by a sovereign, the soul of the body.[49] All, in various ways, associated will with the human and the problem of agency in relation to nonhuman and metahuman worlds. These were thoroughly religious matters, like the fear of diabolical sorcery possessing Descartes's doll.

Francine was not alone. Automaton nearhumans are a standard feature of religious worlds. Aristotle described how Daedalus caused a wooden Venus to move using quicksilver. South Asian tales recount Vishnu statues coming to life, not unlike the Greek story of Pygmalion.[50] Gershom Scholem analyzed the Jewish mystical tradition of the golem centered in Chem and Prague, a "motor soul" with strength greater than a human's but without speech or a "rational soul."[51] Indian kryta dolls—animated by sorcerers to cause the demise of those who embraced them—were similar to Hesiod's Pandora, who functioned as an automaton fabricated by Hephaestus and Athena to wreak havoc on mankind.[52] The tales remind that the manufacture of nearhumans was risky, possibly seditious, even diabolical. They point to the gods jealously guarding their unique office of bestowing movement or language. Even more, they point to the human fascination with nearhuman agents. Nearhuman machines astonished through their movement. Mechanically fabricated motile figures appear across traditions, from the hydraulic and musical automata in the Islamic world of the thirteenth century, as recorded in Al-Jazari's *The Book of Ingenious Devices*,[53] to the Chinese-manufactured automata that worked by using mercury reactions to drive movement. In the Christian West, the thirteenth-century theologian Albertus Magnus reported a bearded mannequin that could play the flute through a bellows mechanism, a form he tried to replicate.[54] One sixteenth-century legend depicts Albert's student, Thomas Aquinas, finding danger in his brass man, "an automaton endowed with the power of speech . . . which served him as an infallible oracle." Albert's android was destroyed by Saint Thomas because it seemed too demonic.[55]

Jessica Riskin explored the impressive divine and diabolical qualities communicated through automata ("inspirited statues") from the late fifteenth and early sixteenth centuries—mechanical devils, a mobile Jesus, ascending angels. She writes: "Early modern Europe, then, was alive with mechanical beings, and the Catholic Church was their main patron."[56] The sixteenth-century "monkbot" crafted by Juanelo Turriano walked, turned, fingered the rosary, and lifted it to his lips as his eyes lolled in a somber trance. The purpose seems to have been to admonish and inspire the emperor's son.[57] John Milton's "animal automatons" also acted with pedagogical purpose. In his depiction of the Garden of Eden, the animals are all automata whose presence allows the two humans to figure out how and whether they are different from the animal.[58] Then, too, the figures could announce the proximity of royal to divine power. Think of the hydraulic automata in the fountains of the kingdoms of Prester John and the Great Khan, described in *The Travels of Sir John Mandeville*, which helped instate sacred kingship and Mongol exceptionality at once.[59] Still another motivation was the desire to fashion the nearhuman and, in so doing, become godlike through the powers of creation. In his 1537 *De natura rerum*, Paracelsus famously recorded instructions for how to make a homunculus from scratch.[60] Cornelius Agrippa's recipe was similar; his homunculi, like Parcelsus's, possessed superhuman strength and the ability to divine secrets but also had no soul and were fit only to be slaves.[61]

To cut a very long story very short, the evidence for religion-like uses of fabricated nearhumans is compelling. The eighteenth- and nineteenth-century versions of automatons were, however, quite different. They were even, arguably, part of a secularization project in which the magical was disenchanted in order to be made into popular amusement and recreation. There was the Canard Digérateur of 1739, a defecating duck that earned its creator, Jacques de Vaucanson, an accusation of blasphemy, and the creamy piano-playing ingénue La Joyeuse de Tympanon, owned by Marie Antoinette and built by Peter Kintzing and David Roentgen in 1784. Most famous of all was Wolfgang von Kempelen's chess-playing Turk, who enjoyed multiple lives, including matches against Napoléon and several tours across the United States. The Turk's career began in 1770 and extended until 1850, well after Von Kempelen's death in 1804, and an even later model named Ajeeb was brought to Brazil and set to work in 1896, as we will see. Von Kempelen's machine-man generated both attraction and fear—often both at once. When one woman first approached the chess-playing man, she crossed herself and ran, fearing that the machine was possessed.[62] Her response serves as more than a casual anecdote. It points to ways quasi-religious responses to automatons carried over into the industrial age. Even in their popular, secular forms, nearhumans retained the ability to enchant in the smog of the city, even under the scrutiny of incipient social sciences being forged to decipher and explain the new boundaries of industrial human life.

Even more, by the late nineteenth century, *the automatic*—both the phrase and the experience—infiltrated large swaths of everyday experience. Identity moved from being secured by social webs of recognition to being measured in photography and fingerprints.[63] Automatic was the camera that recorded human distinction, independent of interest or perspective. The report on the first photograph taken in Brazil was emphatic: "One could easily see that the thing was made by the hand of nature itself, almost without the artist's intervention."[64] Self-acting automatons were now less showpieces of elites than a form of amusement available to all. In Paris, the toymaker Ferdinand Martin sold small automatons by the

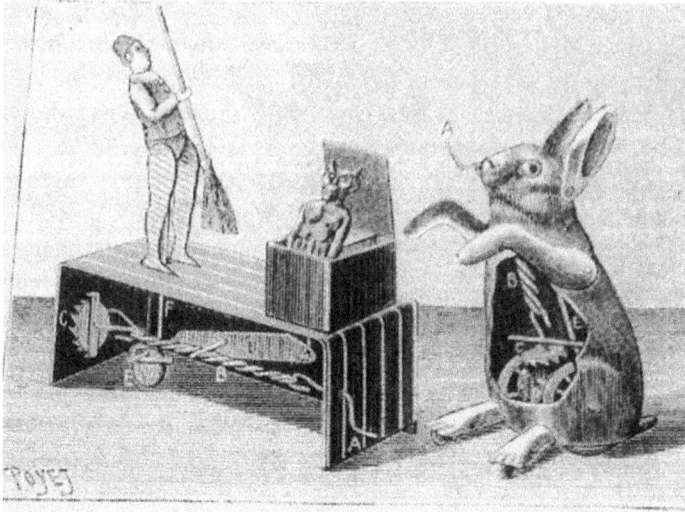

Fig. 4. — Le diable en boîte et le lapin vivant.

FIGURE 0.1. The devil-in-the-box and the living rabbit. Musée des arts et métiers. Photograph by the author.

thousands, the best seller of 1890 being the *diable en boîte,* a little devil that sprang up from a box to be smashed on the head by a neighboring figurine, precursor of the jack-in-the-box (figure 0.1).[65] The same year witnessed the debut in New York of Thomas Edison's talking doll, a commercial failure owing to an uncanny mismatch between the figure and the voice it produced.[66] The Rio de Janeiro newspapers reported that "Ajeeb, the famous card-playing automaton," excited the curiosity of the masses, prompting the opening of a new theater of automatons.[67] A few years later, in 1898, Nikola Tesla awed a crowd at Madison Square Garden with his "tele-automaton," a toy boat he could move and elicit responses from with radio waves.

The automaton was good to play with, but it was also useful to think with. In the late nineteenth century, not only did it enjoy a solid material life in the form of Ferdinand Martin's toys, but it also took on a dynamic literary presence.[68] In fiction, it became a commonplace descriptor of extraordinary acts and actors, as in Jules Verne's tale of 1873, *Around the World in Eighty Days*: "Passepartout rubbed his hands, his broad face brightened, and he repeated cheerfully: 'This suits me! This is the place for me! Mr. Fogg and I will understand each other perfectly! A homebody, and so methodical! A genuine automaton! Well, I am not sorry to serve under an automaton!'"[69] The depiction caricatured overly stiff, rote, scripted, placid, unconscious, or otherwise mechanical human acts. "Oh, you lifeless, accursed automaton!" Nathaniel accuses Clara, in E. T. A. Hoffman's "The Sandman" (1816).[70] In Rio, Machado de Assis narrated a young lieutenant's self-description in his 1882 story "The Mirror" ("O espelho"). At first: "I was like a dead man walking, a sleepwalker, a mechanical toy." Then transformed: "I was no longer an automaton, I was a living being."[71] Euclides da Cunha's classic *Rebellion in the Backlands* (*Os sertões*) described the 1890s military man who led the forces that destroyed a millenarian rebellion, Bittencourt, as "addicted to the typical automatism of those machines composed of muscles and nerves which are so constructed as to react mechanically."[72] In these texts and many more, there appeared a sudden recognition and classification of repetitive human acts *as* automatic and automaton-like and, with that rhetorical gesture, the refurbished profile of a romantic ideal of autonomous personhood, emotive, spontaneous, and free.[73] Such critical uses of *automaton* warned against a creeping invasion of the automatic and how it deformed authentic human being.

In a similar spirit, the automatic was called on to name everyday work within a hardening division of labor. Marx linked the automatic with the devil as an industrial machine "whose demon power, at first veiled under the slow and measured motions of his giant limbs, at length breaks out into the fast and furious whirl of his countless working organs."[74] In his book on suicide, Durkheim cited a worker who described himself as feeling like a mere *automate*.[75] Just so, an obituary in a Rio de Janeiro newspaper of 1898 described the hanging suicide of a man who "lived mechanically" (*machinalmente*), a "perfect automaton and an unhappy worker."[76] In the domain of law, Max Weber described the modern courtroom judge as "an automaton into which legal documents and fees are stuffed at the top in order that it may spill forth the verdict at the bottom along with the reasons read mechanically from codified paragraphs."[77] But, if judges could be cast as automatons, by the end of the nineteenth century the accused began to leverage automatism as a viable legal defense, claiming to be hypnotized or possessed and, therefore, not guilty since a crime required not only an act but also an accountable individual to judge, that is, a body possessed of rational, decision-making personhood and will.[78] This transpired in France in the famous 1889–90 homicide case of Gabrielle Bompard and Michel Eyraud, "l'affaire Eyraud." In the wake of the strangulation of Toussaint-Augustin Gouffé in 1889, Bompard and Eyraud were both charged with homicide. Bompard's defense proposed that she was hypnotized by Eyraud and, therefore, without free will, a pawn rather than an accountable individual agent. The most famous psychiatrist in the world, Jean-Martin Charcot, the protagonist of chapter 1, was summoned to pronounce on the viability of the defense. In Brazil, l'affaire Eyraud was widely reported at the end of January 1891. But the Brazilian press was equally preoccupied with automatism defenses used closer to home, like that of José Ferraz. Ferraz's lawyer, Joaquim Borges Carneiro, defended his client against charges of illegal medicine (*curandeirismo*) by saying that Ferraz was not *himself* the healer but rather only a medium of spirits. Only the spirits could be truly guilty or legally liable since they were responsible for making choices about the cure.[79] Hypnotism and spirits had each become threats to the legal principle of individual accountability, an issue I explore in chapter 5, on the use of spirit testimonies in Brazilian courts. Both psychiatry and religion seemed to unbalance procedures of law. Who was the responsible, liable agent, and where was he?

Crowds were yet another fin de siècle source of automatism, a source of action in which individual agency and will might disappear. Automatism was seen as a collective affliction, agency as an individual virtue. In his best seller *Psychologie des foules* (1895), Gustave Le Bon called the man in a crowd variously *an automaton, a slave,* and *one possessed.*[80] Under the influence of Le Bon's ideas, the Brazilian press exhorted republican political leaders not to be "puppets of the multitudes or automatons of factions," with their disordered convulsions and tumult.[81] Le Bon traveled widely in Europe, North Africa, and Asia and, in 1893, published the work that made him famous, *Les monuments de l'Inde.* Drawing on impressions acquired in his youthful jaunts, he joined vivid portraits of modern massification to fantastic depictions of primitive society.[82] In his scenario, under the force of the crowd modern humanity descended the evolutionary ladder to become a nonrational primitive, a state for which "Ethiopians" and "negroes" played the foil. *Religion* was the name of the process by which this primitive "soul of the masses" became immanent in the individual. The man lost in the crowd is, just like the primitive, blindly obedient and incapable of exercising free will. He is possessed. Le Bon built a powerful racial stratification into his sociology, and Africans were most liable to the crowd sentiments that negated individual will.

Slaves were sometimes referred to in generic terms as *automatons,* bodies without will that could be set in motion like a machine. A Rio daily reported in 1884 on a slave who, "though reduced to the position of an automaton," nevertheless tried to defend herself against sexual assault.[83] Another report detailed a job-training school for children of former slaves who, through their studies, "cease to be brutally unconscious automatons and become citizens convinced of their role in society."[84] The Brazilian statesman José Bonifácio put the matter in like terms: "In truth, primitive man [certainly a reference to enslaved Africans] is neither naturally good nor evil; he is a mere automaton."[85] The association of the automaton with the condition of slavery was not particular to Brazil. Slaves were "labor-saving machines" to the slave owner Harris depicted in *Uncle Tom's Cabin*.[86] Early twentieth-century Japanese and Chinese laborers in Hawaii were likened to "a sort of agricultural automaton," effective only when placed under proper British or American supervision.[87] Yet, while slaves were often represented as automatons, they were abruptly made into liable autonomous individual agents when it was time to be punished or subjected to legal prosecution.

Perhaps no one expanded the lexicon and range of the automatic more than a group of psychiatrists at the Salpêtrière Hospital in Paris led by Jean-Martin Charcot, who was widely imitated in Brazil, the topic of chapter 1. Everyone from Freud to William James to the emperor of Brazil, Dom Pedro II, and the founder of Brazilian psychiatry, Antônio Austregésilo, undertook the pilgrimage to Charcot's laboratory and Tuesday lectures. Beginning in the early 1880s, Charcot and his students redeemed hypnosis from the carnival and salon circuits, transforming it into a recognized medical tool. Charcot articulated new diagnoses by translating historical accounts of demonic possession into the new terms of automatism, hysteria, and autosuggestion, comparing medieval paintings of the demon possessed with contemporary photographs of afflicted patients, mostly female. Freud, Pierre Janet, and others followed suit in drawing on the archives of demonic possession to generate their diagnostic classifications and treatments.[88] The psychiatric arsenal presented a fulsome series of words that entered the vocabulary of Brazilian Portuguese via French: *somnambulism, hysteria, dissociation, automatism, autosuggestion*, among many others.[89] In his 1889 *L'automatisme psychologique*, Charcot's student Pierre Janet used the figure of the *automate* in order properly to frame in the reader's mind the image of the person who acts without will.[90]

There was something particular about the density of this word cloud—*automatic, automaton, automatism*—as it became a transnational assemblage and vernacular, both popular and scholarly, of the late nineteenth century. The automaton as object was past its Renaissance golden age, but that did not mean that it was exhausted. Rather, it became part of everyday language and practice, a cog in the basic classificatory gear of the age.[91]

AROUND THE WORLD

The automatic rendered the world in popular terms, and religion was a legend accompanying the map. While travel writing was already a familiar genre, late nineteenth-century travel writing invested in comparative religion learned at speed. The convention shaped the earth in a particular way. Narratives of journeys around the world flew off the shelves, from writers like Jacques Arago, Mark Twain, Charles Darwin, Andrew Carnegie, and, the best-selling of them all, Jules Verne. Darwin's *A Naturalist's Voyage around the World* went through eleven editions from 1860 to 1890. Descriptions of travels around the world helped produce a novel image of a familiar globality and with it stabilized categories of religions.[92] In his *Following the Equator: A Journey around the World*, Twain discovered in South Australia a land of radical religious cosmopolitanism. He was surprised only by the relative dearth of spiritualists, a mere thirty-seven by his count. Another chronicler of his travels around the world, Jacques Arago, features in chapter 3 of this book. His drawing of a Brazilian slave in *Journal of a Voyage around the World* later came to life as a popular saint and living nearhuman agent, Slave Anastácia. Arago died in Rio de Janeiro and was the mentor of and an inspiration for Jules Verne. He was a keen observer of the religions he encountered, as was Verne.[93] In Verne's *Around the World in Eighty Days*, the heroes Phileas Fogg and Passepartout trade ideas with Hindus and Mormons.

The rash of the books depicting journeys around the world and the seemingly inexhaustible market for them helped form *religion* into a comparative term in ways as important as, and probably more so than, the works of scholarly figures like Max Müller did. The knowledge of "it" gave proof of bona fide cosmopolitanism; colorful descriptions of the practice of "it" served as signs of genuine provincial or exotic authenticity. Religion helped render the world, even as stories of journeys around the world rendered religion in a comparative sense for the first time to general audiences. The genres made each other. Moreover, the assemblages of things and practices described as *religions* were, in the genre of travel writing, caused to appear in rapid-fire sequence, closely adjacent. Religion happened between iron wheels and boilers, according to timetables, at high speed. This was not anything like Marco Polo's discursions on Chinese practices, absorbed over ambling time, or the wind-driven travel narratives of the early nineteenth century. The new regime was steampunk, a goggled ride through many religions observed as a blur. New travel modes and habits produced absurdly flattening similarities and, more commonly, crass polemics of radical difference. In *Round the World in 124 Days*, Ralph Watts Leyland offered staccato reflections on Buddhism, the Jains, Shinto, and the rapport between Hindus and Mohammedans. He gathered his insights on the fly—sixteen days in India, seventeen in Japan, two in Hong Kong. Invoking Verne's fictional eighty-day orbit of the planet, he declared such a hurried circumnavigation difficult but eminently possible: "It is, however, only to be accomplished by a careful preparation of plans before leaving England, in order to make the advertised times of the arrival and departure of trains and steamboats correspond."[94]

The texts convey not only velocity and time compression but also a novel segmenting of views on the divisions of the world, split into specific ways of seeing and narrating in accord with gender, skin color, profession, or transport: for example, Ida Pfeifer's 1852 *A Lady's Travels round the World*, David Dorr's 1858 *A Colored Man around the World*, Darwin's 1860 *A Naturalist's Voyage round the World*, Thomas Stevens 1889 *Around the World on Bicycle*.[95] Thomas Stevens was piqued to find that religions were barely comprehensible at a ride-by pace: "Japanese mythology, religion, temples, politics, history, and titles, seem to me to be the worst mixed up and the most difficult for off-hand comprehension of anything I have yet undertaken to peep into."[96] The world was a mosaic of high-velocity engagements in which religion was part of the show. The agents of the show were traveling European and North American scientists who were, like anthropologists and historians of religion today, afforded cosmopolitan mobility and funds to study "traditional" folk and "nature"—that is to say, those people, animals, and plants that allegedly acted through repetition, habit, instinct, or genetic inheritance rather than innovation or will. To oversimplify, globe-trotting colonial and neocolonial agents "discovered" automatic actors and automatons stuck in place.

William James, Jean-Martin Charcot, Gustave le Bon, and Sigmund Freud were among the travelers. Whoosh! There goes William James to Brazil in 1865 to join the Thayer expedition with Louis Agassiz. Shoom! There goes Jean Charcot to sketch in Morocco. Ho! What pluck we see in young Gustave Le Bon in Nepal. Whump! Now young Sigmund Freud flops down his bags at a Paris hotel and rushes off to Charcot's lecture. All of them were careful observers of both the natural and the religious worlds. William James noted that some humans were *more* liable to automatism than others.[97] Alfred Russell Wallace, the famed naturalist and spiritualist who spent six years in Brazil, ranked animal and spirit life alike in relation to will: Birds' flight is superior to insects' flight because it is the result of will; insect flight is merely automatic. Organizing spirits (willful agents) act on "cell souls," whose work is but automatic, devoted to sustaining "life machinery."[98]

Too, all of them encountered people exhibiting a marked lack of will. Charcot in Morocco in 1887 and William James in Brazil in 1865 were both surprised—or so they said—by encounters with women of color in various states of undress (figure 0.2).[99] One could mount a long list of mobile travelers' discoveries of automatic peoples around the globe. The point is that narratives of journeys around the world composed a

FIGURE O.2. William James in Brazil after an attack of smallpox. Portrait photograph, 1865. MS Am 1092 (1185), Houghton Library, Harvard University.

bipolar network in which certain actors moved only mechanically and in place while others traveled deliberately and willfully. Pierre Bourdieu described world making as a transformation of the vision of divisions.[100] It is in that sense that the automatic world was a twin birth, a division of the world into agents and nonagents. What is more, characters in the script of the automatic were cross-referenced and woven together to become durable. In a different age, Spinoza had joined parrots and automatons; both were beings that mimic understanding but in fact lack it. He joined figures of animality with those of humans without will. David Hume did much the same, setting parrots and "negroes" as comparable in their talent for mimicry.[101] Hegel, too, conceived the human in relation to sup-posed automatons; his description of Africans as nonagentive mimics, people without history, is only the most dramatic example of many.[102] Nineteenth-century social theorists applied a less static but equally perni-cious scale of racial evolutionism and childhood, joining race to age. Gus-tave Le Bon wrote of members of a crowd as both "possessed" and as the "slaves" of a leader's dream, joining affect to enslavement.[103] Slaves were described as *labor-saving machines*, joining mechanics to social domina-tion. Alluring women were linked to automatons in stories by E. T. A. Hoffman, Jules Verne, and Machado de Assis alike. And those considered especially liable to automatism were Africans and Amerindians, lacing together ideas of race, evolution, and the absence of will.

Yet, by virtue of that very lack, these putative bodies without will retained a capacity to become objects of ritual devotion, as mediators of direct, irrational power, and it is the religion-like attraction to the au-tomatic that I want to foreground.[104] This occurred, for example, with the drawing of a slave by the nineteenth-century French traveler and writer Jacques Arago, as described in chapter 3. In fact, it was in the context of the "worlding" effects of the burgeoning genre of travel writing that the figures of affixed and automatic persons took on special significance.[105] What did the nearhuman and nonagency make?

AUTOMATIC RELIGION

In the theory of religion, the idea of the automatic helped make magic. If persons were observed to act automatically, then the religions they performed could be described via the automatic as well. James Frazer characterized magic ritual actions as *automatic*. Religion required wor-shippers and gods exercising will. Émile Durkheim described Aborigi-nals' depictions of totemic animals and their appearance in consciousness as *automatic translation*.[106] Mark Twain put the phrase *automatic religion* in print in 1907, describing a practice "so used to its work that it can do it without your help or even your privity." The phrase designated responses that are ingrained, unconscious, horribly rigid, yet nearly impossible to resist.[107]

Twain's friend William James was more optimistic: "The more of the details of our daily life we can hand over to the effortless custody of au-tomatism, the more our higher powers of mind will be set free."[108] He presented the discovery of automatism—which he located precisely in 1886 with the publication of the psychic compendium *Phantasms of the Living*—as the key to understanding most religious phenomena, expand-ing his idea of automatism out from telepathy and trance to narratives of Methodist conversion. If some subjects are particularly liable to the incursion of experiences from outside the usual field of consciousness, *all* people are to some degree "leaky and pervious," he proposed.[109] Automatic religion, or automatism, described that condition. A key part of the phenomenon of religion and how we think about it is the relative freedom gained and lost, the degree of giving oneself over to metahuman beings and their imagined goals. Religion-like events are always situated between and in relation to polarities of agency and the automaton.

The idea of the automatic shaped the idea of religion in other ways too. James configured religion in the terms of the mechanical: "Every individual soul, . . . like every individual machine or organism, has its own best conditions of efficiency. A given machine will run best under a certain steam-pressure, a certain amperage. . . . Just so with our sundry souls."[110] In this James was hardly alone. In terms of theorizing religion, the turn of the twentieth century produced a sturdy iron-framed mechanics. This was not always the case, nor was it inevitable. Prior to becoming mechanical and automatic, religion was mostly imagined in organic forms. Consider the following from Friedrich Schleiermacher's *On Religion* (1799): "The divine life is like a tender plant whose blossoms are fertilized while enclosed in the bud, and the holy intuitions and feelings you are able to dehydrate and preserve and the beautiful calyxes and corollas that open soon after that secret action."[111] Johann Gottfried Herder employed organic terms similar to those used by Schleiermacher. Religion was "the human soul's most sublime blossom."[112] Like Kant, Herder defined the human in contradistinction to the animal, whose actions, he claimed, were automatic and lacked soul. Contrast that passage with the language of Ludwig Feuerbach, half a century later: "The imperative of love works with electro-magnetic power; that of despotism with the mechanical power of a [wooden] telegraph."[113] To be sure, Feuerbach nowhere invoked automatism and even applied some of the same metaphors as Schleiermacher. Both described religion in relation to the heart, but how unlike were these hearts! Schleiermacher's heart swelled with feeling and depth; Feuerbach's heart was a pump with systolic and diastolic mechanics.[114]

I have something more in mind, however, than grinding religion and the automatic together in a late nineteenth-century mill. I want to consider how the automatic generated not only new codes of description, but also new modes of religious practice and experience: how photography was enlisted in the discernment of spirits, or how phonography was enlisted to hear the voices of the dead, or how the nomenclature of *energy, light, vibrations, electricity,* and *power* began to circulate in and constitute the experiences registered at religious events.[115] The age of the automatic generated new modes of technologically mediated religious practice.[116] It also built new walls. Categories of the anthropology and history of religions fortify theoretical geographies—religion as agency here, religion as automatism there; religion as individual here, religion as collective abandon there.[117] A world split between agents and automatons was effective in the making and reproduction of centers and margins, actors and mimics. The slave, the patient, and the monkey, alongside a photograph of a possession priest, a corpse, and a spirit writer, all being acted through, show the automatic as a twin birth. It marked a division between free and unfree actors, cosmopolitan travelers versus alleged automatons. The firstborn devoured the world on whirlwind circuits of mechanized transport; the secondborn were fixed in place, possessed of machine-like repetition. Such figures were depicted as lacking agency, as like humans but less than human—nearhumans—yet they exerted a magnetism. They could become objects of attraction, even of ritual practice.

Nearhuman

What is the appeal (or horror) of figures or events that present agent ambiguity? How do people *become* agent ambiguous or, to take an older term, *uncanny*? How is the uncanny cultivated and engaged as a technique to disclose something new? Hoffman's "The Sandman" offered the story of a young man who falls in love with a woman whom he discovers to be an automaton. The misrecognition and confusion motivates his suicide. That story gained a South American doppelgänger in Machado de Assis's "Captain Mendonça," first published in 1870. Machado wrote of a man who falls in love with a woman who also turns out to be an automaton. Loving her required that he become like her, at once a genius (more than human) and mechanized (less than human) through brain surgery and ether injection. Machado's protagonist is in agony: "I felt a horribly sharp pain at the top of my cranium; a strange body penetrating to the interior of my brain."[118] Machado posed the automaton and the attraction to it as the topography of familiarly strange dreamscapes. *Uncanny* (*unheimlich*) gained international fame as a term to describe such strange attraction. Despite its familiarity, it holds untapped potential. Most important is that it described and located an affective dimension of nearhuman fascination or horror or both at once. It is worth lingering over this odd term because it came into use precisely to name the problem of the fickle borders of the human and describe the affecting quality of humans' shock at realizing the fact of their own fragile distinction from the animal and the mechanical.

UNCANNY

Friedrich Schelling's 1842 lectures first posed the idea of that which ought to have remained secret (*geheimlich*) but is brought to light, linking the hidden or secret to the uncanny. Published as the *Historical-Critical Introduction to the Philosophy of Mythology*, they invoked the uncanny (*unheimlich*) four times: in relation to experiences of that which is anomalous in nature, experiences of dread, terror, or darkness, figures of childishness and savages, and, in the sole geographic referent given, the territory of South America, in particular La Plata.[119] In his 1906 essay "Zur Psychologie des Unheimlichen," Ernst Jentsch revisited Schelling's idea. He zeroed in on the disorientation and uncertainty caused when the animate and the inanimate are confused by agent ambiguity. A man falls in love with a lifelike woman and goes mad when he realizes his mistake. Or he loses himself among wax museum figures that too closely resemble a natural human. The figures evoke the sensation of the uncanny because of their too-human form, but actual humans also *become* uncanny when they suddenly appear mechanical or not in possession of a unified psyche. Jentsch described someone who meets a person previously known as organic and animate but who now seems guided by a "mechanism" or "mechanical processes."[120] The uncanny as he articulated it groped toward a description of a feeling of an experience of disorientation or an interruption in everyday experience. He described it as mostly disturbing. While such experiences of disorientation may derive from temporary states—drunkenness, hallucination, fear (e.g., darkness in an unknown space)—they may also be cultivated, as when "one undertakes to reinterpret some kind of lifeless thing as part of an organic creature, especially in anthropomorphic terms, in a poetic or fantastic way."[121] A lonely lake is refigured as the gigantic eye of a monster; the outline of a cloud or a shadow is made into a threatening satanic face. Objects come alive by addressing them, carrying on conversations with them, mocking them, or treating them as familiar. Jentsch's cases of uncanny experience focus on dispositions of women, children, dreamers, and primitives, all cast as irrational. He was prescient too in drawing together examples of hysterics, automatons, and gods into a set because of the uncertainty they provoke.

Freud dismissed his own 1919 essay "The Uncanny" as but trifling.[122] It was not just false humility. His effort to circumscribe the term *uncanny* verged on the comic when, as Nicholas Royle observes, he invoked all in one sentence "animism, magic and sorcery, the omnipotence of thoughts, man's attitude to death, involuntary repetition and the castration complex."[123] Following Jentsch's summary of "The Sandman," Freud acknowledged the strange infatuation with a girl who is in fact an automaton but declared the matter of agent ambiguity to be subsidiary to the fear of castration: "The feeling of something uncanny is directly attached to the figure of the Sand-Man, that is, to the idea of being robbed of one's eyes. . . . Jentsch's point of an intellectual uncertainty has nothing to do with this effect. Uncertainty whether an object is living or inanimate, which we must admit in regard to the doll Olympia, is quite irrelevant in connection with this other, more striking instance of uncanniness." The features of the story "become intelligible as soon as we replace the Sand-Man by the dreaded father at whose hands castration is expected."[124]

More revealing than the fear of castration, however, is Freud's use of the word *uncanny* to describe his own experiences of disquieting disorientation. On December 3, 1885, Freud wrote his wife, Martha: "The city and its inhabitants strike me as uncanny; the people seem to me of a different species. . . . [T]hey are all possessed of a thousand demons."[125] Writing from his own experience rather than as an analyst, he helps us see the uncanny in an affective register, confirming Jentsch's initial ideas. For Jentsch, the sensation of the uncanny indexes both the disorientation caused by and the *simultaneous attraction to* the nearhuman, much as Freud found Paris not only uncanny and possessed but also irresistible. Humans seek temporary disorientation in order to see the world differently. Religious events are venues for the production of that shift.[126] Jentsch's vision was, it seems to me, true to Hoffman's. In the novella *Automata* (1814), Hoffman's main character dwells on affect—the reverent demeanor with which people tour wax museums and the "horrible, eerie, shuddery" feeling he experienced in one: "When I see the staring, lifeless, glassy eyes of all the potentates, celebrated heroes, thieves, murderers, and so on, fixed upon me, I feel disposed to cry with Macbeth, 'Thou has no speculation in those eyes Which thou dost glare with.' And I feel certain that most people experience the same feeling."[127]

The gap between visible exterior and a secret interior agent seems key to the fascination with automatons and automatic action. The attraction of the uncanny has to do with this doubling and the affective response to it. It links the automaton, possessed of uncertain agency, to the emerging practice of psychiatry's obsessive late nineteenth-century focus on *double consciousness*, a phrase in play at least since the Mary Reynolds case of 1817, published in *Medical Repository*.[128] An actual person becomes uncanny when he suddenly appears mechanical or not in possession of a unified self. The uncanny here is an experience of disorientation, a mismatch, a shifting of frame that irrupts into everyday experience. In rituals of automatism—scripts involving either becoming or standing in the presence of nonagents or bodies without will—participants become aware of something they mostly cannot name, namely, their own and others' doubleness.

Doubling—*dédoublement*—has been rehearsed in a dozen different ways, and often it has had a specific meaning, as it did for W. E. B. Du Bois in his 1903 use of *second-sight, double-consciousness,* and *two-ness* to describe the internalization of racism: "an American, a Negro; two souls, two thoughts, two unreconciled strivings; two warring ideals in one dark body."[129] But it also afforded capacious readings of agency. Anna Karenina, wrote Tolstoy, "was beginning to feel fear before the new, never experienced state [and] . . . felt that everything was beginning to go double in her soul."[130] Pierre Janet wrote: "Ordinary men oscillate between two extremes, sometimes automatons with determined actions and weak moral force, sometimes worthy of being considered free and moral beings."[131] Religious actors rehearse this kind of oscillation between polarities of the double. She plays the other who is also herself. Ritual encounters with antiagents like the body possessed, the enslaved, the catatonic or comatose, and the mechanical player cast otherwise mostly unspeakable oppositions into relief and sometimes make them available to consciousness: between freedom and constraint, movement and immobility, liveliness and quiet. The pleasure of cultivating automatism or doubling may, to follow Paul Ricoeur, reside in the "hermeneutics of the self" it affords: the receipt of agency through interaction with another by experiencing oneself as or in relation to the other, the nearhuman.[132]

RELIGION AS THE HUMAN

Religion has long been applied as a test of humanness, often with the highest stakes. In South America, determining whether Amerindians had religion—some set of actions recognizable as religion to the Spanish— determined whether these beings could rightfully be considered human (*anthropos*) at all and potentially converted to Christianity. If it was decided that they were closer to animals than to humans, then they could legitimately be killed or enslaved. For the most part, the Europeans imposed their order. Here is the Spanish humanist Juan Ginés de Sepúlveda writing in 1545:

> You can well understand, Leopold, if you know the customs and manners of different peoples, that the Spanish have a perfect right to rule these barbarians of the New World and the adjacent islands, who in prudence, skill, virtues, and humanity are as inferior to the Spanish as children to adults, or women to men, for there exists between the two

as great a difference as between savage and cruel races and the most merciful, between the most intemperate and the moderate and temperate and, I might even say, between apes and men. . . . Although some of them show a certain ingenuity for various works of artisanship, this is no proof of human cleverness, for we can observe animals, birds, and spiders making certain structures which no human accomplishment can competently imitate. . . . Compare, then, these gifts of prudence, talent, magnanimity, temperance, humanity, and religion with those possessed by these half-men (homunculi), in whom you will barely find the vestiges of humanity.[133]

In his defense of the natural slavery of Native Americans, Sepúlveda precises the human—and especially the alleged homunculi or half humans of the New World—in relation to their animal cousins. Yet it was not only Europeans trying to trace the edges of humanness. The Spanish nobleman Gonzalo Fernández de Oviedo y Valdés (1478–1557) reported in around 1525 that the natives of Puerto Rico conducted experiments of their own to test the whites' humanness by killing them, throwing them in the water, and then keeping a vigilant watch to see whether their flesh would rot like their own.[134]

In Europe itself, meanwhile, Kant famously found the moral sensibility and the capacity for comparison to be distinctively human qualities, compared with the merely animal drives of survival and reproduction that nonhumans also pursue. This moral sensibility was especially well expressed in religion, especially ethical Protestantism. Herder too focused on the specifically human gift of the soul. Like Kant, he defined the human in contradistinction to the animal, whose actions were automatic and lacked soul. For him, even reason and language—two capacities often proposed as the distinct qualities of humans—emerged only secondarily in the attempt to comprehend and describe inchoate phenomena like the fate of the soul after death. He argued that reason and language came into existence in and through religion.[135]

A century later, in the late nineteenth century, religion was likewise constitutive of humanness, this time for evolutionary anthropologists, including the so-called father of modern anthropology Edward Burnett Tylor (1832–1917). For Tylor, all humans have religion or something like it, which he called *animism* after he learned that the rubric *spiritism* was already taken. All lower races with which we are acquainted share, he asserted, the belief in spiritual beings. Observations like this one led to his famous and famously short definition of religion: the belief in spiritual beings.[136] Important to note is how this definition was tailored to encompass all known humans and, thereby, help give precision to the moment when humanness occurred in the evolutionary process. When did apes pass into humanness? They became human when they began to wonder about the afterlife or dreams—that is, when they expressed an interest in the soul. For Tylor, as for Herder, *soul* was a crucial marker. Religion emerged out of the human experiences of sleep, dreams, and wakefulness, the animate versus inanimate body, and the mystery of the shifts between the presence and the absence of conscious experience.

The relation can work the other way around: animals can become legal persons, at least theoretically, when shown to have religion. Jane Goodall, for example, argued that chimpanzees have religion and, therefore, warrant the same legal protections as humans. They hold acts of celebration and homage at a waterfall—ritual—with no apparent function other than the celebration of being at that place. Of one chimpanzee she writes: "Standing upright, he sways rhythmically from foot to foot, stamping in the shallow, rushing water, picking up and hurling great rocks. Sometimes he climbs up the slender vines that hang down from the trees high above and swings out into the spray of the falling water. This 'waterfall dance' may last for ten or fifteen minutes."[137] Or take the everyday words of a North Carolinian: "If Bigfoot's real—you know where I live, there's a lot of Bigfoot sightings around here—if Bigfoot's real, what would that do to, say, religion, the economy, all these other things that touch that? Let's just say the DNA on Bigfoot is half-human. Does he have a soul? It helps you think."[138] He is right. It does push us to think.

FREE WILL, THE HUMAN, AND THE ANIMAL

Goodall and the North Carolinian's curiosity about Bigfoot both show how humanness is read in relation to animals and the presence of religion or the soul.[139] At least since Aristotle's *History of Animals*, monkeys have occupied a privileged midpoint between the human and the animal, in labor as in philosophy (whether as mule drivers in Brazil, organ grinders in the United States, or children's playmates in Europe). Monkeys have served at once as a fulcrum for accusations of less than humanness (mere automatic mimicry without will) and as a cipher for the *resistance* to dehumanization—as in the "signifying monkey" described by Henry Gates[140] or in recent cases defending monkeys' rights as legal persons. William James too described how human particularity was worked out in relation to animals—humor, sympathy, language, human will—as opposed to the "automatic" action of a dog.[141] Certain animals helped structure *the human* because of their uncanny proximity to features of humanness, like parrots in their capacity for mimicry and speech but, above all, monkeys in their sociality, expressiveness, and dexterity. The abundance of monkeys and parrots—nearhuman animals par excellence—made Brazil crucial to the project of humanmaking.

Early modern travel accounts from Brazil all invoked monkeys and parrots. In 1511, the Portuguese ship *Bretoa* sailed from Brazil with five thousand "red-trees" (brazilwood), twenty-two parakeets, sixteen callitrichids (small monkeys), fifteen parrots, and three large monkeys. A French ship captured by the Portuguese in 1531, the *Pelerine*, bore three hundred tons of wood, almost two tons of cotton, seeds, and oils, three thousand furs, six hundred parrots, and three hundred monkeys.[142] Hans Staden's captivity narrative, first published in 1557, reported trading with the Tupi on the coast of Brazil for pepper and long-tailed monkeys.[143] Jean de Léry's 1556 account of Brazil mentioned how easy it was to transport certain monkeys across the sea, in comparison with other animals.[144] During the fifteenth and sixteenth centuries, Portugal became the center of the trade in monkeys and parrots in Europe.[145] They began to arrive from Brazil after 1500, and Lisbon became the hub of their trade as Portuguese sailors returned to Sagres, Lagos, and Lisbon with monkeys both as companions and in ample supply for sale. The presence of monkeys in domestic life expanded dramatically in Europe in the late eighteenth century. In Paris, one could encounter them in many homes, and they were common in the major city markets.[146] Capuchin monkeys from the Americas—especially Brazil—were an everyday sight, and monkey merchants emphasized their humanness in their pitches: a ten-month old small monkey, for example, was presented as having "the face and hands of a Negro."[147] Monkeys shared children's bedrooms, raided women's powder rooms, and sat at the dinner table.

Foreign visitors to Brazil in the nineteenth century jammed their accounts with the cries of parrots and monkeys as though the animals dominated the soundscape.[148] Hear the voice of Charles Darwin aboard the *Beagle* in April 1832, disdaining the "miserable" Brazilians but itching to visit "Nature in its grandest form," its "wild forests tenanted by beautiful birds, Monkeys & Sloths." By June, he was out shooting these animals alongside his guides.[149] And there is William James in Brazil on the Agassiz expedition in 1865 with a monkey as his best friend: "Tied to one of the posts of this shed was perhaps the best friend I found in this place, viz. a very large or rather coiatá, or spider monkey."[150] Louis Agassiz himself declared the forest to be "noisy" with howling and Negroes to be similar to long-armed monkeys.[151] He foreshadowed the statements of Count Gobineau, the French ambassador to the court in Rio de Janeiro, who in 1869 called Brazil "a multitude of monkeys."[152] Then too, monkey salesmen were common in the markets of nineteenth-century Rio de Janeiro, and their product was cheap. The American traveler Thomas Ewbank reported being offered a monkey for 6 *milreis*—about $2.50.[153] In the northeast of Brazil, small monkeys called *oustiti* were common children's pets, and *sertanejo* (northeastern) traders from the interior often trained monkeys to ride their transport mules.[154]

Monkeys became common pets in Europe too. By the Belle Époque, they were less common, yet they had come to serve as marks of style and distinction. Thus, the fashion designer Paul Poiret featured them, along with parrots, at a famous party with a "Thousand and One Nights" theme that he threw in 1911.[155] Sarah Bernhardt possessed a parrot and also a monkey named Darwin, among other animals.[156] Introducing the neuroanatomist Franz Josef Gall to his readers, the publisher Nahum Capen quoted Gall as saying: "There are those, indeed, who do not wish that even their dogs and monkeys should be placed in my collection [for anatomical study by dissection] after their death." This suggests that both dogs and monkeys were common domestic partners to which their owners developed sentimental attachments.[157] Chapter 1 below describes the role of one such Belle Époque Brazilian simian in Paris: Rosalie, the beloved pet of the psychiatrist Jean-Martin Charcot.

If the monkey was a New World wonder from Brazil, it was also a figure of diabolical nearhumanness. Satan was imagined as "God's monkey." Demons appeared in the shape of not-quite-human monkeys.[158] This continued into the nineteenth century. In Sheridan Le Fanu's 1872 story "Green Tea," the vicar Mr. Jennings is tormented by his visions of a demonic monkey who follows him, sprawls over the Bible while he tries to preach, and eventually occupies his mind, leading to his suicide.[159] The monkey as demon resembles in key respects the many stories of automatons as devilish figures, from the legend of Descartes's companion to stories by Jean-Paul Richter, E. T. A. Hoffman, Jules Verne, and Hans Christian Andersen. Then, too, the resemblance in the demonic roles played by the automaton and the monkey are hardly accidental. They present two versions of the nearhuman. They blur the boundaries of humanness by their very proximity to it. Both are cast as acting automatically—mechanically or through mimicry—rather than via genuine will or spontaneous acts. Like mechanical automata, monkeys placed the human in question and at risk. So did parrots. These animals in particular posed challenges to the human because of their strange ability to mimic its qualities. Human personhood was worked on and distilled in relation to parrots, monkeys, and spirits as nearhuman automatic actors. All were abundant and readily evident in Brazil, making it a site of dreams for visitors like Agassiz, James, and Darwin.

CYBORG

From the animal to the machine. We are equipped with artificial limbs and rely on transplanted organs. We draw on skin surfaces with plastic, silicone, and ink. We walk with glowing phones affixed to our hands, and soon Internet access will be marketed as a viable prosthetic brain insert, rendering usual ideas of memory moot. Another provocation to the kind of humanism that religion helped produce comes from the present and future prospect of hybrid humans. Bruno Latour, for example, names the way humans, like nonhumans, are constituted in and through the instruments that they use and that are used to learn about them, through their tools and mechanics of discernment. In this respect, human agency is not distinct from the agency of other animals and things. Latour uses *automaton* to describe degrees of self-acting assembly—from the lash-ups between previously disparate entities to those that become so calibrated as to act as one and then, as an automaton, alter the actions of the assemblages' human users.[160]

The truth of our condition in the world, Latour argues, is more like that of an Afro-Brazilian Candomblé initiate than that of a buffered self. Initiation is called *making the god* (*fazer santo*), and initiates make the god at the same time as they *make their heads* (*fazer cabeça*), another phrase describing Candomblé initiation. The reality of the god exists together with the reality of how it was made.[161] Self, world, and religion are all emerging, all being made at the same time. Even more radically, this idea of hybridity asks us to consider the question of whether and to what degree religion is a uniquely human event, or rather a way of perceiving agency that can be shared with other kinds of beings. Nonhuman animals have experiences, suffer pain, feel sadness and joy, take action to seek circumstances different than the present one, even conduct ritual dance. They wield systems of communication, if not usually what linguists would properly call *language*. Can we even imagine nonhuman religions or religion-like events as Goodall did? We should.[162]

Here is one reason. In response to Latour's most famous book, *We Have Never Been Modern* (1991), Donna Haraway deployed the phrase, "We have never been human."[163] Taking as her point of departure the fact that many humans live with companion animals and even think of them as friends on whom they depend, Haraway writes of "natural cultural contact zones" shared between, among others, humans and dogs. Through the infolding of organic and technological flesh, we are all already extra-human, all cyborgs now. Haraway applies the figure of the cyborg to a prophetic project. By attending to our fusions with animals, on the one hand, and with machines, on the other, we can become new beings. "We can learn not to be Man" in the disastrous ways we have "been Man" in the past.[164] Haraway punctures holes in the very "Man" that the category of religion was deployed to discern and define, and with cause. After all, the story of female permeability is an old one, from early models of bodily humors to more recent studies of spirit possession. Haraway exhorts readers to emancipatory politics through technic automatons—a kind of collective, interface vision of personhood—over the shell of mechanical, masculinist, iron-caged autonomy. She takes the old saws of female permeability and automatism and inverts their valence to build something new. I hope this book will add to the effort.

Too often women have occupied an irrational slot similar to the animal's or, when cast as automatons, served as an intermediary between the categories of human, animal, and cyborg.[165] To be sure, there are male automatons in the record: male hysterics, male automatic writers, animate male figurines. What I find interesting, however, is the gendering of even male and female nearhumans. For example, while female hysterics were seen as captive, malleable, and pliant, male hysterics in Paris suffered *fugue*, dissociating their way across vast distances on trains without consciousness of their actions. Female hysterics were stuck in place; male hysterics disappeared over the horizon. Female automatons are coquettish instrumentalists in the style of La Joyeuse de Tympanon, demure fingers on ivory keys. Male automatons are bearded chess masters or superhuman in strength and speed, like *Frankenstein*'s mechanical man. While female simians are playful companions, like Charcot's or James's monkey friends, male simians are overpowering and threatening.[166] In certain respects, even as automatons or monkeys, male nearhumans remain agents. It is harder to make that claim for female nearhumans. The way forward lies in untying the choking braid of the human, untying the knot woven of the individual, agency, and religion.

My hope is that by now the solid association between religion and the human is loosened on both the animal and the cyborg sides. The lines marking out the human—a specificity established through an earlier association of humanness and religion—are now fuzzy. The "anthropological machine"—a machine that continually manufactures the human through the oppositions of human-animal and human-inhuman (or machine)—has broken down, and all the better. For, along with the human, the anthropological machine has always manufactured *exclusions*, the nonhuman.[167] With both religion and the human open to question, we can ask less anthropocentric questions. What is the nonreligion of the human animal? What is the religion of nonhuman animals? What is the religious attraction of the nearhuman? What are religion-like things on the edges of these terms? This book digs in the gaps opened between agentive and automatic action.

Travel Guide

Religion-like things revel in the ambiguity of who or what acts in a given scene and how rarely we know with any confidence. Religion-like situations move across and between attributions of agency, between self-assertion and giving oneself over—a sacrifice requiring a prior claim of individual will—to those projects called *religion*. The distinct attributions rendered in religion are, however, never innocent. Profiles of free and automatic actors built an anthropological divide. This book worries the terms in which humans were converted into automatic machines. I give attention to nearhumans both in their making and in their appeal.

If the early modern West debated individual agency in relation to the figure of the mimic, the possessed, or the animals—think of John Locke's description of the Brazilian parrot who speaks like a person but who might be possessed—by the nineteenth century the nonagent was linked to the automaton condemned to mechanical repetition. But nonagency was also applied to persons *seen* in automatic terms. For example, slaves in Brazil and psychiatric patients in France and Brazil were simultaneously named *automatons*. The difference between agents and automatons was a wall but also a bridge that spanned the Atlantic. Its pilings and rails were composed of human kinds split into agents and nonagents. Mostly the traffic on the bridge flowed from France to Brazil: psychiatric categories made in Paris were affixed onto Afro-Brazilian bodies in Rio de Janeiro or Salvador da Bahia. But sometimes it flowed in the opposite direction—Dom Pedro II, emperor of Brazil, and a Brazilian monkey given by him, played important roles in the Paris salon of the world-famous psychiatrist Jean-Martin Charcot and beyond. Though figures from the Anglo-American world also enter the narrative from time to time—William James, Herbert Spencer, Mark Twain—they mostly speak sotto voce, whispering just offstage. I hope to tell a transatlantic story slightly different than the more familiar one of British and American mechanics and the humanish lives they nurtured.

Epigraphs from Machado de Assis lead every chapter that follows. Machado will be our guide, seer, and bard. Born in 1839, and dying in 1906, the greatest of Brazil's writers lived a life that straddled the merging tracks of the automatic that this book follows. The grandson of freed slaves and a bona fide Francophile who never left Brazil, Machado ranged in stories, novels, and newspaper columns over the issues of slavery, psychiatry, alienism, automatons, speaking animals, and religion, all broached with a dagger wit. The subjects dear to this book first converged in Machado's body and pen, and his writing helped inspire my own reflections on the convergences of seemingly diverse roles around the poles of agency and automatism. In the epigraphs I have chosen, he invites us to the streets of Rio de Janeiro and Paris. In the conclusion, he finally weighs in, adding his voice to the closing arguments. In the meantime, here are the nearhuman agents we will meet en route.

CHAPTER 1: ROSALIE

Chapter 1 uncovers a web of intersections between perceptions of near-human animals like monkeys, nearhuman humans in the form of psychiatric patients and slaves, and nearhuman modes of action like spirit possession, somnambulism, and hypnotism. The story unfolds, on the one hand, between late nineteenth-century French psychiatry, centered at the Salpêtrière under the direction of Jean-Martin Charcot and, on the other, the 1888 end of slavery in Brazil, which posed a crisis of assimilation and religious freedom. Afro-Brazilian spirit-possession rituals were classified, diagnosed, and treated in the terms of automatism, relying on the tools of hypnosis and diagnoses like hysteria, dissociation, and catatonia as minted by Charcot. Charcot, I show, was a rigorous student of medieval and early modern possession and exorcism, and the photographs of patients at the Salpêtrière replicated his careful sketches of possession and exorcism as they appeared in paintings. In this chapter, I map out this network of exchanges. Psychiatric patients on Charcot's ward and their automatic acts were interpreted through the prism of the documented history of European spirit possession. In turn, Afro-Brazilian spirit possession in the wake of abolition was read in the terms of French psychiatric deviance. I show that spirit possession informed diagnoses of French psychiatric patients and of practitioners of Afro-Brazilian slaves. It was via the birth of modern psychiatry that those diagnoses were joined in a shared frame called *automatism* and its subsidiary categories. It was, however, not only discourses and diagnoses that moved between Brazil and France. When the emperor of Brazil went into exile in Paris, Charcot became his personal physician and close friend. His prized capuchin monkey, Rosalie (perhaps named after a prized psychiatric patient), who dined at the family table nightly, was a gift from the emperor himself. Rosalie impinged in certain respects on Charcot's new science, expanding the mediations of automatism to include animal nearhumans, a situation not unlike that of William James, whose early travel journals in Brazil also featured his relationship with a sympathetic monkey. I demonstrate a Brazilian capuchin monkey's role in constituting notions of automatic action in France. In turn, I show French psychiatry's infiltration of Brazilian treatments of Afro-Brazilian possession priests. The category *automatism* was applied to join psychiatric patients, Afro-Brazilian spirit possession, and monkeys in a single ordering frame, with significant social effects.

CHAPTER 2: JUCA ROSA

Photography, like hysteria, arrived in Brazil from France. Chapter 2 investigates the multiple lives of a photograph that depicted a nineteenth-century Afro-Brazilian possession priest—its social life, its ritual life, its legal life, and its afterlives. The photograph was taken around 1870 and is now folded into a faded case file located in the national archive in Rio de Janeiro. It shows a renowned "sorcerer" or fetishist (*feitiçeiro*) named Juca Rosa standing on a proscenium with a devotee kneeling before him. The devotee points a baton or drumstick at the master, expressing humility, homage, and devotion. The photograph represented another kind of nearhuman in that it was deployed as a proxy for the presence of the priest himself and understood by his followers to communicate and carry his power. Telling this story leads to theoretical reflections on the relation of religion and photographs and the management of the religious lives of image-things as vehicles of power. I raise the issue of management to signal how, in fin de siècle Brazil, the coalition between photographs and spirits took shape within forceful regulations and regimes of appearance, legal, social, and cultural. This photograph exerted agency, yet it was far from a free agent. It worked secretly, automatically, through its sheer but barely noticeable presence. Juca Rosa staged and paid for the photograph to use as a particular kind of *carte de visite*, a calling card distributed to followers and clientele as an icon and index of his extended presence and power, even in his bodily absence. The photograph was nearly Juca himself. It offers a window onto a moment of social transformation and intersecting forces: the nineteenth-century abolition of slavery in Brazil and the problem of the assimilation and nationalization of former slaves and their religions as well as the emergence of photography as a new technology of mediation as it was applied to Afro-Brazilian religions and their policing. The goal is to show photography and spirit possession as intersecting, often symbiotic arts of making the previously unseen seen. But it is also to explore the differences in agency between the actual person of Juca Rosa and his iconic photographic likeness.

CHAPTER 3: ANASTÁCIA

Chapter 3 unpacks a different encounter between automatism and agency. It relates an iconic drawing of a human and actual enslaved humans as they were conjoined to produce the spirit saint Slave Anastácia. The story documents a slave turned saint in Brazil via a French traveler's nineteenth-century drawing. This was an instance of a sketch of a dehumanized victim, an enslaved body without will, becoming, through her depicted subjection, an object of ritual devotion. Her images and icons were reproduced in mass media, generating not only pity, trauma, and revulsion but also reverence and attraction. Anastácia was less a historical person than a composite or type. From a sketch, she later metamorphosed into a saint and mass media phenomenon, appearing in myriad shrines and multiple guises, drawing a constant flow of pilgrims and, now, Internet clicks. She is carried on prayer cards, prayed to in shrines, visited on websites, watched on *telenovelas*, and worn on swimwear. Paradoxically, given that her image is one of violent bondage and silencing, she circulates and speaks everywhere. Through the figure of Anastácia, I interpret the ritual attraction to the dehumanized victim-body, the martyr. I show how the kind of agency activated through exchanges with saints is differently emergent depending on the mode of saints' material and social configurations and the *mood* evoked by the saint's manifestation. Slave Anastácia signifies diversely and with varying social effects for different groups of users. In this chapter, I use such radical disjunctures between the forms of presence generated by the same saint to reconsider how saints work by disseminating a mood. By paying attention to a particular unofficial Brazilian saint and her varying settings and moods, I give texture and historical complexity to the notion of automatic agency.

CHAPTER 4: AJEEB

Chapter 4 considers the pull of nearhumanness in the form of human-like machines. It moves from a broad discussion of exemplary religious and literary uses of androids to the narrower scope of the nineteenth-century romance with mechanical chessmen. After a short rehearsal of the story of the best-known figures of that company from Shelley's monster to Von Kempelen's famous Turk, the chapter dwells in greater depth on a lesser-known automaton named Ajeeb as he made his way from Europe to North America and then to Brazil, carried there by a Jewish-Czech entrepreneur named Fred Figner. In spite of Ajeeb's short career in Rio de Janeiro (from 1896 to 1897), he left his mark—a trail of wonder, questions of interiority, and polemics on personhood and fraud. His presence coincided with the large-scale immigration of Ottoman subjects to Brazil, primarily Lebanese and Syrians, in Brazil all labeled *Turks*. I narrate the simultaneous migrations of nearhuman things and actual humans as they collided to generate new religious forms, practices, and systems. When the chess-playing automaton named Ajeeb arrived in Brazil simultaneously with this large new immigrant group of Turks, together they helped launch a new genre of spirit entities called *turcos* into popular religious venues. I use the story of a particular man-machine resident in Rio de Janeiro from 1896 to 1897 to reconsider work on the automaton from a distinctive point of view, namely, that of the ritual attraction to mechanical nearhumans and their powers to generate new religion-like agents.

CHAPTER 5: CHICO X

Chapter 5 recounts the legal uses of spirit testimonies—statements from the deceased as recuperated by spirit mediums, inspired by the French writer Allan Kardec—as they were used in a series of homicide trials in Brazil. The events were precipitated by the celebrity medium and author Chico Xavier. Chico published scores of books via so-called automatic writing. The books were authored by sage deceased souls who, Chico claimed, caused his arm to move like a machine attached to his elbow. He also entered into multiple legal disputes by representing the voices of deceased victims. In this chapter, I explore why people cannot typically be possessed or otherwise act automatically in court since they are obliged to act (or perform) as free, individual persons. Spirits have nevertheless acted in Brazilian jurisprudence by giving testimony, submitted in the form of automatic writing generated by spiritist mediums. They can and do appear in Brazilian court, then, but only in the form of documents. I explore the dedicated semiotic work required for a nearhuman communiqué to transfer a spirit to a document in order to arrive in a judge's hands. Disputes over these legal statements continue to the present. The chapter pivots from earlier discussions of automatic religious potentialities to consider the limits and risks of such engagements. Activating nearhuman figures or approximating them as a deferral of agency presents an effective ritual form, as the previous chapters show. It becomes problematic, however, in contexts that call for a higher degree of reliable or continuous personhood and a more clearly accountable individual than do many ritually circumscribed venues. Academic, legal, and government venues give value to persuasive performances of reliably bounded and continuing personhood—individual or forensic personhood, so to speak—to grant solidity to the currency of declarations, descriptions, theories, hypotheses, and laws issuing from those places. The chapter details the juxtaposition between, on one hand, the *legal* prestige of intent and the kind of individuality such gauging of intent requires and, on the other hand, the *religious* prestige of nonintentionality, the spirits or the Spirit acting on or through a body understood as a vessel of invisible and greater power, with ritual events designed to dramatize the transductions between those conditions. The chapter asks, What happens when those two systems collide in public spaces like the courts? What conflicts emerge when automatic action appears in sites where agentive action and an accountable (and liable) individual are required by the institutional form?

CONCLUSION: AUTOMATIC FREEDOM

Working across the grain of a series of prominent theories to compose a genealogy of agency as used in the study of religion, the conclusion posits a theory of religious agency as craft. Religion is the craft of staging performative events of deferred, suspended, or relinquished individual agency. Seen through this prism, it appears as less the quest after agency as usually conceived than as the quest after automatism, the experience of being acted through. That is itself a form of agency, but one of a quite specific kind.

* * *

Each chapter brings a distinct issue to light, and each follows an unfolding argument rather than a strict chronology. Chapter 1, "Rosalie: Psychiatric Nearhuman," shows how ideas about automatism and agency become intersectionally bundled—in this case, psychiatry, religion, and animal life. Chapter 2, "Juca Rosa: Photographic Nearhuman," examines the capacity of nearhumanness to extend across space and time in certain semiotic forms like photographs that seem to carry within them lives of their own. Chapter 3, "Anastácia: Saintly Nearhuman," considers how fascination and attraction evoke distinct moods through the interactions between specific sites of production and groups of users. Chapter 4, "Ajeeb: Automaton Nearhuman," shows how such moods of agency are materially crafted and expressed through the advertisement of secret interiors, which in turn unleash new kinds of spirit agents, the so-called Turks. Chapter 5, "Chico X: Legal Nearhuman," finally, moves from attraction to the risks of, and necessary limits on, nearhuman agency by showing how given thresholds of reliable personhood are domain specific: the kind of automatic agency that may be desirable in religion-like scenes and situations poses risks to legal ones that need reliable, accountable agents to work. What problems follow when legal thresholds of reliable personhood are transgressed by nearhuman projects undertaken in the wrong place? It turns out—or so I argue—that we still need the individual or a similar threshold of reliable personhood in certain social contexts.

1

Rosalie
Psychiatric Nearhuman

The monkey and the man, the man and the monkey; two inseparable
friends in the house and under the new moon. A thousand stories circulated about this mysterious loner. The most common was that he was
a sorcerer. One person said he was crazy; another saw him as given to
misanthropy.

MACHADO DE ASSIS, "The Straight Line and the
Curved Line" ("Linha reta e linha curva"), 1866

Allow me to introduce Rosalie. Two Rosalies, actually. The first was one
of French psychiatry's most famous patients, Rosalie Leroux. At times
Rosalie's condition—or so reported her celebrity doctor, Jean-Martin
Charcot—took on a posture of religious ecstasy, while at other moments
she snarled like a dog. The second Rosalie was a beloved pet monkey,
and Charcot loved her like a child. Rosalie Leroux was a human acting
bestial, Monkey Rosalie a beastly nearhuman. Given to Charcot by Dom
Pedro II, emperor of Brazil, Monkey Rosalie quickened delight from the
otherwise remote psychiatrist, a perfect gift. Patient Rosalie, on the other
hand, posed a risk and a challenge. Charcot took on the institutional care
of Patient Rosalie in 1871, and she remained hospitalized for the rest of
her life. The gift of Monkey Rosalie arrived two years after the inheritance
of Patient Rosalie. From Rosalie to Rosalie—from prized French patient
to prized Brazilian monkey. Almost surely these two alleged automatic
agents never met, but now they will. Here, I invite them into conversation via the twin stories of late nineteenth-century psychiatry in France
and late nineteenth-century psychiatry in Brazil and of an emperor and
a neurologist. The stories depict adjacent panels across a fold dividing
possessors and the possessed, the master and the slave, the human and
the animal.

I offer the narrative in a series of steps beginning in French psychiatry, proceeding next to a friendship between France's most celebrated psychiatrist and the emperor of Brazil, and ending, finally, in the halls of the first asylum of Brazil. In tracing this crease, I try to show, through a series of key exchanges, how *hysteria* shifted from describing the status of a "female" malady of the "wandering womb" in France to a racial diagnosis of Afro-descendant patients in Brazil. En route we will linger over and mull the role played by a monkey in the middle.

High Priest Charcot

In the early 1880s, no alienist enjoyed the reputation of Jean-Martin Charcot. William James traveled to hear his lectures in 1882. So did Daniel Hack Tuke in 1878 and Wilhelm Fliess in 1886. Freud frequented Charcot's lectures and then salon from October 1885 to March 1886, snuffing cocaine to quell his anxiety, and soon lunched with a troop of accomplished interns like Désiré-Magloire Bourneville, Pierre Marie, Joseph Babinski, and Georges Gilles de la Tourette. Freud's short time in Paris was pivotal. There he turned from the physiology of anesthesia to the study of the unconscious.[1] At public lectures on Tuesdays and Fridays, celebrities and aristocratic dilettantes sat side by side with local scientists and visitors like Freud, Fliess, James, Gustave Le Bon, and, not least, Dom Pedro II, emperor of Brazil.

Tourette, who gained fame for the disease he identified, recorded a time line of Charcot's rise.[2] Born in 1825 to a carriagemaker and his wife, in 1853 Charcot defended his thesis. In 1862 he arrived at the Salpêtrière asylum and began treating a large number of patients, almost all of them women deemed incurably insane. He began giving clinical lessons in 1868. In 1870, following the demolition of a separate building,[3] he was asked to bring the displaced patients into his medical wing. Inspired by symptoms he found in this new captive group, he began lectures on hysteria. After the war against Prussia and the Paris Commune, he was granted his own special ward for these and others he classed as *hystero-epileptics*. The year was 1871, the same year he met the first of his two Rosalies. The hospital walls enclosed some 4,403 people: 580 employees, 87 *reposantes*, 2,780 *administrées*, 853 *aliénées*, and 103 children.[4]

During the 1870s, Charcot's star rose. He made important discoveries in anatomical pathology and degenerative diseases of the nervous system. He cataloged the symptoms of and coined the name for multiple sclerosis and described amyotrophic lateral sclerosis (ALS), aneurisms, and Parkinson's disease. He developed a theory of the localization of brain pathologies in specific neurological sites and published on the secondary effects of neurological lesions like muscular atrophy.[5] Each of

FIGURE 1.1. *Une leçon clinique à la Salpêtrière*, Pierre Aristide André Brouillet, 1887.

these achievements was remarkable; together they were monumental. In 1882, he was rewarded with a new faculty chair and a year later admitted to the Academy of Sciences. Charcot stood at the pinnacle of professional prestige in France. International celebrity was yet to come. It arrived in the last decade of his life with public demonstrations of hysteria and hypnosis.[6] The lectures and displays gave his techniques—and, by extension, the discipline of psychiatry—a public face and provisional legitimacy (figure 1.1).

The disorder of the wandering womb, of course, already had a three-thousand-year pedigree dating at least to Hippocrates and Galen. But hysteria had shape-shifted across the centuries. Charcot's and Freud's attempts to give it a scientific medical frame were the end of the story far more than the beginning.[7] There are many ends still being told, as hysteria in the twentieth century again morphed into a condition of mind, a social frame, even a diagnosis of a historical period. There is an enormous bibliography on the cultures of hysteria and on the work and harm done by both the word and the category.[8] Is there anything that remains to be said? I think so. First is to consider hysteria as nested between versions of nearhuman—the automaton, the possessed, and the animal. Second is to show how hysteria and other categories traveled across the Atlantic to places like Brazil where they were given new, racial forms of classifying use—thus the shift from hysteria as it essentialized gender to hysteria as the mark of the racial other. Third is to situate hysteria in relation to religion-like situations as a form of automatism and uncanny attraction.

While many had studied or written on hysteria in the nineteenth century, none enjoyed the success of Charcot.[9] Hysteria, Charcot argued, could begin in specific traumatic experiences or even suggestion. It was indicated by universal physical symptoms or "stigmata," like changes in sensory perception, disturbances of skin sensitivity, and the susceptibility to hypnotism.[10] Its universality and regularity were crucial. As Jan Goldstein describes, Charcot focused on temporal development—the predictable four stages or stigmata of major, *grand attaque* hysteria. Its "iron laws" included (1) tonic rigidity (the "epileptoid period"), (2) spasms (acrobatics or *grands mouvements*), (3) *attitudes passionnelles* (dramatic renderings of emotions or the "period of hallucinations"), and (4) a final delirium with tears or laughter. These were followed by a return to reality.[11] The fixed stages shaped hysteria into a familiar unfolding story and gripping ritual drama. They made the disease legible and compelling. Their ritual predictability served as the warrant of the procedures' truth.

The secrets of the soul revealed were not unlike the popular dramas of possession and exorcism of an earlier period. The modes and classifications drew on Catholic descriptions of demonic possession. Hysteria was always *the same*, whether across populations, across time, or across place: "Hysteria has always existed, in every place and every time."[12] The possessions and visions of the Ursuline Mother Jean des Anges in 1642 were just like those of Rosalie Leroux. Charcot and the intern Paul Richer reached into the history of art to early engravings of Jesus curing the possessed. They found convincing resemblances between the Salpêtrière's hysterics and figures depicted in Renaissance works like Raphael's *Transfiguration*, where the artist "shows us a young demoniac in a state of crisis."[13] All art history could be pulled into the new anthropological machine of hysterical automatism. So could all places. When the terms of hysteria arrived in Brazil, they were easily applied to descriptions of Afro-Brazilian spirit possession, as we will see.

The universal laws of hysteria prognosticated a secular future when all such phenomena would be set in their proper neurological context. In that sense, Charcot, like the discipline of psychiatry more broadly, mostly played the role of anticlerical positivist and supporter of the secularization of French medical institutions. Yet—to follow an argument forwarded in separate works by Asti Hustvedt and Cristina Mazzoni—in another sense he spiritualized medical practice. His gaze and silent presence "gave [him] the halo of a sacred man by allowing him to reproduce the hysterical attack at will, thus seemingly to perform miracles," according to Mazzoni.[14] He carried the mantle of a shaman. The novelist Maupassant called him the "high priest" of hysteria. There were rumors of miracle cures at the asylum. Freud, too, wrote of Charcot's work with hypnotism, which he learned about in France, as conferring on him a certain reputation as a miracle worker. Is it a surprise that this miracle worker and these religiously invested patients produced a distinct performative and therapeutic synergy? The role of religion at the Salpêtrière seems mostly overlooked, but it was central to the life, thought, and experience of Rosalie Leroux. To see it, however, we need to apply a wider-angled scope to religion-like situations than the questions of anticlericalism or the secular might usually allow.

We should notice, for example, how Charcot and his interns filled their records and diagnoses with religious nomenclature: *transfiguration, stigmata, cruciform pose, demonic possession, ecstasy, aura.*[15] The intern Désiré-Magloire Bourneville's preface to Charcot's last published essay, "The Faith-Cure" (1893), provides an example of the strange hybrids that arose, with his proposals of neologisms like *hystero-demonapathy* (*hystéro-démonopathie*) or *possessed hysteric* (*hystérique-possedée*).[16] Another is the bridging work of the psychoreligious word *stigmata*, at least since Saint Francis associated with Christian spiritual manifestations revealed in skin. Yet another is *transfiguration*, a term Charcot applied with equal enthusiasm to a painting of a biblical scene by Raphael and a patient's distorted face.[17] The terms and procedures of Charcot and his disciples joined two forms of dissociation under new classifications of disease. Demonic possession and hysteria were bound together as participants in the same event, merely with distinct diagnoses: possession from the past, hysteria from the present.

Charcot performed these dramas of possession and pathology— historical as well as diagnostic dramas, I am arguing, for how they seamlessly wove together medieval possession events and contemporary patients in a single strand— in regular public demonstrations. If hysteria itself was made into a compelling ritual drama, so was its public presentation. There were the Tuesday lectures, the more or less improvised interpretations of patients carried out before an audience, and the Friday lectures, carefully written to accompany demonstrations featuring known and reliable patients. A new amphitheater with seating for five hundred was always full. Visitors swarmed the lectures, making stars not only of Charcot but also of his supporting cast of patients. Neurological science became a marvel.

In addition to hysteria's predictable laws, the visual effects provided a second reason for Charcot's public appeal. Charcot emphasized the visual in his own studies—"I am absolutely only a photographer; I register what I see"—and also in his presentations.[18] It was fantastically effective. Like most viewers, Freud was optically inspired: "I found to my astonishment that here were occurrences *plain before one's eyes*, which it was quite impossible to doubt, but which were nevertheless strange enough not to be believed unless they were experienced at first hand."[19] In a different appeal to the visual, patients' poses were rendered in vivid drawings by Charcot himself and by Paul Richer. By the 1870s, the sketches were joined by photographs taken by Albert Londe and Paul Regnard and developed in the hospital's new photograph lab, Le service photographique de la Salpêtrière. Beginning in 1876, these photographs were printed in a special publication devoted solely to patients' bodies, *Iconographie photographique de la Salpêtrière*. Photographs of the fifteen-year-old Augustine, Marie "Blanche" Wittman, Rosalie Leroux, and other women were featured.

The photographs emphasized the women's erotic vulnerability.[20] Doctors' observations did too. Bourneville noted that Blanche was "very buxom" and that Augustine was "well developed."[21] Rosalie Leroux had the "allure" of a simple girl from the country. A doctor from Kansas City visiting a lecture in 1889 described a demonstration that starred "a pale-faced girl, with abundant black hair and a handsome face . . . As she lay helpless against the white pillow, her long lashes curving over her fast closed eyes, she suggested the 'sleeping beauty.'" By the time she was awakened from her hypnotized state, he added, she was "half-dressed before a jovial crowd of [male] medical students."[22] Despite the fact that Charcot expanded the purview of hysteria to include men, only women appeared in the published images of the *Iconographie* volumes. The photographs and demonstrations announced another delicious feature of hysteria, the afflicted women's absence of agency.

These bodies without will fascinated. Blanche, Augustine, Geneviève, and Rosalie—all became familiar public characters by virtue of their void plasticity, as automatons.[23] Charcot sometimes asked hysterics in trance to write his name, a version of automatic writing.[24] A gong sounded; bodies were pierced and posed. But, among the patient stars, Marie Blanche Wittman, who appears in Brouillet's 1887 painting (see figure 1.1 above), was the most famous.[25] Once she achieved a hypnotized catalepsy, Charcot's interns pushed her limbs into various positions to which she showed no physical resistance. Her body would stay frozen in a given position indefinitely until they molded her anew. Wittman was, or so wrote Charcot's students Tourette and Richer, "an actual automaton who obeys each and every order given by her magnetizer." They continued: "[This catalepsy] transforms the patient into a perfectly docile automaton . . . on which one can imprint, with the greatest of ease, the most varied positions. Moreover, these positions are always harmonious, making our automaton something more than a simple mechanism à la Vaucanson."[26] This *man-machine*, as Charcot called her with reference to La Mettrie, could be animated by electricity—a probe touched to her face would spark a series of expressions in a completely mechanical way.[27] "Like another Pygmalion," added Dr. François-Victor Foveau de Courmelles.[28] Besides automatons, the women were compared to animals for their ability to reveal automatic reflex responses; they were "the frogs of experimental psychology."[29] It was a familiar logic: the phrenologist Franz Josef Gall, who studied in Paris from 1807 until his death in 1828, was known to have juxtaposed women's and monkeys' brains in his theory of localized pathology. Woman, machine, animal.

The demonstrations offered new medical considerations of will. In fact, "deficient will power" was one of hysteria's known symptoms.[30] Charcot's student Pierre Janet added, in addition to *dissociation*, the term *abulia* to the tool kit. *Abulia* named the disease of the loss of will. Patients suffer "the invasion of all automatic phenomena which they cannot stop." They become "voluntary slaves."[31] For sufferers of abulia, automatic mimesis was the sole form of action. Thomas Saville, another former student of Charcot's, listed "deficient will power," "want of control over the emotions," and acting "wayward . . . no introspection, nor living by rule," in his *Lectures on Hysteria*.[32]

The Passion of Rosalie

Among the most reliable and dramatic performers of automatic action and the wondrous absence of will, was Rosalie Leroux. She was older than many patients—two years senior to Charcot. She entered the Salpêtrière in 1846, at the age of twenty-three, and was placed in Charcot's care in 1871, the same year that he began to lecture on hysteria. In his first description of her, she was forty-eight and already a "celebrity case in the annals of hystero-epilepsy."[33] So dramatic were the symptoms, wrote Bourneville, that everyone who worked at the Salpêtrière had vivid recollections of her.[34]

She was memorable to others as a famous *case*, a mediator of the specific and the general, a pedagogical tool, an exemplar.[35] We might even say that Charcot helped establish the case study as the proper genre of psychoanalytic research, in part with and through Rosalie and the other celebrity patients. The idea was not so much to cure or heal them as it was to describe, document, and display them. Few of these patients ever left the asylum. They were ensnared in a set of fixed terms and procedures, their role being to body forth as a compelling case *of*. And, like a ritual procedure, that bodying forth had to be done over and over.[36] Rosalie was translated into a series of photographs, diagnostic episodes, spoken lessons, and written reports. All the details of her identity needed to be known and understood, only to then let them recede so that she could represent a regular, even a universal type. But, for Rosalie herself, her memories were more than a case. They seared her, and they bore down. As an eleven-year-old child, she had been chased by a rabid dog while bringing her foster father his dinner in another village. The dog frothed at the mouth; its eyes bugged out of its head. While trying to escape, Rosalie fell and was badly injured. She had recurring panic attacks for eight days, picturing the dog chasing her. She began having episodes of unconscious lethargy lasting minutes at a time. Then, at sixteen, she saw a murdered woman's body with the killer (the woman's husband) standing over it. A third great fright occurred when she was crossing through woods at night in the same area where a girl had been killed a decade before. She carried a sum of money with her, and a robber gave chase in the woods while calling out, "I'm going to get you, you pig!" She suffered violent convulsions and unconsciousness. She came to, wrapped in a thicket of brambles, but again entered another prolonged state of unconsciousness.[37] When she was admitted to the Salpêtrière, she had been in a lethargy lasting three days and nights that was followed by paralysis.

Rosalie's screams blended fears of the three terrors—the dog, the dead body, the robber. Other patients like Geneviève, wrote Charcot, showed signs of *tarentism*, but Rosalie was "a *demoniac*, someone who is *possessed*," akin to the "Jerkers of the Methodist camp-meetings."[38] She became Charcot's exemplar of "violent epileptiform hysteria," or *grande hystérie*.[39] Her appearances became a set piece of public lectures. Her fits of rage, during which she tried to bite those around her, alternated with lethargy. In her delirium, she saw rabid dogs in forests and felt birds in her head and lizards in her stomach. She suffered visual and aural hallucinations: swallows and butterflies on the floor, lizards on the wall, a big black animal like an ox. She swayed before the amphitheater audience, emitting a hoarse sound "like the snarl of a dog."[40]

In 1878, Charcot coined a new term, *zoopsie*, referring to animal visions, to describe some of Rosalie's hallucinations. He described hysterics as sometimes frightened by visions of animals appearing in a predictable part of the visual field: "They see rats, cats, black animals in general, and always on the same side . . . or arriving from behind toward the front."[41] Freud applied the neologism in the case of Emma von N., a.k.a. Franny Moser, who suffered at once from zoophobia and zoopsia.[42] Despite Moser's great wealth, poise, and privilege, she stuttered and had nervous tics like smacking her lips. She was constantly frightened by images of animals: depictions of American Indians dressed as animals, memories of siblings throwing dead animals at her as a child, and visions of such things as legs of chairs transforming into snakes, a hawk goring her with its beak, toads, leeches, worms, horses, a bull chasing her, small lizards that grow gigantic. She described to Freud her reluctance to shake anyone's hand for fear her hand might turn into an animal. She could not take long railroad trips. *Zoopsia* helped describe not only her general fear of animals but also her fear of their nearness—that she could become part animal, as in the story of her hand, or that animals could filter through her skin, as in the idea of chair legs as snakes or the vision of walking on leeches. Her repulsion at seeing American Indians dressed in animal skins played on a similar theme, the prospect of the human becoming animal. The beasts were too close, right up against her, maybe crossing into her. It would explain her chronic stomachaches. Maybe she was already an animal.[43]

Rosalie suffered similar fears, but her pain alternated with religious ecstasy. Bourneville had the most daily contact with her and in 1875 described her case. In Rosalie's *grandes attaques*, she underwent physical contractions that assumed the form of a crucifixion (*crucifiement*). In an attack on October 19, 1872, Bourneville reported: "Her upper limbs are extremely contracted and stretched perpendicularly to her body, ON THE CROSS." The crucifixion lasted from 10:00 A.M. until 2:15 P.M., after which she returned to her normal state and uttered, "My God! I felt so good!"[44] Five minutes later, she returned to the cross for an additional three and a half hours. On October 30, there was another crucifixion attack lasting thirteen hours, from morning until night.

On October 31, 1875, after presenting her stigmata and passing through the ecstatic stage, Rosalie declared that she had visited heaven, where she saw Christ, Mary, and other saints. Bourneville wrote: "Agitation, hiccups, swallowing. The head and then the legs turn rigid. Then the crucifixion is complete. . . . The descent from the cross happens little by little. . . . [Rosalie] seems to wake from a dream: Where am I?" She awakens, stands up, sits down, laments: "I felt so good up there! . . . It was so beautiful!" Bourneville transcribed her description: "She was in heaven, in a dazzling light. Everywhere there was foam, little Saint-Jean, woolly sheep, brilliant diamonds, drawings, paintings, stars of all colors. Our Lord had long brown curls and a red beard. He's handsome, tall, strong, all in gold. The Holy Virgin is golden too [two days before she had been silver]. The Lord spoke to her, but she can't remember his words. She couldn't respond, she was too emotional! . . . She saw Mlle Léontine D [the daughter of a staff person], who told her she was very happy, that there was a place there for her and her mother. She groaned and seemed to regret not being able to have these visions any more."[45]

Rosalie verbally placed herself in heaven, describing herself as with

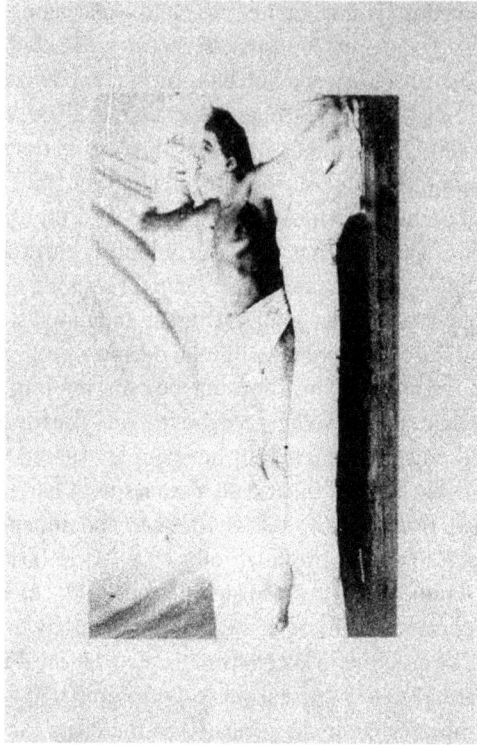

FIGURE 1.2. Rosalie Leroux in the "crucifix" pose. Désiré-Magloire Bourneville, *Iconographie photographique de la Salpêtrière (Service de M. Charcot), par Bourneville et P. Regnard* (Paris: Aux Bureaux de Progrès Médical; V. Adrien Delahaye, 1876–77), 1:39 (plate 6).

Jesus and then "coming down." But the doctors kept her on the cross: Paul Richer's drawing that accompanied Bourneville's report depicted her body turned vertically, as though pinned, even though she had been prone on a bed during the episode. Bourneville published the drawing that way, in vertical alignment as a crucifixion. The photograph that followed in the *Iconographie* was posed the same way (figure 1.2).

Rosalie's religious visions were unusually intense but not unique. After all, many patients at the Salpêtrière were raised in convent schools and had visions filled with religious figures. Two were former nuns.[46] Another, Geneviève Basile Legrande, whom Charcot compared with Rosalie, was born in Loudun, a famous site of demonic possession and exorcism from the seventeenth century—the case of Jeanne des Anges.[47] In the 1876 volume of *Iconographie photographique*, Bourneville and Charcot included a full early account of Jeanne's possession and exorcism. And she was only one model for patients among many. Blanche Wittman and Geneviève admired a contemporary visionary named Louise Lateau of Belgium, about whom Bourneville published an entire volume in 1878, *Science and Miracle: Louise Lateau; or, The Belgian Stigmatic*.[48] Lateau, born in 1850, achieved fame—even crowned as a "hysterical saint" by the Italian criminologist Caesar Lombroso—by bleeding regularly on Fridays from her side and hands. Bourneville viewed Rosalie as having exactly *the same* condition as Lateau: contractions, rigid crucifix poses, visions, stigmata. Rosalie's fellow patient Geneviève called Lateau "her sister" and in 1876 even fled the Salpêtrière to visit her.[49] Rosalie also felt a kinship with Lateau. But, during her *grandes attaques*, her cruciform poses seemed to mimic another celebrated contemporary mystic, Saint Bernadette Soubirous of Lourdes, legendary for the visions of Mary that made Lourdes France's most visited pilgrimage site.[50]

Charcot himself was irreligious and vaguely anticlerical but, in keeping with the social norms of his class, had his children baptized and entertained prelates like Cardinal Lavigerie in his home.[51] Despite his personal disinclination, he was sharply attuned to the history of religion as a source of psychiatric data. I would even say that religion was central to his work. In the lecture "Seizième leçon: Spiritisme et hystèrie" (as transcribed by Tourette), he presented religion as a cause of hysteria—an idea that would be taken up and repeated in Brazilian psychiatry. And, in "The Faith-Cure," he acknowledged religion's capacity to cure, if not in the way devotees believed it did. Both as cause and viable cure, Charcot's hysteria was pervaded by religion. It was built in relation to the history of demon possession, and its emergence as a category was fundamentally an act of the historical translation and revision of possession episodes whose two key features were automatism and visions of gods, animals, or both.

Among the most illustrious of witnesses to these translation cases was the emperor of Brazil, Dom Pedro II. A follower of Charcot's career since the 1860s, and an elegant speaker and writer of French, the emperor was an especially keen and consequential reader and listener when it came to matters of the mind. After all, he had inaugurated the first psychiatric asylum in all Latin America. Understanding his and Charcot's relationship will help shed light on Rosalie, Charcot, and the translation of French psychiatry into Brazilian terms and institutions.

The Emperor and the Doctor

The emperor of Brazil traveled to Europe three times prior to his final exile to France in the wake of the 1889 fall of the monarchy in Brazil—in 1871–72, 1876–77, and 1887–88. Even earlier in his life, he was a keen

follower and patron of science in Europe. The first correspondence between the emperor and Charcot dates to in 1869, when on March 15, 1869,
Charcot wrote to Pedro to thank him for nominating him to receive the
Grand-Croix de l'Ordere Imperial de la Rose, a national medal of honor
in Brazil akin to being knighted: "Sire, I'm proud of this high distinction,
even more precious for how it links me in a new way to a liberal sovereign
who I have long admired as a savant, and who I have recently learned to
love with a lively and sincere respect. From your colleague at the Institute
of France, Charcot."[52] Pedro met Charcot in person in Brussels in August
1876, having enlisted his services to treat his wife, Theresa.[53] Charcot had
been recommended to him by Dr. Charles-Édouard Brown-Séquard,
whom Pedro had met in the United States on the occasion of the Centennial International Exposition in Philadelphia.[54]

So began a friendship and professional relationship that lasted until the
emperor's death. The two men nurtured bonds of care, mutual respect, and
shared interests—a "doctor of state diseases," as Pedro once called himself
in a conversation with Longfellow, and a doctor of the mind.[55] Neither was
much interested in politics. The emperor confessed in a letter to Count Arthur de Gobineau, the racial theorist and the French ambassador to Brazil:
"Politics for me is but the difficult carrying out of duty—I bear my cross."[56]
Charcot took a similar view. He was a friend of important politicians, and
even hosted important state dinners, but remained mostly aloof from the
upheavals of early 1870s France.[57] Work, study, art, and his family filled his
daily schedule. Both were extremely well read and on nearly every subject.
When Gobineau first met the emperor in Brazil, he was stunned, writing
to his wife that it was "unheard of" how much the emperor had read, that
he had read "everything, but really and truly everything."[58]

Pedro II was admitted to France's Academy of Science in early 1875,
and the correspondence between him and Charcot increasingly shared
news from the intellectual front in Paris.[59] "Your Majesty, the science
has gotten lazy [un peu chômé]," wrote Charcot.[60] He reported on Louis
Pasteur's vaccinations for rabies that had been tested only on animals
when in fact testing needed to be carried out on human subjects.[61] One
letter reported on the Brazil pavilion at the international exposition in
Paris and the positive impression it made: Charcot assured Pedro that the
Brazil section was cradled within the French displays, which "seemed to
welcome it like a preferred guest."[62] The two exchanged news and good
wishes for the health and well-being of their wives and children.

When in Paris on his extended sojourns, the emperor attended
Charcot's lectures at the Salpêtrière. He was a regular guest at Charcot's
home, where they dined and played billiards. He joined Charcot's weekly
Tuesday-night soirées, which many other distinguished guests also at-

tended. Charcot's last secretary-intern, Georges Guinon, emphasized his master's unusually warm friendship with Pedro, singling him out as a special guest in the Charcot home.[63] The emperor's routine diary entries let us hear some of the rhythms of their social life:

OCTOBER 23, 1887 [SUNDAY]
. . . 7:10 in the evening. I went to Salpêtrière and watched Charcot's experiments using hypnotism on persons with nervous disorders. Remarkable facts were given that cannot be attributed to pretense.[64]

APRIL 5, 1890, SATURDAY
. . . 10:30. Saw my great grandchildren. I was with Charcot and spoke with him about the projects of the Academy of Science, for which he is leaving for Paris today. Asked him to remember me to my well-known colleagues, including to Quatrefages [a French biologist in the academy] who left me with his article on "Théories transformistes" in the March edition of the *Journal des Savants*.[65]

OCTOBER 10, 1890, FRIDAY
. . . 10:50. Dined well in the company of Charcot, with whom I mostly talked about his hypnotism experiments.[66]

OCTOBER 27, MONDAY
. . . Visited Charcot in his house in Faubourg St. Germain, no. 237. It's like a museum and I couldn't begin to say all I found artistic and interesting. The house has a lovely garden. I was with the whole Charcot family, though his son left before me to attend his course. Going now to speak to a woman.[67]

The emperor's diary notes also give routine details of his life in Paris between his visits to the Charcots. He dressed by 8:00 A.M. and retired to bed by midnight. He slept well and ate with gusto. He noted the rainfall and took photographs. During most of his time in Paris, he seemed blissfully unencumbered by the dramatic changes afoot in Brazil, from the abolition of slavery in 1888 to the founding of the First Republic.[68] Perhaps in a sense he was finally free of the burden of statecraft that he had not chosen and never enjoyed. Now he gave free reign to his aesthetic and intellectual tastes. He played pool at Charcot's or at the Club Nautique; he read scientific articles; he attended shows by Sarah Bernhardt and Georges Sand, took a trip to Cannes with Fustel de Coulanges, chatted with Ernst Renan. He worked on translations from Arabic, Hebrew, and Sanskrit. He read in English from works by Shakespeare (Charcot's favorite writer) and Longfellow, his personal friend. He attended exhibition openings and lectures about apes at the Musée de l'Homme.[69]

Among his many other pursuits, Pedro was deeply interested in psychology. As early as September 11, 1880, he had written to Pasteur in Paris about the course in the anatomy of the nervous system he was following.[70] But his interest in psychology and the nervous system appears likewise in his heavily marked and annotated edition of *Essays of Contemporary Psychology*, by Paul Bourget.[71] And he was impressed by Charcot's demonstrations of hypnotism—so much so that he visited displays of hypnotism by other experts in order to compare them and found them lacking. One of them was by a stage performer called Pickman whose tricks he considered bald chicanery. On November 25, 1887, he recorded: "Dined with appetite. Afterwards watched hypnotic experiments done by Pickman. Seems like a great charlatan, but I had a wonderful time. They made me laugh."[72]

In the late 1880s, Charcot accompanied the emperor as his personal physician on therapeutic trips to Baden-Baden in Germany and Aix-les-Bains in the south of France. He wrote letters detailing Pedro's fickle health to the emperor's personal physician, Claudio Velho da Motta Maia, warning against his psychic and physical overwork and fatigue.[73] This diagnosis, *surmenage*, was an invention of Charcot's student Paul Richer. It built on other maladies of the day like *neurasthenia* (George Beard, 1870) and *degeneration* (Max Nordau, 1892). The terms named a general late nineteenth-century malaise and weariness that gained prominence alongside hysteria.[74] The new illnesses crossed registers, at once naming individual, social, and national fears of decline. They served to draw national distinctions, as in Beard's view of neurasthenia as an especially American disease, or Charcot's diagnosis of the Hungarian wandering Jew ("ambulatory automatism") as an Israelite malaise, or Henri Meige's billing possession delirium as an especially African malady. We can draw a direct line between individual diagnoses like the one the emperor received and sociological theories of anomie and declension from Durkheim's 1897 *On Suicide*, Gustave Le Bon's 1895 *Psychologie des foules*, perhaps even as far as Spengler's 1918 *Decline of the West*. In fact, when Charcot chaired the 1890 World Psychology Congress, Freud, William James, Durkheim, and Le Bon were all in the room, all breathing the air of the automatic as a cipher of human decline.

To counter surmenage, neurasthenia, and degeneration, physicians sought so-called dynamogenous sources of vitality. Beard offered some promising cures—Bordeaux, Claret, and marijuana, for example. Others among his remedies would today give us pause: strychnine and galvanic currents through the head. Still other tonics included hypodermic injections of high doses of caffeine, often administered to Dom Pedro.[75]

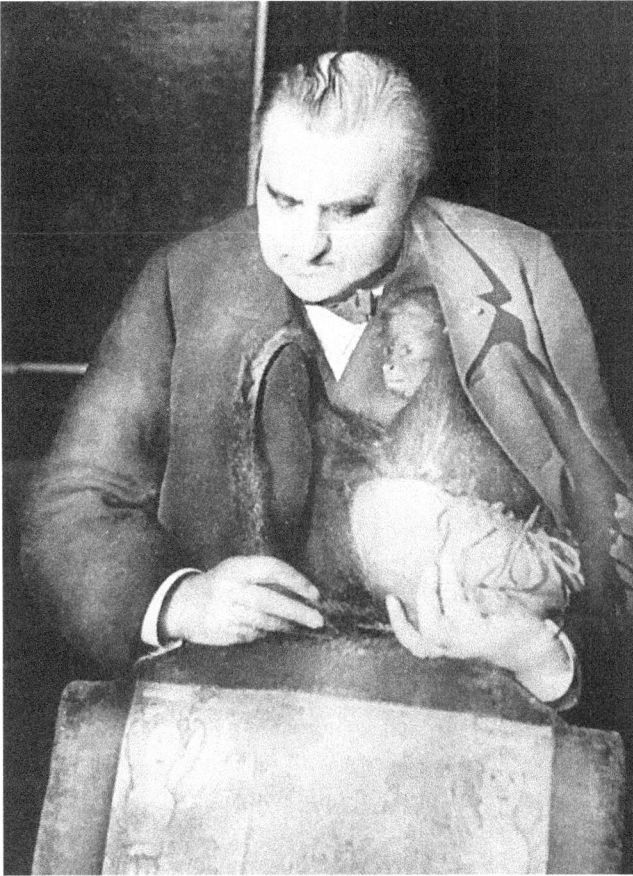

FIGURE 1.3. Charcot with Rosalie. From Christopher G. Goetz, Michel Bonduelle, and Toby Gelfand, *Charcot: Constructing Neurology* (New York: Oxford University Press, 1995).

Charcot's colleague, Dr. Brown-Séquard, reported "rejuvenated sexual prowess" at age seventy-two after "subcutaneous injections of extracts of monkey testis."[76] William James, like Durkheim, saw religion as a possible counter to surmenage and overcivilization. Charcot and the emperor, by contrast, cultivated dynamogeny in the company of animals (figure 1.3).

Monkey Rosalie

Both Charcot and the emperor were members of the Society for the Protection of Animals in Paris. Pedro shared Charcot's repulsion at animal cruelty and a suspicion of the value of medical experiments on animals.

He cast himself as a patron of Brazil's natural world and engaged experts to catalog the birdlife of Brazil. He hired a French landscape designer to oversee his gardens and parks, including those at his main palace at Quinta da Boa Vista, Rio de Janeiro, which he filled with diverse species. Prevailed on by the baron of Drummond, he created a zoological garden in the neighborhood of Vila Isabel, in Rio. His exchanges with Pasteur on animal experiments related to research on rabies and cholera show him to have been more flexible than was Charcot. In one exchange from 1884, Pasteur, pondering how to move from experiments on animals to experiments on human subjects, expressed envy of the emperor's position as head of state and asked him to consider offering him the chance to experiment on subjects convicted of crimes and sentenced to death. Instead of being condemned to death, he proposed, they could choose to become experimental recipients of vaccines against rabies or cholera, an option they would almost surely accept. The emperor wrote back that he had suspended the death penalty but begged Pasteur to come to Rio de Janeiro to develop a vaccine against yellow fever. This time it was Pasteur's turn to decline, claiming that at sixty-two he was too frail.[77]

For his part, Charcot imagined himself in terms of animals and identified others in relation to animals. As a student sitting for his *agregé* exam, he left drawings on his test including the faces of some members of the faculty of medicine drawn as monkeys. Once he drew a self-portrait of himself in the form of a parrot with a beaked nose.[78] A bear was his personal totem and he had one mounted on the wall of his summerhouse in Neuilly and one in his Paris study as well.[79] The family's summer household hosted multiple cats, at least two dogs (including a Great Dane called Sigurd and a Labrador named Carlo), a donkey (Saladin), a parrot (Harakiri), at first two monkeys (Zibidie and Rosalie) and then a third (Zoë), and a duck.[80] Harakiri and the monkeys were gifts from the emperor, brought from Brazil.[81] "He loved animals, or rather he had a tenderness toward them and a great respect for living things," observed Charcot's personal secretary, Georges Guinon.[82]

Charcot was also a strident defender of animal rights laws.[83] At an international event in London in 1881, he denounced the British Cruelty to Animals Act of 1876, which exempted the aristocrats' precious foxhunt.[84] At the same event, he witnessed a debate between Friedrich Goltz and David Ferrier, the first displaying decorticated dogs, the second brain-lesioned monkeys. The question at hand was whether mental functions were localized in specific parts of the brain. Participants traveled to the laboratories of both doctors to see their actual animals. When one of Ferrier's monkeys limped into view, Charcot gasped, "But it's a patient!" ("Mais c'est une malade!"), recognizing and announcing the similarity between human psychiatric patients and the animal subjects.[85] In his published lessons, even when he made reference to research on monkeys—such as the restriction of range of vision as a result of cortical lesion—he insisted that it meant little without seeing direct evidence from experiments on humans.[86] If he stood against the use of monkeys' bodies as experimental fodder, the form of the monkey was sometimes applied as a diagnostic prism for a human condition, as in his description of a patient he attended in December 1874 with a "monkey hand" ("main de singe"): "The thumb is thrown back and out on the same plane as the other fingers."[87]

A sign mounted over the entrance to his laboratory announced, "You will find no dog laboratory here."[88] At the summerhouse in Neuilly another placard cited Shakespeare's King Lear: "As flies to wanton boys are we to th' gods. They kill us for their sport."[89] He abhorred the bullfight and the hunt. He reproached his intern Gombault for his studies of toxicity on guinea pigs. He enlisted in an antivivisection league.[90] What is more, his animal ethics pervaded the household. The Charcot children would never hurt a butterfly or a frog or disturb a spider's web. Their neighbor at the Hotel Chimay from 1875 to 1884, Marie-Louise Pailleron, recalled that, when her poodle broke a foot and, unable to be healed, was chloroformed by the veterinarian, young Jean Charcot lamented that she had not brought the dog to him since he would certainly have saved it.[91]

Léon Daudet, a friend of the family and a frequent visitor in the Charcots' home, juxtaposed the doctor's misanthropy with his rare love of the company of animals and his hatred of any form of animal cruelty.[92] Like Daudet, the emperor was surprised by the contrast between Charcot's love for animals and his comparatively distant treatment of his patients.[93] It was especially apparent in relation to Charcot's monkey, or, rather, monkeys. The emperor seems to have sent the Charcot family monkeys on at least two occasions: first Rosalie and later Zoë, a capuchin.[94] Monkey Rosalie joined the family in the 1870s after Charcot's treatment of Pedro's wife, Teresa, in Brussels 1876. Marie-Louise Pailleron recalled that Rosalie liked to hang by her tail from the lights in the high-ceilinged apartment, unnoticed until she dropped abruptly into the lap of an unsuspecting guest.[95] Jean Charcot, the psychiatrist's son, described Rosalie as a guenon monkey, gift from the emperor of Brazil. He offered a telling anecdote. The year was 1881. A special dinner was given at the Charcots' residence in honor of the Russian grand duke Nicholas. The grand duke wanted to meet in private with President Léon Gambetta to discuss a Franco-Russian alliance. As a close friend of Gambetta's, Charcot agreed to host them at his villa in Neuilly, outside Paris. At the illustrious occasion, the Brazilian monkey chewed on all the perfect apples in the fruit bowl and then replaced them all in such a way that the marks were turned down and invisible. The trick was discovered only when the fruit was served. Madame Charcot was embarrassed, but everyone else burst out laughing when they realized who the guilty culprit was and that she was hiding in the piano.[96] Rosalie was brought back to the table, where she dined with her human family while sitting on the grand duke's knees.[97] She was even an agent, altering the conditions of her surround: the initial awkwardness now broken, a warm informality replaced the former chill and set the stage for an informal détente.

Years later, the Charcot family received a new nearhuman guest. Charcot wrote to the emperor's main Brazilian physician: "Imagine that the large black monkey (a guenon) that you sent to Mlle. Charcot is a wonderful creature—*sweet*, intelligent, easy to raise, we hope. . . . In a while she'll start speaking—she eats every day with us at the table, seated in a high chair!!"[98] Georges Guinon, who was frequently in the Charcots' home, also described her:

> I heard about the first monkey; I only got to know the second, a little guenon with a gripping tail, quick as gunpowder, smart as . . . a monkey, cuddly as a cat, clean as a penny. The patron loved her very much and was entertained by all her pranks. He had set her a place at the table right next to him in an infant's chair with a tablet, and he was enthusiastic when Rosalie stole a hazelnut or a sweetmeat from his plate or, at a moment when he wasn't looking, took a banana with her tail from the fruit bowl. Then the patron laughed, that kind of silent laughter that shook his knees, his chest and his whole body, and suddenly enlivened and cleared his normally concentrated look.[99]

Jean-Martin was "enlivened" and "enthused" by his monkeys' company. It is less clear that his wife shared the same attraction. Perhaps life with all the animals overwhelmed Madame Charcot at times. She was horrified by the incident involving the Russian grand duke and, in 1887, when Charcot and his daughter traveled to Morocco, gave the larger monkey, Zibidie, to the zoo across the street from their home.[100] There Zibidie would have been displayed next to human nearhumans: Ashantis, Nubians, Bushmen, Zulus, Eskimos, and others exhibited at the human zoo that opened in 1877 and closed in 1931, the Jardin Zoologique d'Acclimatation.[101]

Dianne Sadoff argues that Charcot used a static idea of nature on which to paint his dynamic stories of psychosis.[102] This nature included the bodies of patients at the Salpêtrière, a vast repository of experimental material. The idea is that Charcot's fascination with animals as well as their close proximity functioned as a stable *tableau vivant*, a baseline against which to see and measure deviance and illness. This makes sense, but I want to add another perspective, a simpler and more direct route. Charcot felt most human in the company of his animals. It was with animals, wrote his students Alexandre-Achille Souques and Henri Meige, that he most expressed his emotions and seemed most at ease.[103] He was enlivened and clarified by them, wrote his personal secretary.[104] It is even possible—though I have not been able to confirm it—that his monkey Rosalie was named after his patient Rosalie. If so, it would suggest that the two overlapped and converged in his thinking, even that he *identified* the one with the other.

Identification is, of course, a freighted word to apply in these circles. Freud wrote of it in his letters to Wilhelm Fliess, beginning in 1897. Freud himself identified with Leonardo da Vinci and Hamlet (including Hamlet's hysteria). Identification was central to his Oedipal theory, in which children learn to identify with each parent in distinct ways that we need not rehearse here. In his later *Group Psychology*, identification is "the earliest and original form of emotional tie." But it is also the basic structure of hysteria. A person so identifies with another that she feels and enacts that person's pain or hostility. Such identification can spread and become "contagion," even a "hypnotic order" taking over an entire group and leading to the absence of will: "The conscious personality has entirely vanished; will and discernment are lost."[105] *Identification* refers to how characteristics of one being are taken up into another, a kind of possession. What I propose for the case at hand is that the two Rosalies' identities were taken up and triangulated with Charcot's, that the Rosalies were identified in his own thinking, even related to each other through the issues and emotional ties of animality, nearhumanness, and will.

Monkey Rosalie in a high chair at table, Zibidie with Ashantis in a zoo. Agency, structure. As we leave Paris, I want to call attention to another contrast. For patients like Rosalie Leroux or Franny Moser, animals were terrifying. Charcot's and Freud's zoopsia crawled with animal automata that swarmed with blind, hungry instinct. Patient Rosalie ricocheted between visions of the bestial and the beatific. In Charcot's experience, on the other hand, animals were sublime extensions and mirrors of himself, part of his composite agency. For Charcot, Monkey Rosalie was authentic, unmediated, and true. People were the problems.

Brazilian Salpêtrière

"The head monkey at Paris puts on a traveller's cap, and all the monkeys in America do the same," wrote Henry Thoreau.[106] In our case, the head monkey at Paris built a hospital to treat psychiatric alienation, and all the monkeys in the Americas followed suit. The first psychiatric asylum built in Latin America was in Rio de Janeiro. Prior to his journeys, the emperor was long engaged with building a system of care for the insane in Brazil, inspired by France. He founded the first asylum for nervous disorders in 1841, among his very first acts as sovereign. It opened on December 5, 1852, and it bore his name—the Hospício Dom Pedro II. The Hospício was modeled after the Salpêtrière and dotted with statues of its most famed alienists, like Philippe Pinel and Jean-Étienne Dominique Esquirol. The names of the Brazilian institution's salons likewise paid homage to the legends of France: Pinel, Esquirol, Bourneville, Calmeil, Morel. French visitors repaid the homage by visiting the new institution and writing about it. According to one such visitor in 1880, it was well appointed, even *luxe*, the most impressive building in the city. The massive structure housed about 350 patients. "Most were racial Europeans, relatively few *métis*, barely any *nègres*, and a total absence of *indiens*," wrote another French visitor. It caused him to wonder whether there was a racial factor involved in mental illness.[107]

The most frequent diagnoses were various versions of mania, dementia, alcoholism, and epilepsy.[108] From 1853 to 1890, out of 2,088 patients admitted, 846 received the diagnosis of mania in various forms. Mania and monomania—an obsessive preoccupation with one thing—were diagnoses also diffused from the Salpêtrière, in the work of Esquirol, a student of the legendary Pinel. Hysteria barely registered as yet, though in nine cases it crept in via hybrid terms like *hystero-mania*. The handful that received a diagnosis of hysteria proper were white, privileged, and female. For example, Maria da Pureza Guimarães was admitted in 1872 at age twenty-one and died in the Hospício in 1907. She was Portuguese and wealthy, a "first-class"-status patient requiring private service, separate food preparation, and luxury quarters.[109] Afro-descendants constituted a large population in the early period of the Hospício. Among patients registered at intake, 996 were described as white (*branco*), 483 as black (*preto*), and the rest as either one of at least eleven color categories of remarkable precision—for example, brown (*pardo*), tan (*pardo claro*), darker brown (*pardo escuro*), a bit dark (*moreno*), dark (*escuro*), mixed (*crioulo*), and crossed (*cruzado*)—or unnamed. Close to 20 percent of inpatients were slaves or *libertos*, freed slaves. Fully 235 were African born.[110] Presumably, some slaves were pushed into the sanitarium simply to be rid of them because they were troublesome or seen as without value. A *crioulo* named Marcolino was committed in 1865 by his master Joaquim Maria Carlos Verani for reasons of "monomania." Joaquim attested that Marcolino suffered "hallucinations of ambition, making it practical [*con-*

veniente] to have him treated at the Hospício."[111] Owners often freed their slaves upon institutionalizing them to avoid paying the pensions for their sustenance.

In the period from 1890 to 1917, the Hospício became much more crowded, both with patients (7,360 cases) and with newly popular diagnoses. The late century crowding of asylums seems to have been typical in Europe and North America as well. As Anne Harrington writes, the asylum "created its own expanding clientele."[112] The expanding population of patients may have been due to syphilis and its mental effects, as yet unrecognized. In the case of Brazil, we can also point to more specific causes: the end of slavery in 1888 and the sudden migration to cities like Rio, both factors contributing to the sudden precarity. In the admission registers, mania and monomania diminished, and the most frequently attributed illnesses were epilepsy (976 cases), hysteria (573 cases), and insanity (*loucura*; 541 cases). Afro-Brazilian religion, never named as such, became a prime contributor to the rising admissions. The proportion of patients of color rose to over half.[113] To be sure, there was always uncertainty about such classifications. Even among personnel trained in detection, diagnosis, and treatment, the sort of ongoing internal life or consciousness that we call *identity* remained fluid and hazy. Race and color were malleable when it came to the Hospício's intake registers. The journalist Afonso Henriques de Lima Barreto was admitted for his first visit as "white" but then a few years later, picked up drunk on Christmas Day while blathering citations from his favorite French poets Bossuet, Chateaubriand, Balzac, Taine, and Daudet, as "brown" (*pardo*). Perhaps his skin color was seen differently because he was a confirmed alcoholic and returning patient (figures 1.4 and 1.5).[114]

Consider also Alexandrina Maria de Jesus, who was first admitted in 1894. She was brown (*parda*), forty-five years old, and diagnosed with hysteria with alcoholism. In 1899, she was still forty-five, but her race was *fula* (from Fulani), a capacious ethnonym in Brazil applied to African Muslims. In 1905, she was forty-eight years old, and her color was black (*preta*). In 1910, however, she was once again registered as brown but had abruptly turned sixty-three and assumed a baroque diagnosis of insane/manic/depressive. In 1913, she remained brown, but she had regressed to the age of fifty, and her diagnosis had shifted to "periodic psychosis." The point is that her diagnoses, perceived skin color, and age were constantly in flux, even among those with records and expertise to discern and define them. Identity remained mysterious and inscrutable even when forensic techniques like photography were applied to measure it. Photographs were arguably used more to support and confirm interns'

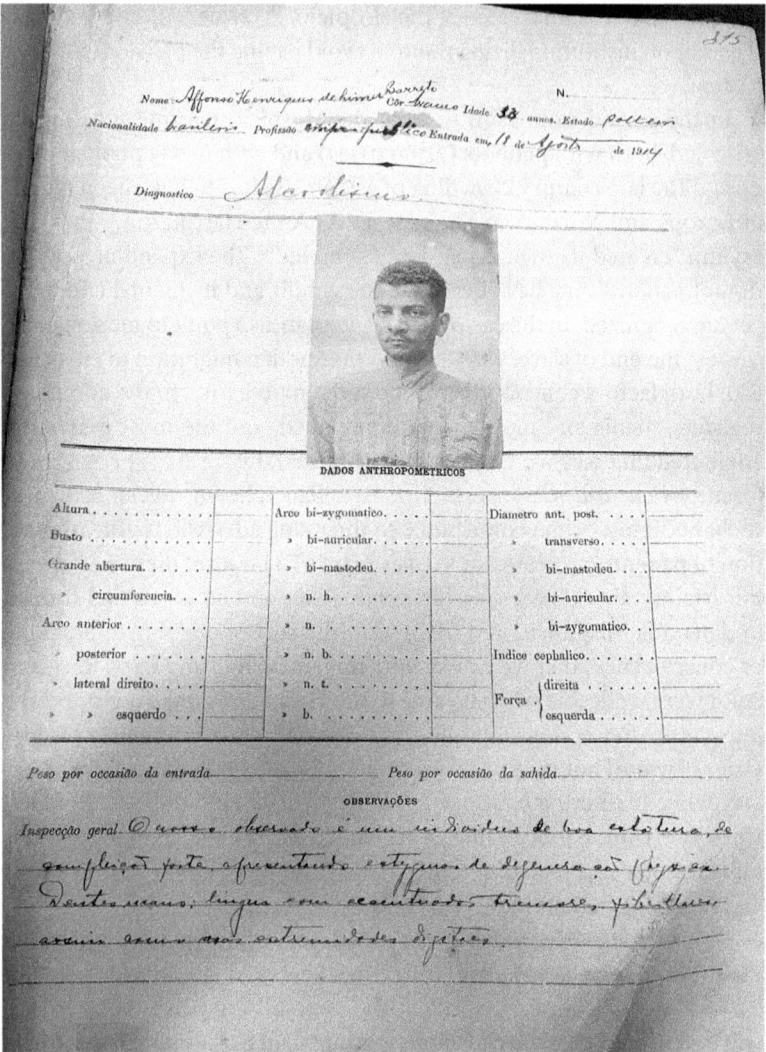

FIGURES 1.4 AND 1.5. The two different Lima Barreto intake files. Núcleo da memória, Instituto de Psiquiatria Universidade Federal do Rio de Janeiro. Photographs by the author.

subjective psychiatric judgments than to anchor patients' identities in enduring and reliable ways; much as photographs had worked in Rosalie Leroux's case at the Salpêtrière to justify and document her crucifix pose. Each fulfilled its mandate to mark Alexandrina as a hysteric, as insane, and as a periodic psychotic. The photographs did not so much express her diagnoses as they performed or helped make them. What strikes me in

Estado civil *solteiro*

Profissão *jornalista*

25 de Dezembro se 819

em 26 de Dezembro de 1919

Causa mortis

Diagnostico *Alcoolismo*

8 de Agosto de 191 4 tendo observação no livro n. 161

de 19—

cases like Alexandrina's is the odd disjuncture between, on one hand, the slipshod rendering of identity in terms of external personal characteristics and, on the other hand, the obsessive care taken to discern and name the multiple identities occupying one physical body. The latter was what really counted in Alexandrina's translation into an exemplary *case*, the former far less. As for Rosalie at the Salpêtrière, who really cared where she came from or where she would end her days? What mattered was that she be affixed to the cross, that she *give evidence* of a regular stage in the ritual process of hysteria.

Religious themes appear in many patients' admission records and documentation. I am curious about the ways the religious lives of patients were seen as deviant even though, on the face of it, they read much like many of the religious experiences described by William James in his Gifford Lectures of 1901–2, where, I note parenthetically, the term *automatism* appeared nineteen times. In his 1881 novella *The Alienist*, Machado de Assis parodied this supposed deviance in a sanitarium clearly modeled on the Hospício:

> A young man of twenty-five by the name of Falcão was convinced he was the morning star; he would stand with his legs apart and his arms spread wide like the rays of a star, and stay like that for hours on end asking whether the sun had come up yet so that he could retire. . . . There were several interesting cases of delusions of grandeur, the most notable of which was the wretched son of a poor tailor, who would recount to the walls (for he never looked anyone in the face) his pedigree, as follows: "God begat an egg, the egg begat the sword, the sword begat King David, David begat the purple, the purple begat the duke, the duke begat the marquis, the marquis begat the count, and that's me. . . ."
>
> I won't mention the many cases of religious megalomania, save for one fellow who, on account of his Christian name being João de Deus— John of God—went around saying he was John *the* God. Then there was Garcia, a university graduate, who never said anything because he was convinced that if he uttered so much as a single word, all the stars would fall from the sky and set the earth on fire, for such was the power which God had invested him.[115]

In Machado's story, patients pursue their religious projects with heroic dedication. They labor to locate themselves in a divine project and carry out their special part. They work to map the strange figures of their imagination onto the grid of a higher plan. Though written as satire, Machado's tale was not far from the truth. Actual patients were extraordinarily devoted to their visions and their spirits. The clinicians' work must have been exhausting. Apparently, it was almost impossible to disabuse patients of their religious commitments. Pinel reported in 1806 that the religious maniacs and melancholics were by far the most difficult to cure, perhaps even incurable.[116]

If so, certain aspects of patients' religious dedication were mirrored by the staff. This has been overlooked because of the emphasis placed on the anticlerical efforts of certain doctors, but that is too limited a view.[117] Pinel had observed already that most of the history of the treatment of "mental affections" was associated with priests and the duties of the "sacerdotal office."[118] Perhaps we could say that there was a dialectical exchange between the religious goals of patients and those of the staff. In Machado's story, the Director explains: "The asylum is like its own separate world, with a temporal authority and a spiritual authority [*governo spiritual*]."[119] The Hospício Pedro II's treatment philosophy was inspired by Pinel and Esquirol, the famed doctors of the Salpêtrière, who approached alienation as organic—caused by cerebral lesions or other failures of the nervous system—but also experiential, mental, or even spiritual.[120]

In the mid-1860s, according to Dr. Manoel José Barbosa: "The alienist doctor prescribes little but observes the hygienic conditions of the sick, consoles, animates, seeks by every means in his reach to restore their spiritual calm."[121] It is clear that interns and doctors had strong normative ideas about religion even later in the century. Thus, of two different patients admitted on the same day, April 1, 1897, one was documented as having "incoherent religious ideas," while another was described as "manifesting perfectly coherent religious ideas."[122] And, as at the Salpêtrière, psychiatry and religion overlapped through notions of healthy spirit versus religious delirium. The historian Lilia Schwarz reported one doctor's recorded observation: "Presents as calm; obedient attitude; tranquil mood; asked about reason for interment said she doesn't know, has a sense of how but not place or time . . . said that on the Isla do Governador, where she lived, she was taken as a sorcerer [*feitiçeiro*], and that for that reason the priest often came to bless her . . . has religious delirium and assumes a mystical attitude."[123]

In 1914, the writer and reporter Lima Barreto was, as we have seen, admitted for his diligent alcohol abuse and reported that to be part of the Hospício community was to live the "show of insanity" (*espetáculo da loucura*). Half the patients suffered from a hereditary illness, and 10 percent were alcoholics, but the remaining 40 percent were spiritists of one type or another. You could not count all the patients with heads peopled by spirits and things of the otherworld, Lima Barreto wrote: the dead of their families, enlightened great ones, astral forces, all alive, touched, heard, seen. Even he dreamed of an otherworld. In the asylum library, he revisited his love of Jules Verne and dreams of voyages in a zone apart, at sea on the *Nautilus* under waves of cachaça.[124] In this hospital, he wrote, "everything is black [*tudo é negro*]" because most patients were black; the color black "cut" and imposed itself in that place. Lilia Schwartz noted that the diagnosis of religious delirium was always associated with degeneration. At the Hospício, as abroad, religious delirium, degeneration, automatism, and blackness were gathered.[125]

Patients' vivid religious lives were surrounded by the institution's religion. The main daily caregivers were Catholic sisters, and the treatment model was intended as both medical and moral, "mixed therapy" (*tratamento misto*). Masses were said daily; patients were allowed to attend once a week and on religious holidays. The asylum was officially under church direction, linked to the Sisters of Mercy (Irmandade da Misericórdia) until the founding of the republic and the separation of church and state in 1890. The second in command at the asylum was the mother superior, and she was in charge of the finances and the daily functioning of the institution. A priest who lived at the Hospício ran the chapel, located at the very center of the building, directly above the pharmacy.

When the asylum tried to modernize its care and professionalize its staff as secular, here again the model was the Salpêtrière. In 1881, the director complained that his authority was undercut by the sisters charged with patients' care.[126] He demanded nurses trained at the Salpêtrière in Paris for their specialized skill but also for their cultivated subservience. As Manuella Meyers describes, psychiatrists aimed to laicize their institutions by purging the staff of nuns. But, at the same time, instead of sharing responsibilities with nuns, they hoped to institute a proper gender hierarchy—male psychiatrists and female nurses. Director Andrade, like the other Brazilian doctors—all male—envied the French-trained nurses' university preparation and their deferential compliance to medical superiors. He sought to replace the old religious order with what the inmate Lima Barreto called another *fetichismo*, the sacralization of university degrees.[127] Even in 1920, many of the medical texts the staff had on hand were written in French. Lima Barreto, who had never finished his university studies, translated instructions for doctors and nurses alike.[128]

Brazilian zoopsia

The word *zoopsia* appears abruptly in the observation records at Brazil's founding asylum on June 1, 1897, became common in 1898, and then faded away by the turn of century.[129] Of course, *zoopsia* could not mean exactly the same thing for Rio's patients as it did for the Parisians or the Viennese. It was inhabited by a tropical menagerie composed of monkeys, parrots, jaguars, snakes, and butterflies. The patient Canisio Baptista de Magalhães, diagnosed with "psychic degeneration," saw visions not only of Jesus nailed on a cross but also a meeting of monkeys whose leader, a demon, tied Canisio up—perhaps, he said, because he had not confessed his crimes.[130] Another patient reported visions of monkeys, dolphins, dogs, and bulls and attributed his troubles to witchcraft.[131] João Simões, admitted on November 17, 1899, suffered hallucinations of wolfmen (*lobishomens*) together with swarms of small monkeys. He could hear them calling his name and screamed for help to be saved.[132] Often, the visions of animals and spirits appeared side by side. Manoel Caluleo, suffering "delirium," sensed the presence of a spirit and at night "had zoopsia" featuring cockroaches, rats, and a portion of frogs under his bed.[133] Eliza Maria Allina de Mello suffered hysteria. She saw demons all the time and also heard them speaking into her ears. At night, she too had zoopsia: enormous uluas, a voracious saltwater fish of Brazilian waters, wrapping themselves around her neck.[134] Candidio Pinto felt fire ants running over his body and saw animals turning into people.[135] America Borges da Silva, diagnosed with epilepsy, reported cockroaches entering his body through his ears.[136] What is noteworthy in these reports is the problem of animals' proximity to the human. Patients sensed animals against their skin, in their ears, drumming on their heads, pushing through their beds, much like Freud's patient Emmy von N., who felt a vulture's beak tearing into her skin. Brazilian patients too seemed to fear being at any moment penetrated by animals that might then occupy and direct them. Many describe transmutations between animals and humans or their body parts. One patient reported seeing human and animal penises changing places.[137] Another, Lydia Paes, diagnosed with hysteria in 1899, described seeing a wax figure transform itself gradually into Saint Michael.[138] In fact, the terms *transfigure, transmutate,* and *transform* litter the record. In this respect, animals were like spirits but different from human-like demons or ancestors. Their main characteristic was their raging physical force— swarming without thought, giving chase without cause or reason.

As in the case of Rosalie Leroux at the Salpêtrière, animal life infused Brazilian interns' observations and diagnoses of patients. Margarida, diagnosed with "idiocy," was described as seeming to act under the influence of some outside power; her voice was automatic and monotone, "like the voices of parrots."[139] Another patient, Elvira Monteiro, a hysteric, had zoopsia but was also described as showing a "bestial air."[140] Patients not only saw animals; they were also often treated like or in terms of animals.[141]

AUTOMATISM

In the 1890s Brazilian asylum, automatism was not merely a symptom ("movimentos automaticos") but its own diagnosis ("ambulatory automatism"), as in the case of Domingos Bonito, white, forty-two years old, admitted on June 27, 1896. Domingos disappeared, unconscious for fifteen days: "He took a train, but then began to feel dizzy. . . ."[142] Ovidio José de Sant'Anna, a delirious alcoholic who entered the asylum in 1899, was admitted because, having attended a spiritist session to see the invocation of spirits, he became perturbed, lost consciousness, and then felt himself being transported somewhere without using his own will.[143] Hysteria—absent from earlier decades' admission records—also became a standard criterion. In Rio de Janeiro, it was often associated by interns and doctors with spiritism. And, in fact, *hysteria with spiritist delirium* became in 1896 a diagnosis in its own right. Reports included standard descriptions of Afro-Brazilian religions. Here is Emiliana de Jesus, *preta* (black), admitted on May 29, 1896, displaying hysteria and spiritist delirium: "Invents spirits in her head. . . . Feels the spirits of others, which she sees enter her body. . . . Has made [*feito*] various offerings to different saints to be cured of these invasions."[144] Another hysteric, José Braz Guimarães, likewise "invokes the saints."[145]

Saints was a term that cut in multiple directions—for example, toward popular Catholic practice and toward Afro-Brazilian spirit-possession religion—referring to possessing deities as saints (*santos*) alongside other terms like orixás. It is clear from the intake records that interns routinely asked about patients' participation in Afro-Brazilian religions, generically referred to by the hospital staff as *espiritismo,* and that it was seen as deviant. That is why patients are described as *confessing* their participation as such ritual events. These intake interviews were part of the rites of passage that turned people into proper patients and cases, through what Harold Garfinkel called "successful degradation ceremonies."[146] Joanna Philomena Ribeiro—black (*preta*), forty years old—became a case as follows: "Constant doubling of personality. . . . Manifesting religious ideas, making reference to things before her life. . . . *Confesses* frequenting spiritist sessions at Abala's house, and it was there she was taken by mental disturbances. . . . She seems to be acted on by one or more spirits. When they enter her body, they make her whole body tremble. Then she feels as though one or more people are inside her, playing, fighting, talking about different things."[147] The hysteric Maria Enéas Ferreira, brown (*parda*), "speaks of religious subjects, invoking God as her protector": "Was taken to a spiritist session. There she saw only bad spirits of women wanting to do her harm. Talks about marriage and about sorcery [*feitiçaria*] she's been a victim of."[148] Deolinda Ferreira dos Santos, thirty-eight, registered as black (*preta*) and a hysteric, also suffered visions, describing them as caused by sorcery (*feitiço*) for which acquaintances who were jealous of her happiness and her employment were responsible.[149] Paulo Claudinhos told interns that he had *feitiço* in his body that caused his epilepsy, sent by a black man (*preto*) who worked on the farm where he lived.[150] Eugenia Felicia da Silva, white (*branca*), 27, "complains about being tormented by spirits, and [claims] to be herself a medium": "She says she gets along with [the spirits]. She sees the shadows of the spirits of people she knows. . . . The spirits speak to her in her chest."[151]

In many cases, zoopsia and spirits appeared together. One evaluation begins with a diagnosis of hysteria accompanied by visions of insects climbing the walls. It goes on: "Recently he cured his ills by resorting to spiritism, and now, wrapped in spiritist theory, he considers himself a medium of the first rank, with celestial power over every saint of the earth."[152] A woman named Thereza, diagnosed with hysteria and religious delirium in 1898, saw a lizard on a plate. The lizard was, she asserted, her guardian angel. The intern noted that she had been involved with *feitiçaria* (fetishism or sorcery).[153] Manuel Bernardo da Silva Rosa, also admitted in 1898, believed himself to be at once a monkey and a spirit.[154] Notice the repeating terms indexing Afro-Brazilian religion—*feitiçaria, espiritismo, blackness, animality*—being psychiatrically sutured together.

NEARHUMAN GENDER, NEARHUMAN RACE

It seemed obvious in the nineteenth century that, in Brazil as in Europe, the treatment of mental alienation might vary among patients of different races. "A Russian peasant, or a slave of Jamaica, ought evidently to be managed by other maxims than those which would exclusively apply to the case of a well bred, irritable Frenchman," wrote Pinel.[155] The earliest French visitors to the Hospício likewise discerned a racial stratification in the early population of patients in Rio. But Afro-Brazilian patients proved especially hard to read. In 1896, less than a decade after the abolition of slavery was completed in Brazil, the psychiatrist and forensic criminologist Dr. Raimundo Nina Rodrigues published the first detailed descriptions of Afro-Brazilian ritual practices. He focused on the dangerous and the exotic, the "extravagant, strange dances," their "savage and mysterious poetry."[156] In Brazil the founding of the republic in 1890 just after emancipation in 1888 meant that, when Nina Rodrigues's first anthropological study of Afro-Brazilian religions appeared, it was framed by a nervous national question about the possibility of assimilating former slaves and the risks of contagion posed by former slaves' sudden social proximity, including the risks posed by their religions. A medical doctor by training, Nina Rodrigues published a series of eight articles in an 1896 issue of the *Revista brasileira*. In his introduction to the French translation of 1900, in which the articles first appeared in a single volume, he dedicated the work to the improvement or perfecting (*perfectionnement*) of peoples for the sake of the nation.[157]

In the book, Nina Rodrigues described how authentic possession was verified within ritual communities by the total amnesia and lack of will it produced. He noted how neatly it matched the work of the French psychologist Pierre Janet, whom Nina Rodrigues greatly admired. Like Charcot and then Janet, Nina Rodrigues tried to regularize the procedure of hypnotism, but with only partial success. Take this extraordinary sequence of events: One day, while observing a Candomblé ritual, Nina Rodrigues notices a young black woman next to him, also watching with rapt attention. He strikes up a conversation: "Do you have a *santo*, and which?" The girl replies that she does not have the resources for her initiation and therefore had no *santo* seated in her head. Perhaps he would like to help? He agrees to become her patron and fund her initiation. She begins to dance in the *roda*, the ritual circle of dancers, wearing an expression that leaves him with "no doubt that she was not in a normal state." When he later *interrogates* (his term) her, he discovers a gap in her memory precisely at the moment of her possession dance. He trusts her description implicitly; surely she will "confess" the truth. Days later, he encounters her again, this time on the street. Persuading her to adjourn to his office, he hypnotizes her on the first try. She enters a "somnambulant state." Since they are alone in his office, he resolves not to try further experiments until he can assemble additional colleagues as witnesses. The girl returns the next day, when he has arranged for another professor to be present, Dr. Alfredo Britto. Once she is again hypnotized, Nina Rodrigues suggests to her that she is now in the Candomblé temple (*terreiro*), the same one where they first met. He asks her to hear the ritual songs to the gods, to call them to mind. When she hears the music of her saint, Obatalá, he forcefully tells her that she should now "fall into the saint" and be possessed. She begins to sway in the correct manner.

Nina Rodrigues calls her by name: Fausta! What's wrong? She replies that she is not Fausta but the Yoruba/Afro-Brazilian god Obatalá. He tries to make her dance in the form of the god Obatalá, but now she refuses. Obatalá-Fausta does not dance, a departure from the script. She instead lectures Nina Rodrigues on Yoruba mythology and its relation to Catholicism. Now, however, he suspects something. He discerns that the views of the spirit seem quite like the views of Fausta herself—a bit too much like her, in fact. Fausta awakens from her trance, confused and stunned. Even many hours later, she was still so dizzy, she says, that she lost the money Nina Rodrigues had given her.[158]

What a scene! The Brazilian psychiatrist studies Afro-Brazilian spirit possession inside the frame of hypnotism, induced in his office using methods imported from France. I am less interested in the diagnoses Nina Rodrigues assigned to these episodes—from familiar terms of demonic possession and hysteria to his own creative inventions, like "neuropathic mysticism"—than in the situation as such, one in which a remarkable series of encompassments has taken place. The Yoruba gods were brought into the laboratory, called in and out at will. Possession was encompassed by hypnotism—it was Nina Rodrigues who manufactured the descent of the sky god Obatalá by the force of his suggestion. And his book itself, which ended up being directly cited in legal cases in the decade that followed, disciplined Candomblé within the new republic's parameters of tolerable, legal religion. In this triple encompassment, Nina Rodrigues revealed his mastery of idioms, moving nimbly between worlds. Note the way old words were juxtaposed with new ones—*demon/interro-gate/confess/truth*, on the one hand, and *hypnosis/hysteria/psychology/experiment*, on the other—tidily folding the primitive up in the modern and Fausta's experience into his own diagnoses. She was remade as a *case study*, in accord with the new medical genre. But Nina Rodrigues remade himself here too. It was through his relation to possession—the ability to discern it as truth and as fraud (for it is under the suspicion of the decep-tion of public credulity that Afro-Brazilian religions were to be regulated in the early twentieth century) and to translate possession so assuredly into the emerging terms of public health—that he established himself *as* a medical anthropologist, a doctor able to scale up from a case to the collective and universal and, thus, tend the nation's body.[159]

These hypnotic events were not, however, as safely contained as the good doctor hoped. As Michel de Certeau described: "The possession rekindles former conflicts, but transposes them. . . . It reveals some-thing that existed, but it also, and especially permits—makes possible—something that did not exist before. . . . Thus what takes place becomes an event. It has its own rules, which displace previous divisions."[160] My view is that Nina Rodrigues was not able to tell real from simulated possession. Fausta apparently received money from him on several occasions. When she was dizzy even hours after the possession episode, refusing dance and instead lecturing him on Yoruba myth, she lost the money, perhaps warranting another payment. She mimicked the look, just enough. Even Nina Rodrigues remarked on how uncannily her movements resembled those of other priestesses. She played on his unshakable faith in his ability to sift real consciousness and will from mediated versions. Possibly—we cannot finally know—she got him to pay her twice and then never saw him again. "Roll your eyes in ecstasy, and ape his every move," Zora Neale Hurston advised.[161]

Nina Rodrigues tried to make sense of Afro-Brazilian spirit possession by drawing on the powerful vocabulary of French psychiatry. *Hysteria* proved especially useful. He used the word liberally to pull Afro-Brazilian rituals into a comparison with another site, Paris and its world-famous asylum. "The tam-tam of Salpêtrière is not more effective for Charcot's hysterics [than the music of blacks to induce possession]," he wrote. He emphasized the specifically African talent for mimicry. But, in fact, he was a mime in his own right, carefully imitating French techniques. He sought out and found his own hysterics in Brazil. And, just like the famous Jean-Martin Charcot at the Salpêtrière in Paris, he hypnotized subjects in order better to assess their automatisms—their somnambulant states, their suggestibility, their trance-like catalepsies, and, following the term coined by Janet, their dissociations. Much like another of Charcot's students in Paris, Henri Meige, Nina Rodrigues worked the transatlantic fulcrum to answer pressing questions of African hysteria.[162]

Bridge

Dom Pedro II died in the Hotel Bedford in Paris on December 5, 1891. Charcot was one of the three signatories of the death certificate.[163] He himself died not long thereafter, in 1893.

Charcot never visited Brazil, though his son docked in Rio de Janeiro during his expedition to the South Pole and posted a letter from the city recalling honors paid to his father by the Geographical and Historical Institute of Brazil. Both Charcot and Dom Pedro II enjoyed afterlives as spirits. Dom Pedro II continued to pass on words through the medium Chico Xavier, the subject of chapter 5.[164] Charcot's postmortem animation was shorter lived. The writer León Daudet recalled his spectral glide: "At about four in the morning, before dawn, I woke up in my hotel room over the park, filled with the songs of birds. I felt a presence, and without the door opening, Professor Charcot appeared to me, his familiar form grave and serious as he crossed the wide room. His luminously white shirt was open at his powerful neck, and he held his hand to his heart. He disappeared, evaporating into the singing of the birds, he who had loved beautiful music so much. Right away I had the intuition that something terrible had happened."[165] Daudet found the music in the vision significant. What strikes me, however, is that Charcot evaporated into birds.

And what of the song of hysteria? Hysteria's emergence and rise seems, in hindsight, a bizarre accident, a chronotope of a particular decade. Ian Hacking detailed the disease's strange contingency, posing the question: "How can a form of mental illness emerge, take hold, become an obsession in some place and time, and then, perhaps, fade away?"[166] The Salpêtrière generated far more recorded instances of hysteria than did other institutions during the same period, suggesting an odd local concentration.[167] Hysteria was at least partly local in space, despite its successful emigration to Brazil. Even more, it was local in time. The diagnosis of hysteria grew in prevalence at a particular moment and then dramatically declined after Charcot's death. Once Charcot was gone, his most famous patient-performer, Blanche Wittman, abruptly ceased her hysterical crises and instead worked in the photographic and radiology labs. When asked about her earlier life as a hysterical performer, she was barely interested. Yet she denied that her performances been sheer fakery. In a curious statement, she said: "If we were hypnotized, if we had the crises, it's because it was impossible not to have them. For one thing, because it was not at all pleasant. Simulation?! Do you think it would have been so easy to deceive Monsieur Charcot?"[168] And, in fact, Charcot had paid close attention to techniques of simulation. He marveled at patients' inventiveness and the body's capacity for "neuromimesis," the capacity to simulate organic disease.[169] Hysteria, Wittman seemed to suggest, was a real fake. Authentic automatism.

The critics were harsher than were former patients. A sham and a show, reinforced by self-confirming logic and charisma, claimed Daudet.[170] Charcot's Polish student Josef Babinski disavowed organic causes of hysteria after the master's death and proposed instead a new term, *pithiatism*, "from [the Greek for] 'I persuade,' and 'curable'; or, a disease fixable by the power of suggestion."[171] It had all been nothing more than conjuration and contagion. Two other students, Alexandre-Achille Souques and Henri Meige, cast "l'hysterie de la Salpêtrière" as a homegrown sickness, an indigenous malady tasting of its own *terroir*. Even Charcot himself had questioned his model at the end.[172] Charcot's main rival in France, Hippolyte Bernheim of Nancy, claimed that the susceptibility to hypnotism had nothing to do with hysteria, contra Charcot; rather, it was hypnosis that presented a universal human capacity, a position Freud ultimately sided with. Though Freud translated Charcot's essays into German and published a respectful eulogy and homage, he kept a wary distance. He had misgivings, not least about the regularity of Charcot's terms. For Freud, the genre of the case study retained its unique, idiosyncratic features, even though case studies eventually served as evidence of broader disorders. Another contemporary, Guy de Maupassant, felt no such compunction: "We are all hysterical, since Dr. Charcot, the high-priest of hospital-harvested hysteria, spends a fortune maintaining a race of nervous women whom he infects with madness, provoking a demoniacal frenzy."[173]

Writing with a century's distance, Georges Didi-Huberman is gentler, though not much: "The hysterics of the Salpêtrière were so 'successful' in the roles suggested to them that their suffering had lost something like its basic credibility. They were so 'successful' as *subjects of mimesis* that, in the eyes of the physicians who had become the directors of their fantasies, they entirely lost their status as *subjects of distress*."[174] Even admirers worried that Charcot had invested too much trust in hypnotic technique and the organic theory of hysteria, with good reason. Rivals like Bernheim and then Freud established that almost anyone could be hypnotized under the right conditions. The great Charcot's reputation flopped. His shrinking status was evident not only in France but also in Brazil, where press stories citing him in particular and hysteria as a diagnosis peaked in the period from 1890 to 1920, and crashed thereafter.[175]

Ian Hacking argues that debates about whether something like hysteria was real or socially constructed miss the point. The relevant question is not, Was it true? Rather, we should be asking, In what ecological niche did the terms of this illness thrive? Into what larger taxonomies did it fit?[176] My answer is that hysteria, dissociation, monomania, zoopsia, and many others ultimately come down to questions of agency. What was the nature of consciousness and will? How did trauma, like gods and demons, act in us? In the spirit of those wider questions of religion-like things, the very questions of agency and the automatic asked by Charcot left lasting contributions. Beginning in the early 1880s, he directed attention to the role of traumatic experiences, emotions, and ideas—"an active but unconscious mental process elaborating symptoms"—including those he called *hysterical* for the lack of obvious organic genesis and sometimes maintained by dissociative mental processes.[177] Conscious will was not as stable or consistent a feature of human experience as people had thought. It was riven by automatisms.[178]

* * *

I have tried to show how figurations of nearhuman, automatic actors were stacked on a social, religious, and medical bridge spanning France and Brazil. In part, that bridge was built from the copresence of human spirits and animals in patients' and doctors' experiences and the diagnoses that classified those experiences. Patients felt animals against their skin, wrapping their neck, tearing in. In Rio, too, patients' zoopsia indexed the fear of being enveloped by or becoming animals that might occupy and direct them, of losing humanness, crossing a thin line. Animal life served to define human psychic life and its fragility. At the same time, it could serve as a salve for late century exhaustion, surmenage, as in the case of Monkey Rosalie.

William James's diary from Brazil offers possible insight into why. While in Amazonia in 1865 on the Louis Agassiz mission, James described a spider monkey (*coiatá*) as his best and only friend in town: "The excessive mental mobility of monkeys, their utter inability to control their attention or their emotions . . . they are as completely possessed by whatever feeling happens to be uppermost in them at the time" (figure 1.6).[179] He dismissed the idea of monkeys as mere mimics or comic fools. Instead, he focused on their directness and fullness of expression, without filter. This idea, I think, gets at the flip side of automatism as mechanical repetition, namely, the idea of the automatic as unfiltered, direct, and genuine, "automatic freedom" as James called it. If the automatic was a symptom of late century industrial sickness, it could also become its cure. James's

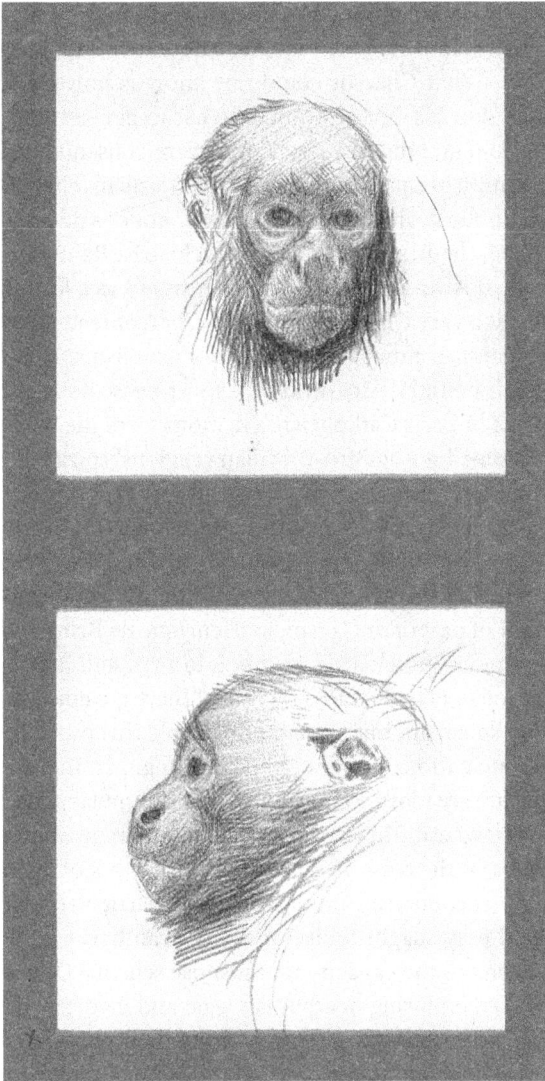

FIGURE 1.6. William James's drawings of his "best friend" in an Amazonian town, Brazil, 1865. Houghton Library, Harvard University.

and Charcot's experiences in the company of monkeys mirror each other in that respect.

This version of automatism, much like Monkey Rosalie herself, helped cut through the crust of overcivilization, neurasthenia, and surmenage. Automaton action was revised into a kind of cultivated skill and craft.[180]

Charcot's agency was made and extended in relation to two Rosalies, the inversions and juxtaposition of a human made animal and an animal made almost human. What Charcot could not know is how this composite agency would after his death continue to act to generate durable ideas of nonagency and automatism. The terms were consequential. In Brazil after the separation of church and state, Afro-Brazilian religions were regulated under public health and hygiene laws, not considered religion at all. And, in 1896, the Brazilian criminal psychiatrist Raimundo Nina Rodrigues classified Afro-Brazilian possession rituals as a form of hysteria. In a way, his was a very Charcot-like move. Charcot read hysteria in relation to seventeenth-century French Catholic exorcisms; Nina Rodrigues read nineteenth-century Afro-Brazilian spirit possession in relation to Charcot. But, if in Paris Catholicism's demons were the stuff of hysterical visions, in Brazil it was Afro-Brazilian religions' spirits and so-called fetishism that offered raw materials for diagnostic experimentation. And, if in Paris hysteria was mostly a disorder of women, in Brazil it became mostly a syndrome attributed to Afro-Brazilians and their religions.

Little changed in the psychiatric view of these religions for decades. A later director of part of the Hospício, Henrique de Brito Belford Roxo, drafted the standard psychiatric textbook in 1921, and it was still being printed and used in 1938. In it Roxo wrote: "There are episodic deliriums not caused by spiritism, but among our people this cause is extremely common. Hallucinations surge without warning. . . . These episodes of spiritual delirium are more common among the popular classes of Rio de Janeiro than elsewhere. They are also much more frequent in Brazil than in Europe. What is the reason? It has to do with a lack of instruction. . . . It is frequently encountered among *negros*, in particular, in part due to the beliefs and easy suggestibility of the African heritage."[181] Charcot's and others' agency—the capacity to transpose schemata across domains easily—produced enduring nearhuman legal and medical structures for Afro-Brazilian others an ocean away. Despite their oppression and legal constraint as a contagious crisis of so-called public health, however, these possession practices and hybrid visions of spirit-infused agency were objects of desire for Afro-Brazilians and Euro-descendants alike and accordingly patronized. As the journalist João do Rio wrote in 1906: "It is we [the middle and upper classes] who assure her [Afro-Brazilian religion] existence, like the love of a businessman for his actress-lover."[182]

On the day Freud left Paris in February 1886, Charcot gave him a photograph of himself. It was inscribed: "À Mssr. de Dr. Freud. Souvenir de la Salpêtrière. 1886. 24. février." The portrait had been professionally taken in a studio, Photographie Champs Elysée. Charcot posed with a grave expression, hands tucked in his dark, long coat. Freud surely kept it, like he kept a copy of Brouillet's painting of Charcot hypnotizing Blanche Wittman on the wall above his desk, where it remained throughout his career. In this way, Charcot lived on, not only as a spirit haunting Daudet, but also as a photographic trace. Chapter 2 looks in more detail at the intersection of these versions of automatic nearhumans: photographs and spirits.

2

Juca Rosa
Photographic Nearhuman

I retired to my study, where I stayed longer than usual. Escobar's photograph, which I had there next to my mother's, spoke to me as if it were he himself.

MACHADO DE ASSIS, *Dom Casmurro*, 1899

Photography and spirits collided in the body of José Sebastião da Rosa, known simply as Juca Rosa. He was born in Rio de Janeiro of an African mother in 1834; his father is unknown. As a young man in the slave society of monarchic Brazil, he earned his keep as a freeman tailor and coachman. By the 1860s, he had also built a cross-racial clientele for his work as a possession priest of prodigious skill. Yet his success and relative fame—not least as a prolific seducer—also brought him enemies. In 1870, he was denounced to the police in an anonymous letter. For a full year thereafter, the story of the celebrity priest provided a steady stream of gossip and news. After the most famous trial of the decade, he was convicted of fraud (*estelionato*) and sentenced to six years of prison labor. He disappeared from the historical record after that, but his name lived on as his story became a cautionary tale—"that fellow's a real Juca Rosa"; "the fatal Juca Rosa epidemic."[1] News reports of imitators and followers even a thousand miles away appeared—one "Juca Rosa adept" in Rio Grande do Sul, another in the state of São Paulo.[2]

The long-lived phrases show that much more was in play than a single alleged con. His was a multiform affair, blurring genres. The Juca Rosa event crisscrossed issues of race, sex, class, and religion and the genres of newspaper reports, legal documents, photographs, and rumors. Reports of his deflowering several white women and his marriage to a Portuguese *senhora* were part of what made the story irresistible. Even more, Juca Rosa was a crux for debates about Afro-Brazilian religions and their place in a nation moving toward emancipation. The criminal investigation opened a window onto Afro-Brazilian spirit-possession practices and ritual work usually closed to outsiders. Juca Rosa's theft of Catholicism was especially noted—the fact that he performed baptisms and marriages and used Catholic saints in an Afro-inspired possession religion, taking control of their look but then insidiously transforming them.[3] That he was possessed by *foreign* spirits also incited concern. One newspaper article noted: "The sorcerer says he is inspired by an invisible power that is not God, nor any saint known to us."[4] As the public prosecutor, Antonio de Paula Ramos, summarized the matter, the defendant presented himself as a master of supernatural powers, dressed in a "special manner" before the altar of Our Lady of the Conception to celebrate crude ceremonies, and then, claiming to be inspired and infallible by virtue of this illuminated state ("saint in the head"), received money and presents. Through claims of spirit knowledge, he "deceived uncultivated, weak and superstitious spirits [of his followers]."[5]

By the 1880s, as we saw in chapter 1, *feitiçaria* (lit., "fetishing," though mostly translated as sorcery) and spiritism were accused of causing hysteria.[6] But, in 1870, the pivot of the accusation—whether under the fading legal terms of sorcery or the new, nineteenth-century ones of fraud—rested on the issue of possession, the moment when Juca Rosa donned a special outfit, assumed a new persona—saint in the head—and spoke in a supernatural voice and with enhanced authority. In his possessed state of doubled, hybrid agency, he was said to deprive "weak spirits" of their individual judgment and autonomy. He was depicted as a possessed actor overpowering women who were liable to respond automatically, proffering sex and money with no will of their own. This subversive "social adventurer," as he was called, was emblematic of Afro-Brazilian religions infecting the national body. They threatened to sabotage Brazil's rational evolution. A growing parasite, the Juca Rosa epidemic seemed bent on taking over from within.

The life and case of Juca Rosa has been documented in rich detail in Gabriela dos Reis Sampaio's *Juca Rosa*, and I rely on her work for the framework I employed here, though I do have my own reading of the judicial documents. A feature of the case that has been largely overlooked, however, but that I consider critical is the role of a specific photograph used in the investigation and trial. The photograph remains nestled in the case file to this day. It is, in fact, the only photograph in that case file or, indeed, in any case file from the period that I have encountered. When the image appears from among the many pages of yellowed handwritten reports, it is as though the priest himself suddenly leaps into view. He returns our gaze, holds a pose, turns real in ways he did not as a text, a name, a category, a crime, a social epidemic. Much like the multiperson mind of the psychiatric patient, the difference motivates a question: What is in the photograph?

Juca Rosa's image had one life as a ritual object, another as a police document. In fact, it enjoyed multiple lives—social, ritual, legal—and several afterlives too. Telling the story of this nearhuman, an automatic light trace that acted on its own even at a distance from the body of its human subject, exposes the religion-like uses of photographs and the management of the religious lives of images. If chapter 1 addressed the nearhuman configuration of animals and psychiatric patients, this chapter brings the nearhuman alliance between photographs, spirits, and possession into focus. The coalition between photographs and spirits took shape within forceful systems of appearance, legal, social, and cultural. This photograph exerted the force of the automatic yet was far from a free agent. Like Juca Rosa's spirit powers, the photographic powers of mediation were constrained, regulated, and controlled. They were also put to work.[7]

The convergence of photographs and possession by spirits may appear unlikely. When we examine this case, however, it becomes difficult to avoid it. What was at stake was the question of whether Afro-Brazilians— slaves and former slaves—could become fully human and fully citizens, accountable, contract worthy, rational, and autonomous, but also sufficiently loyal to the nation that had enchained them. Photography developed at the same time as the gradual emancipation of slaves from 1850 to 1888. Afro-Brazilian slaves and freemen alike were understood as uniquely gifted in the arts of possession and uniquely in need of interpretation. There were state interests at stake in learning to read possession, in seeing, standardizing, and reforming the secret forces that lay under the skin and, toward that end, in that inner life's anthropological documentation. Afro-Brazilians in the age of gradual emancipation would require strategic assimilation and containment through police and medical surveillance. What role would photographs play? The new truth-telling machine, joined to the emergent social sciences of anthropology and criminology, offered the promise of rendering internal states, mental capacities, and even religious sentiments in visual form.

Photomaton

A familiar refrain: "Photography was heir to the enlightenment project in its untiring urge to cancel the obscurity of the world."[8] And in that sense it was a disenchanting machine tooled to expose the formerly mysterious and occult. We know, however, that that is only part of the story since visual technologies also opened new vistas of enchantment. Far from erasing spirit-possession practices with ideas of objective ocular truth born of the mid-nineteenth century, the birth and spread of photography helped populate the modern world with spirits and cause them to circulate.[9] From one perspective, the intersection of spirits and photography even seems obvious. Spirits depend on visual and material technologies for their manifestation. They appear in bodies, things, images, and sounds. More surprising is the inverse point, that quests for congress with spirits took part in the rendering present of modern technologies of visualization and materialization, like photography, and of ensoniment, like phonography.[10] They produced not only new media but also a new kind of priest, "the photographer medium, specialist in the capture of spirits."[11] I want to resist the bipolar juxtaposition of secular and religious, disenchantment and enchantment, in favor of other temptations, namely, the attraction to religion-like situations that fall somewhere on a near-human, automatic spectrum. No technology was as prolix in generating nearhumans as photography. None benefited more from the prestige of the automatic. According to Lorraine Daston and Peter Galison, the camera, alongside other machines, would "let nature speak for itself": "Where human self-discipline flagged, machines or humans acting as will-less machines would take over." Here was the prestige of *mechanical objectivity*: "the insistent drive to repress the willful intervention of the artist-author, and to put in its stead a set of procedures that would . . . move nature to the page through a strict protocol, if not automatically."[12]

Like hysteria and spiritism, photography came to Brazil from France. The first daguerreotype in Brazil was made in 1840, just a year after Daguerre announced his new technology in Paris. It was taken by Louis Compte, a French abbot who arrived in the Brazilian port of Salvador da Bahia on the ship *L'Orientale*.[13] And, as in the case of psychiatry in Brazil, photography took on new roles, capacities, powers, and significations in the transatlantic crossing. It did not simply arrive; it was taken apart, remade, and deployed in new projects and to different ends. Obviously, not everything changed. As in Europe, photography gained fame in Brazil by virtue of its claimed automaticity, the capacity to replicate and represent without the distortions of human interpretation or art. On both sides of the Atlantic, it enjoined an evidentiary function. It offered a technology of memory work, a visual way to register bodies that was especially popular in the wake of wars and the abrupt mass mortality they caused: the Paris Commune of 1870–71, the American Civil War of 1861–65, the Brazil-Paraguay War of 1865–70.[14] The early decades of photography transformed the idea of memory from an imprint of personal recollections and a consensual story cobbled together from various sources attributed with less or more legitimacy, including painted or written versions, into a harder idea of truth. Photographs were considered a document of what transpired independent of human perception and the photographer to be but an extension of the lens. Recall Charcot's confidence in his laboratory's visual evidence of patients' inner lives from chapter 1: "I am absolutely only a photographer; I register what I see."

Photography showed the world automatically—not a report or an interpretation but what was objectively there. The first newspaper report on the camera in Brazil, from January 17, 1840, suggests the optimism: "In less than nine minutes appeared the fountain on Paço Square, the plaza of Peixe, the monastery of São Bento, and all the other circumstantial objects, all reproduced with such fidelity, precision, and detail that one could easily see that the thing was made by the hand of nature itself, almost without the artist's intervention."[15] Nature itself! After reviewing Samuel Morse's report on his 1839 visit with Louis Daguerre in Paris, the *New York Observer* wrote: "With what interest shall we visit the gallery of portraits of distinguished men of all countries, drawn, not with man's feeble, false, and flattering pencil, but with the power and truth of light from heaven!"[16] Secrets of nature heretofore invisible to the eye were now made visible, from Muybridge's 1877 images of a horse galloping to the first photographs of lightning, front-page news in Brazil in 1889.[17] As Alfred Stieglitz wrote in 1899: "It was generally supposed that after the selection of the subjects, the posing, lighting, exposure and development, every succeeding step was purely mechanical, requiring little or no thought."[18] Photography offered the world itself, by itself, or so it seemed, a prestige of authenticity that lingers still in the Photomaton booths that pock Paris shopping malls today. No photographer needed, only a face and a credit card. Here comes the image, two-dimensioned, nearhuman, supine in the tray.

Its perceived automaticity granted photography an "epistemic privilege" of truth in journalism, law, forensics, science, and historical archives, a status it still enjoys even in spite of the fact that photography is no longer seen as artless or unmediated.[19] This epistemic privilege made the photograph of Juca Rosa a key witness in his own prosecution, as we will see. At the same time, the aura of automaticity endowed photography with a religion-like force based in automatic agency. André Bazin's celebrated 1945 essay on the ontology of the photographic image argued roughly what Stieglitz had written a half century earlier: "For the first time between the originating object and its reproduction there intervenes only the instrumentality of a nonliving agent. For the first time an image is formed automatically." Bazin pointed to the religion-like impulse of representation, the need to overcome time. Thus, photography resembles the partially automatic quality of a death mask molded from the face of a corpse whose image now lives on. Just so, a photograph is "the object itself . . . freed from the conditions of time and space that govern it," a "magic identity substitute." Photographs are "phantomlike . . . the disturbing presence of lives halted at a set moment in their duration, freed from their destiny . . . by the power of impassive mechanical process."[20]

Writing in 1977, three decades later, Susan Sontag also pointed to the dual features of automaticity and the power to overcome time. She cites an advertisement from the 1970s: "The Yashica Electro-35 GT is the space-age camera your family will love. Take beautiful pictures day or night. Automatically. Without any nonsense." She also noted: "Photographed images do not seem to be statements about the world so much as pieces of it." They were indisputable evidence that fun was had, a place was visited, you were there, these people exist, others were killed. Sontag pointed out the aggression in the uses of photography to "collect," even to "shoot." In the Juca Rosa case, as we will see below, police inspectors presented his photograph during interrogations and demanded forensic evidence from its visual cues. What is happening in the image? Why is he dressed in this way? On the other hand, photographs convey an immortality of persons and events, converting them from time-bound into timeless agents. Here, like Bazin, Sontag is drawn to the religion-like character of photography: its talismanic uses as a memento mori, as a mode of participation, as an imprimatur of the real, even as a ritual compulsion.[21] Analogous swings between the fact-finding, scientific, and forensic power of photography and its religion-like powers appear in Roland Barthes's *Camera Lucida*, with his division of the labor of photography into the roles of operator (the one wielding the camera), spectator (the consumer of images), and spectrum (the object of the shot). Spectrum hovers between spectacle and the return of the dead. It heralds a present being as a future corpse and a haunting specter.[22] Many have argued in similar terms, tugged back and forth between the forensic, evidentiary side of photography and its power to haunt.

Juca Rosa's photograph played both parts: evidence for the police and a spectral extension of himself for his followers, who carried his image on their bodies or into their homes. The point is to note the juxtaposition between claims of the automatic and observations about religion-like capacities. Perhaps, then, we should see photography and religion-like situations less as in tension than as thoroughly interdependent. A photograph's automaticity invites religion-like attractions and ritual uses. The image arrives from beyond, direct from nature, untinged by human bias or time-space limits. Religion-like situations of spirit possession rely on this sense of immediacy, too. It is not the human who speaks but only the god through her. In the case of Juca Rosa, these *techne*—the photograph and the possession—were forcefully pulled into alliance. Until his arrest in 1870, it worked fantastically well.

The work of photographs as authentic carriers of presence has been important in forensic and legal settings but equally so in religion-like operations. The multiple lives of photographs are part of what, since their invention, has made them important ritual tools. They work miracles of numination, causing things to appear that are otherwise invisible to the eye. Giordana Charuty calls this photography's capacity for incarnation.[23] I like to think of spirit possession and photography as two forms of poiesis, both in Plato's sense of the kind of making that fights mortality and in Heidegger's sense of an emergence from one state to another, an *ec-stasis*, standing outside oneself. Spirit possession and photography are dual arts, sometimes intertwined, of bringing forth or making what was hidden seen. Applied this way, poiesis matches Schelling's notion of the unheimlich discussed in the introduction, the moment when that which once was secret is secreted. Both spirit possession and photography are techniques of enlargement or extension of presence across space. Like the portrait of one beloved, a spirit's arrival and sudden departure indexes absence as much as presence. Both afford "the advent of myself as other," to take Barthes's memorable phrase.[24] In that sense, photography inherited religious potentialities from practices and doctrines of representation that long preceded it in painting, statuary, and the uses of reflective surfaces. Bazin, Sontag, and Barthes each pointed to something transcendent and immortalizing in photographs. We shall see below how Juca Rosa's portrait shaped and extended his perceived spiritual abilities.

Given the apparent tension between the documentary, rationalizing intent of photography and the religion-like motives of spirit possession or mediumship, it may seem contradictory or anachronistic to link spirit possession and photography as coeval, tangled arts of revelation. Yet that is what they became in the late nineteenth century, notwithstanding spirit possession's millennia-long history compared with photography's recent birth. Spiritualists, Afro-Brazilian priests of Candomblé, and other ritual actors applied scientific evidence provided by photographs to their own claimsmaking, as did the Catholic Church. João Vasconcelos showed that the new Catholic assertion of papal infallibility (at the First Vatican Council, convened by Pius XI in 1868, and ending in 1870) was accompanied by the photographic evidence of the Virgin's apparition at Lourdes, which confirmed the change. Modern disenchantment, he proposed, has less to do with the decline of religion than with its integration with regimes of evidence.[25] But sometimes it worked the other way. Scientists reached into religion-like scenes and situations to cross into unknown horizons of evidence. To take a prominent example, Alfred Russell Wallace prefaced the third edition (1896) of *Perspectives in Psychical Research* with the ironclad assurance: "What are termed spirit-photographs . . . have now been known for more than twenty years. Many competent observers have tried experiments successfully." A decade letter, in 1908, the famous Italian criminal anthropologist Cesare Lombroso argued similarly, calling photography a "transcendental artistic power." A decade later, Sir Arthur Conan Doyle was still arguing the same.[26]

If photography allegedly disenchanted the world with forensic evidence from the world itself, it also offered new pleasures of mediation, nearhuman images from the spirits themselves. Like the two Rosalies, photographs presented agent-ambiguous events and scenarios that attracted viewers and held their attention. Parenthetically, digital photographs of today do this too, albeit in another way. Though photographs retain a certain evidential authority in the academy and mainstream news, we now regard them with suspicion owing to their digital malleability. Any digital photograph today elicits questions. Is it real? How real? What is the real? Religion-like questions. The questions arise because photographs replicate and imitate but they also contain residues of that which was imaged, what Sontag called the trace—"something directly stenciled off the real, like a footprint or a death mask."[27]

The uncanny sense of a person being *in* the photograph is an idea as dear to twentieth-century modernists as it was to nineteenth-century colonial subjects forcibly subjected to ethnographic cataloging. In the third edition (1911) of the *Golden Bough*, Frazer presented (in just three pages) a list of twenty cases of different ethnic groups that resisted photography for fear it could carry away or otherwise take possession of the soul. He traced such fears to older ideas of locating the soul in shadows or reflections seen in water, mirrors, and drawn and painted likenesses.[28] At least some of his named cases point to the aggression and colonial violence entailed by the drive to collect. William James, whom we encountered in the Amazon with a monkey friend in chapter 1, was embarrassed by Louis Agassiz's demands to shoot subjects of all Brazilian "racial types" in the nude, sometimes against their will and despite their plain discomfort.[29] At the Salpêtrière, too, there are indications that patients resented and resisted their capture and public display in images. Paul Richer recounted an inmate who stole multiple photographs of patients. Caught with the photographs stashed in her pocket, she was abruptly transfixed by catalepsy and offered no explanation for her behavior, but it is not difficult to imagine her and other patients' rage at such an invasion of their bodies.[30] Roger Bastide, the French anthropologist who spent much of his career in Brazil, kept a letter in his records about resistance to photography. A villager in Corsica refused to allow a photograph of himself and his donkey. The man explained: "Last year a tourist like you took a picture of my grandfather and said he would send him the photo. My grandfather received it three months later. And in fifteen days he was dead! In the apparatus [*appareil*] was the evil eye. The photo made him die."[31]

Resisting the demand to be photographed may bring groups into conflict with nation-states. The Amish in the United States, for example, have sometimes refused to be photographed on the grounds that photographs spur pride or that they count as the graven images proscribed in the Bible.[32] In some instances, the courts have disallowed the right to refuse to be photographed, claiming a compelling government interest in cataloging the citizenry in order to protect public safety.[33] In all these cases, the fear of being photographed points to the medium's potential power. Photographs rouse dread because they embody and capture the subject. And, once images are captured, photographs can shape-shift, taking on new lives far from their subjects' will or control. A diagnostic photograph at the Salpêtrière was converted into a personal effect when a patient stole it and made it her own. Photographs of hysterics from the Salpêtrière were redeployed as images of surrealist transgression in Salvador Dali's 1933 collage *The Phenomenon of Ecstasy*. Georges Bataille took Alfred Metráux's photographs of Vodou spirit possession and repackaged them in his study *L'erotism*. An ethnographic photograph taken by an anthropologist was placed on an altar, to be treated or apotheosized, or situated among salient spirits. Karen McCarthy Brown described the Brooklyn Vodou priestess Mama Lola hanging a photograph of herself possessed by the god Ogou by her altar to Ogou.[34] A photograph of a ritual scene can be made into a legal evidentiary document, as we will see in Juca Rosa's case. The power to transport presence but also to shape-shift it, to drop the trace scraped from the skin of one scene into other venues, makes photographs valuable but also dangerous tools. Accordingly, photographs—and their interdiction—are often involved in religion-like scenes and situations.

In "The Faith-Cure," Charcot wrote about images used in votives to describe how photographs extend personhood.[35] The trace of the healed person remains forever at the shrine, bearing witness, even as the rest of the person walks on. Portraits gather light infused with traces of a person and project it into other spaces—a pocket, a wall, a desk, a locket worn against the skin. And the insertion of the religion-like powers of photographs into everyday life transformed social relations. As we have seen, Charcot gave Freud a photograph of himself on the day Freud left Paris, wanting to send a bit of himself with Freud, but not just any version of himself, only a stylized and perfected one, a blown-up collage of visual clues to an ideal, not Charcot but "Charcot." Hardly the real, in other words, but rather Charcot as demigod. Emperor Dom Pedro II constantly sent and received photographs between Brazil and Europe: images of spouses and children and carefully arranged portraits of himself along with images of engineering works advertising progress. He often welcomed photographs of art from abroad in the mail: photographs of paintings by Luiz Montero (in 1867), a photograph of a bust of Béatrice de Portineri (in 1873), photographs related to Linnaeus (in 1872), a photograph of work by the Italian sculptor Magni (in 1878). In 1881, he wrote to the princess of Germany to request photographs of the sculptures of Pergame.[36] Photography was for him a route to European cosmopolitanism, a technique of feeling a part of it all even at a bodily remove. And it worked. He was well-known in Paris society even prior to arriving in the city, having already been rendered present, and had had Europe rendered present to him, in images taken with a camera.

Arts of Appearance

The image of Juca Rosa that was confiscated by the police blurred the genres of scientific and aesthetic photography.[37] It was a creative work, an unusual portrait that contained forensic clues in its posture, clothing, and props. Juca Rosa was hardly unusual in having or distributing copies of his own image. Portrait photographs had been fashionable in Brazil for a decade. In 1840, Father Louis Compte printed a daguerreotype of Emperor Dom Pedro II with equipment he had brought with him from France. The fifteen-year-old Pedro immediately ordered his own gear and commissioned daguerreotypes of all members of the royal family. The new technology had gained a very public imperial imprimatur, and every family of means followed suit.[38] Also in 1840, the first photography studio was opened in Rio de Janeiro. By the early 1860s, small, cheap cardboard-backed *carte de visite* photographs were in wide circulation, followed by the slightly larger "cabinet photographs," almost as popular in Brazil as they were in Europe.[39] These images—almost all in carte de visite form—were devoted to the production and advertisement of respectability.[40] They could be given to others, arranged in the salon, attached to one's front door, worn on the body, given to pay tribute, or used to arrange a rendezvous.[41] In 1870, there were thirty-eight photographic studios operating in the central district of Rio.[42] The fashion was not only in or of the capital city, either. Beginning in the 1840s, itinerant photographers with daguerreotype equipment ranged from city to city, stopping to work the smaller towns in between.[43]

In the context of the waning decades of slavery and the positivist climate of order and progress, a period of defining and forming the modern republic, photography gained protoanthropological authority. Its authority, like that of the sciences, was based on the principle of the copresence of the observing machine with the thing observed. The camera was like Charcot—"I register what I see"—and vice versa, the sense of sight without the biases or frailties of the human eye. The camera would help document, bound, and define human groups.[44] Much as it worked at the Salpêtrière, photography's role was to serve as compiler of objective facts. Just as facts were applied to the classifying and publicizing of psychiatric diagnoses, states deployed the camera to register citizens, slaves, and former slaves, collecting and cataloging "the people," including their religious lives, on a grid of standardized classifications. Photography was in Brazil central to the project of documenting and defining the nation, not only by recording and broadcasting its technological progress, but also by inventorying, ordering, demonstrating, and exerting control over national territory, "not just as an ally of science, but [as] an enactment of it," a control that appeared graphically in the 1882 Anthropological Exposition, held at the Museu Nacional in Rio de Janeiro.[45] The exhibition of indigenous Brazilians, held up for the nation as both founders and sacrificial victims, was shot by Marc Ferrez, at the time Brazil's most talented photographer, and disseminated in the early photography magazine *Revista illustrada*.[46]

"To collect photographs is to collect the world."[47] It was not only to name and accurately describe the state, however; it was also to enforce state power. This became clear in France with the first use of photographs of dissidents by police enjoined to round up the rebels of the 1870–71 Paris Commune, in the wake of which Charcot opened his new unit, began his lectures on hysteria, and initiated his care of Rosalie Leroux.[48] Comprehensive photograph albums of prison inmates were collected during the 1870s in Russia, the United States, and Brazil. The technology of photography was harnessed to the positivist vision of a legible and governable world, a total world present in objective evidence. It reached even the inner life of persons, including psychiatric patients, prisoners, and possession priests. The total world became imaginable in part through the camera, making the camera not just a machine but also a moral artifact that set social, legal, and material effects in motion. Within this strange new world, photographic portraiture in Brazil, as elsewhere, helped produce an image of "singular individuals endowed with interiority and presented as though [individual interiority] were a fact."[49]

By far the primary use of photography was in the making of portraits for everyday, private use and distribution. The affordability of small photographs made them widely popular, and they transformed the means of making and maintaining networks. In Brazil, as in France, those networks included saints, spirits, and the dead, and photographs were applied to a range of ritual uses devoted to their gathering. Charcot, for example, took note of the role of photographs at Catholic shrines as testimonies of miracles. While visiting the Church of the Holy Maries in the South of France, he discovered a plaster cast of the leg of a miraculously healed twelve-year-old girl (the age is his conjecture and was based on the cast's contraction), a hysteric who suffered from clubfoot. Alongside the cast was posted a photograph of the girl standing on the afflicted limb just after the healing.[50] The votive was composed of the plaster cast and the photograph joined together. Catholic churches in Brazil often contain similar shrines where votive objects and photographs are juxtaposed; piled casts of healed limbs are now liberated to climb the shrine walls in the lissome body of the photographic image. Mattijs Van de Port writes: "The 'photographic real' was picked up in religious-magical practices, where it came to substitute [for] the body."[51] To take another example, sometime in the 1930s on the occasion of a Catholic mass given on September 27, the day of the twins (Cosme and Damian), a young girl brought a photograph of her family to the front of the church and placed it on the altar to receive the saints' blessings.[52] And in Bahia, it was a common custom to photograph dead infants posed as still living and to refer them as *anjinhos*, "little angels," the images then being paraded in the streets.[53] The photograph substituted for the bodily presence of the departed. It held something in reserve, something of the soul of the child. By the late nineteenth century, children taking their first communion received a photograph of themselves, presumably their only one, as a rare and precious gift.[54]

Meanwhile, Afro-Brazilian Candomblé temples used photographs to signal and announce their lineage, hanging portraits of founding priests and priestesses on the wall in keeping with a baroque ethos that privileged visual representation in nineteenth-century Brazil. But they also deployed photographs for a range of other purposes, like rituals related to securing or restoring love. In these cases, photographs *become* the people being ritually treated. Importantly, too, photographs and the right to take them divide public from private spaces and parts of rituals. In that sense, photography helped map sacred space in subtle but significant ways. As Roger Sansi put it: "The control over the mechanical reproduction of images in Candomblé is first and foremost an issue of privacy and intimacy. . . . [O]bjects that stem from the body, including photographs, as a part of the distributed person, can be used to throw spells against the people they index. Intimacy and sorcery are in many ways coextensive: the question is who will use the image, what for, and to what extent these images can be considered a part of the person."[55]

Spiritism did not migrate from France as quickly as photography did, but, by the turn of the twentieth century, Brazil had become the international center of spiritism, a status it retains today.[56] Perhaps no religious tradition was as possessed by photography as spiritism, in Brazil inspired by the French mystic Allan Kardec, a.k.a. Hyppolyte Léon Denizard Rivail. *Espiritismo* offered the promise of Afro-Brazilian spirit-possession practices with none of the social liabilities. Even if it was not quite respectable, it was thoroughly French, cosmopolitan, and à la mode. Copies of Kardec's *Le livre des esprits* (1857) were to be found in Rio by 1860 and had been translated into Portuguese by 1866.[57] Spiritist groups like the Groupe Confucius, also called the Société des Études Spiritiques, were meeting regularly by 1873. The monthly review *Revista espirita* began publication in 1875, and the large-scale spiritist organization the Federação Espírita Brasileira first convened at the beginning of 1884.[58] By the 1880s, spiritism stood alongside reports of Afro-Brazilian *curandeiros* (practitioners of *herbal healing*) and *feitiçeiros* like Juca Rosa as the stuff of everyday news.

In France and the United States, as in Brazil, photography and possession were tangled in spiritism. Spirit photography—the exposure of spirits behind or next to living subjects in portraits—was important in the expansion and public profile of spiritism after 1860, beginning with William Mumler's images.[59] Pierre Janet, writing on automatism in Paris, was impressed—and perhaps bemused—by the story from the United States of a photograph showing a man surrounded by twenty-three spirits. His reaction helps us see how these images circulated around the Atlantic.[60] Spirit photography's influence and then its debunking—since, like Édouard Buguet in Paris, Mumler ultimately stood trial on charges of fraud—were a descant to portrait photography's emergence in everyday life.[61] Followers of spirit photographers like Mumler in the United States and Buguet in France were hardly dissuaded by court testimony levied against the imagemakers. Many were convinced that the spirits of the deceased appeared in spite of or even through practices intended to defraud clients. I have not found evidence that spirit photography played as important a role in Brazil as it did in both France and the United States, perhaps because in Brazil the visual evidence of spirits would not have been as novel or surprising. Yet a photograph called *Portrait with Spirit*, taken by Militão Augusto de Azevedo in the still-sleepy town of São Paulo around 1880, depicts a satirically posed dandy with an Egyptian vase on his desk and an enormous white ghost hovering behind him. Given the ironic antispirit photographs like Militão's, there must, then, have been spirit photographs taken in Brazil, mimicking the work of Buguet in Paris.[62]

The religion-like uses of photographs depended on their materiality. Though photographs may convey transcendence, until recently they were (and in many respects still are) objects with all the qualities of things: edges, shape, texture, solidity, and varying durability over time. They had not only visual but also haptic and even olfactory qualities. As at once an image and a thing—an object that attracts the gaze, has weight in the hand, takes up space in a file, or pulls on the nail pinning it to the wall—a photograph mediates a scene or person in a place and time different from those in which the photograph is viewed and the here and now. The quality of being at once an image and a thing is important because it enables photographs' multiple lives, crossing dimensions. One dimension is sensorial: photographs were possessed of a visual life, a tactile life, and so forth. Another dimension is spatiotemporal: they enjoyed a first life in relation to both the time and place of their making and their framed subject, a person or a landscape, and a second life in the sites and psyches of their viewers. In fact, they have many other possible lives enduring long after the living subject has died or the architecture of their initial display has shifted. Juca Rosa's photograph still acts today, hailing us from an 1871 case file, spurring new ideas and words.

Father Quibombo

Let us set the scene as we bring the main protagonist back on stage. In Brazil, emancipation was a long, drawn-out process. While the transportation of slaves was officially illegal after 1836, at least "for the English to see" (*para inglês ver*), it continued with only partial disruption from the British navy until 1850. After 1850, the transportation of African slaves was dramatically reduced, but the institution of slavery and the internal trade in slaves continued, a great migration from the northeastern sugar zones of Bahia and Pernambuco to the burgeoning coffee plantations in the southeastern states of Rio de Janeiro and São Paulo. Slaves who fought in the war against Paraguay from 1865 to 1870 were offered their liberty, but the old institution's grip began to loosen only with the 1871 "Law of the Free Womb." Full emancipation was finally decreed with the "Golden Law" of 1888, passed by Princess Isabel while her father was abroad in Paris with Charcot. It was at the precise moment the Law of the

Free Womb was being debated and then passed that the most notorious nineteenth-century case of illegal fetishism was tried in Brazil's capital (figures 2.1 and 2.2).

Juca Rosa's case is unusual in the legal files from the period, distinguished not only by virtue of the abundance of documents that have survived but also by virtue of its inclusion of a photograph of the accused. The photograph was found by the police in the home of one of Juca Rosa's followers, and it was used to prompt depositions from witnesses.[63] Its material form is that of the carte de visite. The distribution of such cards would have been affordable for someone of Juca's resources given his wide network of clients, at least some of whom were wealthy. He displayed and increased his status by sharing in the bourgeois pastime of exchanging such cards. Most cartes de visite exchanged in Brazil offered sober portraits of the subject, almost always alone, posed in noble dress against one of the standard backdrops available in a studio. Portraits of slaves taken during the period focused less on poses or bucolic settings; rather, slaves were photographed in documentary, anthropological style, in plain unadorned garb and wielding the tools of their labor. Juca Rosa's purpose seems to have been different from either the aim of displaying respectability or that of production. The pose he elected to depict and craft with care did something else entirely. The image portrays him and a companion standing on a proscenium painted with flowers, set against a bare white background, creating an unusually open space. The space is filled by a ritual scene, or its imitation. A devotee, João Maria da Conceição, kneels before Rosa on the proscenium—whether in homage, in deference, in supplication, or to present a ritual hierarchy graphically we cannot say—and points toward him with a staff. Sampaio finds it likely that the staff was a drumstick called a *macumba*, the same word given to the drums it struck, used to call down the gods manifested at spirit-possession events.[64] Under interrogation, João gave testimony that he had simply assumed the position Juca Rosa demanded of him, without having any idea about what it meant.[65]

Despite the action conveyed, the image is silent in its fact making, as João's statement attests.[66] We know that Juca's clients possessed this photograph and that Rosa also kept portraits of all his clients and devotees. What did he do with them? Their uses remain opaque to us. But the idea of the personal trace contained in the image and our knowledge of other ritual events in Brazil that made use of photographs as containers and conveyors of personhood together offer clues. Threats reported by a participant named Leopoldina Fernandes Cabral in her deposition hinted that Juca Rosa's possession of followers' portraits served in part as a means of their ritual control. Leopoldina told the police investigator Tavares that, even when she wanted to break free from Rosa's influence,

FIGURES 2.1 AND 2.2. The photograph of Juca Rosa in the police file of 1870–71, Arquivo Nacional, Rio de Janeiro (photograph by the author), and the same photograph digitally edited, as published in Gabrielle Sampaio, *Juca Rosa: Um pai-de-santo na Corte Imperial* (Rio de Janeiro: Arquivo Nacional, 2009), 188.

she could not because he had threatened her, "telling her that if she does [leave], he, with the spirit that he ruled for good as for harm, would disgrace her and make her end up in at Mercy Hospital." Juca Rosa was said to be able to give or take fortunes from his clients at will. There was also a report of a death threat made against one Henrique de Azurar.[67] Perhaps the holding of Leopoldina's photograph and those of all his clients was part of what made the threat seem real. Legal records in Brazil leave ample clues as to how photographs were used in curing practices of various religious traditions. In 1930, for example, Ubaldina D. Rodrigues sent a photograph of her husband to the famous "Dr. Mozart" in order to have him cured of the "bad path" he was following.[68] And, also today in Brazil, petitioners frequently leave photographs along with notes and money at saints' altars, including that of Slave Anastácia, who features in the next chapter. Juca Rosa likely used carte de visite images of his devotees as proxies for their bodies. His ritually acting on the photograph for harm

or benefit would affect the person as well. Several depositions stated that he had admitted as much. At the same time, his own photograph may also have served as an avatar that extended his presence and power into clients' and devotees' homes and bodies. But also put him at risk.

The photograph held a quite different meaning for the police—as testament to the performance of illegitimate ritual and potentially illegal practices. It was first mentioned in the report of Inspector Ignacio Ronaldo: "I succeeded in obtaining the portrait which I am pleased to send with this report . . . which shows the creole in his fetishist costume, accompanied by his assistant."[69] For the police investigation, and then at trial, the photograph served as visual evidence of Rosa's possessions, the fact that he ritually engaged African spirits on behalf of clients from whom he then profited, with the issue of profit being key to the accusation of fraud or charlatanism. But it also shows how police work had become invested in the turn to the visual and the use in it of the camera. Ritual practice and police practice were equally caught up in the visual turn and dependent on this specific photograph as proof of Juca Rosa's bona fide powers of possession. Both were swept up in the *photography effect*, to borrow Jonathan Crary's phrase, a "new cultural economy of value and exchange," a "totalizing system" of novel desires.[70] The investigator and the public prosecutor seem to have been little interested in the songs that were sung, for example, or the foods that were prepared and offered to the saints. "Diverse herbs, roots, powders and liquids" were confiscated and sent for examination by two medical doctors, but the concoctions were found to have only everyday ingredients. No descriptions of drums, icons or food entered the record. Major ritual procedures were barely glossed: they drank during consultations; there was a ceremony called *play* (*brincadeira*) and another called *binding* (*amarração*). Participants danced to *macumba* music and sang in African languages.[71] Dances were in a circle (*roda*). Beyond that, the details recorded are thin gruel—unless, that is, one happens to be specifically interested in the question of Juca Rosa's body possessed. In that case, the archive offers a feast.

The investigation was resolutely focused on the question of Juca's posturing as one wielding spirits and able to exact undue fealty from his followers on that basis. Moreover, it was resolutely focused on that specific photograph, his distributed carte de visite, when Juca Rosa's ritual family was interrogated. The very first question directed to Henriqueta Maria de Mello—who hosted ritual events and kept ritual tools and objects at her home—was whether she was familiar with the image. She responded that she knew it to be Juca Rosa and that she recognized the clothing as what he last wore at a large ritual event that took place overnight on August 14–15. In fact, every interrogation began with the photograph. Another witness, Miguel, was asked whether he knew it. He responded that he did, having already been shown the image by another person, Julia Adelaide Havier. From these initial questions, investigators composed their case. Wearing the clothing depicted in the portrait, Juca Rosa became possessed by spirits and (as shown), in a state of exalted status and expanded power, deprived others, especially women, of their autonomy. By making himself master of their souls, he became master of their bodies; even, or so he was accused, "enjoying the women in an unnatural way."[72]

If the photograph helped produce new modes of sociality and religious experience, its material form also neatly fit the procedures of police work as new forms of legal bureaucracy were coming into being.[73] Police work was now visual work, often photographic work. The object's flat shape and flexible paper construction made it a congenial fit for the hand, in interrogations, and for the flat rectangular shape of the legal file. This quality of the image-thing's material fit in the court file is what allows me access to the photograph still today, unlike anything else that may have been confiscated during Juca Rosa's arrest. Between the photograph and the surrounding text emerged a symbiosis between photography, the terms of filing systems, and bureaucratic institutions surrounding policing and the public sphere. All three converged as emerging technologies of the nation-state by 1870. The attraction of the photograph—not just as a revelatory thing but also as an archival thing, an evidentiary thing, a neat, compact, and clearly bounded thing—was at least part of what led authorities to focus on it. But what, exactly, did it give evidence *of*?

At a specific moment in ritual gatherings in the home of Henriqueta Maria de Mello, most recently on the night of August 14–15, 1870, Rosa retreated to a separate chamber in the company of a woman named Ereciana in order to change into his special attire of blue corduroy and silver fringe. On reemerging, he was transformed into a powerful authority named Father (Pai) Quibombo. He would then fall to the floor and be "taken" (*tomado*) by a range of additional spirits, among them "Santo Zuza" (Saint Zuza) and "Pai Vencedor" (Conquering Father).[74] The photograph depicting Rosa wearing the vestments of possession provided the evidence and was used to cue verbal depositions by witnesses confirming the precise events and their order. Key to the investigation was the description of his transformation from rational individual into a person possessed, wearing the garments that appear in the photograph. Crucial too was the language applied to this altered state—that he was taken and thereafter became something other than a human agent. The basic sequence of events at the ritual was confirmed by multiple participants. Juca Rosa himself, however, never confessed. In his second interrogation, when specifically asked about his unusual garments, he denied that they had any ritual use. He claimed that they were a Carnaval costume. When asked to explain his possession of the photographs of many of his followers, he insisted it was just for play or a joke (*chalaça*). And, of course, there were no live photographs of Rosa in the state most in question, that of being possessed.[75]

Later ethnographies, however, offer a rough idea of what likely transpired at Henriqueta Maria de Mello's house in August 1870. Roger Bastide described a mid-twentieth-century possession event:

> Every mystical trance is transformed into a party, and every party ends in mystical trance. Trance is the supreme moment of the religious festival, that to which everything leads. . . . Accompanied by the deafening thunder of the drums . . . the faithful sing the songs. . . . Meanwhile the members of the fraternity, men and women—but many more women than men—dance the steps appropriate to each of the different songs. In the course of these songs and dances . . . a being suddenly stirs. The dancer's shoulder blades shake with convulsive tremors, the body shudders and may fall to the ground. The god has mounted his horse. . . . When a believer becomes possessed, she is taken into . . . another little

room. . . . There the person is redressed in the liturgical garments of her god. . . . From then on, the possessed is not an ordinary being, she has become the god itself.[76]

This is very similar to what the police pieced together from the photograph of Juca Rosa. There were circular dances driven by music, retreats to another room, changes in costume, a priest who enters a trance state, and his transformation into a god bearing an African name—in this case, Father Quibombo. His title in this state is a West Central African variant of *kingombo*, the Kimbundu term for *okra*. Stephan Palmié has documented the same word also appearing in Cuba, as *quimbombó*.[77] The spirit arrives from elsewhere—from Africa, or a Yoruba otherworld (*orun*), or Bahia, or the place of the ancestors. Once in that state, the priest wielded special authority and the power to cure illness, divine the unseen, bestow fortune, inspire love, or exact revenge.

I can also speak to my own ethnographic work on spirit possession in multiple sites in the Afro-Atlantic world. The gods *manifest* or *descend*, and those possessed are described as *being turned, rolled, mounted, taken*, or *leaned on*. The metaphors of weight, force, and directionality cue us that spirits cannot be rendered present to consciousness except through shifts registered in material transductions.[78] The outward marks of spirit incorporation include bending at the waist accompanied by trembling shoulders, verbal cries that announce a given deity or spirit, stylized dance steps demonstrating the god's character or natural domain, shifts in voice register, accent, and cadence, superhuman tolerance of pain or alcohol, and the donning of special vestments borne with regal bearing or another demeanor befitting the character of the god. *Possession* describes an experiential shift, a perception of the descent of the spirits seen, heard, and felt in material and bodily acts through which spirits (in Brazil, orixás, *voduns*, or *inquices*, depending on a given liturgy's putative African nation) are rendered present.

Spirits and the modes of their appearance are chronotopes—forms of nearhuman presence that are also markers and anchors of a given time-space juncture, in this case linking Rio de Janeiro to the kingdom of Kongo. Spirit possession contains histories. It is a genre of history making, a reckoning of the present in relation to a specific past.[79] Yet, because spirit presences are contingent on material sites of appearance, the histories that spirits help compose and, when incorporated, dramatize and stage are necessarily malleable and shifting. New gods bring new territories and new pasts into focus. States and statecraft, of course, also select certain places and times to elevate while erasing, suppressing, or trivializing others. In the case of Juca Rosa and his followers, it is not too much to suggest that a part of what was happening was a battle over Brazilian history. One version, a ritual one, celebrated an African past; another, a nineteenth-century legal one, sought to efface or limit the power of that past. As Juca Rosa's defense attorney pointed out, the police investigation and initial denunciation were both carried out within an antiquated legal framework, the Portuguese Philippine Code, dating from 1603. In that anachronistic version of the accusation, the issue of feitiçaria was foregrounded and harnessed to nineteenth-century fears of social contagion. Against this, the defense reminded the judge that the modern and properly Brazilian category was no longer fetishing but rather fraud (*estelionato*), with a legal verdict of guilt hinging on the fact of not only making false claims but also, and more importantly, profiting from them. The judge agreed with the defense's argument that feitiçaria was an invalid legal category. Nevertheless, he condemned Juca to the full sentence of six years of forced labor—to the status of a slave and an automaton—on the basis of his having been established by the prosecution as being a "true fraud."

What role did the photograph play? Among other things, it served as a hinge or shifter from the earlier Philippine Code, which outlawed working with spirits, to the modern Brazilian Criminal Code, which outlawed pretending to work with spirits for monetary gain. It helped register the shift to the new crime; not of spirit possession, as under the old terms of feitiçaria, but of fraud, *acting* possessed. And, in truth, possession often begins in such a subjunctive mode, acting as though the spirits have arrived in the body. Spirit possession is a learned response to a specific material context and the social expectations of a social group. Every spirit-incorporation event is at once a repetition and a revision of earlier editions since even the same spirit's or god's performance is slightly altered with every appearance. Every possession performance is constitutive of a genre but also of a specific event because contingent on a given material context and moment of a spirit's or a god's appearance or, perhaps better, a god's coming into being. Spirit possession is a form of ritual work. Becoming an adept at carrying and performing a god in a human body is a craft and skill as much as a predisposition. It often requires elaborate and secretive initiations within a tight-knit community of practice called the family of saint (*família de santo*). As an adept learns to incarnate her god, she also remakes herself. Roger Sansi writes: "Candomblé people 'construct' their saints as autonomous agents, at the same time that they build themselves as persons. 'Making the saint' is a dialectical process of continuously constructing the person, in relation to the spirits that she embodies and to the 'other body' of these spirits, the shrines."[80] Why learn this craft and do this work? Why did Juca Rosa's followers gather for the all-night projects that exacted significant physical and financial tolls? Their purpose was to protect participants' basic everyday needs—their finances, health, love lives, and fecundity—against the forces of anomie, sickness, death, bad luck, and the master class by rendering the gods present in human bodies. We can only imagine that Juca Rosa's ritual events worked. Participants wanted to take part, at least initially. If they became subject to a certain kind of automaticity, as the police and the press asserted, they also acted as agents by assenting to the ritual terms.

Cameras able to capture spirit-possession events in live-action, photojournalistic style emerged only after 1930. When in 1936 Edison Carneiro sent photographs of Candomblé to Arthur Ramos, he apologized for their being too dark, adding in explanation: "You know that participants aren't allowed to dance outside the temple."[81] Prior to photojournalistic shots of ritual, enormously popularized by Pierre Verger by the end of the 1940s, something as abstract as spirit possession could be read only by its external visual cues and their narration. Without such an image, inspectors and prosecutors used Juca Rosa's portrait to try to discern the agency hidden within the possessed body—evidence of one who works with a saint in the head—with reference to the objects appearing in the image and the stories witnesses summoned to describe them. They found all the requisite parts of the accusatory narrative: African garments, primitive acts indexed by Juca Rosa's bare feet, the tools for a drumming ceremony, unwarranted social hierarchy, hidden powers associated with the mysterious sack hanging from Rosa's belt, and inexplicable Afro-Brazilian self-aggrandizement. Rosa had, after all, gone to a studio and carefully staged this portrait to depict a religion-like situation.

We cannot be sure why Juca Rosa had the portrait made in the way he did. Surely one motivation was the solidification of his authority. With the imposing image of the priest in the garments of power standing before a kneeling acolyte, he expanded and extended his presence. Other, additional uses seem likely, especially in view of the small pouch he hung from his belt as a symbol and source of material power. Sampaio points out the similarity to Central African *nkisi*, a pouch, packet, pot, or statue containing an assemblage of ingredients. Cast in the threads of its material confluences, a *nkisi* spirit is contracted to protect its user. I think this interpretation makes sense, given that the majority of enslaved Africans who disembarked in Rio de Janeiro were taken from that region. Juca Rosa's mother at least was very likely of Kongo ethnicity. And the name he adopted when possessed, Quibombo, also suggests a Central African origin. This possible *nkisi*—another kind of container with a hidden interior—relates to how we think about Rosa's photographs, both the ones he distributed and the ones he collected. Photographs, including his carte de visite portrait, were, under certain conditions, *nkisi* power tools. A photograph of someone could be used against her via contagious magic, much like a hair clipping, a piece of clothing, or a signature or written name. This is why Juca Rosa kept photographs of his devotees and clients in his possession. Images that contain something of the person they represent exert power, for good or ill. Such photographs were religion-like tools that cut in at least two ways. They circulated a public persona, anchored memory, and solidified reputation and pedigree, but they were and are also ambiguous, dangerous things with lives of their own, that can be turned against you.[82]

The Priest's Two Bodies

The idea that photographic portraits manifest and transmit power is surely correct, if not necessarily for the reasons given by Juca Rosa's community. Wittgenstein's notes on Frazer's *Golden Bough* remind us that it is not necessary to resort to magic to explain the power of photographs since the ways in which we interact with them already contain their own satisfaction—burning, kissing, arranging, or hanging them creates an experience of emancipation, intimacy, or order.[83] This must have been so for Rosa's followers, who felt his presence in his image. Photographs circulate beyond the scene of their making, granting them unintended powers. They make secret things potentially public, and their circulation cannot be easily managed. For practitioners of subaltern religions, in particular, there is always a threat posed by photography. For at least a century in Brazil—from roughly 1871 to the 1970s—photographs could be and were used as evidence in police cases involving sorcery and, later, fraud. That memory persists in spite of Candomblé's recent popular acclaim and transformation into a national patrimony.[84] Until recently, photographs were mostly forbidden during initiation into Candomblé, for example, and photographs of states of possession were always forbidden, though that has now begun to change. That does not mean that photographs were completely banned. By 1890, stately portraits of temple founders graced the walls of ritual spaces as indexes of *axé* (transforming power) in the sense of the authority created by proper lineage and also as advertisements of a given house's prestige. By the 1930s at the latest, photographs of ritual objects were sometimes permitted, provided the photographer was sufficiently trusted, though ethnographers often pushed the limits of that trust. In 1936, Edison Carneiro took many photographs in Bahian *terreiros* and commented on the anger they might cause owing to the ritual secrets they might reveal: "Last Sunday, I took some photos that

FIGURE 2.3. Here, Verger's subject is in the midst of an initiation during which she learned how properly to incarnate the god of love, beauty, wealth, and fresh water, Oxum. Note the portraits of prominent priestesses from the past hung on the wall behind the initiate, including photographs. The photographs of former and current priestesses announce the prestige and tradition of the temple (*terreiro*) to the public and, through them, help constitute the temple's legitimate genealogy (*axé*). One of many photographs of spirit possession taken by the French photographer Pierre Verger, this one was shot at Candomblé Cosme, Salvador, Bahia, sometime between 1946 and 1953. Used with permission of Fotos Pierre Verger, Fundação Pierre Verger.

would have caused a furor if they had turned out. . . . But the film was old and damaged. I lost everything. Will try again next week."[85] And the live possession shot of ritual dancers became standard by the late 1940s, in the famous images captured by Pierre Verger and in a thoroughly evidentiary way (figure 2.3).[86]

The portraits are not just a record of the past, for they also circulate *axé*, life force, in the present. Photographs not only document; they help generate a desired reality.[87] The Juca Rosa photograph, likewise, was not just a document of a past event; it was an agent in everything that transpired in the case, animated by various frames of speech and action. I suggest, expanding still further, that technologies of recording possession and playing it back to its actors, extending spirits' possible reach through secondary semiosis, began to play an important role in constituting what it means to be possessed at all in the age of the automatic. This was certainly true of spiritism. Despite his misgivings about the premature promotion of spirit photography as evidence, Kardec incorporated photographic terms in his depictions of the appearance of spirits, as "an image daguerreotyped on the brain" (in *Le livre des mediums* [1861]). Consider also *La Genèse* (1868): "As thought creates fluidic images, it is reflected in the perispital envelope as in a mirror; it is embodied and in a sense photographs itself there."[88]

In fact, spirits have never appeared but through techne of their unconcealing, whether in spirited bodies, cameras, or computers, and the manifesting materials are always changing, producing spirit possession differently over time. Writing about the moment he took his possession photograph in 1931, Michel Leiris described the subject as a poseur and speaking with a "voice like a phonograph."[89] He recorded another moment when his colleague Marcel Griaule's magnesium flash *caused* a spirit to appear, in response to the apparent military danger.[90] To oversimplify for a moment, photographs serve as ritual tools and also as ethnographic tools, and the two may inflect and infiltrate each other: ethnographic photography may begin to carry ritual effects and ritual photography ethnographic ones. Juca Rosa's photograph demonstrates this loop. Used ritually, among other ways, during his lifetime, it has now acquired ethnographic force, giving us clues to Afro-Brazilian priestly couture, tools, and postures in 1870.

There are many examples of how photography has entered into and even helped recalibrate spirit possession in relation to photographic automatism. Consider the words of a twenty-four-year-old university student and practitioner of Brazilian Umbanda residing in Portugal as she details her experience of possession: "All my friends in the *terreiro* [temple of Candomblé] that see my *pomba gira* [female spirit] tell me how nice and funny she is, and how she helps women getting over their ailments. I have even asked them to take a photo of her when she incorporates me, so that I can have an idea what she looks like. I know it is my body, but one does not know what happens: the *time-lapse of incorporation* is like a blank. . . . I just feel a little trembling and dizzy afterwards, but at the same time one has a great feeling of peace and having done something worthwhile, being incorporated by such important entities."[91] The famous photographer Pierre Verger offered yet another example: "The *adosu* [new initiate of Candomblé] can be compared to a photographic plate. He holds within the latent image of the god, at the moment of initiation imprinted on a virgin spirit innocent of any other imprinting, and this image reveals itself and manifests itself when all the right conditions are reunited."[92] Henri-Georges Clouzot, meanwhile, also applied ethnographic photography to authenticating spirits' possession of the body but in a different way—by observing the lack of response to a magnesium flash explosion a mere two meters from the spirit-possessed subject's eyes.[93] Reaching beyond Afro-Atlantic traditions, Birgit Meyer showed how Ghanaian Pentecostals suspect the capacity of images, including photographs, to see you. The devil and other spirits can work against you through the eyes of photographs.[94] Tanya Luhrman interviewed a member of the Chicago Vineyard Church who described the vividness of his or her prayer life as "almost like a PowerPoint presentation."[95] Of course, photography's terms inflected many other domains, too, including studies of the brain. In 1878, for example, Edward Clarke compared brain cells to a negative: "Let a number of brain cells, impressed, like the negative of a photograph, with past events. . . ."[96]

The spirits and the Holy Spirit are now rendered present and interpolated through the conventions of the photographic view, a process that began in the time of Juca Rosa. These technological mediations of spirits do not diminish their agency, but they do change it, rendering it ambiguous in new ways. In this sense, Jonathan Crary recalls the original, sometimes religious sense of *to observe, observare*: "to conform one's action, to comply with." Similarly, Lorraine Daston and Peter Galison describe how the emergence of photography entailed not only a new way of seeing but also a new ethic, a new epistemology, a new form of scientist, in short, "a commitment."[97] The anthropologist Katherine Hagedorn explored how Afro-Cubans performing in folkloric shows or documentary films requiring faked Santería rituals are often really possessed by the gods as they attempt to mimic their bodily movements.[98] Hagedorn is interested in how these stagings are infiltrated by the real, but it would seem that we could invert this to explore how real possession is increasingly infiltrated by media to become spectacular performance.

"What does my body know of Photography?" Barthes began his reflection on the splintering of his person into its images, each of which seemed to freeze and carry off a part of him into arcs of actions out of his control. His body no longer seemed to be quite his own, and it was not. He was, in part, an automaton—his body and its work became the extension of other operators. Possession priests know this better than anyone, for their bodies are never solely their own. They know, too, that iconic representations like photographs have their own agency, acting independently of their subjects, and can be acted on by those who wield them. That is why they require careful management. The doubling of body and its mirror image can be deliberately applied: Juca Rosa distributed his carte de visite image widely, to all his followers, as a way of extending his presence and power into their bodies and homes. But the split can also be taken as a loss, even a death, when forcibly imposed.

The experience of losing ownership of one's body in both photography and spirit possession presents a symmetry and, sometimes, a symbiosis. Through the study of a photograph confiscated in 1870, I have tried to show that photography had dramatic effects on the making and regulation of a certain kind of automatism in possession practices. Police, priests, tourists, ethnographers, and others came to know and regard possession differently through the agency of photographs. But, even more, automatic photography infiltrated religion-like situations and practices itself as its meanings were increasingly experienced as if through a lens, verbally narrated, and even experienced in the camera's terms. Just as early photography was touched by the traces of spirits, spirit possessions were now summoned by flashbulb explosions or recalled as "time-lapse incorporation" exposures, calculated portraits on a proscenium, PowerPoint presentations, or instances of other photographic techniques through which the gods are enabled to appear.

* * *

Harbinger of the modern automatic, photography dovetailed with the enormous influence of Comtean positivism and its mantras of technological and scientific development. The photograph was a "form of expression adequate to the times of the telegraph and the steam locomotive."[99] It matched the mantra, "Order and progress," Auguste Comte's phrase embossed on Brazil's first republican flag in 1889.[100] Photographic evidence of the new order arrived in the capital city in 1897. That year saw the first Brazilian war mediated by photography, the war of the state against religious dissidents in the backlands of Canudos. The photographs taken at Canudos were all still lives, literally, since many of them were of corpses. Once the state had exterminated the settlement at Canudos—home to a population near thirty thousand, all of them poor, many of them former slaves and Afro-descendants—the images were shown in a public, electric-projection show that debuted on Rua Gonçalves Dias in Rio on Christmas Eve 1897. It promised the thrill of enlarged images, "lifesized."[101] "Curiosity! Amazement!! Horror!!! Wretchedness!!!!" read the advertisement. "THE CADAVER OF THE FANATIC COUNSELOR."[102] Electrically projected photographs were the major automatic attraction on Rua Gonçalves Dias. But two streets over, on Ouvidor Street, the main entertainment district of the city, another attraction held court from 1896 to 1897, a checkers-playing automaton named Ajeeb. The two were parallel, near contemporary attractions: the photographed corpse of the fanatic and the automaton Turk going head to head. Automatic photography helped inaugurate modern, republican Brazil, and so did the marvelous automaton Ajeeb, whom we will encounter again in chapter 4. Both were instrumental in establishing and securing the other against which the people—the agents, the humans, the bodies with will—would be defined. But, before we encounter Ajeeb, let us meet a drawing by a French traveler of someone who became a living saint in Brazil: Slave Anastácia.

3

Anastácia
Saintly Nearhuman

From that point things proceeded automatically. . . . All the saints, tremendous psychologists, had penetrated the soul and life of the faithful and shredded the fibers of each, like anatomists dissect a cadaver. Saint John the Baptist and Saint Francis of Paola, fierce ascetics, showed themselves somewhat surly and rigid. But Saint Francis de Sales wasn't like that; he listened and spoke with the sympathy you see in his book *Introduction to the Devout Life*. In that way, according to the mood of each, they continued their observations.

MACHADO DE ASSIS, "Among Saints" ("Entre santos"), 1896

Saints share something in common with slaves. Both are bodies filled with another's will, carrying out labor not their own.[1] Like psychiatric patients, monkeys, and possession priests, slaves were often considered automatons and nearhuman by virtue of being like animals—mechanical bodies empty of soul, ancestry, name, or family.[2] Saints' automaticity comes less from their proximity to the animal than from their nearness to a god. These distinct vectors of the automatic—proximity to the animal and to a god—converge in this chapter around a hybrid slave-saint. This story is about not a saint as such but a drawing of a slave who became a saint by a French traveler who settled in Brazil. The traveler's name was Jacques Arago; he was one of the around-the-world writers we met in the introduction.

The saint, Slave Anastácia, was never recognized by the Catholic Church, and in fact the church aggressively denied that she ever existed. And what it means to exist is what is at stake, for she clearly exists in certain respects. Devotees pray to her and receive responses. They feel her presence through ritual acts of contact. She exists, too, in a variety of material forms, from ink to wood, plastic to fabric. She occupies space and attracts acts of supplication, remorse, and hope. She exists in multiple different ways. What she lacks in will she recoups in temperament, situated within clusters of objects and constellations that conjure distinct moods.³ Like other saints, Anastácia is an assemblage, a suturing together, a "jointure of the somatic and the normative," to quote Eric Santner, that gathers moods and directs people to certain dispositions and forms of action.⁴ Considering saints as suturing—saint as assemblage—will help us consider differentiated experiences in the presence of saints and the ways the very same saint can gather multiple different social groups around distinct dispositions.

Perhaps a way to rephrase the question of what it means to exist is to ask, What histories and forces appear and come into being in and through Anastácia? What is the genre of her automaticity? Surely, she speaks to the barely reckoned history of slavery and its legacies, to issues of mixture and miscegenation, signaled by her flashing blue eyes, and to the meanings of emancipation since, as we will see, Arago's drawing first attracted the masses when it was posted alongside the corpse of Princess Isabel (who, as we have seen, ended slavery). It is as though the residue of Isabel's body and the bones of dead slaves somehow attached to Arago's drawing, filling it with emancipatory and healing potencies. Yet, even as she speaks to the history of slavery, Anastácia is also a slave herself, responsive only to the prayers of others. Her very ambiguity makes her a religion-like figure, even for those who do not reach out to her with ritual techniques or gear.

Slave Anastácia—or, rather, Arago's drawing of her and its many later reproductions—shows how coming to life always happens in a certain mode and with a particular mood. The kind of agency activated through exchanges with images of saints is not simply there or absent. It is always differently emergent. By paying attention to Slave Anastácia as she appears in varying modes and moods, we can give texture and nuance to the notion of automatic agency. Of course, all the protagonists appearing in this book are situated within a certain affective field. Rosalie Leroux was surely tragic. Monkey Rosalie, by contrast, evoked a sense of child-like playfulness and Juca Rosa a mystique of wonder and transgressive intrigue. Freud described the experience of Paris as uncanny. Mood is always part and parcel of the arts of appearance, but it is especially in this chapter that it takes center stage.

To Mood Upon

On rare occasions, *mood* has even been deployed as a verb, *to mood upon*. A letter from Sir John Duckworth, aboard the *Leviathan* off Saint Domingue during the Haitian Revolution, includes the declaration: "We returned to Port au Prince to mood upon our absurd indigested and blundering plan."[5] Duckworth's phrase suggests how mood does not preclude questions of individual volition. Rather, it sets the question of enacted will and its deferment within clusters of relations including people, spirits, things, places, senses, and situations that together evoke a disposition. What saints *do*, from the perspective of mooding upon, is induce states of being in their devotees: benevolence, forbearance, rage, horror. They trigger desired possibilities and dispositions through the moods they help create.

Heidegger's notion of being thrown into the world famously described how existence always occurs in tandem with a mood; being is incarnated through an emotional prism.[6] Saints are not thrown in the sense that Heidegger argued for humans, pressed into relationships as part of consciousness. Still, they are interpellated into a situation, a time, a predicament, a valence, a *perspective* on the world that confers a mood, a mood that is potentially shifted by virtue of the saint's summoning and presence. This attunement mostly goes unperceived. Walter Benjamin, for example, described how, in the act of reaching for a lighter or a spoon, "we hardly know what really goes on between hand and metal, not to mention how this fluctuates with our moods."[7] The reaching toward a saint likewise entails a mood linking hand to metal, wood, or plaster of paris—of reaching toward a solid edge. What mood emerges in the interval, the reach? If the ritual labor of summoning is a technique of being with, mood gives contour to the bridging of the known and the enigmatic, actuality and possibility. Being with is inflected by mood: guilt, love, estrangement, hope. Stated otherwise, a saint's presence is never simple thereness. It is never still. Presence always has direction, movement toward, and mood.[8]

Mood and mooding upon have to be put into words, set in a narrative frame. Saints, like other incarnates, are emplotted. On this score, Hayden White famously described the various moods of nineteenth-century histories—benign irony in Tocqueville, the perverse mood of Gobineau, onetime ambassador to Brazil and close friend of the emperor's, the optimism in Ranke, the tragic in Spengler. He perceived that a given historical drama is always cast in an emotional color carrying ideological implications, depending on what a given social drama is alleged to have been a revelation of. Moreover, histories are drawn from primary representations that are themselves possessed of mood, like Burckhardt's reliance on Giotto's paintings of Saint Francis.[9] Drawings or paintings of saints like Giotto's carry mood, and those materializations are, in turn, embedded in narratives that also have tone, valence, color, and direction. This has implications for the dispositions to action that may follow from any given incarnate's presence. It means that we need to attend not only to the aesthetics of saints' appearances and the affects they generate around them but also to the kinds of stories that bring saints to life.

Saints seem to be possessed of mood across traditions. In Islam, saints (*wali*) can follow one of several paths to authority: "sober saints" are models of extreme piety and scrupulous attention to law; "ecstatic saints," by contrast, sometimes exceed the law and are possessed (*majdhub*) or rapturous.[10] In South Asia, saintly visions were, June McDaniel noticed, accompanied by a mood: "In visions they saw specific deities, places, or situations while in trance they would be overcome by a feeling or mood." Sometimes the mood was of intense separation, at other times of erotic love. The mood evoked in saints' communion with a given deity could shift depending on the space—Kali in one room did not produce the same mood as Kali configured in another space.[11] In his classic *The Cult of Saints*, Peter Brown similarly documented how in late classical Christendom the presence of a saint's relic could inspire, variously, "a mood of solidarity," "the joys of proximity," "a sense of the mercy of God," and "moods of public confidence."[12] Saints' modes of presence convey a mood, though not neatly or consistently. A yogi's ascetic mode can be linked to a mood of horror, tenderness, or passion.[13]

Afro-descendants in Brazil revered humans and nearhumans of sublime power, including leaders of runaway slave settlements like Zumbi, orixás like Ogum, Xangô, and Iansã, inquices like Matamba and Nkosi, and folkloric tricksters like Zé Malandro. But there are also instances of dehumanized victims, bodies without will, who became saints. Their very passivity, ritually transfigured into agency, is the problem of this chapter. Their images and icons generated not only pity or repulsion but also reverence and attraction. Some were actual historical personages. An eighteenth-century woman, Rosa Maria Egipcíaca da Vera Cruz, began to have mystical visions after twenty-five years of slave labor, abuse, and forced prostitution (as a so-called profit slave, *escrava-de-ganho*) and recounted them in vivid detail. Initially subjected to whippings and exorcisms as one accused of being possessed by demons, she was ultimately revered as a saint, and common people sought her out for healing miracles.[14] Other saints were less specific historical persons than composites born of the nineteenth-century collective imagination. One of them was Slave Anastácia, a "precarious saint" denied official status by the Catholic Church but alive to her devotees nonetheless.

Precarious saints are often effective because of their marginal status. Stuck in purgatorial limbo, they work overtime to gain credit through benevolent acts and advance toward heaven.[15] Then, too, lacking official recognition, they remain unbound by the rules of decorum governing official saints. They are free to act with malice when necessary, and this makes them useful too. Precarious saints are unusually motivated, energetic, and effective, activated along unofficial and unlikely paths. Saints can also be precarious in their unstable figuration. Philippe Descola considers figuration as the sole shared quality of phenomena denoted as *religious*: "[Figuration is] the public instauration of an invisible quality through a speech act or an image. Under all guises chosen to consider it, religion embodies, religion incarnates, religion renders present in visible and tangible manifestations the various alterations of being, the manifold expressions of non-self, and the potencies which contain all their acts."[16] What I want to draw attention to in this description is the fickle quality of figuration. Descola's pithy declaration leaves a lot of work to ethnographers: discerning how people render things like *invisible quality*, *alterations of being*, and *expressions of nonself* in tangible ways. Yet it is just this uncertain, always-unfinished, agent-ambiguous quality that evokes religion-like situations. The very imprecision of not knowing exactly what happened renders religion-like scenes and situations emotionally compelling.[17]

Perhaps this is especially so for saints, who may enjoy official sanction and recognition but can also exist without formal, top-down legitimation or imprimatur. They emerge through informal processes of consensus, reputation, and some combination of sentiments of fear, attraction, and awe. How do they do it? The work of emergence requires, first of all, stuff. Like all incarnates, saints have to be materialized. Catholic saints depend on visual and material technologies to move from past corpse to present agent, to re-present, allowing special favor to be felt as near under certain circumstances.[18] In their quality as present-day forces, saints exist in and through bodies, things, images, and sounds. Devotees make creative use of objects, senses, and postures to enliven contact: ceramics, burning candles, flowers, written notes and photographs, genuflected knees, hands pressed to glass. Machado's novel *Iaiá Garcia* depicts a slave named Raimundo who even eats saints:

> "Raimundo," the girl would say, "do you like saints that are meant to be eaten?"
> Raimundo would straighten out his body, begin to smile, and, giving his hips and torso the movement of his African dances he would answer, crooning:
> "Pretty saint! Delicious saint!"
> "And a working saint?"[19]

Modes of making contact with saints mimic human-to-human techniques of touch, taste, or speech. After all, saints are superhuman powers but also thoroughly human bodies—typically distant and, in the Catholic tradition (unlike others), always bodily deceased—rendered in plastic or graphic form. They exist through both their visual and their material nature as human-like forms, endowed with many of the qualities of fleshly bodies: shape, texture, a degree of permeability, and vulnerability to decay over time.

But here is the trick. While a given saint's presence is materially entangled with the media through which it appears, such media are erased from religion-like experience even as they generate it.[20] Birgit Meyer calls this the phenomenon of *disappearing media*. The physical form is part and parcel of the saint's presence, though that material frame is seldom recognized as constitutive; rather it disappears or recedes, allowing the experience of presence to emerge in and of itself.[21] Or it is reconfigured as itself spiritual, as a tradition-boosting technology or a spirit accelerator.[22] Some media convey and amplify immediacy, and many ritual events cannot proceed at all without sensory amplifiers, typically sonic or visual.[23] The hybrid nature of saints' being at once a historical person, a living presence, a localized material thing, and a mode of national or global flow is important because it means that, like the photograph of Juca Rosa discussed in chapter 2, saints live multiple lives across multiple dimensions, diversely reproduced to circulate even centuries after their birth as saints.

Further, the transfer of presence demands proper techniques of discernment or "knowledgeable seeing" in order to recognize saints' blessing or benefit—a "saint's signature" to confirm that one has gained it.[24] As images and things, saints convey a presence from some other place and time: typically, in the Christian tradition, attesting to historical persons who witnessed or directly experienced the living presence of Christ as God, a testimony for which they were martyred. (And, in fact, *martyr*, from the original Greek for *witness*, is for the Catholic Church an official title preliminary to being considered as a saint.)[25] Saints can be used to recruit available pasts into present-day ideological projects, as we will see. Yet they also exist in and through a sensory here and now, as an object that attracts devotees, holds attention, draws financial gifts, and takes up space in a niche, narthex, shrine, or *velário* (the candle-burning room) and emits a mood. Holding these points in mind—saints' dependencies on materials, groups of discerning users, techniques of ontological transfer, and moods of incarnation—let us now bring Slave Anastácia back into the frame.

Anastácia was first incarnated in a nineteenth-century French traveler's sketch. Only after 1971 did she become a phenomenon. But just look at her now! She debuts at myriad shrines and in multiple guises, drawing a constant flow of pilgrims and Internet clicks. She poses on prayer cards, demands her own shrines, is visited on websites, frolics on telenovelas, and gazes from bikinis. Her image is one of violent bondage and silencing, yet, a superstar, she circulates, speaks, and invites devotees to feel her everywhere she goes.

"Inkarnation" and Sainticide

Anastácia was born of ink. Key to the generation of official Catholic saints is their entextualization in a trail of testimonial and catechistic legal records that serve to justify their actual physical existence. In the case of Slave Anastácia, however, her graphic birth was likely her only one: That is to say, unlike most saints, whose careers began as carbon-based bodies of flesh, Anastácia's genesis was a nineteenth-century drawing of an unknown male slave in Rio de Janeiro. Part of a polemic on the brutality of slavery in Brazil, it was drafted by the French traveler Jacques Arago. Arago drew a powerful image. The slave is girded by an iron shackle around his neck and a muzzle or shield (a so-called flanders mask) covering his mouth. Over a century later, the drawing was reimagined and figured as a female saint. The figure's mute suffering mimics and in part replicates Christ's founding sacrifice. Yet the image is a particularly forceful depiction of sheer disempowerment and passive victimhood. While, following the template of Christ, many Catholic saints willfully submitted to pain for an envisioned larger cause, part of their heroism derives from the idea that they could have resisted or accommodated, had they wished, but chose not to. Anastácia's story allows little space for individual will. This helps explain why her suffering passivity rendered her a saint non grata for many members of the Movimento Negro (Black Movement; also Consciência Negra) in Brazil. Yet this tragic figure—in fact, a figuration of a figuration—of a nonagent, a person without will—managed to become a living saint.[26]

Many parts of Slave Anastácia's animation have been well documented, and here I depend on this body of work.[27] Anastácia was born of an unlikely confluence of a tradition, a drawing, a building, and a situation. She was born of a tradition of Afro-Catholic saints, but she came into being in a specific building, the Igreja do Rosário e de São Benedito dos Homens Pretos (Church of the Rosary and Saint Benedict of Black Men). The Church of the Rosary began with a land donation in a central part of the city in August 1701. On February 2, 1708, the land was blessed and the first stone placed, and the church, built by slaves, was completed in 1710. The brotherhood it housed was founded even earlier, in 1640. As a testament to the political importance of the church, when the Portuguese court arrived in 1808, fleeing Napoléon's march on Lisbon, it was the first church they visited. From 1710 to 1825, the Senate convened in the church's consistory chamber, and it was from the Church of the Rosary that it presided over the independence of Brazil in 1822, when Dom Pedro I remained in Brazil against his family's wishes after his father's return to Portugal.

Next, the drawing. An unidentified slave was drawn in Rio by Arago between 1817 and 1820. It appeared with the caption "Châtiment des Esclaves (Brésil)" and was published in Arago's *Souvenirs d'un aveugle: Voyage autour du monde* in 1839. In chapter 6 of this book of travels around the world, one of three chapters on Rio de Janeiro, Arago presented detailed narrative descriptions of the slave market and the treatment of slaves. They appear just adjacent to discussions of the library and the quality of the theater (figure 3.1).

Arago described Brazil as the cruelest slave society he had witnessed, and, in that context and the wake of the Haitian Revolution, he marveled at slaves' apparent indifference: "Saint-Domingue, Martinique, l'Ile-de-France and Bourbon have seen many days of revolt, fire, and killing.

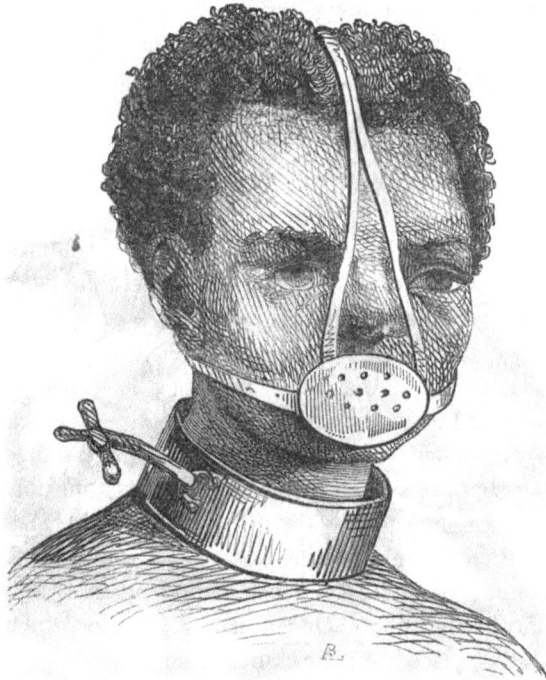

FIGURE 3.1. Jacques Arago, "Châtiment des Esclaves [Brésil]," in *Souvenirs d'un aveugle: Voyage autour du monde* (Paris: H. Lebrun, 1842), 1:76.

Only in Brazil have the slaves kept quiet, immobilized under the knotted whip."[28] He surmised that revolt was on the way, but in the meantime (*en attendant*) he offered his eyewitness report of torture: "As we wait [for the inevitable revolt], look at that man passing, with an iron ring to which has been adapted a vertical iron knife, all forcefully tightened on his neck; it's a slave who tried to run away, now marked by his master as a vagabond."[29] Then he described a second male slave: "And here's another with the face entirely covered by a mask of iron, with two holes left for the eyes and closed at the back of the head with a strong chain. This one was truly miserable: He ate dirt and gravel to stop the whipping; but now he may well expire under the whip for his criminal suicide attempt."[30] These are the sole descriptions of instruments of torture appearing in the text that correspond in some respects to Arago's drawing. Noteworthy is that both textual descriptions are of male slaves, whereas the image that became an object of devotion and reverence as a saint was of a female. There is also no eye color in the original black-and-white drawing, in contradistinction to the saint's later depiction with piercing blue eyes.[31]

The drawing that became Anastácia's image was registered in the context of travel writing. Like other examples of the budding genre of world travel, Arago's journals drew the world in dualistic print, juxtaposing his own mobility with Brazilian subjects fixed in space. Slave Anastácia indexes just such an encounter between mobility and immobility, between Europe and the Americas, between France and Brazil. Arago described slaves engaged in endless repetition, chained and without the will even to direct their own bodies. Yet he was sympathetic to their plight. Despite his surprise that they had not risen up, some appear as heroes of endurance and strength in his descriptions. One was the slave who, after a brutal and extensive whipping that ripped off his flesh, smiled, yawned, and stretched and then announced to the watching crowd: "By my faith, I just couldn't sleep." Another survived a long whip count and demanded the same number again, to demonstrate his disdain.[32]

Arago concluded his section on slavery by insisting on the superior intelligence of Africans and Afro-Brazilians compared with the lazy, cruel masters. These latter are the real slaves, he wrote. Savaging their crowded, mad religious processions and fanatic Catholicism, he closed the chapter: "Ignorance and superstition make only slaves."[33] Despite his criticism of it, Catholicism would remain the law of the land until the birth of the republic, in 1890. Following the 1822 declaration of Brazilian independence from Portugal, in 1830, about when Arago sketched the image in question, the new criminal code stipulated consequences for offenses against "religion, morality and good custom" (chapter 1, article 276). The law had little direct or specific bearing on the practices of Afro-

Brazilians since the institution of slavery itself sufficiently restricted slave activities, including ritual events. Then, too, slaves' religious gatherings were at times viewed positively by masters as a useful technique for blurring sentiments of slave unity and focused efforts at rebellion.

Paradoxically, the gradual emancipation of slaves was correlated with the development of repressive police institutions. Monarchic absolutism began to unravel after independence. The cosmopolitan savant Pedro II, born in 1825, had inherited the crown but remained as yet too young to occupy the throne. With colonial rule gone, new, national demands grew in strength. Individual liberties and public order suddenly became values that required institutional enforcement. As classes and races began to mix more freely in the streets and public spaces, the upper classes pressed their new, liberally defined status as citizens rather than mere subjects and demanded protection from all contact with slaves and the poor.[34] The nineteenth century leading up to the emancipation of slaves saw the emergence of a new social order, of which previous chapter's saga of Juca Rosa was a dramatic marker. The Intendancy of Police, first brought to Brazil from Portugal in 1808, was followed by the Guarda Urbana (City Police) in 1866 and then the National Guard and the civil and military police units. For as long as slavery lasted, the police forces acted to maintain a kind of public order as defined by slave owners, but they also learned to treat others of dubious status in a similarly violent fashion: all could be subject to arrest for challenging the terms of their subjugation.

As emancipation unfolded over the course of the second half of the nineteenth century, then, slaves endured new versions of harassment in a context of expanding police control. But liberty did come. First, the Queiróz Law of 1850, passed under the duress of British ships patrolling Brazilian harbors, officially abolished the slave trade. Next, in the war against Paraguay of 1865–70, slaves enlisted as soldiers were rewarded with freedom following the restoration of peace. Then, under the Law of the Free Womb of 1871—the year in which the Juca Rosa trial unfolded—children born to slave mothers were considered free.[35] In the 1885 Saraiva-Cotegipe (Sexagenarian) Law, all slaves over the age of sixty were liberated. And finally came the Golden Law (Lei Áurea) of May 13, 1888. With the emperor away in Paris and soon to be exiled there, his daughter Princess Regent Isabel, "the Redeemer," abolished slavery completely with a slash of her pen. Brazil was last of the New World slave societies to abolish the old institution.

In many respects, the twofold emancipation from slavery in 1888 and from the monarchy in 1889 did not alter the social hierarchy all that much. If the Golden Law's arrival was relatively anticlimactic, this was because by 1888 most Afro-descendants in Brazil were already free. In Rio de

Janeiro, the proportion of slaves had between 1850 and 1872 already declined from 42 to 17 percent of a population of around 275,000.[36] The precipitous decline points to the dramatic social transition that was already under way in Rio, from a city dependent on slave labor to a mostly free city. The sudden gap in slave labor was quickly filled by wage labor and land-tenure relations based on a patronage system. Outside principal cities, and particularly in the northeastern interior, abolition brought little change. To be sure, with the political transformation from monarchy to republic, shifting ideas of the nation were set in motion. But the new terms of public space invited other forms of restriction. Those displaced from the city center by reforms undertaken by French architects brought to create the parks and airy boulevards of Rio as a "tropical Paris," including a direct replica of the Parisian opera house in the city center, were mostly former slaves. Entire neighborhoods were razed. Public space, like the new republic, demanded the drawing of margins, the labor of boundary work.

The nineteenth century documented by Arago was long gone. But his drawing of a slave abruptly reappeared in public view at the Church of the Rosary, more than a century after its making. In the years leading to abolition, the church was the meeting place for key political activists, even perhaps including Princess Isabel. By virtue of its political history, coupled with its association with slaves and former slaves, it was in the twentieth century also associated with labor and the political Left. A working-class cafeteria operated from its outside walls. The Museum of the Negro (Museu do Negro) functioned in a rear corner upstairs, operated by the Brotherhood of Our Lady of the Rosary. After the coup of 1964, it was a site of resistance to the dictatorial regime, host to clandestine meetings. Several members of the brotherhood told me that the fire that half destroyed the church in 1967 was arson, ignited by agents of the dictatorial police. The cause of the fire was never discovered and barely investigated. Much of the church, including most of the museum's artifacts and records, was destroyed.

The fates of Jacques Arago's drawing and the Church of the Rosary converged in 1968. Following the church's reconstruction in that year, a man named Yolando Guerra who was the director of the Museum of the Negro removed the image from a copy of Arago's travelogue and hung it on the wall of the museum. We cannot know why he did so. No doubt he felt a certain aesthetic pressure. As the director of a museum with a specific pedagogical mission, what could he find to fill the gap in the collection left by the fire? Like previous regimes, the dictatorship made much of Brazil as a unique "racial democracy," the only country to have solved the problems of race, through its allegedly benign miscegenation. That patently false but powerful national myth had to be somehow countered. Also, it was an important year, the eightieth anniversary of abolition. Detaching the page from Arago's book and installing it on the wall must have been motivated by the need to compensate for the objects lost in the fire, replacing them with the artifacts and images at hand to tell the story of slavery. Guerra regarded the image as instructive of everyday torture, but he likely saw more in it than that. It was uniquely moving. Arago somehow had captured a deeply human expression buried under the most inhuman apparatus.

Certain visitors appreciated the sketch, but mostly it remained unnoticed—until July 1971, that is. In that year, the remains of Princess Isabel were placed on display in the museum for two weeks prior to her body's relocation from Rio de Janeiro to Petrópolis, the summer palace and her true home, in the mountains above the city. The casket was paraded through the city center, accompanied by the Brotherhood of Our Lady of the Rosary, dressed in solemn regalia, and carrying her to their church, the oldest and most traditional black church of the former capital (figure 3.2).

Isabel's body lay in state for two weeks with Arago's drawing posted just next to her. During that time, thousands visited the museum. There, they encountered not only the body of the princess but also the drawing, which, through its proximity, seemed related to her and to abolition. In

FIGURE 3.2. The brotherhood accompanying the arrival of the body of Princess Isabel to the Church of the Rosary, 1971. Photograph displayed at the Museu do Negro.

the 1970s, too, the church was in yet another way physically linked to the history of slavery and, by extension, Slave Anastácia. During the process of laying track for the nearby subway line, bones of former slaves were discovered. Devotion to "the Souls" (*as Almas*)—and in particular to "the Souls of Slaves" (*as Almas dos Cativos*)—gained in popularity. They were viewed as suffering incarnates, conveying the force of martyrs. From this unlikely assemblage—Arago's drawing, the corpse of Princess Isabel, the bones of slaves, the Church of the Rosary, and a moment in time when the Movimento Negro was gaining traction against the myth of racial democracy—was born a saint.

Arago's sketch of the masked slave was launched into action. Oral reports of miracles in the wake of Princess Isabel's stay at the museum began to circulate. The miracle-working image gained a name, Slave Anastácia. Anastácia began to be written about in popular tracts that created a story of her life and history. Along with other Afro-Brazilian figures of historical legend like Zumbi, the rebel king of an independent seventeenth-century maroon city (*quilombo*) called Palmares, she became a central character in the surging 1970s Movimento Negro, a civil rights project that placed religion, music, and cultural performance front and center.[37] In 1984, two activist brothers who were part of the movement, Nilton Santos and Ubiraraja Rodrigues Santos, sponsored a petition to have her beatified and then canonized as an official saint. The documents requesting the promotion in status were gathered by May 17, 1984, and included a rationale and a series of personal testimonies. The file was submitted to John Paul II on June 22, 1984. The rejection arrived just as swiftly, sent from the desk of Cardinal D. Eugenio de Araujo Sales on August 3.

The application and its rejection each directly addressed the question of the slave-saint's historical existence. The petition for sainthood proposed that Anastácia represented a "lacuna in the history of Brazil." She was born "sometime between 1770 and 1813," probably in Bahia. She was punished and tortured with the instruments depicted in Arago's drawing yet somehow made it to Rio de Janeiro—"with the help of philanthropists"—and was then medically treated at the Church of the Rosary until she recovered. In the application, Anastácia existed as a specific flesh-and-blood, historical person. The petition invoked existence in another sense as well, declaring that Anastácia enjoyed the enormous devotion "of the people," that she was, in fact, "more venerated than the actual saints." She was the recipient of the "constant celebration of masses for the souls of captives," of which she is the sole black effigy in the church ("a única representante negra em effigie na igreja"). She was by rights a "legitimate" salve to people's suffering, akin to other recognized Virgins like those of Salete, Lourdes, and Fátima.

Next, the petition invoked Anastácia's recognized miracles. To that end, the beatification request assembled a set of hand-drafted personal testimonies to her healing power. One letter reads as follows:

Dear Slave Anastácia,

I'm writing to you to thank you for all the blessings I've received from having faith in you. Especially about the sickness of my mom, thanks to God and you she's well, and I ask that you keep looking after her and all of us. Thanks also for helping with the job for my husband. Lately I'm facing some business problems, and I ask that you give light to choose the right path. I visited you over there in your temple in Madureira, and I have lots of faith in you and ask that you keep watching over my family.

I love you, Marisa.

However, despite many such testimonies and the detailed argument for Anastácia's authentic historical existence, the church rejected the bid in short order.[38] The letter from the archbishop declared that there was no possibility of canonization because there were no documents giving secure evidence of an actual past, either of her life or of her death. "Historical rigor is the first and indispensable legal requirement," it scolded. In addition, it continued, there is no support from canon law for the kind of public devotion accorded to this person. That fact that she was a saint of the people simply had no standing in the matter of canonization. Somewhat ominously, the letter then expressed the sentiment that practices of popular reverence should even be stopped by the archdiocese. The faithful must be alerted to ecclesiastic norms, it claimed, which do not allow for devotion to unrecognized saints.[39] It called for the petitioners' collaboration in diminishing Slave Anastácia's sainthood: "Toward this end, we hope also to be able to count on the intelligent cooperation of both signatories [i.e., Nilton and Ubiraraja]."[40] It directed a jab at the two activists, alleging that they enjoyed no rightful status to lay claims: "We inform you that the use of an alleged status, 'agent of social pastoral,' is inadequate."[41] The letter ended with the pro forma recognition of the petitioners' good intentions as fellow Christians and Brazilians.

The next step in the church's attempt to rid itself of Anastácia took place in the court of public opinion. An official notice from the Rio diocese issued on August 26, 1987, announced: "It has been determined and conveyed to priests to abstain from accepting solicited masses of thanksgiving for 'Slave Anastácia' or for any other reason. This determination does not impede the accession to perform masses for the souls of slaves."[42] Ritual engagements with the souls of slaves were permitted, just not with *this* slave. The cardinal then took further action, appointing an archivist, Monseigneur Guilherme Schubert, to investigate the source of the upstart. Schubert filed a devastating report stating baldly that Anastácia never existed, that the image derived from a drawing by the French writer Jacques Arago, that Arago had in fact drawn a male and conjoined two corporal punishments and instruments of torture he witnessed, that the idea of Slave Anastácia as a female, blue-eyed saint was an invention of Yolando Guerra, and, finally, that regarding this saint as a "god" (*deusa*), as her followers sometimes seemed to do, was counter to the church's notion of sainthood. Schubert's blunt conclusion, printed in a major daily of the time, read as follows:

> Thus we must arrive at the conclusion that, though it is just to feel pity for the suffering of black slaves, we cannot accept the liturgical cult of a figure that never existed, based solely on a drawing that did not even present a woman but rather a man (or, rather, two men). A popular movement began from an inventive fantasy of Mr. Yolando Guerra. This fantasy might serve for a novel or even a film. Whether the religion of Umbanda accepts this we cannot say. The Catholic Church does not.[43]

Schubert's mistake was not in his assessment of the specific origin of Anastácia, most of which, in narrowly historical terms, seems correct. Rather, it lay in an impoverished idea of what it means to exist and his cavalier dismissal of the role the popular imagination plays in the careers and moods of saints. And so his intervention had little effect. Even in the face of the church's attempted sainticide, devotion to Slave Anastácia continued to build in the lead-up to the centenary of abolition. With further confrontations looming between the church and the people, other agents of the church pressed the case against Anastácia. On March 25, 1988, Dom Marcos Barbosa reiterated the official line: Anastácia "simply did not exist."[44] Cardinal Eugênio Salles joined the fray on May 12, 1988, the day before the centenary anniversary of abolition: Anastácia had never existed and, therefore, could not be beatified or treated as an object of legitimate devotion. It had nothing to do with politics or racism, he insisted, and everything to do with the need that the church "not foment popular credulity." A year later, as yet another anniversary approached, sculptures of Anastácia were removed from the Church of the Rosary by the metropolitan curia. Parish priests offered homilies on the nonexistence of Slave Anastácia as a saint.[45]

Why was the church so worried about this illegitimate arriviste? And why was she suddenly so popular? In spite of the attempts to empty and *thingify* Anastácia, her cultivation had ballooned beyond any oversight. In 1981, a particular devotee, Dona Marieta, gathered donations from friends and neighbors to have a bust of Anastácia erected on a public square, the Praça Padre de Sousa. It became a busy location for Anastácia's cultivation.[46] Meanwhile, Nilton da Silva opened a "Temple of the Slave" in the neighborhood of Madureira, in the working-class north zone of Rio, and there founded the "Universal Order of the Slave Anastácia." By 1985, the temple was visited by thousands on Anastácia's saint's day, the day of emancipation, May 13, when the entire street was decorated with streamers and jammed with pilgrims. All the major newspapers covered the proceedings. Events began with clarion blasts at 5:00 A.M. and ended with fireworks in the evening. Masses for Slave Anastácia were celebrated by two priests of the Syrian Orthodox Church, Geraldo dos Santos and Agostinho José Mario; Nilton da Silva himself conducted the most popular event of all, a giant "mentalization" session. The exercise showed the extension of Slave Anastácia into Umbanda—a possession religion combining Afro-Brazilian Candomblé and French Kardecism—as a spirit akin to the class called *pretos velhos* (old blacks). Two additional temples devoted to Anastácia were opened in Olaria and Vaz Lobo, suburbs of Rio, with services led by clergy of the Catholic Church of Brazil, a dissident, national catholicism separate from the Roman Catholic Church.

Photograph spreads featuring Slave Anastácia were printed in mainstream publications like *O jornal*, especially around May 13.[47] Personal advertisements in newspapers announced blessings (*graças*) received from her in exchange for offerings (*promessas*). A favela neighborhood was named after her.[48] Soccer players, managers, and clubs claimed her as their patron saint.[49] Famous samba schools like the Unidos de Vila Isabel elevated her to a starring role in Carnaval spectacles, televised nationwide. A decade later, in Bahia, the all-female percussion group Banda Didá paraded and performed wearing her mask. Her profile grew against a shifting national backdrop in which black history was being newly instituted in the country as a whole—through the National Black Consciousness Day (Dia Nacional de Consciência Negra), and the addition of Afro-Brazilian history to the public school curriculum.[50] Slave Anastácia was the history of slavery incarnate, but a version that was alive and active, her blue eyes blinking, ever ready to forgive or redeem.

At the Church of the Rosary itself, devotees flocked to the Museum of the Negro to see the image of Slave Anastácia, along with other suffering incarnates like the Unknown Slave (Escravo Desconhecido).[51] The devotion to Anastácia expanded in the buildup to the 1988 centennial of abolition and its aftermath. Completely novel mythistories emerged with details of her life story, as if out of nowhere. Some continue to circulate today, even in encyclopedia entries: "From the little historical evidence recorded, it can be said that this great martyr was one of the many examples of Afro-Brazilian resistance. . . . Her martyrdom started on April 9, 1740. . . ." The entry goes on to detail her arrival from Congo on a specific ship, her beautiful mother named Delmira who was purchased and raped, the subsequent birth of Anastácia in Pompeu, Minas Gerais, on May 12, and the sexual violence perpetrated against her despite her heroic resistance.[52] Other versions cast her as a former Yoruba princess and avatar of the goddess Oxum. The stories multiplied and spread.

Perhaps at this juncture we should summarize Slave Anastácia's similarities and differences from other saints. Like other popular Catholic saints in Brazil, Anastácia is recognized both in orthodox Catholic and in Afro-Brazilian cultic settings, if on the margins of both. Like other saints, she is understood as having suffered in the past for a just cause and as offering present benefits for other bodies owing to the past suffering that her body endured. Gaining those benefits requires following one of several familiar techniques of conveyance or exchange—through contact, mimesis, written petition, material and financial offerings, or prayer. Unlike those of other saints, however, Anastácia's narratives do not necessarily mark her as Christian. Like other saints, she serves as a mediator but not of the reality of Christ's living presence. Her martyrdom attests not to the experience of Christ as God but rather to the pain of enslavement and sexual assault, both her own and her mother's, as her blue eyes—indexing miscegenation through rape—dramatically announce. Slave Anastácia is also characterized by a reduced personhood. Whereas many saints are characterized by heroic acts of will, the defiant refusal to renounce, her fame lies in her sheer endurance—mute, bound, raped, gagged, locked in metal. She moves only within strict limits. She sees but cannot speak. She heals but cannot taste. Unlike many Afro-Brazilian *santos* who dance in the bodies of living humans, she does not manifest and, thus, remains immobile.[53] She is a saint who is a metal-flesh hybrid, encased. Her saintly heroism lies in being able to signal persisting personhood even in and through the cage. In sum, whereas officially recognized saints were typically actually existing humans who bore witness to a mythic being, Anastácia is the inverse—a mythic being who bears witness to the actually existing history of slavery in Brazil.

Techniques of Presence

Despite her rejection as a canonical saint, Anastácia regularly comes to be. She *is* even if, according to the church, she never existed. Because she is a never-existing yet ever-present, precarious not-quite saint—interstitial in every sense—the possible modes of her appearance remain wide open. She signifies diversely and with varying social effects for different groups of users. John Burdick's work is especially incisive on this score. He points out that white, middle-class women engage Slave Anastácia by emphasizing her dramatic difference from them; they focus on the saint's dark skin, benign good nature, and solicitude in a more or less patron-client (or master-slave) form of exchange.[54] Black or mixed-race women's engagement with her, however, is premised on proximity and likeness—"She suffered in ways I suffer"—and on reading her suffering as being less about her victimhood than about the white pathology that caused it. It should be noted, however, that many black activists reject her as a pernicious glorification of submission.[55]

Here, I want to propose three modes and moods by which the incarnate Slave Anastácia is animated and brought into existence in spite of the church's insistence that she lacks it. First, she is activated in the Museum of the Negro as a martyr whose suffering points to the actual history of slavery in Brazil, a history she both indexes and sanctifies. The mode is biohistorical, pointing, if in imaginative ways, to actual bodies in history. The mood is trauma. Second, she is activated in the Sanctuary of Slave Anastácia, where she is a composite saint and spirit. In that space, whose owner, visiting priest, and congregation are mostly white, the history of slavery slips from view. Her suffering is encased in glass, available for consultation and exchange, and grouped with that of other saints, detached from the history of slavery or racialized violence. She is ethereal and constrained to the role of attending to personal petitions and the masses held in her name. The mode is spiritual—personal, sanctimonious, restricted to the terms of private exchange. The mood is less one of historical trauma than of resigned serenity. Third, she is activated in the market, on television, in fashion, and online. In this broader arena of circulation, her deployments and significations are as varied as her sites of use. A cab driver hangs her image from a rearview mirror for protection, someone else carries it in a wallet as a promise made in exchange for a cure. In the most public domains of her transmission, however, a predominant theme is her bound and boundless sexuality, combining fantasies of domination, including her inability to speak, and the right to her violent abuse.[56] The mode is mechanical, in which a body as machine is endlessly reproduced in downloads, textile prints, reruns, mimeographs, and equally copyable sex acts. The mood is erotic submission.[57]

ANASTÁCIA IN THE MOOD OF TRAUMA

In the mood of trauma, Anastácia's primary ideological locus is the history of slavery. Her home church and birthplace is Our Lady of the Rosary in downtown Rio, which receives an unusual amount of traffic. There is a constant flow during workday hours, with twenty to fifty persons seated in the sanctuary at any given time and hundreds attending the popular midday masses on Monday and Thursday. The church is the hub of Afro-Catholic history in Rio de Janeiro. It was here that Slave Anastácia first appeared or emerged as a saint. And it is here that she today appears, in several guises. Though the church is most famous for Anastácia, her icons are nowhere on hand at the entrance or in the sanctuary. Rather, there are icons of Saint George and Saint Benedict. Notes left at their feet ask for their help with exams, household conflicts, health problems, etc. Many petitions are lists of names. Small images of Saint George, Saint Benedict, and many other saints, including the unapproved Slave Anastácia, can be purchased at the entrance.

In the church annex, on the second floor, Anastácia plays a much larger part. With no fewer than seventeen different icons or instantiations, here she is ever present, nested within clusters of Afro-Brazilian indexes: slavery, Carnaval, Candomblé, the brotherhood. Still, she is the clear focal point. One of her instantiations is as a pedagogical figure teaching the history of slavery in Brazil. In the Museu do Negro, also in the Church annex, the museum director, Ricardo Passo, has her placed her strategically, if precariously (figure 3.3). There, devotees and museum visitors

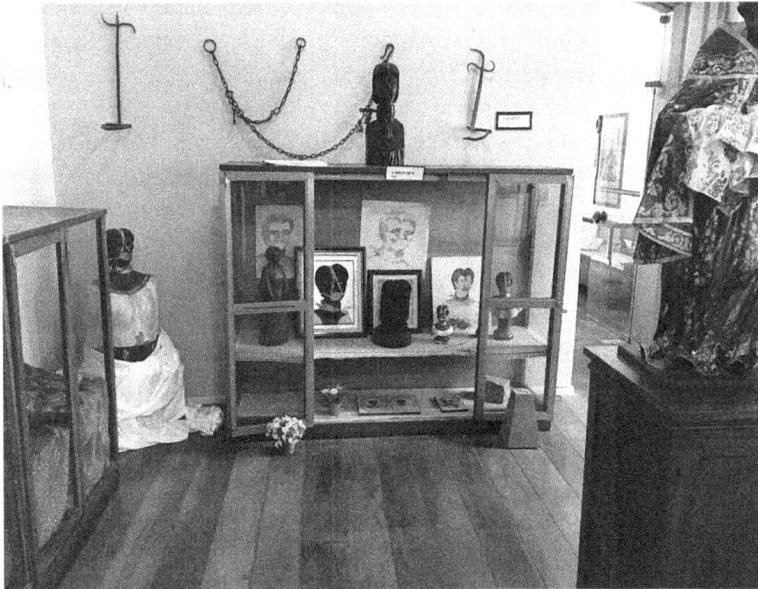

FIGURE 3.3. Slave Anastácia at the Museu do Negro in May 2016, simultaneously a shrine and a historical exhibit. Photograph by author.

approach her images joined centrally in a large armoire. A discreet box for petitions or money gifts is placed at its base. On top is a stack of mimeographed prayers to gain Anastácia's favor with instructions for their use. Museum administrators patrol the line between deploying Anastácia as an exhibit and deploying her as a saint, and they remain vigilant about this boundary work. The church was once nearly closed because of her unsanctioned presence there, and the museum was closed from 2001 to 2011. Hence the need to keep her out while still remaining attentive to the fact that she is the reason many parishioners visit at all. The line dividing the inside of the church from the outside is unclear, a delicate negotiation in space of the issue and location of her existence. Though the museum is housed under the same roof, is it still in the church? How about the velário, open to the outside air, where candles are burned to her? Or the stalls that are outside the church but back up against it? The ambiguity renders the museum and Anastácia's various installations vivid religion-like negotiations.

To avoid possible conflicts with the diocese and make clear that the museum is outside, above the figures of Anastácia the display includes unmarked tools of torture—manacles, shackles, chains, iron rings. Passos explained to me that this arrangement allows visitors to pivot easily. The assemblage might be a shrine, but it could also be an informative exposition. To maintain this useful fuzziness, he is careful to remove offerings of money, flowers, and written notes and deposit them downstairs in the velário, where the material presentation of Anastácia is clearly for ritual and not pedagogical purposes. Yet there is clear evidence that even Anastácia as historical exhibit is also used as an altar, a site of exchange, since flowers, notes, and money are left below her head daily. Moreover, her presence expands at auspicious times of year and diminishes at others. The altar exhibitions are living things, modulating, expanding, contracting, posing challenge and reply. When I left Rio last year, Passos took an icon of Anastácia off the armoire shelf and gave it to me. I protested, taking the site to be a sacred one worthy of protection and preservation. He put it back in place but then picked a smaller one and extended it toward me. "People always lend a hand," he said, meaning that they bring new editions of Anastácia. Even my writing would "take part in making her altar" ("fazer parte do altar dela"). Perched on the edge dividing history and religious practice, Slave Anastácia's altars are able to expand or shrink, to adopt new media of extension or refuse them.

In the museum, Anastácia's presence expands in May and November, when abolition and the National Day of Black Consciousness, respectively, are celebrated. The number of visitors jumps tenfold from about fifty a day to five hundred.[58] Anastácia serves as at once a political signifier and a ritual signifier. At the museum, that hybridity appears in very graphic form. One poster presents a simultaneous historical narrative and prayer: "Goddess-slave, slave-princess, princess-goddess . . . give us your force to fight, and never to be enslaved."[59]

Even in the velário, Anastácia remains slightly undercover. Her figure is cased alongside a much larger image of Saint Michael the Archangel. Like Anastácia, Michael is concerned with justice. He bears the cross of souls (*cruzeiro das almas*) and protects the dead. Under the Church of the Rosary are—or so it is asserted—the bones of deceased slaves, discovered when the tunnels were dug for the nearby metro line. In this sense, Saint Michael Archangel and Slave Anastácia's roles are joined as the protector of the souls of slaves. And, while Michael's bulk fills the glass case, the figures of Anastácia outnumber him, and the vast majority of written petitions left for the saints' consideration are addressed to her. This site gets more traffic than the museum itself. At any given time during the day there are several people present. They usually remain for five or ten minutes, time enough to light a candle, approach the icon's case, and spend a brief period in contemplation or prayer. I estimate that during the week over one hundred people visit Anastácia daily and more on Mondays and Thursdays, when large midday congregations gather for mass.

Just outside the velário—technically outside the church wall—three different Afro-Brazilian diviners practice their craft. The most sought after, Tia Rita, has a constant line and charges from fifty to one hundred *reais* (somewhere between $15.00 and $30.00) per consultation. Dressed as a *baiana*, in stylized Afro-Brazilian priestess couture, Rita is also a member of the church brotherhood. She told me some of Anastácia's uses in her practice. Slave Anastácia is invoked to deal with legal issues and with matters of love "because she suffered so much injustice." But she is also solicited for help with physical ailments like a sore throat, presumably because of the painful bands of iron encircling her neck. Tia Rita explained that someone seeking the aid of Anastácia might need to do more than just make offerings of candles, money, or fruit: "When you ask something of her, you should spend three days mute, making your request [*fazendo pedido*] silently." By mimicking her muteness, the petitioner fortifies that quality, and Anastácia gains in presence. On the other side of the church, Rita's mother is likewise practicing, divining with cards as well as plying her trade with cowrie shells (*búzios*). She has a bust of Slave Anastácia on her table. She warned me against the evil eye, a rival's jealousy. The diviners often direct clients to visit Slave Anastácia inside the church. They instruct customers to perform tasks (*tarefas*) there, to make petitions or express thanks for jobs saved, debts repaid, and sicknesses or vices cured.

When I last returned to visit with Tia Rita, in August 2018, she had died. Her stall, backed against the velário of Anastácia, was padlocked. All her saints and gear were still present, though covered by a cloth. Neighboring vendors told me that it had been that way for months: "Nobody wants to touch her saints. Someone has to do it who knows what they're doing." Respect.

Perhaps the most common method of contact with Anastácia is visiting her at a specific site and placing a hand against the glass case housing her image. The physical contact—palm on glass—is accompanied by a slight lowering of the head, in deference and petition, and the mouthing of prayers. One must always "ask with faith." If, like all saints, Anastácia resides most forcefully in certain places, she also achieves extralocal extension. From Rio she moved to Bahia, where she also has a shrine at the church most associated with Afro-Brazilian history in Salvador da Bahia, the Church of Our Lady of the Rosary of the Blacks (Igreja de Nossa Senhora do Rosário dos Pretos). Her role there, as in the Museu do Negro in Rio's Church of the Rosary, combines didactic and ritual functions (figure 3.4). As an important historic site in one of the most visited parts of Salvador, the church attracts both tourists and parishioners. One sign identifies different black saints and explains the reasons for their cultivation. Known and officially recognized black saints like Benedict or Iphigenia serve as examples of martyrdom; others, like Santa Barbara, provide syncretic links between Catholicism and Afro-Brazilian religions like Candomblé (in Bahia Santa Barbara is also known to be the orixá Iansã).[60] Anastácia does not fit either category. The sign continues: "In addition, we observe in Brazil the belief that martyrs of captivity and slavery are good intercessors for petitions, and act as intermediaries for obtaining sought-after graces. In exchange for these favors, masses for the rest of their souls are given, along with money, flowers, and candles set out around their tombs and icons. It is in this sense that the devotion to Slave Anastácia in this brotherhood can be understood."[61] Note the special care taken to justify and bracket the presence of Anastácia's image within the church by emphasizing her link to the souls of the dead and employing hedging phrases like *in this sense*. Not an actual saint, she is nevertheless a "good intercessor."

ANASTÁCIA IN THE MOOD OF RESIGNED SERENITY

In the mood of resigned serenity, Anastácia's benevolent mercy trumps any hint of the trauma of slavery.[62] At the Santuário Católica da Anastácia, in the northern sector of Oswaldo Cruz, Anastácia is juxtaposed both with Saint Michael and with Saint George, another champion of justice. But there the similarities between the Church of the Rosary and

FIGURE 3.4. Anastácia as part of a didactic display with labels and explanations at the Church of Our Lady of the Rosary of Blacks, Salvador da Bahia. The blue eyes shine. Photograph by the author.

the Catholic Sanctuary of Anastácia end. Masses are held at the Sanctuary of Anastácia three times a week, led by a priest of the Brazilian Catholic Apostolic Church (Igreja Católica Apostólica Brasileira). This church was founded as a dissident breakaway from the Roman Catholic Church in 1945 and welcomes Slave Anastácia as a bona fide saint.[63] The sanctuary was opened by the owner of the house a decade ago after Anastácia bestowed a miracle on her by allowing her stolen car to be recovered. At this temple, icons of Anastácia are sometimes grouped with pretos velhos (the familiar spirit of "old blacks" in Umbanda). There were multiple niches where written notes and burning candles were left, some for public use, others for household devotion. One note, open and legible, beseeched Anastácia for a "clear conscience" (*lucida consciência*), "free of sickness" and all evil, so that the petitioner would be happy with the "path" (*caminho*) his or her life has followed. Another asked for a job for a husband. Others provide lists of names. Anastácia's blackness and torture are strikingly cast in contrast with a field of unusually white versions of saints and intercessors, including Christ.

At a Wednesday evening mass for Slave Anastácia and Saint George, from 6:00 to 7:00 P.M., eighteen people were in attendance, six men and a dozen women. Despite the small group, the priest, Padre Fabio, used a headset microphone, an informal, colloquial style, and no Latin. The Eucharist was served; three women went directly from receiving the sacrament to kneeling before Anastácia. All gathered around the life-size effigy of Anastácia for recitations and prayers. Next followed recitations and prayers to Saint George. Men lined up to have the cape of Saint George placed on their shoulders by Padre Fabio while he prayed, asking Saint George to transform them into defenders and protectors, like he himself. The men then held the cape aloft while the women walked beneath it, reaching up to touch it as they passed. If Anastácia and Saint George are joined in their thirst for justice, here their juxtaposition also instantiates dramatic gender differences. The ritual linked men with Saint George and his role as a defender and women with submissive Anastácia. Men defend women, who in turn suffer for all. This "politics of serenity" is controversial for those in the Movimento Negro, John Burdick writes, because Anastácia allows for little structural or historical critique; yet devotion to her, even in these kinds of spaces, "helps negras in small, everyday ways to value themselves physically, challenge dominant aesthetic values, cope with spousal abuse, and imagine possibilities of racial healing based upon a fusion of real experiences with utopian hope."[64]

Not far from the sanctuary is the Mercadão de Madureira, the main commercial site in Rio for the purchase of the gear central to Afro-Brazilian ritual work. Here, one encounters a range of nonexistent but very-present beings, including agents of Afro-Brazilian traditions across a wide spectrum from Espiritismo to Umbanda to Candomblé. The market is enormous, a hall filled by hundreds of vendors selling everything from herbs to clothing to live animals for sacrifice. Figurines of virtually every spirit—orixás, *exus*, pretos velhos, *pomba-giras*, and angels—are for sale. Everything! Except perhaps Slave Anastácia.

I inquired at dozens of stalls and stores and found only three small images of Anastácia. Her relative absence amid such an abundance of powers was surprising. A few stalls reported that they used to have some but ran out after her high season, around May 12–13. Many more reported that they never carried her. One salesclerk told me in no uncertain terms that I was wasting my time, committing a category mistake: "Anastácia pushes too much toward the Catholic side." She did not fit the genre of sales in Afro-Brazilian religions per se. However, if I went down the block, outside and over to the Catholic bazaar (Bazar Padre Normand Artigos Católicos), there I would certainly find many Anastácias. Hardly. There, the owner also looked at me askance—again a category mistake—and told me that Anastácia was not "really Catholic." Only one product—a plastic-bead Anastácia rosary—was for sale. What I want to call attention to in the short description of these markets, so crucial for both Afro-Brazilian and popular Catholic practice, is the fact that Slave Anastácia was marginal but present at each venue. At the Afro-Brazilian religions market she was "too Catholic" but still occasionally peaked out, while at the Catholic store she was too African but still, barely, hanging on in the form of plastic rosary beads. This very ambiguity makes her unusual, odd, a generator of religion-like scenes.

In any given Umbanda temple, meanwhile, Anastácia takes on a less interstitial but more metaphysical mood. Here is one example, from the website of an Umbanda center located six hundred miles west of Rio de Janeiro, in Paraná, the Centro Pai João de Angola: "The spirit of Anastácia is gifted with vigorous LIGHT and EQUILIBRIUM; with her heart sweet and enlightened she distributes forgiveness, love for the creator; she finds hearts imprisoned by egoism and spiritual blindness. This is her most profitable area of work and blessings. She liberates from the goads of illusion and, like a solitary, inexhaustible star, lights the paths of those who seek emancipation, in the name of Jesus. Humility and an aura of love are the marks of her presence."[65]

ANASTÁCIA IN THE MOOD (AND MARKET) OF THE EROTIC

In the mood of the erotic, Anastácia's transformation into Yoruba royalty—the daughter of Oxum, a popular Yoruba and Afro-Brazilian deity—launched her into superstardom by emphasizing her sensual intrigue. A television miniseries based on her aired in 1990 and continues to be easily available on YouTube, where it has been viewed millions of times.[66] The show took its narrative from a short story by Maria Salomé, a white member of the Brotherhood of Our Lady of the Rosary, emphasizing Anastácia's history as an African noble and her extraordinary beauty.[67]

In Salomé's story, Anastácia appears as a Christ-like figure whose birth is preceded by an annunciation. This point was picked up in the miniseries version, where Anastácia was played by Angela Corrêa, a spiritist. In the first episode, a *babalawo* (Yoruba diviner) tells the royal parents that a blue-eyed child will be born, a daughter of the Yoruba and Afro-Brazilian deity Oxum. In a later episode, Anastácia raises a slave owner's child from the dead, after which she dies and ascends to heaven as a white dove, a female African Christ.

Whereas other textual accounts cast her as Bantu or as arriving on a Kongo slave ship, the television series—timed to launch on May 15, 1990, roughly in conjunction with her celebrations around Abolition Day—portrayed her as coming from the part of Africa most familiar to Brazilians, though also one that, parenthetically, did not figure prominently in the slave trade to Brazil until the end of the eighteenth century and the beginning of the nineteenth. The production paid careful attention to the question of historical fidelity, however much the history involved was invented: "The quest for origins and consequent fidelity to the reconstruction of the past is evident in all the details."[68] The director, Paulo César Coutinho, elaborated: "What most fascinated me was the possibility of a historical reconstruction of one of the most incendiary periods of our past."[69] But, apart from the question of historicity, it was Ângela Corrêa/Anastácia's sex appeal that featured in the press, one reporter writing: "[She] could make herself the 'Ebony diva' of Brazilian television. This is confirmed in the scenes where she appears nude, in a gorgeous setting of her 'honeymoon' in a waterfall. Perfect body and impressive expressions."[70] Another newspaper likewise focused on sex: "The legend of the slave Anastácia, sanctified by popular belief, nevertheless unfolds in a context of human torture and sexual and moral perversions."[71]

As Marcus Wood describes, Anastácia took up space in hair salons, cafés, shopping malls, on cigarette lighters, key chains, T-shirts, and swimwear, even BDSM and fetish doll porn sites.[72] A bikini store in Copacabana named Anastácia played on a similar provocation between suffering abnegation and erotic fascination. In this valence, juxtaposing the nearhuman tropes of the automatic and the animal, Wood notes that Anastácia is "frozen eternally within her terrible machinery" and reduced to the status of "dumb animal."[73] The sadomasochistic excitations played on by Anastácia were visible in certain commercial deployments, but they usually remained contained. They exploited her strange ambiguity as at once a figure of protest against slavery and a slave herself, acting at the bidding of her devotees with no apparent will of her own.

This tension became explicit at São Paulo Fashion Week in June 2012. There, the designer Adriana Degreas launched a new line of beachwear prominently featuring Slave Anastácia in a garment draped on the body of the blonde supermodel Shirley Mallmann. Anastácia's muzzle was likewise shown on the runway, as a coy bikini accessory covering the navel instead of the mouth. Fashion commentators gushed. The host of weekly fashion show *GNT Fashion*, Lilian Pacce, enthused:

> All this with Bahian spice: a baroque brocade here, some lace there, colors of orixás, prints for Iemanjá, and even a slave's iron mask. Liberated from their master, these "slaves" float in silk gowns or two-pieces with conic brassieres, creating a 1950s silhouette. For the prints, there are strong images of Anastácia (the slave-saint), Nega Fulô, and lots of margarita flowers. . . . The feeling is that Adriana is totally at ease, from sunbathing to strolling on the ship and—even more—stripping down to white lingerie panties and a baby doll miniskirt [*bunda rica*], totally transparent. As Adriana reminds us, they reveal the color of sin, of those negras who drove their white masters crazy.[74]

Not all viewers were as excited. In late September 2015, the African British woman Tanya Allison mounted a petition drive from London on Change.org with these words: "Fashion Designer Adriana Degreas has displayed a dress on her runway emblazoned with a Black slave on the front in a shackled contrapment over her face & mouth which would enable them to not be able to speak. This is not fashion, this is fetishising and commodifying racial abuse. We need to put a stop to this can you believe in 2015 we are still subjected to this form of racism & imagery. It would not be acceptable to emblazon a dress with a Holocaust victim & we will not accept this form of disrespect to our ancestors."[75] The petition gained 1,733 signers within a few weeks, and elicited a response from Adriana Degreas' design company:

> The Adriana Degreas brand does not promote, endorse or accept any racist or any other discriminatory practice or bias regarding gender, race or religious belief. The Collection was created in homage to the Brazilian state of Bahia, particularly to honor the culture of the women from Bahia. The particular image that has created distress (only outside of Brazil) is that of a Saint called Escrava Anastácia, a very important religious figure in Brazil, both for Catholics and Umbanda (Afro-Brazilian religion) practitioners. Escrava Anastácia's figure is always represented as such (with the horrible muzzle collar) and she is known in Brazil as symbol for women's strength, resilience and the struggle for freedom. As many other Saints in Catholicism, she is depicted in a situation of martyrdom.[76]

Two issues demand attention in this fashion show display and the charged exchange that followed: the trope of Slave Anastácia's sexuality and, by extension, that of the sexuality of "Bahian women," that is, black and mixed-race women. The display was cloaked as homage to Bahia, women's strength, and Catholic martyrdom, three emphases that stand in substantial tension with each other. Still, the contrast between white users of the image—whether as models, clients, or imagined male objects of seduction—on the one hand, and a black martyr and a black-authored petition against such uses, on the other, left unresolved questions. The design company's solution was to say that all *Brazilians* recognize the homage and that only foreign Afro-descendants are opposed. The accusation of racism was absorbed into a difference of national culture.

Despite its obvious evasions, there was something to such an argument. Slave Anastácia was, in fact, a celebrity icon and a television star, in addition to being an Afro-Catholic saint and a slave. Official Catholic saints, like orixás of Candomblé and spirits of Umbanda, are printed on textiles and take other graphic forms regularly. But the resistance to Slave Anastácia among Movimento Negro activists in Brazil suggests that, like Tanya Allison, they still find the slave-saint to have limited heuristic value for bringing the history of slavery to public consciousness at best and to be a pernicious white fantasy of black sexual servitude at worst. They argue that, however fictitious she may be, Anastácia should not be so easily detached from the site, mode, and mood of her making.

Moody Materials

Each mode-mood alliance draws on and activates a different feature of Anastácia's material being. In the first instance, the instruments of torture are called out: the muzzle and neck ring. In the second, her blue eyes feature, gazing gently upward with sympathy, forgiveness, and understanding toward white masters. In the third, her torso is featured. The distinct modes of incarnating the saint's moods call different physical features to the fore. Those material forms in turn impinge on her mood and her capacity to structure social groups and their predispositions to certain kinds of action.

Different sites seem to allow for the emergence of Anastácia in one sort of mood but to foreclose it in others. The beachwear saint, driving white masters crazy, could never appear at the Church of the Rosary. The full-length icon of a sweet, spiritual Slave Anastácia could not stand among the bones in the rough-hewn velário. Each materialized version of the saint emits and is sheathed in mood. It has a fit. *Fit* has many parts, including historical residues that stick to the incarnate and shape its form.

Even the skin color Anastácia is depicted in is correlated with special and social fit. Prints of her come in different shades of blackness—mulatta, quadroon, dark skinned—so that everyone can find himself in her image.[77] Still, the residues are thicker and stickier in some sites than they are in others and are not so easily slipped or effaced.

Certain modes of Slave Anastácia's appearance cause the actually existing history of slavery to be amplified, while others cause it to be downplayed. As one devotee declared: "I'm devoted to the slave because she was a slave, get it?"[78] The Brazilian Catholic temple in Oswaldo Cruz, the Umbanda and spiritist centers, and the São Paulo catwalk offer examples of Anastácia's progressive streamlining and movement away from a historical mode. By *historical mode*, I mean not the kind of forensic history demanded by Monseigneur Schubert in the church inquisition but rather a more generous cast of history that recognizes how a thousand flesh-and-blood stories of actually existing slavery might be forcefully condensed and made thinkable and affectively available in the never-existed form of Slave Anastácia. In this historical mode, Anastácia's suffering is redemptive because it speaks possibilities into the present. Robin Sheriff proposed that Slave Anastácia symbolizes or expresses the actual here-and-now experience of Afro-Brazilians being muzzled.[79] It amplifies the history of slavery in a fashion that exposes the unevenness of gender, the fact that enslavement bore down on female bodies in ways it did not on male bodies.

Perhaps we might say that as Slave Anastácia moves further from her site of accidental origin at the Church of the Rosary—further from the bones of slaves, the molds of where the abolitionist Princess Isabel lay in state, the ashes of the fire that arsonists sparked, or the diviners casting shells in the shadow of the walls—the more permeable and open-ended she becomes. Her capacities as an automaton or a nearhuman expand and contract with the mood of where and how she comes into being. The risk, for her as for many nearhumans, is of becoming ever more streamlined, fluid, and pixelated and being made into a servile mammy, a wispy spirit, a Yoruba princess, or a cruise-ship fantasy, caricatures mostly unthinkable closer to her material home and place of origin.

* * *

When I last visited the Church of the Rosary in August 2019, Tia Rita's stall had been replaced by a barbershop, and the church's doors were locked shut. It had been that way for six months. There were reports that pieces of the ceiling were falling down on pews. In addition, several members of the brotherhood were accused of illegally selling burial plots. The city had closed the building and suspended all its functions until structural work could be done and the malfeasance resolved. But there is no telling when or if that will happen, given the lack of funds or political support. What will happen to this hardworking, much-petitioned saint? There is no guarantee that the most important site devoted to Anastácia will ever open again. She may be permanently unhinged from her place of origin, her historical ground. Whether this status as a saint in exile will lead to an expanded or a diminished presence or simply a different, more shape-shifting one cannot yet be predicted. Her status is as precarious as ever. Yet the very uncertainty of her agency—its shifting modes and moods—seems a part of her beguiling force. She will endure; that is what she does. She exists.

The next chapter considers the agent-ambiguous, religion-like biography of another incarnate drifted dangerously far from home, a checkers-playing automaton, a Turk in Rio fabricated as another fantastic, near-human thing.

4

Ajeeb
Automaton Nearhuman

[Rio] will always be our New York. . . . They'll never take away our vast bay, our natural and industrial wonders, our Ouvidor Street with its checker-playing automaton and its ladies.

> MACHADO DE ASSIS, *Gazeta de notícias*,
> "The Week" ("A semana"), June 7, 1896

A giant Turk, a chess-playing automaton, sits atop a compartment closed by a beckoning door. What lives inside? A folded person or a mechanism? A mind, pulleys, and cogs? Or possibly nothing at all? A feint, a whiff, a hoax, a vacuum? The box pulls us close. We are seduced into imagining someone or something inside, even against our will. No one is sure what the unseen agent is like.

Religion-like objects across multiple traditions announce hidden inner compartments as a recurring theme. The gap between a visible exterior and a secret interior agent was a quality shared by a psychiatric patient and a monkey in chapter 1, by a photograph, a possessed body, and an *nkisi* amulet in chapter 2, and by a drawing by a French world traveler that was enlivened by contact with a Brazilian princess and then became a saint in chapter 3. It was likewise vital to the charisma and special effect of automatons, including the protagonist of this chapter, Ajeeb.

This chapter considers the pull of nearhumanness in the form of human-like automatons. It moves from a discussion of exemplary religious and literary uses of androids to the narrower scope of the nineteenth century's romance with mechanical chessmen. After a short rehearsal of the story of the best known of that company, Von Kempelen's famous Turk, we will zoom in on a lesser-known machine-man called Ajeeb as he made his way from Europe to North America and then to Brazil. In spite of his short career in Rio de Janeiro (which lasted only from 1896 to 1897), he left his mark—a trail of wonder but also one of polemics on personhood and fraud. This automaton Turk arrived around 1890, the same time as the mass migration of actual Turks to Brazil from the Ottoman Empire began. The chess-playing Turk meant something very different in Rio than he did in Paris or New York. Even more, he took part in a moment that birthed a new family of spirits in Brazil, the *turcos*. Ajeeb shows how nearhuman attractions launch new religion-like situations, entities, and modes of evocation into motion. The closed compartment under the magic man was jammed with more than a hunched-up chess whiz. It was dense with other whorls, too, social forces animating the Turk's turbaned head in ways few could foresee.

"Soul of the Automaton"

A series of famous nineteenth-century literary figures advanced religion-like projects through wood or metal frames around enigmatic interiors. They were objects at once of horror and of fascination. To clarify this particular ethos, let us begin by looking at the most famous such story of all, Mary Shelley's *Frankenstein*, from a different point of view: the creation of the monster as a religion-like situation.

FRANKENSTEIN TO R.U.R. ROBOT

Frankenstein was woven most immediately from a parlor game but also from Shelley's earlier encounters with actual automatons.[1] The tale's hold over us derives less from the monstrous quality of the inventor's spawn than from its familiarity, its uncanny proximity to humans. The monster thrills to the sublime beauty of nature just as humans do. He is overcome by emotions—loneliness, remorse, longing, and rage cause him to weep. Like the humans he studies closely, he imagines a future with a partner. He learns to speak and is moved by reading *Paradise Lost*. The tragedy lay in that, while he is human in many respects, he can never be fully human. He speaks eloquently, but a strange, rattling hoarseness betrays his voice.[2] His limbs are "in proportion" and his features were selected to be "beautiful," his face even a figure of wonder, but his appearance still causes "breathless horror and disgust," like a "demoniacal corpse." Worst of all, he understands and feels the tragedy of his nearhumanness all too well: "My form is a filthy type of yours, more horrid even from the very resemblance." If, however, he is in some ways less than human, in others he is more. Eight feet tall, he has supplies of superhuman strength and endurance, "more than mortal speed," and unusual powers of persuasion, "as if possessed of magic powers."[3] He vacillates between declarations of sub- and superhumanness, between slave and master.[4]

The creature's presence evokes both fear and awe, horror and wonder, even all at once. Proximity to this nearhuman generates a response captured in Rudolf Otto's curious phrase *mysterium tremendum*, an unwieldy, discomfiting sensation of being in the presence of something eerie, incomprehensible, awful, yet also powerfully magnetic, "like stored up electricity."[5] Otto struggled to name it but noted its affinities not only with electricity but also with a word conveying the vast, huge, or monstrous, *ungeheuer*.[6] We encounter such tensions in descriptions of the creature's creation: "tremendous being . . . unearthly in his ugliness." The combination of magnetism and repulsion holds the protagonists, maker and made, caught in one another's orbits. The creature cannot do without his maker, Victor F., just as the maker is compelled to stay close to his device and double. The two exchange parts and qualities—like Victor F., the monster thrills to the sun and songbirds and imagines a future with a partner, a nearhuman like him. Meanwhile, Victor F. begins to mimic his machine, becoming mechanically driven and filled with the voices of others: "I pursued my path towards the destruction of the daemon . . . as the mechanical impulse of some power of which I was unconscious."[7] The "strange resemblance" between Drosselmeier and his automaton Nutcracker, in a story published two years before Shelley's, suggests the same idea of a magnetic attraction between a man and his offspring machine.[8] The two stories point to the ritual attraction to nearhumans and to their capacity to signal at once the subhuman diminution of the human, on the one hand, and the superhuman extension and expansion of human powers, on the other. Dr. Victor Frankenstein sought not only the power to create life, following in the wake of an Agrippa or a Paracelsus; he also felt driven toward its company.

The monster contracts with his maker: "If you consent [to make the requested female companion], neither you nor any other human being shall ever see us again: I will go to the vast wilds of South America."[9] He never made it to the southern continent, however, having been last seen traversing the ice floes of the North instead. A few pages ahead, we will go instead.

A century after Shelley, the Czech author Karel Čapek conjured a new vision of sacred nearhumans with his neologism *robot*, from the Old Slavic *rabu*, "slave." It appeared in the script for his play *R.U.R (Rossum's Universal Robots)*, first performed in 1921. These artificial persons too perambulate humanness, tracing edges to etch it into view. Their differences at times raise them above humans and at others set them below. Their memories are much better than people's, for example, but they never laugh or experience happiness. They are nearly invariant—though the company sent 500,000 *tropical* robots to South American to raise wheat on the pampas. They have a larger intellectual capacity than biological people do and succeed at mounting a rebellion that sets them up as masters instead of slaves, yet they enjoy no concept of history. They assemble together to form governing institutions. Still they seem like "unhumans," as one character calls them, because they cannot reproduce and have no fear of God.[10] And there is the familiar and persistent refrain that they have no souls.

Two humans—the head of research at the robot factory, Dr. Gall, and a visiting young woman, Helena Glory—are drawn to the elusive project of endowing the robots with souls. Early in the play, in response to a robot's seizure, Dr. Gall interjects: "That was no good. We must introduce suffering."

HELENA: Why—why—If you won't give them souls, why do you want to give them pain?
DR. GALL: For industrial reasons, Miss Glory. . . .
HELENA: Will they be happier when they can feel pain?
DR. GALL: On the contrary. But they will be technically more perfect.
HELENA: Why won't you make souls for them?
DR. GALL: That's not within our power.

Over time, however, Helena persuades Gall to alter the "physiological correlate" of a few robots. Under the robot leader Damon—demon—a revolution ensues. Robots become more human, learning defiance, hate, and strategy. Ultimately, they kill all humans but one, Alquist. Alquist has shown himself as the most human of all by virtue of his prayers, his love of tradition, and his ability to labor with his hands. As the very last human, he witnesses the rebirth of a new version of hybrid humanness:

ALQUIST: Robots are not life. Robots are machines.
SECOND ROBOT: We were machines, sir, but from horror and suffering we've become . . .
ALQUIST: What?
SECOND ROBOT: We've become beings with souls.
FOURTH ROBOT: Something is struggling within us. There are moments when something gets into us. Thoughts come to us that are not our own.

The robots' nearhumanness is most fully realized when two of Gall's modified robots express emotions and sense the sublime natural world. What surprises in the dialogue is that, on their becoming human, soul is experienced as inspiration, even possession or becoming another. To be human is to be capable of becoming another: "Thoughts come to us that our not our own." Robot Helena says to Robot Primus: "Hear that? Birds are singing. Oh, Primus, I would like to be a bird!" Helena and Primus fall in love, and their exaltation appears to Alquist as an epiphany: "O blessed day! ... O hallowed sixth day! 'So God created man in his own image. ...' The sixth day! The day of grace. [*He falls on his knees.*]"[11]

The themes shared between *Frankenstein* and *R.U.R.* bookend a long nineteenth century: the question of soul, the conflict between fabricated and fabricator (in both cases articulated in terms of master and slave), the risks of humans' inventive hubris, the inevitability of scientists' attempts to make nearhumans. Most striking for my purposes is the composite attraction-repulsion evoked by proximity to the machines, a set of sensations layered with religion-like situations, questions, and pursuits, like the inquiry after the soul or, expressed otherwise, the uncertain anxiety over which agencies possess or occupy uncannily nearhuman beings. Both stories narrate plans for such machine lives in South America. Soon we will see what became of a mechanical nearhuman that actually arrived there.

MARVELOUS TURKS

Actual automatons of the period, like literary ones, catalyzed religion-like situations around them. It is not only that, in interaction with an audience and a place and time, automatons themselves produced a religion-like reaction. It is also that they sparked innovations in religions more narrowly construed. Take, for example, Robert-Houdin's draftsman, put on display at the Exposition of 1844 in Paris's Palais de l'Industrie. His most prestigious visitor was the comte de Paris, king of France. When he was set to drawing a crown in honor of the king, his pencil broke, and the drawing was left unfinished. Some saw this as an augur or prophecy: "The pencil broke in its hand, and left the crown a mere unfinished anticipation, almost a prophecy."[12] Charles Dickens wrote: "And there was Robert-Houdin's own automaton, that drew so ominously—for the pencil broke in the act of tracing the figure of a crown for his dispossessed heirship, the Count of Paris."[13] Another observer added: "A Roman augur would have derived an omen from this simple incident."[14] Note the terms: *prophecy, augury, omen.*

How about the most famous machine of all, Wolfang Von Kempelen's? The introduction called attention to the exclamations and ritual gestures that occasionally erupted on first encountering Von Kempelen's chess-playing Turk in Europe: recall the woman who made the sign of the cross over her heart and exhaled a prayer, believing the figure to be possessed.[15] Johann Maelzel purchased Von Kempelen's automaton and adorned it with new flourishes like a vocal announcement of victory in French,

"Échec!" Maelzel's revamped Turk found success in Paris (1817), London (1818), Amsterdam (1821), and other European metropoles before arriving in New York. He disembarked on February 3, 1826, and opened soon after at the National Hotel at 112 Broadway, where Maelzel also slept. Maelzel seems to have felt complete only when near his machine. "For such was his habit or his system—he liked always to live in the closest connexion with all his agents, animate and inanimate," wrote George Allen in 1859.[16]

Installed in New York, the Turk elicited no less of an uncanny aura. "The chess automata enchanted the credulous and the skeptical alike. . . . [S]ome spectators fled the room, or even fainted when an automaton began to stir."[17] The automaton acquired fame as a formidable champion. So did the few candidates who managed to beat him—young Benjamin D. Green in Boston and eighteen-year-old Samuel Smyth in New York (after which, or so it was said, an observing gentleman was "so far beside himself" that he ran out and up the street without his hat to report the news).[18] The figure's longest-employed internal operator was the Alsatian champion Wilhelm Schlumberger. He too gained substantial repute as what Maelzel once called the "soul of the automaton."[19] Again, notice the terms: *animate* and *inanimate agents, enchantment, possession, soul of the automaton*. Religion-like situations.

Given the Turk's success, several copycat androids were fabricated in the United States—one by an inventor named Walker, another by Balcom. Unfortunately, the secret of the automaton's soul first came to light in 1827 when several boys witnessed an operator exit its internal compartment. Fleeing the setback, Maelzel resolved to take the figure to Havana and then on to the South American capitals.[20] On November 9, 1837, he and Schlumberger sailed for Havana aboard the *Lancet* with the goal of getting the automaton up and running for business by around Christmas. They had to rush: Carnaval season, between Christmas and Lent, was the festive time. After Ash Wednesday, at the end of February, no one was likely to play the Turk. They arrived on schedule, but within a period of months Schlumberger contracted and then succumbed to yellow fever. And Maelzel himself became a victim of the same malady on July 21, 1838, off the coast of Charleston during his return journey to the United States.[21]

The Turk lived to see another day, cared for by a new owner, and installed in the Chinese Museum in Philadelphia. His semiretirement lasted an additional fourteen years before he was consumed in an 1854 fire, "a sublime departure."[22] His last owner wrote a solemn elegy: "Already the fire was about him. Death found him tranquil. He who had seen Moscow perish knew no fear of fire. We listened with painful anxiety. . . . [W]e thought we heard, through the struggling flames, and above the din of outside thousands, the last words of our departed friend, the sternly whispered, oft repeated syllables, 'Échec! Échec!' "[23]

James Cook summarized many of the narratives that gathered and came into focus around the Turk and helped power his spectacular as- cent, including "the increasingly fuzzy moral threshold separating artful imitation and criminal deception; a wide variety of geo-cultural rivalries symbolized and contested through a caricatured non-Western other; the socioeconomic and gendered implications of playing, beating, and con- trolling Maelzel's diligent laborer; and the increasingly provisional and unstable status of printed information in the emerging urban-industrial society."[24] We can add even more. The language applied to descriptions of the Turk and the responses he inspired—phrases like *beside himself, soul of the automaton, agents animate and inanimate, augur* and *prophecy*, and *the sublime*—hint at religion-like situations, an agent-ambiguous aura that gathered between the machine and its users. Edgar Allan Poe's 1836 essay debunked the figure's illusion of agency but also tried to name the precise source of his wonderful strangeness. He called it a "[potentially] 'pure machine' unconnected with human agency" but one whose movements were not quite lifelike.[25] But Poe doth protest too much. The tension he names—the space opened between *potentially* and *not quite*—is impor- tant. The being was not obviously a pure machine; it was only potentially one. It lacked human agency, even though it was almost (not quite) life- like. The very betwixt-and-betweenness of the Turk was what motivated Poe's essay at all. The need to debunk served only to emphasize the power of the automaton's draw.

Following Poe's terms—*potentially* and *not quite*—I set the attraction to the chess-playing Turk in relation to nearhuman agency. The Turk dwelt in the "uncanny valley," to take Masahiro Mori's 1970 phrase, by virtue of a dissonant combination of humanlike appearance and inhuman mo- tion.[26] He was close enough to humanness, but not too close, that mostly he charmed and enthralled without shocking. As Mori argued, figures too distant from the human—say, speaking but bearing tentacles instead of limbs or forty eyes instead of two—evoke repulsion, a desire to flee. Just so with figures *too* close to humanness. Think of Philip Dick's *Do An- droids Dream of Electric Sheep?* (1968), in which the bounty hunter Rick Deckard is attracted to Rachael Rosen, whom he initially cannot quite mark as nonhuman, and then repulsed by her when he learns the truth. (Parenthetically, religion is the main cipher of their difference. Rachael is unable to practice Mercerism, which requires mystical empathy, a gift that androids lack.) The Turk was, by contrast, like humans yet also, in transparent ways, nonhuman and, therefore, according to Mori's curve, well positioned in the uncanny valley and attractive to the observer's eye. Through his machine-man and its cast of operators, Von Kempelen gained fame as a "modern Prometheus," much like Victor Frankenstein.[27] The mechanical Turk sat on a throne spanning machines, humans, and gods. Some saw him as diabolical. Under his massive, silent, turbaned gaze, balanced astride a secret compartment of whirring gears, some must have perceived a vaguely godlike being.

From the ashes of the first Turk's incineration, new machine-men bearing names born from Orientalist vapors arose: Mephisto, Hajeb, As-Rah.[28] Then came Ajeeb.

Ajeeb From London to Rio

Built by an Englishman, Charles Alfred Hooper, in 1868, the machine-man Ajeeb was called by the Arabic and Urdu word for *strange, unusual,* or *wonderful.* The name was likely drawn from *The Thousand and One Nights'* "Story of Noor Ed-Deen and His Son," in which the character Ajeeb was esteemed for his elegance of form. We could add that Ajeeb was born at roughly the same moment as mysticism and the study of Eastern religions in Europe and of an Orientalism that positioned the "mystic East" as wondrously irrational, in contrast to which the industrial West imagined itself and its bodies as self-possessed and impermeable.[29]

Hooper operated his automaton in London for five years and then brought him to New York, where he began to operate at Manhattan's Eden Musée on August 1, 1885. Ajeeb consisted of a papier-mâché body set cross-legged, with a head of wax topped by a white turban and a torso accented with a red velvet cape. Like Frankenstein's machine, he was larger than life, seven feet tall, and seated on a three-foot-high platform. The museum catalog offered a description:

> Visitors while on the gallery should not fail to see AJEEB, the mysterious chess and checker playing automaton. It represents a Moorish figure seated on a cushion, beneath which is a perfectly open table; in front is a small cabinet and doors, which are all open, as well as the back and chest of the figure. Any stranger is at liberty to play a game with the automaton; the movements of the figure are free and easy, and it shifts the pieces with as much accuracy as its living opponents and with much greater success, generally coming off the conqueror. In giving check to the king the automaton makes a sign by raising his head twice, and for checkmate three times.[30]

Ajeeb held a hookah in his immobile left hand and wore a stuffed cockatoo on his right shoulder (figure 4.1).[31] He was a great success, lasting

FIGURE 4.1. Cabinet-card image of the chess automaton "Ajeeb the Wonderful." Cropped version. 1886. TCS 1.183, Harvard Theatre Collection, Harvard University.

a decade at the Eden. Wherein resided his appeal? His trade card did not even bother advertising his skill at chess. Rather, it was his "séances extraordinary and mysterious" and his strange, almost human qualities that were announced: "Its movements are so life-like, that it is difficult to believe that it is not endowed with life."[32] Of course, he also played chess. In fact, he played all the time, against opponents from Sarah Bernhardt to O. Henry, and easily earned his keep. Entrance to the museum was $0.50. It cost $0.10 more to enter Ajeeb's chamber and another $0.10 to play. Altogether, he produced between $50.00 and $70.00 per week, his olive skin variously occupied by chess masters from Albert Beauregard Hodges to Harry Nelson Pillsbury. Charles Moelhe, another virtuoso of the game, operated a different Ajeeb in Chicago. By 1895, the version at the Eden had been replaced by a new player and a new automaton figuration of the mystic East named Chang, a "Chinese Mandarin . . . with a spiky mustache [and] a blue and green embroidered satin robe."[33]

Even so, Moorish Ajeeb returned to work and remained in operation at the Eden on and off until 1915. Even during the decades thereafter, he still sporadically returned to service and gave off a supernatural frisson. Frank Frain became coowner of Ajeeb in 1932 and kept him boxed up in his Cadillac. He exclaimed: "Why, one time, the pieces in those boxes in the Cadillac got to jumping up and down, so help me God! And three times, when I went to fix Ajeeb's head on him, I fell down like somebody shoved me!" A staunch Irish Catholic, Frain took Ajeeb to be blessed at the shrine of Saint Anne-de Beaupré, near Quebec City—a shrine much visited by Native American and Roma communities. And, as late as 1943, he kept Ajeeb's head in his Queens apartment, at times massaging his cheeks, combing his beard, and moistening his eyelids with Vaseline: "When I set him up in the right light, with mirrors and drapes, there's a lot of controversy as to whether he is alive, so help me God."[34] Religion-like situations: séance, mystery, blessed, shrine, endowed with life.

Though the original Ajeeb never left New York, peripatetic copycat versions were long in motion. In 1896, an Ajeeb was purchased by a Czech-born Jewish emigrant to the United States and shipped to Brazil.

AJEEB IN BRAZIL

This part of the tale begins with an adventurous entrepreneur. Fred Figner was born in 1866 in Milevsko, Bohemia. After emigrating to the United States as a teenager in 1882, he settled in San Antonio and supported himself as a traveling salesman.[35] He first encountered an Edison phonograph in San Antonio and purchased his own in San Francisco in 1891 as part of a business venture launched with his brother-in-law. The two envisioned turning a profit by acquiring technological inventions of the North and bringing them to Latin America, where their novelty would likely still hold. The wager paid off. Figner moved to Brazil permanently, never re-turning to the United States other than for short business trips.[36] Figner imagined himself bringing techno wonders to the benighted tropics. In fact, what happened was something different. In Brazil, those wonders took on whole new meanings, uses, and scenarios. They were converted into something new, and Figner was too. He became the founder of the record industry in Brazil, a pillar of Rio society, and a spiritist patron and adept, as we will see in the next chapter.

In 1891, Figner brought the phonograph with him to the growing tropi-cal town of Belém (Bethlehem), located on the north coast of Brazil on the edge of the Amazon region. There, he launched his new career with street demonstrations of Edison's miraculous new machine, powering it with a foot pedal to play waltzes, ragtime, and opera. Most impressive of all, he could make cylinder recordings of people's voices.[37] He gained fame as the man with the "talking machine" (*máquina falante*), a strange device able to speak and even outflank time by capturing human voices of the recent past and launching them into the sonic present. At least four thousand residents of Belém paid to see it, attending five-hour shows that lasted all afternoon. A smash success, the performances were repeated in town after town as Figner wended his way down the coast to the capital.[38] So closely was it tied to Fred Figner that the talking machine started to be called the "Figner machine" (*máquina figner*).

Figner disembarked from a steamship in the harbor of Rio de Janeiro in April 1892, and, by early June, he and his marvelous machine were installed at the Hotel Freitas.[39] His demonstrations included discourses he had recorded in the north on famous deceased figures like Dom Pedro II, who had just breathed his last in Paris. The sonic victory over both space and time, together with the quality of sound, attracted widespread attention, and it was only the start.[40] Figner made the capital city his home, establishing his business and, beginning in 1897, a large family. He traveled frequently to the United States and Europe. Once, in 1892, it was to escape yellow fever, but mostly it was to acquire the latest sight-and-sound gizmo. For a decade, he made his living bringing technological sensations found abroad back to Brazil. First to arrive was the phonograph, then the first cinematographic device—the Edison Kinetoscope—in 1894, likely acquired at the 1893 Chicago World's Fair. These were topped by the Kinetophone in October 1895, described as "the marvelous appliance [*aparelho*] that allows us to see and hear at the same time."[41] The first film projection show followed on July 8, 1898, another "Figner machine"; the new attraction always came with his name attached. Alongside his growing investments in sound and film, Figner offered visual spectacles to lure the curious.

A voyage of early August 1895 took Figner to New York, and there he likely purchased an edition of the automaton Ajeeb.[42] By early December of that year, he was in Montevideo, Uruguay, showing off the new checkers-playing wonder.[43] A few weeks later, he was in Buenos Aires, displaying the Kinetoscope together with Ajeeb in a small theater on Florida Street. In May 1896, he was back home in Rio. With fitting fanfare, the arrival of a bona fide automaton, a mechanical checkers-playing genius, was announced.[44] Figner determined a location in the busiest nightlife and entertainment district, the rollicking Ouvidor Street—the first street to have been lit by gas, in 1860, and the first to boast electric lights, in 1891 (figure 4.2). It was by far the liveliest avenue in town. Lima

FIGURE 4.2. Rua do Ouvidor, Rio de Janeiro, ca. 1890, where Ajeeb was first displayed. Photograph by Marc Ferrez, Instituto Moreira Salles, RJ.

Barreto, the famed journalist, tippler, and asylum patient from chapter 1, needed few words to convey the vibe: "I'm much appreciated on Ouvidor Street, but then, who isn't, really?"[45] Figner invited reporters from every newspaper.[46] Ajeeb made a dramatic first impression:

> Yesterday we had the opportunity to witness the ingenious automaton who plays drafts with precise expertise, defeating all adversaries presented to him. It's a mechanical device representing a richly dressed Turk with a large silk turban, seated cross-legged in Oriental-style, with

a game board on his lap. The figure's expression is magnificent, and his physiognomic attitude is that of someone meditating. . . . His game is perfect, as is the playing apparatus. What is the secret, what is the soul of the automaton? It resides in an expert homunculus insinuated in the large cavities of the automaton. But this doesn't diminish the machine's curiosity, which most definitely merits a visit.[47]

Ajeeb's visual impact was joined to sound, drawing on Figner's past successes. One reporter described first encountering Ajeeb through a synesthetic penumbra of aural-visual magic, watching him while simultaneously listening to an aria from Bellini's opera *La sonnambula* played on the latest and best phonograph.[48] Clearly, Figner was no fool. Linking the images of somnambulists and the checker-playing Turk, both cloaked with the mystique of automatism, was a brilliant move. What a debut! Ajeeb presented more than simple entertainment thrills, profit, and a place for ambitious checkers players to measure themselves against the perfect opponent. There was something more. As had occurred with previous versions of the Turk, commentators lingered over the question of Ajeeb's soul, the soul of the automaton, even as Ajeeb himself, stoic in his robes, kept his secrets. Not incidentally, Ajeeb's arrival in Rio coincided with that of a large group of actual human Turks from the Ottoman Empire, especially Syrians and Lebanese. Brazilians referred to all these arrivals as *turcos*. But few *turcos* made the impression that Ajeeb did.

In one sense, Ajeeb's superhuman aura dimmed too soon in Rio. The great Ajeeb lost at least three times. One time he lost to one Augusto Guimarães. Another time he lost—and very publicly—to a customs agent named Claudino Alves de Castilho.[49] Castilho played against Ajeeb for six nights in a row, mostly tying his nemesis in hung games. On the seventh night, however, something changed. He returned for yet another round and played with focused concentration from 8:30 P.M. until 9:00. Things were advancing in his favor when the game was abruptly halted, under dubious circumstances. The event earned an exposé and a rebuke in the popular daily *O país* (The nation):

> Yesterday, however, [Ajeeb] was completely demoralized . . . to the point that the police were called and directed to attend to his empresario. . . . The game was interesting from the start. After a quarter hour, unbeatable Ajeeb found himself seriously weakened; and, after twenty minutes had passed, o glories of Ajeeb!, all the spectators trembled with emotion. Only two plays remained available to the doll, and either one would bring a terribly embarrassing defeat. Castilho's victory was secure, that was clear. Ajeeb wasn't sweating only because he's made of plaster. But

the discomfited empresario looked like a firework display: from green he turned yellow, then red, blue, to the devil. The automaton hesitated with his hand suspended, as though it were made of meat and the pieces on the board were hot coals.[50]

Abruptly, the master of ceremonies drew the crowd's attention to a clock announcing the hour, 9:00 P.M., purportedly the end of the exhibition. He swept his hand across the board, wiping it clear.

With that single stroke, it suddenly became clear that Ajeeb would never in good faith submit to defeat, that, rather than let him lose face publically, the operators would end the game through deception. The crowd erupted in disbelieving fury. A reporter from *O país* called the police to report Ajeeb for exploitation of public faith, ironic given that the exposition was premised on playing with the very idea of trust. A day later, the playwright Artur Azevedo added to the uproar with a poetic jab:

Ao Ajeeb	*To Ajeeb*
Ó turco, se assim te escamas,	*Say Turk, if you're going to escape like that,*
É bom que arranjes as malas. . . .	*It's time to pack your bags. . . .*
Pois sabes jogar as damas	*How is it you know how to play the game,*
E não sabes respeita-las?	*But not how to respect it?*

His outrage seems peculiar. After all, everyone knew there was a person hidden in the Turk, guiding the play. Human losers quit games to save face all the time, even in front of witnesses in public spaces. No one thinks anything of it. Certainly it would not normally be considered newsworthy. What kind of compact had been violated, then, causing Ajeeb to bow out so abruptly? The anger that followed the abandoned match suggests that the Turk was much more than the man playing inside. The automaton's presence was extrahuman, even if the player was not. He had a larger-than-life aura, a special effect of his size, his dress, his hookah, the strange way he moved, the hidden and unsure nature of his agency. He was not a god, but he was not quite a mere human or machine either. He was something in between, nearhuman. For such a being, the expectations of just play and moral conduct were set higher and the intrigue of seeing him lose tantalizing. A nearhuman agent falls to an everyday customs agent? It was epic, like the spectacle of a king getting his cape stuck in a door. No wonder the crowd rebelled.

The furor pushed Ajeeb to depart Rio for more sympathetic climes. Within weeks he left town, this time under the direction of Figner's brother, Gustavo. But, if Gustavo and Ajeeb anticipated an easier time of it elsewhere, the trip brought little relief. In São Paulo, Ajeeb lost again, to Dr. José de Toledo Piza. On this occasion, Gustavo Figner was at least prepared for a gracious exit. Piza was directly placated by a photograph of Ajeeb with the inscription: "To my conqueror" ("Ao meu vencedor"). (Piza's daughter, incidentally, guarded the photograph like a precious relic, even after her father's death.)[51] And then January 1897 found Ajeeb in Argentina. His ignominious exit from Rio still had not been forgotten, however. The newspapers tolled the "sad memories that Ajeeb left us."[52]

In February 1897, Ajeeb continued on the road, touring a series of cities in the Brazilian state of Minas Gerais. Much as he had in his early, honeymoon weeks in Rio, the machine-man evoked awe. Under the storyline "Ajeeb, the Turk," readers in Minas Gerais learned: "It's an extremely strange machine that must be seen, as it is difficult to convey a sense of the precision with which the pieces are moved by an unconscious player. The competition among the curious [to see Ajeeb] was extraordinary yesterday, and all left without being able to explain the marvelous companion of Mr. Fred Figner, his worthy owner."[53]

Absence made hardened hearts grow fonder. By March 1897, the automaton was back in Rio, resurrected, "the new Ajeeb." To help win this round, he was joined by two novel attractions. One was "Inana," named after an ancient Mesopotamian goddess akin to Venus. Billed as a *sylphorama*, Inana was a trick of mirrors that created the illusion of a goddess floating in the air without benefit of strings. She was described as a great beauty whose "celestial" form was part of the draw. The other attraction was Vulcan, a "human volcano" able to breathe fire. The mysterious and indomitable Ajeeb, the celestial Inana, the mighty son of Vulcan. Juggernaut trinity, "the three phenoms."[54] Marvelous, perfect, precise, unbeatable, celestial. It was in that moment that Machado de Assis penned the epigraph I have given this chapter: "[Rio] will always be our New York. . . . They'll never take away our vast bay, our natural and industrial wonders, our Ouvidor Street with its checker-playing automaton and its ladies."[55] Machado's phrase, it should be noted, pulled Ajeeb and women into parallel. Perhaps it had the unintended effect of at once humanizing an automaton and nearhumanizing the "ladies." Both had the look of thing-like wonders and superhuman attractors.

Should we be surprised that Ajeeb so quickly regained face—and profits? Even prior to losing a few matches, he had long been exposed in the most obvious sense. Most members of the audience knew very well that the automaton carried a human operator within. Over a century had passed since the tours of Von Kempelen's Turk. By this time, the only real mysteries were how the human hand could be so well concealed and how the theatrical contract binding audience to illusion was sealed and maintained, however tenuously. Why would people flock to see an illusion whose premises they knew to be a fraud and whose real workings they all understood? There are clues. In the first week of play, in May 1896, the *Jornal do comércio* waxed rapturous over Ajeeb's likeness to a human—his ability to indicate impatience with a shake of his head, for example—even as it was forthright in revealing his "secret" and "soul" as a "homunculus . . . insinuated in the cavities of the automaton."[56] A few days later, the paper doubled down on the debunking. The soul of the automaton was, it wrote, a dwarf in the Turk.[57] Still, the revelations seemed to accentuate the figure's strange presence more than undo it. Only ponder the ideas and images: the soul of the machine is a homunculus insinuated in an automaton's cavity or a dwarf inserted in a giant Turk. The descriptions fascinate and mystify more than disenchant.[58] They make him sound like a god, one that is also nearly but still not ever human, but one that can be subhumanly impatient and petty and superhumanly creative and destructive all at the same time. Not an inexplicable or transcendent god, in other words, but more like a Greek or a Yoruba god or a popular Catholic saint—not quite human, strange, wondrous, bizarre, uncanny.

DOUBLED BODIES

Ajeeb the nearhuman installation offered attractions not offered by the human, the divine, or the obviously machine. His in-betweenness mattered. Poe's essay highlighted just this point, pointing to the Maelzel automaton's merely almost humanness as a reason for its plausibility as a thinking machine: "Were the Automaton life-like in its motions, the spectator would be more apt to attribute its operations to their true cause (that is, to human agency within)."[59] Recall again Mori's uncanny valley. Poe emphasized the machine's *distance* from the human as much as its proximity as key to the attraction. Perhaps we should ask, What is the work of this gap, the attraction to the distance? Why seek the presence of even an obviously fraudulent nearhuman? The reiterated phrase *soul of Ajeeb* offers another clue. Ajeeb gave material and theatrical form to the problematic quality of agency. More concretely, he embodied and helped articulate and make conscious the question of what or who is acting in us. As Philip Thicknesse had described Von Kempelen's machine a century before, the automaton is "a man within a man . . . he bears a living soul within."[60] The prospect of fraud does not undermine the force of the question of hidden agency. To the contrary, it fragments agency into layers of external, internal, and the layers in between. It gives expression and form to a truth of personhood, the unnamed gap between performance and internal state. Erving Goffman tried to describe the division of every individual, split between roles of performer and character. The *performer* presents an external impression that is supposed to represent, with more or less reliability, a *character*, an internal set of enduring qualities.[61] But Goffman's insight begs further questions. Where is the operator behind or within an external body? And who controls *that* operator? The figuration of a homunculus working inside a towering Turk unfolded further renderings of the matter of soul, of inside and outside, inner life and external action, character and performance.

As we saw at the outset of this chapter, the problem of the authentic and the penetrable interior is a recurrent object of religion-like thought and key to the spectacle of Ajeeb. In that sense, Ajeeb resembles many religion-like nearhuman agents. The golem's animation depended, at least in some literary renderings, on the drafting of a secret name that was inserted into the cavity of a clay head.[62] An Afro-Brazilian Candomblé initiate advances into deeper secret knowledge through rituals of "making the head" that include incisions in the body and herbal insertions. An *inquice* (*nkisi*) sculpture of Angolan Candomblé in Brazil is animated by the substances that reside within. In a famous, early 1870s trial of an Afro-Brazilian sorcerer (*feitiçeiro*) in Rio, a photograph of the priest was revealed to have not only an external representative force but also an internal, hidden capacity to act as an extension of the priest's body, as we saw in chapter 2.[63] What is more, a participant in an Umbanda ceremony in Brazil today may be possessed by a Turk, inverting the order of a man within a Turk, and rendering instead a Turk within a man or a woman. A body within a body, the doubled form, is a thoroughly religion-like trope, an unseen agent in an impressive external form.

Religion-like situations and scenes show their doubleness. Religious-like people are adept users of such things and scenes and adepts at the craft of recasting themselves as hybrid agents. For example, Fred Figner's friend Chico Xavier, shortly to become Brazil's most famous spiritist and automatic writer, presented himself as an appliance (*aparelho*). By writing automatically, as an appliance, someone like Chico approached the uncanny nearhuman from the flip side of Ajeeb, becoming a man possessed by a machine. He was as beguiling as a homunculus in a Turk.[64]

Ajeeb flourished in Brazil only for a little more than a year, from about May 1896 until July 1897. Thereafter, Figner kept celestial Inana in play but mostly moved decisively toward sound recording and sales in recording and other technologies. By 1901, his advertisements announced a modern, twentieth-century paradise of phonographs, graphophones, gramophones, Franklin typewriters, magnetic soles to cure rheumatism, electric alarm clocks, electric table fans, sewing machines, incandescent lights, and other things on a long list of "American novelties." By 1902, he had recorded and secured the rights to several thousand Brazilian songs. He expanded from selling the phonograph to making records and film and acquired enormous fame and wealth as the pioneer of music recording in Brazil. He established the Casa Edison, the first recording studio in Brazil, and Odeon, the first record manufacturer, both in Rio de Janeiro. He was a titan of the early recording industry, not just in Brazil, but globally. Moving into the twentieth century, then, Fred Figner had little further need for his automaton or, for that matter, his sylphorama or human volcano. I have not been able to discover what happened to Ajeeb—if, like his namesake in the North, he continued to thump and push, to be waxed until he glowed, and to be chauffeured in a Cadillac to be blessed at the gypsy cathedral of Quebec. I doubt it.

In hindsight, we might consider Ajeeb a transition object, in relation to which Rio de Janeiro—or at least certain bourgeois sectors of it—moved from a tropical Belle Époque to a twentieth-century industrial mode of life. As in Europe, where, citing Paul Lindau, Walter Benjamin registered an automaton fatigue that marked the moment when "the motif of the doll acquires a sociocritical significance. For example: 'You have no idea how repulsive these automatons and dolls can become, and one breathes at last on encountering a full-blooded being in this society.'"[65] But I have not found much evidence for nearhuman fatigue in Brazil. Ajeeb lived on as a legend, incarnate in new guises. Already in July 1897, there appeared a new book for sale, *Alma de Ajeeb* (Soul of Ajeeb), by Moysés Benhazen, on expert strategies for checkers by another invincible player.[66] Even more, the automaton became mythic. He may even have acted as tributary to the river of spirits—not deus ex machina but something else, a weirder apotheosis, like a human in a mechanical body occupying the cavity of a god. Hominum in machina in deus? Or, even better, hominum in machina in deus in patrinum?

Spirit Bodies and National Bodies

Ajeeb the automaton Turk directly accompanied the first wave of actual immigrants to Brazil called *Turks*. Their temporal convergence pushes us to plot Ajeeb in a social history register, as a cipher not only of new urban leisure for the middle class but also of the domestication of the exotic Orient, which was just beginning to make its presence felt in Rio and elsewhere in Brazil.

Between 1879 and 1947, 80,000 mostly Catholic and Greek Orthodox Syrian-Lebanese immigrants settled in Brazil.[67] Disparate ethnic groups, whether Lebanese, Syrians, Moroccans, or actual Turks, were, in the host society, all conjoined under the ethnonym *turco*, which denoted, roughly, anyone carrying an Ottoman passport. That migration accelerated precisely when Ajeeb took up residence in Rio. Whereas the decade from 1884 to 1893 saw only 96 Turks (in fact, mostly Syrians) arrive in Brazil, that from 1894 to 1903 found 7,397 Middle Easterners taking up residence, a number that expanded more than sixfold in the decade following.[68] The roving journalist João do Rio, whose words closed chapter 1, unsheathed his acid pen in 1904 to parody elites' hand-wringing over the number of Syrians—especially Christian Maronites—in Brazil: "When the first ones arrived here some twenty years ago, people believed them canni-bals. People antagonized them, and in the countryside many fled under stoning. Even today, almost nobody detaches them from this general and depressing adjective: Turks. They—those who show up—are all Turks!"[69]

Many of these Turks supported their families as peddlers and were, along with Maghreb Jews, associated with itinerant petty commerce.[70] In the wake of abolition in 1888, small towns in the interior were left with no mechanism or manpower for the distribution of goods. The new class of peddlers filled the gap. They were called *mascates*, a word that became synonymous with *peddler* in Brazilian Portuguese but had initially de-rived from a town on the Arabian Peninsula, Muscat. If many remained *mascates*, however, some also founded businesses. The number of Syrian and Lebanese companies in São Paulo rose from six in 1895 to five hun-dred in 1901, and the first Arabic newspapers in Brazil were printed in 1895, in São Paulo State.[71]

Though outsiders, these Turks were familiar strangers; they were, so to speak, safe exotics. For one, they were mostly Christians. In addition, the so-called Moor was part of Portugal's history. Prominent writers seek-ing to define Brazil's national character sometimes traced key qualities back to Moorish Portugal.[72] Journalistic reports appealed to Brazilians' similarities with Turks, as in their protectiveness toward women with "Turkish vigilance and jealousy," unlike North Americans.[73] At the same time, however, the Turk posed a threat. Though the Ottoman Empire projected power and wealth, social Darwinist theories of race and fears of national decline or exhaustion, *surmenage*, were in vogue and highly in-fluential. Some commentators stoked dread of a potential mongrelization among elites already lamenting their nation's perceived lack of purity.[74] By 1891, Rio's newspapers mention the "abuse of peddling" by *turcos* on the streets and plazas of Rio on Sundays and a "swarm" (*enxame*) over-running the capital with ill effects on established businesses.[75] One edito-rial from 1888 went even further: "Lock the doors so that they do not infiltrate our organism, [bringing] instead of strong blood, the evil virus of an indolent people."[76] The *turco*, in sum, at once conveyed Oriental mysticism, decadent wealth and luxury, sensuality, and a dangerous inva-sion of the social form. In these polemical editorials, Brazil was variously imagined as a body and as a house. Both had insecure, permeable exteriors vulnerable to invasion and interior occupation. The national body or house, one might say, mirrored Ajeeb's shape, composed as it was of an exterior frame directed by a hidden inner force. It begged the question of the agent or manager within.

In 1899, the North American journalist and short story writer Ambrose Bierce—in some respects a Northern mirror of Machado—published a tale called "Moxon's Master." It presented an automaton chess player in familiar Orientalist props: "not more than five feet in height, with proportions suggesting those of a gorilla—tremendous breadth of shoulders, thick, short neck and broad, squat head, which had a tangled growth of black hair and was topped by a crimson fez."[77] Machine, animal, red-fezzed lack of control, unknown opaque interior, danger. On losing to his maker, the automaton erupts in rage, reaches across the board, and locks his throat in a fatal grip. Some in Brazil viewed the arrival of migrants from the Ottoman Empire in roughly Bierce's terms. National anxieties led to an attempt to fashion a closed body against a dangerous homunculus that might be growing inside—restrictive immigration laws against arrivals from Africa and the Middle East, incentives to Europeans.

But this was not the only recourse. Resistance to actual immigrants was accompanied by fascination with mechanical and spirit Turks. We have, after all, seen the popular magnetism of Ajeeb. A very different route was to adopt the Turk as a source of spirit power. This should sound familiar: In the United States, the end of any actual Native American sovereignty by 1890 directly corresponded with the sudden popular attraction of Native American culture, most emblematically in Buffalo Bill's Wild West shows, where the former shaman Black Elk found a new hokum career. Something similar was taking place in Brazil as Turks were being assimilated and imagined as, among other things, spirits.

By the time of the emperor's exile and the birth of the republic in 1890, Brazil had a number of established spirit-possession traditions, ranging from African Candomblé to the French spiritism articulated by Alan Kardec. All entailed the manifestation of spirit bodies in human bodies as scenes of enchantment, healing, inspiration, luck, and revelation. At the end of the nineteenth century, the Turks joined the repertory of available spirits. To be sure, in Maranhão, in the Afro-Brazilian religious traditions of Tambor de Mina and Pajé, there had long existed a class of spirits known as Turks, commanded by a spirit leader called the King of Turkey. The Turks are known as *encantados* (lit., "the enchanted"), a word whose practical sense was translated by Seth and Ruth Leacock as *guardian spirit*.[78] They were born at least in part from popular Portuguese narratives of battles between Moors and Christians brought to Brazil during colonization, like the *Song of Roland* or "The Stories of Charlemagne and the Twelve Peers of France."[79]

Around 1890, a specific temple devoted to Turkish spirits was founded by Anastácia Lúcia dos Santos, an Afro-Brazilian woman. These spirits were a class of *caboclos*, usually understood as rustics of mixed indigenous and European descent. They are widely present as a common type of possessing spirit in Afro-Brazilian traditions, not only in Tambor de Mina, but also in Pajé, Batuque, and Umbanda, where they possess the bodies of mostly Afro-Brazilian or mixed-race participants. In ritual contexts, the Turks are valued as "noble pagans."[80] Indigenized and subject to the more central African gods, they gesture toward the history of Islam among former slave groups and the history of Jesuit missions, but, in rituals, venues, and mythic narratives, they never overpower. Mostly they wait like sentinels, solemn and stoic. But the most beloved Turkish spirit of all, Mariana Turca, is identified with a species of parrot (*arará*), with which she is commonly pictured, not unlike Ajeeb with a parrot on his shoulder. The *turcos'* spirits were an appealing spirit type, conveying exotic yet safely domesticated force.

In Belém, where Figner had first hawked his Edison phonograph, practitioners of the Afro-Brazilian religion Batuque also engaged with *turcos* as a spirit family. In fact, the Turks made up the largest family of spirits. These *turcos* hearken back not only to the Moors of Portuguese history and folklore but also to representations of Brazilian Amerindians and mixed-race *caboclos*. They emerged as a refraction of popular seasonal performances of the romance of battles between Christians and Moors. They are formidable warriors, but, given the historic oppression of Africans, Afro-Brazilians, and indigenous groups of the Amazon region, their popular narratives also incorporated an idealization of the typically losing Moorish or Turk side.[81] That is, Afro-Brazilians may have valued the legend and the image of the Turk as an underdog, for the same reasons that elites feared or resented them, and not only in Brazil. Afro-Uruguayans celebrating Carnaval in 1832 apparently sometimes dressed as Turks.[82]

Through acoustic, visual, and mechanical masks, the figuration of a sacred Turk emerged not only in the far north—Belém and Maranhão—but also in centers of immigration like Rio. Spiritism and then Umbanda in and around Rio incorporated the Turk into ritual performance, sometimes with the so-called Oriental Line, as an Arab or, more commonly, as *ciganos* (gypsies).[83] In Rio de Janeiro today, the Turk is less visible but still very much present. He lingers as a variation of gypsy spirit, as Cigano

FIGURE 4.3. Ritual icons of the Cigano Saraceno (Saracen Gypsy) for use on altars, at the Mercadão de Madureira, Rio de Janeiro, August 2018. Photograph by the author.

Saraceno (Saracen Gypsy), together with his consort, Cigana Saracena. Their figures are widely available in the Afro-Brazilian religious markets like the Mercadão de Madureira in the north zone of Rio (figure 4.3).

We cannot say that the automaton Turk Ajeeb directly morphed into the spirit family of *turcos* or the spirits known as Saracen Gypsies. After all, the important priestess Mãe Andresa had already begun receiving the King of Turkey spirit and opened her Turkish temple in 1889, several years before the arrival of Ajeeb.[84] What we can say is that the phenomena of Ajeeb and the spirits called *turcos* were born of a shared moment and of common sources of fascination with the exotic. The Moorish (*mourisco*) architectural style became popular in late nineteenth- and early twentieth-century Rio de Janeiro, for example: the Moorish Pavilion was a major attraction on the beach of Botafogo, and a "Moorish" tower was featured in the design of Figner's mansion, built in 1912.[85] Moors and Turks were at once less than human and surcharged with strange, inscrutable force (figure 4.4).

Spirit Turks were activated in response to the history of the Moors in Portuguese and then Brazilian legend but also in response to the arrival in Brazil of actual flesh-and-blood migrants from the Ottoman Empire. After all, the spirit *turcos* often mirrored actual features of the late nineteenth-century migrants. João do Rio described the incoming population before 1904 as being composed of mostly Maronite Christians with some Muslims; it was likewise in the spirit family.[86] The spirit Turks became mixed-race *caboclos*, learned from *índios*, and mingled freely with Afro-Brazilian pretos velhos.[87] So did the actual Turks, who had to find their place in relation to, and miscegenation with, the existing groups of Brazil. In their trances, the spirit Turks present a story of harmonious integration that expressed the actual aspirations of arriving migrants. In the Batuque tradition, the Turks are conquerors, victorious even over Brazilian kings and Americans.[88] But another catalyst that generated both Ajeeb and the spirit Turks is the one salient for the ideas in play in this chapter, namely, the sudden widespread exposure to new technologies of mediation like a strange, not-quite-unbeatable automaton.

Is it possible that the machine-man Turk infiltrated the spirit Turks that now routinely inhabit bodies in Brazil, a machine in the spirit in the man? Many of the qualities that were set and cast in the character

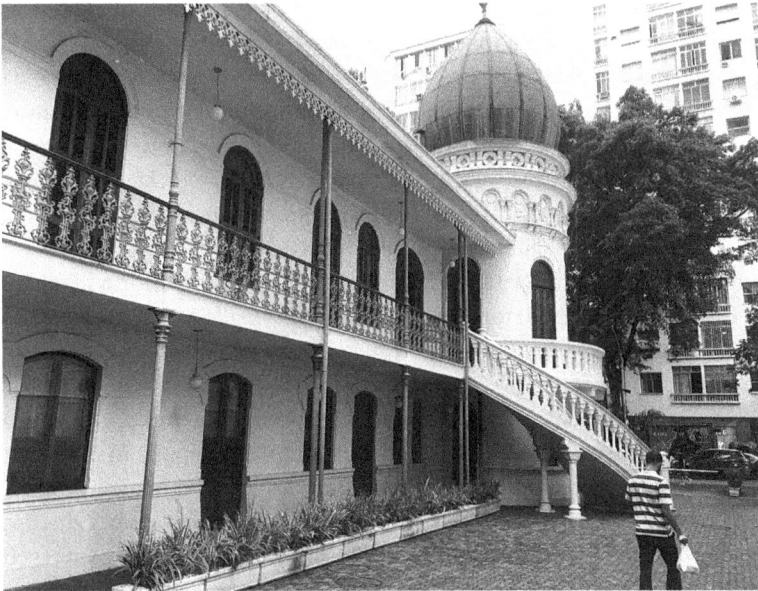

FIGURE 4.4. Fred Figner's mansion, built in 1912, featured a "Moorish" (*mourisco*) tower. Photograph by the author.

of Ajeeb are reproduced in contemporary ritual practices of Tambor de Mina, Pajé, Batuque, and Umbanda. Probably they have been in play since the first part of the twentieth century. For example, in Batuque, the *encantados*, among which the *turcos* are the most numerous, have human foibles but also superhuman capacities—covering space in a hurry, hearing and seeing at a distance, instigating calamities like automobile accidents, shutting down factories, causing unwilled human action.[89] Perhaps not incidentally, spirits' potency is perceived very much in the terms of the technological forces that became available in the 1890s, at the same time that the Turks—human, automaton, and spirit—together arrived on the scene. Turks can take over a human body to present the compelling spectacle, like Ajeeb, of a body within a body. And, finally, a medium who receives and transmits the *encantado* is referred to as an *apparatus* (*aparelho*), the same label applied to the sound and light technologies Figner displayed in 1895, as in *aparelho phonográfico*, the "phonographic apparatus," or *aparelho cinetógrafo*, the "cinetographic apparatus."

Apparatus

Expanded ritual uses of the term *aparelho* came into currency in Brazil through spiritism, in the writings of the French spiritist author Allan Kardec (a.k.a. Hyppolyte Rivail), who used *apparatus* to refer at once to electric devices and to the human body: "We have an image of life and death still more exact in the electric battery. The battery, like all natural bodies, contains electricity in a latent state: but the electrical phenomena are only manifested when the fluid is set in motion by a special cause. When this movement is superinduced, the battery may be said to become alive; but when the cause of the electrical activity ceases, the phenomena cease to occur, and the battery relapses into a state of inertia. Organic bodies may thus be said to be a sort of electric battery." And elsewhere: "Incarnation has another aim . . . of fitting the spirit to perform his share in the work of creation; for which purpose he is made to assume a corporeal apparatus [*appareil*] in harmony with the material state of each world into which he is sent."[90]

It was in Kardec's *Le livre des esprits* (1857) that *apparatus* (*appareil*) was applied to spirit mediums. The book circulated rapidly in Rio, both in French and, after 1866, in Portuguese translation.[91] The new religion spread rapidly across Brazil thereafter, between 1870 and 1900. Adjacent notions of mediation—mechanical, religious, and migratory—converged and produced a new hybrid in which the Turks were one of the familiar spirits in the repertoire of the apparatus, the medium. Different domains were being translated into one another—the immigrant's body, the automaton's body, the spirit body, the national body. Bruno Latour used *translation* to describe how the qualities of one entity are at once projected into and taken up by a second entity. Politics and science, he wrote, become inextricably meshed as projects like *waging war* and *slowing down neutrons* are conjoined; or, rather, it turns out that politics and science were never discreet to begin with.[92] The same is true for nineteenth-century notions of the automatic and religion-like situations. They were fluidly translated, meshed, taken up from one mode to the other: possession to hysteria to possession, as we saw in chapter 1; automaton Ajeeb, *turco* spirits, actual Turk migrants, Ajeeb. I argue for considering talking machines, an automaton checkers-playing Turk, actual migrant Turks, and spirits Turks as intercalibrated in a process of ongoing translation. The spirits, Turks, took on the basic appearance of Ajeeb even as Ajeeb was styled according to familiar legends of the Moors. The spirit Turks conducted themselves automatically, carrying out mechanical missions, and manifesting themselves via battery-like human apparatuses.

Evidence from a comparative situation shows such translation occurring elsewhere in the Americas. Stephan Palmié documented how, in 1908 Philadelphia, Afro-Cuban practitioners of the tradition called *abakuá* relied on sophisticated sonic technologies to announce the presence of the spirits, or *potencia*. He cites a journalist's report from that year:

> From under the water a speaking tube stretches across the room to a converter. It is filled with wheels, has a glass front, and a bit of stovepipe sticks out the top. Leading into the converter, from the western end of the room, is another speaking tube. Still another tube finds its way into the converter from a kettle drum in the east. This kettle drum is made of a china washbowl covered with a skin. A final tube is carried out into Fairmount Avenue. This has a megaphone exit, and it is from this megaphone that the people in the neighborhood get notice that the spirits are busy.[93]

Sonic technologies and religious ideologies converged in the manifesting of the spirits in what Palmié called their *acoustic mask*.[94] Following this line of thought, we might imagine Ajeeb as, among other things, a visual and kinetic mask of *turco* spirits. The spirits gained automatic capacities via him even as he was, unknown to him or Figner, stocked by customers with the tropes and images of the Moors and Turks who preceded and accompanied him. In this series of translations, the chess-playing automaton became an entirely new and different kind of being than what Von Kempelen first imagined and built, a version now packed with an entirely different historical life. Then, too, at the same time, the spirits of Brazil called *turcos* were filled with a dose of Ajeeb's marvelous automaton powers.

* * *

The fabulous Fred Figner! We will meet up with him again in the next chapter. He enjoyed a long career post-Ajeeb, including after his death. His close engagement with sound, light, and electric energy helped guide him toward spiritism, which saw these properties as vehicles or, better, batteries of the sacred. He became officially affiliated in 1903, through the influence of Pedro Sayão, the father of the opera singer Bidu Sayão.[95] He worked out of the spiritist center Casa de Ishmael and became vice president of the Brazilian Spiritist Federation. It became his religion, and he became a close friend and confidante and the financier of Chico Xavier. He also wrote his own newspaper column, "Chronica espírita" (Spiritist chronicle), in the newspaper *Correia da Manhã* starting around 1920 and continuing until his death. In these weekly or biweekly columns, he continued to explore questions of sound, light, and transmission, but now less with regard to the show and the attractions of Ouvidor Street than to the materialization of spirits. He also criticized the Catholic Church as often as he could. And, on rare occasions, spirits of the deceased came to him to use his arm and pen to gain a new public hearing. This was the case on April 9, 1931, when he allowed the deceased appellate judge and legal theorist Lima Drummond a chance to hold court again by writing about him—or, rather, allowing Lima Drummond to write through him—in his column.[96] I will return to this issue of how the dead—and which dead—gain the right to speak in chapter 5.

Figner himself could not keep quiet after his own demise, either. After his death in 1947, his spirit appeared to Chico, who gave it a voice through his own pen. Even disincarnate, Figner remained invested in matters of sound and light. According to Chico's automatically written book, the disincarnate Fred Figner, now known as Brother Jacob, traveled to a celestial California in 1947. In that otherworld he met Thomas Edison, whose products he had sold and profited so handsomely from in Brazil. Edison occupied a more elevated sphere but allotted the visitor fifteen minutes of his time (and not a minute more). He glowed, a techno saint: "Light crowned his [Edison's] venerable head." Edison told Brother Jacob about the end of the nineteenth century and the phonograph. He warned about the splitting of the atom and the atomic bomb. Brother Jacob asked whether Edison would return and be incarnated and what great trick might follow his invention of the electric light. Edison responded that only God was the real creator and that it was time we invent a divine, eternal light that would shine forever inside of us. After a last embrace, they separated. Note the mediations: Chico writes (automatically) as Brother Jacob, who is the spirit version of Fred Figner, who reports his conversation with Thomas Edison.[97]

Such radical metamorphoses do not happen without friction. Figner's family contested the viability of Chico's authorship, his legal right to write—automatically or not—*as* Fred Figner. As we will see in chapter 5, law may require a higher threshold of accountable individual personhood—or a different notion of a legal person—than did the nearhuman play of Ajeeb or Chico's automatic meditations drafted from Figner's corpse.

5

Chico X
Legal Nearhuman

It may be that there is in me something like an echo of the past. Spirit-ism hasn't yet arrived at the point of admitting to incarnation in animals, but it will have to in order to reach the full conclusions of its doctrine. Thus it may be that I was a rooster in a previous life, years or centuries ago. If I concentrate right now, I hear a remote sound of something like a rooster's crow. Who can say it wasn't me that crowed three times after Saint Peter denied Jesus? That would explain a lot of my predilections.

MACHADO DE ASSIS, "The Week" ("A semana"), May 20, 1894

Humberto de Campos died in December 1934, the best-known Brazilian author of his day. A poet, short story writer, and chronicler, he was by the end of his career also famous for a newspaper column authored under the nom de plume Counselor X.X. He occupied seat 20 in the Academy of the Immortals, the pantheon of greats modeled after that of Paris, when he reached his untimely death at the age of forty-eight. Humberto proved more resilient than his mortal flesh and in more ways than one. He left a speech to be read to the other Immortals after his demise, naming his pre-ferred successor as president of the Academy, Múcio Leão.[1] In the form of this *posthumous note*, as he called it, his will carried on even without his body.

Humberto also lived on as a spirit. In March 1935, three months af-ter his death, he began to speak to a boy in the state of Minas Gerais, Francisco ("Chico") Xavier. Chico recalled hearing the spirit's words, "Prepare yourself, boy, we have lots to do tonight." After finishing work at his day job in Belo Horizonte, he spent several hours nightly in a state of trance, writing down Humberto's words. To describe the process of spirit writing (*psicografia*) he offered: "It is as though someone applied an electrical device to my right elbow with its own automatic will. It's not me who writes. I obey a superior force."[2]

The statement is as intriguing as it is opaque, not unlike André Breton's description of his fate as "to have written and not to have written books."[3] How did this kind of writing that is not writing actually work? Reporting on her experiments with William James, Gertrude Stein described her dissociative writing as possessed "of a decidedly rhythmic character" that set her in a different relation with time than usual. Chronological sequence collapsed; past, present, and future blurred.[4] Henry Olcott likewise described the automatic-writing process of Madame Blavatsky, the founder of Theosophy, as a stay in the unfolding of time: "Her pen would be flying over the page . . . when she would suddenly stop, look out into space with the vacant eye of the clairvoyant seer, shorten her vision as though to look at something held invisible in the air before her, and begin copying on her paper what she saw."[5]

When they describe their capacity to work not only in but also *on* time, automatic writers sometimes spoke of their ability as a gift, something that simply came to them, but they also described it as a craft or a technique. In 1920, for example, Anne Lane and Harriet Beale published an account of their experience learning to write automatically: "At first we obtained only circles, words and fragments of sentences. . . . It was more like opening a window to a crowded street and listening to the chance words one could catch, than like anything else in the world. On the eleventh day came a decided change. From the moment we began, the writing was firmer and more impelling, and we were told at once that whoever was using our hands had come with definite intention, and meant to stay with us. We had, in technical phraseology, 'found our control.'"[6] In Lane and Beale's case, automatic writing had a learning curve, a period of discipline before the words began to pour out. Chico, too, practiced his craft, developed his technique, and then found his control. From there things moved quickly. By 1944, he had published five books "authored by" the famous deceased writer Humberto de Campos.[7]

Perhaps Humberto would not have minded. His own view of individual authorship left room for ambiguity: "The human soul is a cave so dotted with hiding places and twisted with zigzags that there's never been a man on earth, no matter how meticulous, who came to know even half of his own heart. Just when we suppose we've found a simple life without complication or subterfuge, that's when an abyss opens in front of us, a volcano, a subterranean mouth capable of swallowing whole the pilgrim seeking to unravel the mystery."[8] If the individual soul was a mystery to Humberto, his description of writing further muddled the idea of the individual self. "How do I write? . . . I write mentally at first: the machine doesn't do anything but copy the phrase that already exists in my head, the velocity of whose construction the fingers can't match."[9] His description of the body as but the machine-like scribe of the mind reads much like Chico's description of automatic writing as akin to having an electric device bolted to the elbow. The problem, in terms of the law, was that Humberto's family took a stricter view of individual authorship and its legal meaning than did Humberto himself. This tension between the automatic writer, the possessed or inspired author, and the legal person, a reliable, durable, and accountable individual agent or author, gives grist to the mill of my argument here.

In 1944, Humberto's widow and three children filed suit against Chico Xavier and the Brazilian Spiritist Federation (FEB).[10] The trial made headlines as the "Humberto de Campos Case," becoming almost as renowned as the Juca Rosa case of 1871, discussed in chapter 2. Humberto's family asked the court to render a definitive decision as to whether the works were or were not drafted by the spirit of their deceased husband and father. They accused Chico of exploiting Humberto's fame to sell his own books and, in the process, confusing the reading public and cutting into the sales of the books he actually had written. The automatically written works were inferior, the suit continued, and, when not deficient, then obviously plagiarized. Finally, if Humberto *was* determined to be still writing, any royalties from those books should still go to the family. If he was determined *not* to be still writing, Chico should be prosecuted for fraud.

FEB's defense tried to show that the postmortem books were indistinguishable in style from the premortem books and, thus, that Humberto was clearly still writing, just in spirit form. The defense document—"Two Humbertos: One Style, One Soul, One Feeling" ("Os dois Humbertos: Um só estilo, uma só alma, um só sentimento")—was widely circulated. It argued, among other things, that the courts have no rightful place in adjudicating the matter at trial since the asserted presence and voice of a postmortem spirit is a matter of the constitutionally mandated freedom of religion. This bold argument set the terms of freedom of religion and legal authorship at odds. Yet it was far from clear that such an argument would work. How could a legal decision even be rendered on matters so ethereal?

The family's lawsuit proposed that all parties appear in person: not only Chico Xavier but also the spirit of Humberto de Campos, whose "operationality" should be demonstrated and verified. On August 23, 1944, however, Judge João Frederico Mourão Russell declared the suit invalid, arguing, first, that on death the individual forfeits his or her civil rights and that the entity "Humberto de Campos" therefore no longer carried legal standing and, second, that inherited authorial rights were limited to works an author produced prior to death. Finally, he noted that the judicial system is empowered to pronounce only on entities already existing within a judicial relationship, presumably limited by the beginning and the end of biological life and the works produced within that span. The courts are ill equipped to decide whether the entities of such a relation exist in the first place.

The family appealed but to no avail, and the decision was reaffirmed in November 1944. In the wake of the trial, Chico went on to publish another seven books under the authorship of Humberto de Campos, the last in 1967. On the new books' covers, Humberto was not explicitly named. Rather, the spirit source was called "Brother X" in order to avoid further legal entanglements with the deceased author's family. Brother X, however, was widely known to be Humberto de Campos. The title even seemed to mimic and draw from Humberto's own pen name, Counselor X.X. Without his assent, or at least without the assent of his family, Humberto continued to write despite being bodiless.

Striking in this highly publicized case was how, by problematizing authorship, the legal definition of the individual was called into play and clarified. The court made it clear that, at least in terms of certain rights, individual identity ceases to exist with bodily death. But the question of legal authorship in relation to spirit-written texts, not to mention the question of freedom of religion in relation to authors' descendants' property rights, continues to expand. Thousands of books produced by automatic writing are now in print, responding to an eager and expanding market demand. Even today some legal theorists argue that, though mediums are receiving rather than generating ideas, their writing still should be seen as their own and legally protected, given the processes of selection, compilation, and organization and the very negotiation of static necessitated by responsible mediumship.[11]

In spite of the unusual notoriety of the Humberto de Campos case, the late writer was hardly unique. In fact, several protagonists of previous chapters lived on as spirits, also channeled through the arm and pen of Brazil's most famous automatic writer and best-selling author ever, Chico Xavier. We should place *author* in quotes, however, because, according to his own report (and much like Bispo do Rosário, the artist with whom this book began), Chico was not himself the source of the words he wrote. Rather, deceased persons wrote *through* him including Dom Pedro II and Fred Figner. Taken over by the spirit of Figner, as recounted at the close of the last chapter, he crossed time and an ocean to pose questions to Thomas Edison in a shimmering California. There is something marvelous and audacious in these written incarnations, these grafted extensions of human reach: Chico as a comic book X-man *avant la lettre*, sprouting new faculties from his body to face down any critic or crisis. As we saw at the end of the previous chapter, however, while Dom Pedro II had already been long enough in the crypt not to oppose being animated against his will, Figner was not quite dead enough. Like Humberto's family, the Figner family challenged Chico's right to write as Fred Figner. It was only one of many legal challenges he would face.

The encounters of an automatic spirit writer and the law offer a rare opportunity. What kind of legal person does the law require, and how do religion-like scenes and situations, like automatic authorship, contravene those rules? What happens when legal persons and religion-like persons interact? Academic, legal, and government venues—legal culture—give value to persuasive performances of reliably bounded and continuing personhood or individual personhood, justifying and anchoring declarations, descriptions, theories, hypotheses, or laws issuing from those places. The usually unspoken rules of personhood become in these contexts vividly clear as soon as they are transgressed or someone is possessed in the wrong place. Such moments reveal a gap dividing, on one hand, the *legal* prestige of intent and the kind of individuality such gauging of intent requires and, on the other hand, the *religious* prestige of nonintentionality, the spirits or the Spirit acting on or through a body understood as a vessel of invisible and greater power, in ritual events designed to dramatize the transductions between those conditions (figure 5.1).[12]

FIGURE 5.1. "Heroes of Brazil: Chico Xavier, Superman," May 6, 2009. Photograph by Alexandre Possi. Graphic art by Ricardo Tatoo. Used with permission of the artist.

Previous chapters addressed versions of the ritual attraction to nearhumans—their making in uneven transatlantic encounters and the ambiguous agencies they helped launch. This chapter turns from potentialities to the limits—even the risks—of engagements with such beings. Activating nearhuman figures or seeking such status oneself is all well and good in a temple, a theater, or a game hall, you may be thinking, but perhaps less desirable in contexts that call for a higher degree of reliable, continuous personhood than these circumscribed venues do.[13] In Rio de Janeiro, I recorded stories of possessions happening "out of place" that suggest the risks. One person described a harrowing experience of being a passenger in a car whose driver suddenly was possessed by an *orixá* and became a different being. Who knows whether such spirits can drive or care about traffic laws? he wondered. In a second case, a man dancing with a woman in a club noticed her face taking on a different expression as she became a *pomba-gira*—the spirit of a woman of the streets—and then striking him sharply and cackling, shifting to another being without warning. I also heard the story of a girl who was initiated into Candomblé and a regular vessel for the gods in the temple. One day at school, in order to play at doing ritual, some boys put a wrap on her head in the style she wore when possessed. With that invitation, the *orixá* took over her body and would not leave until her priestess (*mãe de santo*) could be summoned. When the priestess did not arrive for over an hour, the boys received a stern reprimand since the regular school routine was disrupted. Another person described a sexual encounter with someone who, when the moment had passed, suddenly morphed into the trickster god Exú and demanded a cigarette in an unfamiliar voice. At the end of 2019, the singer Karina Buhr accused a priest of Candomblé of having raped her, allegedly while possessed by a randy spirit named Malandinho.[14] The priest claimed that he had no memory of the incident and therefore had committed no crime. Disturbing, disquieting events.

Misplaced possessions create new dangers and new possibilities. The anthropologist Gilberto Velho described an incident he witnessed of spontaneous possession overcoming a person on a busy Rio street in the 1980s. Strangers organized themselves into lines to ask advice of the abruptly inspirited person. A bystander designated himself the facilitator, and the consultations with the spirit continued for two hours.[15] Though deprived of qualities of will or intention, this nearhuman was supercharged with other special capacities, like divinatory knowledge that enabled him to decipher the troubles of random people queuing up to talk to a spirit. But that midday rush-hour transfiguration was, it is fair to say, a somewhat unusual event. More often, multipersonated bodies or multibodied persons seem to pose a hazard in public space—thus the institutionalization of Rosalie Leroux, the incarceration of Juca Rosa, the encasement of Anastácia, and the careful staging of Ajeeb. Though many ritual contexts give value to and even work as factories for the making and staging of multipersonated bodies or multibodied persons, misplaced possessions in public space are often seen as awkward, unwelcome, or even dangerous. Why should this be so? Phrased differently, what kind of personhood and attendant notion of agency do law and civil society require?

Law and governance seem to require different versions of identity and agency, less beholden to the automatic than the agency of the figures we have met so far. This chapter shows that the legal person is a shifting target. As we saw in chapter 2, Juca Rosa's possessed personhood—a shape-shifting personhood with saint in the head—rendered him a transgressor and helped placed him outside the law. More recent cases involving spirit testimonies have, by contrast, placed mediums' work and their documentary revelations at the center of at least some legal decisions. All the cases involving possession or mediumship, however, entail and allow a deferral or complicating of individual accountability that presents legal challenges and potential risk.

Locke's Brazilian Parrot

It is an old problem. In early modern political theory, the discussion of what kind of individual was needed to make up civil society relied on reports from the New World, a laboratory of nature, to map out the terms of the debate. Tropes and stories from the colonial world—the cannibal, the slave, the monkey—helped set the so-called rational, autonomous person into relief. Hobbes's contemporary Robert Boyle cast into doubt the doctrine of individual resurrection through stories of the Caribbean cannibal. When an individual body is eaten by others, with the flesh of the first now reconstituted as the flesh of a whole series of others, in what form would the original body be resurrected? Boyle extended the challenge of cannibalism much further, describing an infant's nursing, for example, as the ingestion of the "blanched blood" of the mother, the implication being that so-called individual life is in fact nothing but a constant process of the cannibalizing and hybridizing of bodies.

In the fourth edition of *An Essay concerning Human Understanding* (1700), in part in response to Boyle, John Locke added the tale of a possessed Brazilian parrot.[16] The Dutch colonial governor of Pernambuco (the primary seventeenth-century sugar-producing region of Brazil), "Prince Maurice" (Johan Maurits van Nassau-Siegen), had heard about a famous talking parrot. On entering the chamber to be presented to the governor, the parrot first observed, "What a company of white men are here!" "Who is this prince?" the parrot was asked about the governor. "Some general or other," it replied. The parrot was then asked where he was from ("Marignan"), to whom he belonged ("a Portuguese"), and what he did ("je garde des poulles" [I take care of the chickens]).

Locke borrowed the story from William Temple, who cast it as an "idle question" that "came in his head." Locke also used the story as a digression, but one with a purpose. Could a parrot have personal identity? Locke seems to say no since personal identity hinges on reason, reflection, and consciousness, the ability to consider oneself as the same thinking thing across different times and places and hence a self that may "be continued in the same or divers substances." He decided that a parrot is but a mimic, able to parrot personhood, so to speak, but not generate it. The right sort of civil person could not simply be found; rather, he had to be cultivated. In *An Essay concerning Human Understanding*, Locke presented another thought experiment. Assume that the consciousness of a prince is inserted into the body of a cobbler; after the cobbler's own soul deserts the body, is the resulting being the prince or the cobbler? The answer for Locke is clear—the prince.[17] What makes the person is consciousness, not soul or body. Even more, personhood consists of consciousness over time, a series of actions reckoned in relation to their consequences. This precise bounding of consciousness was crucial. The soul is too fickle; we cannot be sure we retain the same soul while we sleep or while we are inebriated. Bodies, likewise, are a shifty foundation—an infant becomes an elder, the slim fatten up, a worker loses a hand in an accident. The self that previously extended its sympathy to the fingertips now adjusts to end in a stump, to take Locke's own example, and the consciousness occupying that changed body continues to accumulate memory and experience for which it is accountable in the future. This last was, it seems, the crucial point. Law, including the eternal law of rewards and punishments, depends on this kind of accounting. Effective civil participation, requiring lawful behavior, must be anchored in the individual *person* rather than in the soul or the body.

For his part, Kant began to work out his opposition to multiperson bodies in his early writings on the mystical visionary Swedenborg.[18] His complaint against Swedenborg focused on the risk of private interest and special revelation. Particularist versions of illuminism—or "fancied occult *intercourse* with God"—subverted the hope of a public religion and a shared standard of morality and truth.[19] Kant's idea of a public spirit is, by contrast, a social and moral force capable of sustaining society. Leibniz's *Theodicy*, a book Kant knew well, had formulated the matter similarly. Morality and law depend on the firm status of the "I," grounded in free will. Free will, for Leibniz, includes three features: the spontaneity of action, the assurance that action originates from the one who acts; the contingency of action, the fact that other courses not taken were possible; and the rationality of action, the guarantee that it follows from the deliberation of alternatives. These three qualities of action—spontaneity, contingency, rationality—ensure law. Turned the other way around, law ensures a continuous accountable self, an "I" possessed of identity that endures and is liable *over time*.

Once established, these ideas of legal, individual personhood became far more than philosophical exercises because, at the end of the nineteenth century, they came to inform new social science programs and legal regimes. William James directly engaged Locke's argument. As James described, Locke was first to propose that personhood was not a principle but a process, something made from moment to moment through consciousness.[20] James noted how, when it appeared in 1689, Locke's essay "Of Identity and Diversity" created a scandal for affirming that two different persons could occupy one body. But, in James's opinion, Locke's view now represented the status quo, amply confirmed by psychologists like Charcot, Janet, Freud, and James himself. James thought that automatic writing, in particular, posed important questions about personhood, and it became one of his main theoretical laboratories, including in work with his student Gertrude Stein. In addition to the process of how messages are received, he attended to the look of the writing itself. He described the "freakiness" of the pages of automatic writers—often filled with features like mirror script, backward spelling, and writing from right to left, bottom to top, or in some other geometric figure—that would be difficult to achieve without *automatic freedom*, a curious and, for me, critical phrase.[21] The very freakiness was evidence of the experiences' authenticity. A simple fraud could never pull it off. These kinds of phenomena resemble the demonic possessions of the past but mediate more optimistic messages from the beyond than hell and damnation. Automatic writing was far "humaner," James wrote.[22] James followed Locke, then, in taking an expansive, processual view of personhood. Despite being centuries apart, however, both recognized the pragmatic and legal need for strong assertions of individual identity in certain places and for certain purposes.

If James's proposal opened out to a wide-angle vision of agency, in Brazil his contemporary Raimundo Nina Rodrigues took a more telescopic view. Nina Rodrigues set to work studying criminal psychiatry in the context of Afro-Brazilian religions. He confirmed the conflict between legal culture and religion-like situations more than he threatened it. As we learned in chapter 1, in 1896 he published a series of articles on "animist fetishism" in Afro-Brazilian ritual practice, later gathered in the book *O animismo fetichista dos negros bahianos*. Fernando Ortiz's inaugural study of Afro-Cuban religions, *Los negros brujos* (1906), was informed by similar ideals of psychology, identity, and personhood. The twin studies by these two pioneering criminologists, penned a decade apart and in Brazil and Cuba, respectively, informed legal treatments of the religions they described. For Ortiz, Cuba's turn-of-the-century "mala vida"—the gray zone of prostitution, crime, and vice, defined in opposition to the "vida honrada" and the "vida buena"—was the direct consequence of lingering African spirits. The African remained "slave of his passions," stuck in his "moral atavism," as evidenced above all in rites of possession.[23] Nina Rodrigues, for his part, underscored the civil risks related to Afro-Brazilian Candomblé in grappling with Brazil's republican problem. First, he argued, Afro-Brazilian religion interrupts the regularity of work and justifies vagrancy (*vadiagem*).[24] What is more, Candomblé is in part inspired by the Yoruba religion of West Africa and is copied from a form of foreign civil government under which the king corresponds to the high god and mediating ranks of nobles correspond to the mediating deities called *orixás*. Therefore, Africans, *crioullos*, and *mestiços* who practice the Yoruba religion in Brazil are all already living within a rival political system. Nina Rodrigues declared that he had even heard of possession's power in motivating battle and sedition, thus the reason for prohibiting African immigration. Afro-Brazilians are in a state of transition from fetishism to idolatry and, given their *hybrid* religion, as "mestizos of spirit" not liable to conversion to a pure Catholicism. That is, because of their religion, it is not clear that they are assimilable to the nation of Brazil whatsoever. Next is that religion involves possession—the loss of individual personality, memory, and accountability—but also, and even worse, the faking of possession. Finally, Candomblé has already taken possession of the country; it is embedded "no ânimo publico," in the public spirit, and risks further expansion via social contagion, as the dramatic story of a possessed white girl conveys.[25]

Nina Rodrigues's descriptions were not only an anthropological project but also a legal project, nationally applied and enforced. His terms—ranging from the familiar, like *possession*, to the hybrid religio-psychiatric, like *somnambulant spiritist* (*espirita sonâmbulo*)—began to appear in police reports prosecuting cases of illegal religion at the close of the nineteenth century and the first decades of the twentieth, just as republican Brazil was taking legal shape. It is in this light that we should read the new public health laws instituted in the penal code of 1890. The code included the newly written articles 156, 157, and 158.[26] Article 156 prohibited the practice of medicine or dentistry without the necessary legal certification. Article 157 prohibited the "practice of spiritism, magic and its sorceries, the use of talismans and cartomancy to arouse sentiments of hate and love, the promise to cure illnesses, curable and not curable; in sum, to fascinate and subjugate public belief." Article 158 proscribed "administering or simply prescribing any substance of any of the natural domains for internal or external use or in any way prepared, thus performing or exercising the office denominated as curandeiro." In short, article 156 addressed illegal medicine, article 157 sorcery, and article 158 *curandeirismo*.

The addition of these three articles to the penal code posed a legal paradox that would endure for much of the twentieth century. The new constitution of 1891 declared the freedom of religion and the separation of church and state. Because Afro-Brazilian religions were considered a dangerous contagion, the solution was the repression of Afro-Brazilian traditions under an alternative category, namely, *public health*. Afro-Brazilian ritual actors closely linked healing and medicine, then, but so did the state and the state's law.

Spirits, Static, Documents

By the turn of the twentieth century, Brazil had become the center of spiritism, a status it retains today. That tradition began as a late nineteenth-century import from France. It offered the promise of Afro-Brazilian spirit-possession practices with none of the social liabilities. To the contrary, even if it was not quite respectable, it was thoroughly French, cosmopolitan, and à la mode.[27] As such, spiritist mediums were granted more legal space in which to act than were the priests of and participants in Afro-Brazilian traditions.

In the period dividing Juca Rosa from Chico Xavier—the last third of the nineteenth century and the first half of the twentieth—the default legal person was remade in the terms of a bio person. Between 1850 and 1900, her identity began to be verified in photographs, fingerprints, and anthropometric signs acquired in techniques pioneered by criminologists like Bertillon in France and Galton in England. But this did not mean that other kinds of persons abruptly ceased to exist. Multipersonated bodies continued to act and endure today in the religions of Candomblé, Vodou, Santería, and many others with saint in the head. They work on everyday crises of love, health, fertility, and financial success. Spiritism, by contrast, adapted itself to the terms and procedures of the bio person, applying photography, stenography, and medical sciences to its authorizing procedures, and building elaborate bureaucracies in hospitals and legal associations that neatly matched the rationalizing institutions that characterized the early twentieth century. Spiritists positioned themselves as not even members of something as lowly and partial as a religion; rather, they spoke in terms of science. They rejected the primitive term *posses-sion* and embraced the techno term *mediation*. Thus, while our guide, Machado de Assis, was critical of spiritists, and while in 1898 the Catholic Church added automatic writing to its list of injunctions, elites were in general receptive to this new religion-like fashion.[28] One reason is that French Kardecism and its quasi-scientific articulation of spirits resonated with at least some members of the judiciary, with the result that symbiotic juridical-spiritist associations were forged. And this elective affinity between spiritists and jurists was materially built on the shared reliance on and everyday practice of living with documents.

Documents are things that draw people into associations and help constitute them, becoming part of their reality.[29] In the cases considered here, documents help constitute spirits and people's associations with them, but they also become part of spiritism's overall notion of spirits.[30] One spirit—the deceased audio-recording magnate Fred Figner from chapter 3—described the challenge of getting messages through from the beyond in a book he authored a year after his death under the nom de plume "Brother Jacob," with, as we have seen, Chico Xavier serving as scribe and automatic writer. In that text, called *Returned* (*Voltei*), the spirit of Figner named sources of telepathic static that spirits face: a medium can be insensitive, requiring herculean labor from a spirit; a "receptor" can be surrounded by waves of distraction; the "instrument's" mind may be already filled or preoccupied; a medium can attract competing force waves that contaminate the communication and make the "apparatus" unreliable; the necessary natural elements of mediation, like "radiomagnetic fluid," may be lacking; social organizations to regulate these variables and sharpen the instrument may be inexistent, persecuted, or weak; and, finally, there can be as much "noise" in the spirit world as in the living world, causing the spirits to err. All these issues mean that transmissions from the dead are vulnerable, slivered, and noisy. This makes spirit *documents* crucial—at least according to Figner's spirit, as written (in a document) by Chico—because they are uniquely able to cut through the static to render a communication substantive and definitive.[31]

Of course, such documents can themselves be challenged, as we will see, because the authorship linking them to a legal person is not clear. In Erving Goffman's terms, mediums of spirit documents are *animators* rather than *authors*; that is, they speak or write words that they did not create.[32] For Goffman, the originator of the words constituting a speech act is the *principal*. But the matter of authorship in a case like this is considerably more complicated than that, as Judith T. Irvine has described.[33]

Spiritist animators' written messages are directed to an audience, the *addressee*. They are also citational, incorporating personae from the past. Moreover, the process of automatic writing presents varying degrees of consciousness, allowing for the prospect of "self-talk"—a speaker and an addressee in the same person—and what Goffman called *role distance*, a divided self with one part commenting on another's utterances. The medium may have been invited or even hired to transmit a message— meaning that, in Irvine's terms, a *sponsor* is also party to the message, along with the *transmitter* and the *formulator/composer*.[34] A medium's writing, already multivocal, is then cited in court and, thus, reanimated by a judge or otherwise amplified before a jury, adding further participant roles to the communication. Then, too, a message written automatically by the medium conjures an image of the spirit source in the jurors' minds, or the *figure*.[35] There is also the *accused*, in defense of whom the spirit communication may be offered. Irvine calls this participant-role the *fingeree*.[36] Thus already: principal, animator, figure, sponsor, addressee, multiple selves, and fingeree.

We could continue to multiply possible participant roles as spirit-writing events unfold in real time. What is important, however, is that spirit possession and spirit writing do *not* appear in court as performances in real time. Rather, they must assume a very circumscribed, conventional legal form, as a document. As a document, spirit medium-ship becomes an object "detached from ongoing pragmatic relations," as Irvine puts it.[37] Assuming this conventional genre, as document, a spirit's words take on an independent legal existence that, like other features of legal culture, *appears* to transcend time and become transferable in space. Yet even such "transcendent texts" still rely on the authority of the conversational event they purport to supersede, in this case spirit mediumship and automatic-writing events.[38] One might say, then, that, in arguing for the rights of the animator as (legal) author, Brazilian legal theorists have considerably reduced and oversimplified matters in the interest of legal-rational authority. That they are able to do so depends on the transduction of spirit speech, whether experienced as an electric impulse attached to the arm, a collapse of time, or a cacophony out of which a control finally appears, into the recognizable legal form of a document.

Let us now turn to two cases in which this transpired and documents written by spiritist automatic writers entered into and acted in the legal domain. While the Humberto de Campos case discussed above considered the problem of spirits of the dead continuing to act as authors, these two raise the challenge of so-called spirit testimonies—narratives transmitted ("psychographed") by the dead through mediums and committed to some written form—as admissible legal documents in court.

There have been many such cases, but in these two the issues are sharply brought into focus.[39]

JOSÉ DIVINO NUNES CASE

Spirits entered the legal process through the work of Chico Xavier on several occasions. Among them was the first time in Brazilian law that a spirit's testimony was admitted as part of a legal defense, in this case against a homicide charge.

On Saturday morning, May 8, 1976, in the Brazilian city of Goiânia, a sixteen-year-old boy named José Divino Nunes killed Maurício Henrique.[40] Maurício found the gun in José's father's bag. A few moments later he was dead. Two years later, while in a spirit-writing trance, Chico received a message from the deceased and drafted a letter from the victim to his family asserting José Divino's innocence. The message said: "Dear Mother, Father and Sisters. I came here today asking for your courage. I ask you not to think of my trip here with sadness. Neither José Divino nor anyone was to blame for what happened. We were playing with the revolver thinking that with a loaded gun you could wound someone by aiming at his image in a mirror. I was wounded as a result of this foolish game, and the rest we all know."[41]

Judge Orimar Bastos of the Sixth District Court verified that the spirit's signature was "identical" to that of the deceased teenager. The defense (citing article 121 of the penal code) reminded the court that, under the modern penal code, it is "the motives . . . that are the touchstone of crime": "There is no crime without intent; it is only there that a crime exists."[42] Judge Bastos then pronounced Nunes innocent. The legal foundation he named was the lack of any apparent intent or premeditation in the homicide, but he added in his written statement: "We must give credibility to the spiritual message even though it is unprecedented in judicial circles that the victim himself, after his death, comes to relate and furnish facts . . . that correspond with the declaration of José Divino himself. . . . This frees the accused of guilt." And later: "Mauricio's message not only enlightened me, but also backed up all of the defense's testimony. . . . The message had to be mentioned in the ruling because it helped me make my decision. . . . I am not a spiritualist. I judged Nunes innocent because the killing was not premeditated. Mauricio's message said the killing was a foolish mistake, no one was to blame. The decision was easy for me."[43]

Bastos makes plain that the psychographed message from the dead played a role in his decision. It was equally clear that, despite his denial, he embraced the doctrines of spiritism and, moreover, that he considered the stance unexceptional. Perhaps one reason he could assume this was that Chico was by now a national celebrity. Indeed, his authenticity as a *legitimate medium* was supported during the trial by a public statement read by a representative of the Public Prosecutors' Office of the state of Goiâs.[44] If that was the first time in Brazilian history that a spirit had helped a judge decide a case, however, it would not be the last. Additional cases involving spirit testimony were tried in 1984 and 2006.[45]

ERCY DA SILVA CARDOSA CASE

The 2006 case spurred public debate on the future of Brazil's judiciary. I redact the story as it appeared in Brazil's most respected news daily, *Folha de São Paulo*:

Two spirit-writing letters were used in the defense's argument for the case in which Iara Marques Barcelos, sixty-three, was acquitted of homicide, by a [jury] vote of five to two. The letters were attributed to the authorship of the murder victim. . . . The defense lawyer, Lúcio de Constantino, read the documents in court last Friday, seeking to absolve his client of the accusation that he had ordered the killing of the notary public Ercy da Silva Cardosa. Though it has caused controversy in the judiciary, spirit-written letters have already been accepted in judgments. . . .

The lawyer's reading of the letter [from the deceased victim] was heard with careful attention by the seven members of the jury. He read: "What most weighs on my heart is to see Iara accused like this, by dissimulators and fakers who are just like those who killed me. . . . I send Iara a fraternal embrace from me, Ercy."

The notary public was seventy-one at the time of his death. He died in his home in July 2003 as a result of two gunshots to the head. Iara Barcelos was accused when Ercy da Silva's twenty-nine-year-old housekeeper, Leandro Rocha Almeida, stated that he had been contracted by Iara Barcelos to scare her patron, with whom she also maintained a romantic relationship. . . . Almeida was condemned to fifteen and a half years in prison, though he denied having committed or ordered the crime.

The letters from the victim were psychographed [*psicografada*] by the medium Jorge José Santa Maria. One of the letters was addressed to the husband of the accused, who was also a friend of the victim. The other letter was addressed to the defendant herself. The accused's husband initially sought help regarding the case at a spiritist meeting.

The defense lawyer claims to have studied spiritist theory in order to prepare the defense, though he himself claims no religious affiliation. He cited the letters as the turning point in the trial, playing a key role in his client's acquittal. *Folha de São Paulo* was unable to speak with the medium. Because jurors are not asked to comment on the rationale behind their votes, it is difficult to evaluate the influence of the spirit letters. The documents were accepted in court because they were presented within the proper time frame and because the prosecutor did not attempt to prevent or impugn their status.[46]

Remarkable in this case was the fact that the defense lawyer admitted using spiritism and spirit testimony as a defense ploy and emphasized how well it had worked. In the failed appeal, Judge Manuel José Martinez Lucas affirmed that the use of spirit testimony in the trial was constitutionally protected under the freedom-of-religion clause and that the jurors had been free to evaluate the letter in accord with their own private convictions.[47] Judge José Antonio Hirt Preiss of the appellate bench likewise confirmed the jury's acquittal but offered a different comment on the spirit testimony entered at trial, asserting that Brazil is a secular republic: "Religion remains outside the court chamber, in accord with Brazilian laws."[48]

It remains unclear whether spirit testimonies constitute an intrusion of religion into legal procedure, but the question motivates concern. *Folha de São Paulo* ran a story on May 19, 2008, under the headline "Association Wants to Spiritualize the Judiciary." The report addressed the "polemic" surrounding the multiple and increasingly forceful associations of spiritist judges and lawyers. The largest of these is called the Brazilian Association of Spiritist Magistrates (Associação Brasileira de Magistrados Espíritas) and numbers over six hundred judges of the court.[49] Among them is Francisco Cesar Asfor Rocha, who sat on Brazil's Supreme Court from 1992 to 2012. A newer organization composed of police deputies, prosecutors, lawyers, and judges called the Association Juridical-Spiritist (Associação Jurídico-Espírita) was recently founded in São Paulo and counts several hundred members.[50] The association advocates for a judiciary that is "more responsive to humanitarian questions" and able to engage controversial issues like abortion, euthanasia, same-sex marriage, the death penalty and stem-cell research. It states, "God is the greatest law," and defends the use of spirit-written letters in court. One of the association's founders, the prosecutor Tiago Essado, declared: "The State is secular [*laico*], but people are not. There is no way to dissociate enough to say: I'll use my faith only in the spiritist center." Meanwhile the president of the Brazilian Association of Spiritist Magistrates, the retired federal judge Zalmino Zimmerman, stated that the association's objective is "the spiritualization and humanization of law and the judiciary." When the Ministry of Justice (Conselho Judiciario Nacional) was asked to address the question of spirit testimony and the apparent growing power of spiritist judiciary associations, the judge and spokesman Alexandre Azevedo dismissed the concern: "I don't see any difference between a declaration given by me or you, and a declaration given by a medium, psychographed [*psicografada*] by someone."[51]

By some measures, then, spirit writing as testimony is being normalized as a part of the legal process in Brazil.[52] Spiritists counter the claim that they are infusing religion into law by arguing that spiritism is not a religion so much as a science of knowing, an epistemology, a way of seeing, a method of inquiry. For those judges and lawyers holding this position, practicing spiritism is much like practicing law: an attempt to apply practical techniques to the discernment of otherwise hidden truths. The ambiguity of authorship embedded in the practice of spirit-written documents contributes to their opacity. Mediums allege different kinds and degrees of inspiration, as is the case in other genres of mediumship practiced in Brazil and elsewhere. Alejandro Frigerio called attention to the fact that most possession involves some degree of conscious awareness and that even emic descriptions make this plain. The Umbanda practitioners in Argentina among whom he conducted fieldwork used at least three grades of possession on a scale of most to least conscious awareness: *irradiación* (irradiation), *encostimiento* (being beside), and *incorporación* (incorporation).[53] A similar scale holds true for spiritism, complicating greatly Goffman's notions of authorship, principal, and even animation. One mode, so-called pneumatographia, is considered as direct spirit writing, with no consciousness enjoyed by the physical writer whatsoever. But most spirit writing is indirect—involving some participation of the medium's consciousness—and graded as *mechanical, semimechanical*, or *intuitive*.[54] Intuitive psychography, involving normal but focused consciousness of the medium, is no longer even mediumship, strictly speaking, but rather better viewed as heterography, indicating a document holding traces of multiple authors.

Declarations of the degree of self-consciousness expressed in such terms also serve as claims to the relative status and signature of personhood. As Matthew Hull writes, a signature physically references a person as a node in the chain from which a file or a document is produced. Bureaucracies often have multiple signatures indexing various degrees of involvement of an individual, from full typed name and title with signature and stamp to a scribbling of small initials.[55] Mediumship also relies on a scale of signature. Claims of *indirect* psychography communicate that human editorial craft took some part in the testimony. That very signature of personhood, however, invites the problem of human interest and legal prejudice. *Direct* spirit writing is alleged to include no human consciousness whatsoever. As we have seen, in the famous medium Chico

Xavier's description, it is as though an electric apparatus is attached to the elbow: "It's not me who writes." In this form of speech, the spirit is the principal, the medium's *body* is the author, and the reader of the document in court becomes the animator. Paradoxically, the weak or absent signature of personhood—the notion that the principal and the author are unhinged—potentially imbues the document with greater testimonial force. Such authority works exactly inversely to normal legal standards of testimony, according to which value hinges on an indelible and authentic signature of accountable individual personhood.

Perhaps we could say, then, that monography—an authentic single-principal document—may be legally effective at either end of a spectrum of agency, whether as a spirit message or as an individual human message. The weakest legal documents are those whose agency is mixed or of unclear spirit influence. They carry neither the authority of transcending the human signature nor that of being indelibly linked to an enduring human signature.

Perhaps this very ambiguity should render spirit testimonies legally suspect. Either they are documents with no testimonial value, since the author did not actually witness the event, or—in the case of *pneumatography*, a claim of pure spirit writing without human impediment—they are religious documents and challenge the official secularity of the state.[56] But it seems to me that this very ambiguous, heterographic, interstitial character is precisely the source of the strange legal force of spirit testimonies. They wield the extrahuman authority of religious documents without quite disqualifying themselves as such. They serve, that is to say, as files or archives of nearhuman attraction.

Reckoning Intent

The culture of legality is the system through which state actors conjure order or the appearance of an objective, universal standard. Multipersonated bodies throw the ideals of legal culture—which is based on individual accountability—into disarray. In contrast to legal culture and its situations, religion-like situations are factories of agent ambiguity and permeable persons. Religious persons are composed of ever-changing interiors, with different abilities and ideas of possible action than they had before their engagements with gods, ancestors, and spirits. From this perspective, persons acting religiously are the direct opposite of the kinds of individuals that legal culture seeks to make. Most of what persons acting religiously *do* is designed to transform individuality instead of render it continuous. Religion-like scenes seem crafted to shake autonomous free will instead of buttressing its reliability. As in the Humberto de Campos case, such scenes blur the limits of the natural body and its death instead of taking them as given. Then, too, if legal persons are conceived of as possessing authenticity in the sense of a verifiable continuity between exterior and interior being, religion-like situations propose the opposite, the prospect of an interior different from the exterior. In certain situations, this makes religious persons non- or extralegal persons. For example, in Brazil's 1891 constitution, Catholic monks or *religiosos* were prohibited from voting, along with women, the illiterate, beggars, and minors (those under twenty-one), because "they had renounced their liberty as Individuals."

The example gives pause, but few of us would disagree with the proposition that some form of gatekeeping around legal personhood in civil life is necessary. There are simply so many kinds of persons, human, near-human and nonhuman, colliding in the world that rules of engagement are warranted. Perhaps Hegel's idea of God as "absolute person" and that of animals, or even trees and rivers, as potential legal persons bookend the spectrum under consideration here.[57] Human collectives can, even in highly abstract form, be legal persons, most imposingly in the form of states and corporations.[58] But notions of what constitutes a legal person are at times baroque. Consider the doctrine that the legal person is distinct from the natural person. This doctrine, by which corporations act as legal persons, descends from the thirteenth century and the simple phrase attributed to Pope Innocent IV, "since the College is in corporate matters figured as a person." This underscored that a given community within the church could be collectively represented as a legal person and, moreover, that this personness exists beyond any natural person, as *persona ficta*. It was a spiritual, not a material, reality. In other words, we can read a quasi-mystical quality back into the early legal formulation of incorporation as well as ideas of legal personhood.[59] Legal personhood construed as the multiple masks worn by a single biological body seems to posit an excess of persons against intuitive and inherited ideas of natural personhood.

The discomfiture of some with the recent US Supreme Court decision on the corporate personhood of anonymous collections of political donors is not altogether different than the surprise at hearing of spirits of the dead finding voice in the Brazilian judiciary. Both present the challenge of seeing across a gap—from natural bodies to *personae ficta*, the figure of many persons acting as or *in* one body. They cut against the grain of the more familiar "fabrication of man," as the philosopher of law Pierre Legendre described it: "Biological individuality is not an automatic guarantee of subjective existence. Institutional structures anticipate the subjective construction of individuals by attributing to them ab initio the status, in terms borrowed from Roman law, of a person (persona).

In other words, the institution of genealogy establishes the line of destiny in which, from life to death, the existence of each subject is played out. It establishes the framework of the law of persons. . . . The dogmatic fabrication of man begins at that point, with the tracing of a line of kinship and law's masking of the newborn being as the issue of two speaking subjects."[60] The jump from the sort of fabrication that mostly informs state law to multipersonated and extrabiological bodies may evoke fear, suspicion, disbelief, horror, wonder, or multiple sentiments at once. The response depends, at least in part, on the venue and the associated expectations of personhood involved, legal persons serving, then, as a "device or contrivance for making livable a certain political situation."[61]

Multiperson bodies and the traditions that cultivate them as sources of special revelation pose special challenges and risks for legal institutions and procedures. Because such religions and their manifold invisible agents are prevalent across most of the world, those challenges will have to be addressed. Following Annemarie Mol's work on medicine and the body multiple, I do not hazard here an epistemology—how legal situations come to know personhood—but rather focus on legal *enactment*, the question of how personhood is shaped into a certain form through the procedures of specific cases.[62] Spirits can act in jurisprudence by giving testimony submitted in the form of automatic writing generated elsewhere. They can and do appear in court, then, as documents. But it takes dedicated semiotic work for a nearhuman communiqué to make it to a judge's hands. If it is not on paper, in legal-rational terms it does not exist.[63] As in medicine, in law enactments are shot through with implicit normative judgments, not least with respect to the question of accountable and legally liable or *forensic* personhood. Spirits and spirit testimonies straddle medical and legal versions of the normative.[64] But they are not randomly deployed. A general pattern exists. Spirit testimonies have mostly appeared in cases involving violent crimes tried before a jury, always on behalf of the defendant. Usually they convey a message from a murder victim, vindicating the accused. They seem to reassure jurors or give them license to acquit when they are on the fence or are so inclined but in need of a transcendent or at least a supralocal guarantor of truth. Ismar Garcia interviewed one lawyer-medium who said that, from a spiritist perspective, the reason for these trends is that spirits do not manifest for things as insignificant as property, nor is it in their nature to accuse.[65] In addition, spirit testimonies mostly serve as secondary evidence, a kind of character witness presented to the jury, rather than as direct evidence. At least that is what its defenders claim. The actual influence on a jury is hard to measure, though, in every case I have encountered, spirits weighed in on the winning side.

The cases suggest a question that I hope has by now been made more strange than it was when I began: What, exactly, is a legal person? In other words, what kind of personhood and attendant notion of agency does law require? The case studies reviewed in this chapter show that the legal person is fluid and historically contingent. As we saw in chapter 2, Juca Rosa's possessed personhood, a shape-shifting personhood with saint in the head, rendered him a transgressor and helped placed him outside the law. More recent cases involving spirit testimonies, by contrast, have placed mediums' work and their documentary revelations at the center of at least some legal decisions. All the cases involving possession or mediumship, however, entail and allow a deferral or complicating of individual accountability. How so? First, spirit mediums complicate the time sequence usually required in legal reckonings of causality. For example, in one of the cases, the appearance of a victim's spirit in 1978–79 helped determine what happened in 1976. In the third case here entertained, two letters written in 2006 from a man killed in 2003 helped secure the defendant's innocence. In both instances, spirits acted on legal time and seriality, achieving a temporal collapse by which a victim three years in the grave was enabled to speak in the judicial present.

While personhood ends with natural death, natural death is not, according to the Brazilian civil law verdict in the 1944 Humberto de Campos case, a self-evident or consistent boundary. Certain later cases suggest the possibility of intelligent human agency persisting beyond the body's demise. In multiple homicide cases described above—in 1978, 1984, and 2006—deceased witnesses' testimony was admitted in court after being written down by a different, living human medium's hand.

Most importantly of all, spirit documents act on legal reckonings of *intent*. Spirit testimony is effective in influencing Brazilian juries' understanding of it. José Divino, for example, was shown by a spirit's testimony not to have acted with intent and therefore to be not accountable. Now, to be sure, Brazilian and other legal systems are chock full of subtle adjustments based on putative intent. Religious commitments affect intent and can, as we have seen, change legal status. Then, too, crimes committed in a fit of violent rage after being provoked—when one is not oneself—can reduce a sentence dramatically. Conversely, crimes committed with too much personhood and personal intent—for egoistic motives—can receive particularly harsh sentences. Madness or insanity claims present legal extremes of nonintentional action, and sentences are modified accordingly.[66] There is also the automatism defense, like that applied in the case of José Ferraz. Ferraz's lawyer, Joaquim Borges Carneiro, defended his client against charges of illegal medicine (*curandeirismo*) by saying that Ferraz was not himself the healer but only the medium of the spirits who carried out the work.[67] Karina Buhr was not raped by a priest. Rather—or so the accused claimed, as we saw above—the crime had been committed by the vile spirit, Malandinho.

Spirits present multiple complications of intent: Perpetrators who were hypnotized or possessed may not be liable for their acts as accountable individuals. Or spirits may tell stories or offer legal opinions that, once transformed into the legally recognizable form of a testimonial document, help shape jurors' opinions of a defendant's intent. Given all these complications of intent and the measuring of defendants' interior states that they require, spirits may be seen less as a full departure from other legal calibrations of the internal person than as an especially complex problem of how to gauge inner motivations.

Perhaps, then, we can use these cases to think comparatively about the issue of legal personhood. Charles Taylor famously argued that the Western individual is characterized by the notion of the buffered self, a form of personhood that is impermeable to possession by external agents and, therefore, by virtue of its very insularity, at least relatively enduring over time.[68] The temporal dimension of enduring accountability is key to the very notion of *identity*. The legal historian Susanna Blumenthal described the "default legal person" in the United States as something much like Taylor's buffered self.[69] Versions of a default legal person exist in every national legal culture, and legal systems may even require a default legal person in order to function at all. Lacking one, they apply techniques to create one. One method of creating a default legal person is by contrasting him (and it has mostly been a him) with the "weak spirits" that appear in, say, the descriptions of Charcot's patients, Juca Rosa's initiates, those easily seduced by Ajeeb, or devotees of Anastácia or, for that matter, in Frazer's accounting of primitive magic, Kant's discussion of Swedenborg, or Locke's possessed Brazilian parrot. In the writings of figures like Hobbes, Locke, and Kant, the accountable individual person acquired its silhouette over and against another type, namely, the "dividual," or the *very permeable person*.[70]

Very permeable persons must be made or translated into legal persons if and when they enter the purview of the state. Some argue that legal culture even requires this submission, a disfiguring rite of passage. As Judith Butler wrote: "To be dominated by a power external to oneself is a familiar and agonizing form power takes. To find, however, that what 'one' is, one's very formation as a subject, is in some sense dependent on that very power is quite another."[71] Butler's description has often been too casually cited, but what intrigues me is how, like Taylor's description of the buffered self or Blumenthal's of the default legal person, it plays frictionally over and against the figure of the possessed. In Butler's formulation, becoming a political subject is every bit as much of a possession (and dispossession) as discovering a god in one's body.[72] Colin Dayan calls the attempt to define and distinguish the legal individual an *idiom of servility*: "State-sanctioned degradation in America is propelled by a focus on personal identity, the terms by which personality is recognized, threatened, or removed. I treat the legal history of dispossession as a continuum along which bodies and spirits are remade over time."[73] Dayan seeks leverage by assessing how the spirit of law and laws about spirits were intertwined. The critique seems to be that personal identity is always less than clear but that certain editions of opacity—say, corporate personhood or the legal extension of one's name as a commercial domain—are given a legal pass more readily than others, say, those related to Afro-Brazilian spirit possession.

While I agree with that assessment, to leave it at that strikes me as too easy. After all, most everyone views spirit possession and other mediations—at least when applied by subaltern groups like Afro-Brazilian temples of Candomblé—with sympathy. Spirit possession can interrupt a given oppressive frame of life and express contradiction, give voice, or offer respite. It offers a platform to show that, just as the state is split, so also is the citizen, who (like the state) mostly performs reason and reliable personhood while holding in reserve the possibility of resistance, whether acted on or not. This holding in reserve of another, internal sovereignty is important.[74] We can conceive of spirit testimonies in court serving a similar purpose, holding a sovereignty in reserve from the fully subjectified citizen-person.

But what shall we do with spirits and spirit documents when they are wielded by the wealthy and powerful, as in the Brazilian associations of spiritist judges? These present-day spiritist judges are already cloaked in institutional power and hardly need superhuman avatars to further extend themselves and their judgments across time and space. They deserve our critique, attention, and concern. For, as it turns out, just as we seem to need venues of nearhuman attraction and automaticity, we also need domains of accountable personhood to know who pulled the trigger, who is responsible for the child, who committed rape, who signed the contract, who wrote the book.

Even more: Who can decide exactly *which* dead have the right to speak, in law or elsewhere? In Machado's end-of-the-year address to the Academy of Letters in 1897, he invoked the responsibility to language, to tradition, and to the dead. "The authority of the dead does not afflict and is definitive."[75] But I am not so sure. The dead can be killers, especially in the form of a legal document.

Conclusion
Agency and Automatic Freedom

I looked in the mirror, moved from side to side, stepped back, waved, smiled, and the glass reflected everything. I was no longer an automaton, I was a living being.

MACHADO DE ASSIS, "The Mirror" ("O espelho"), 1882

"The Mirror." A usually taciturn fellow, Jacobina, describes a new theory of the soul to a group of friends in the middle of the night. Each person carries within him two souls, he expounds, "one that looks from the inside out and the other that looks from the outside in":

Now, the external soul can be a spirit, a fluid, a man (or many men), an object, even an action. There are cases, for example, of a simple shirt button being a person's external soul, or it could be the polka, a card game, a book, a machine, a pair of boots, a song, a drum, etc. Clearly, the function of this second soul, like the first, is to transmit life; together they complete the man, who is, metaphysically speaking, an orange. Whoever loses one half, automatically loses half of his existence. . . . There are gentlemen, for example, whose external soul in their earliest years is a rattle or a hobbyhorse, but later on life it will be their seat on the board of a charity. For my part, I know a lady—and a charming creature she is too—who changes her external soul five or six times a year.[1]

Jacobina continues on to his main proof case for the theory, his own story. His grave mien claims full attention; he threatens to leave if his friends' focus flags. They lean in, rapt. He begins. As a young man he was made a lieutenant, a life-changing event for a poor lad from the country. His aunt and extended family treated him differently, even calling him Mr. Lieutenant. Slaves looked at him and spoke to him with more respect than before. His aunt ordered them to move an antique mirror that once belonged to the Portuguese court to his bedroom so that he could see himself in uniform and adjust to his new status. One day, however, the entire household abruptly departed to attend to a distant daughter's imminent death and funeral. Jacobina was left with only the slaves to flatter him. A day later, the slaves too fled the plantation, and he was completely alone. Being a lieutenant did not mean anything without someone there to admire it. Jacobina began to fall into psychic illness: "I was like a dead man walking, a sleepwalker, a mechanical toy." He scribbled on paper without awareness, like an automatic writer. As he watched himself in the mirror, his body turned fluid, dispersed, a mass of shapeless lines. He began to go mad, as though his soul had fled along with the slaves. Finally, in desperation, he remembered his uniform. Hurriedly he dressed, then lifted his head: "I looked in the mirror, moved from side to side, stepped back, waved, smiled, and the glass reflected everything. I was no longer an automaton; I was a living being."[2] The uniform reshaped him; the mirror recognized him.

The listeners came back to themselves, as though they had entered something like a trance during the telling. Jacobina was already gone.

Machado too reflects and recognizes. He observes quietly, Virgil above the fray. But he was also *in* it. As much as anyone in late nineteenth-century Brazil, he occupied a position between categories. Surely he felt his doubleness and the agent ambiguity of his own skin. He was the son of a housepainter and the grandson of a freed slave, a mulato (as he was and is known in Brazil) married to a white Portuguese woman from the Azores island of São Miguel, and the first president of Brazil's Academy of Letters. He was also a critic of slavery, but he mostly addressed it only indirectly. Slavery is determinant in his work, wrote Roberto Schwarz, but slaves rarely appear as agents.[3] Yet he was a master of the subtle critique of "seigneurial will"— how it emptied others of their own autonomy when it could be exercised only through masters' concessions.[4]

Machado was a boy who studied at a girls' school, where his mother was employed, and never graduated, but he was among the best-read people in Brazil.[5] He was a man who never traveled outside Brazil, but he learned French from a baker and then English and German and studied Greek late in life. He was a literary celebrity with a lively social life, but he was also awkward, reticent, stuttering, skinny, bespectacled, and occasionally convulsive.[6] He was a master of Portuguese but a Francophile. In the 1860s, he translated several French plays for performance. He received newspapers to keep up with news from France.[7] He was a Francophile, yes, but one who loved Shakespeare best. He was a man who loved children but had none of his own, who adored his wife, Carolina, yet may have had affairs with actresses. He was an irreligious, even antireligious freethinker, yet he filled his work with religion-like scenes. In his most famous novel, *The Posthumous Memoirs of Bras Cuba*, the narrator's delirium, hypnotism, and twenty-minute-long trance launch the three hundred pages that follow. During the episode, Bras Cuba describes his idée fixe and his monomania—diagnoses minted at the Salpêtrière—that frame the narration told from beyond the grave.[8]

Machado's very body sutures together the chapters of the book. In 1869, Dom Pedro II bestowed on him the Imperial Order of the Rose, and Machado knew and admired the emperor as a man of learning.[9] As a journalist himself who got his start writing for the Rio daily *Diário das notícias* and then wrote columns for the *Gazeta de notícias* and other papers, he surely followed the case of Juca Rosa. He would have visited the Church of the Rosary many times, the site where Anastácia came to life, as it was one of the most important cathedrals in the city. By the late 1890s, in spite of his advanced age surely he passed Fred Figner on Ouvidor Street, where each, after his particular vocation, presided—Machado in words, Figner in sound and image—perhaps exchanging a nod or a handshake. He knew Ajeeb and thought him a point of civic pride since he mentioned him in print. And he discussed spiritism more than thirty times in his newspaper chronicles, mostly with acid wit. Spiritism has multiple faults, he wrote. When you want to talk to your old pal Vasconcelos, the spirits instead give you a mossback blowhard like Nostradamus. He called spiritism "a factory of idiots and psychotics [*alienados*]" and a maker of dementia.[10] He satirized psychiatry in similarly brutal fashion in a novella set in the Hospício Pedro II—a building he must have visited at least once on a day when it was open to the public—but was far more sympathetic to curandeiros, "the original cells of medicine."[11] As a founder of the Academy of Letters, Machado occupied seat 24; a few years after his death, Humberto de Campos moved to Rio and was voted into seat 20. Though Machado and Humberto never crossed paths, their Immortal seats were just adjacent. Machado bridges chapters 1–5 not only in the epigraphs but also in the very cells of his skin that remain at each site or event described in this book. What can he say from this privileged, posthumous vantage?

Machado himself thought that everything interesting about him was in his writing, not in his life. He hoped that his words could serve as avatars, extenders, and scramblers of his own person, to that end even sometimes writing, like Chico Xavier, under a pseudonym, "X."[12] Like such absent-present authorship, his stories offer scenes and situations of agent ambiguity, the elementary forms of religion-like life. The automaton, the psychotic, the spiritist, the testimony of the dead, animals that speak—all are mirrors of the human that, by pushing the terms of agency off balance, unleash new possibilities for what the human can be.[13] Writing is another such prismatic mirror, a technology for crafting religion-like scenes and situations to bend the terms of agency. Machado's writing did this.

The lines from "The Mirror" that constitute the epigraph to this conclusion pose a curious tension between self and mirror, between self and the nearhuman likeness that appears there. The mirror was, by the end of the nineteenth century, a familiar tool in the study of self-awareness and personhood. Machado's tale followed in the wake of Darwin's observations of children's first recognition of themselves in mirrors and preceded later theories of the mirror as necessary to ego formation, especially as proposed by Jacques Lacan.[14] The protagonist moves from automaton to living being, but the metamorphosis does not happen through his own subjective effort or will. It happens, Machado seems to suggest, in an interaction with at least three other actants: a uniform, an ancient mirror, and an automaton version of the protagonist himself. This latter is a two-dimensional iconic resemblance, a "me" that imitates but lacks intent. In the exchange that ends the story—one that anticipates the contract in Oscar Wilde's 1890 *The Picture of Dorian Gray*—the mirror image becomes the automaton while the Lieutenant's living body turns human again. If the protagonist is a living being, however, he remains split and doubled, alive and human only through a complex alchemy like that in Latour's description of the Candomblé initiate being made in relation to the *orixá* seated in her head and much like the ritual work of Juca Rosa. The initiate "receives [its] autonomy by giving the autonomy it does not possess to entities that come to life thanks to this conferral."[15]

It is not as though there is no individual agency involved. After all, at some point the Lieutenant must decide to don the uniform and look in the mirror, giving full attention to the reflected image. Yet even his act of looking in the mirror carries within it the residue of previous actions of others, like the words and admiring looks of the slaves and the aunt who addressed him with such deference and respect in the past. They helped constitute Mr. Lieutenant, the character who rushed back into his body as he gazed into the mirror. Even this apparently human agency, then, ends up as nearhuman, jointly made between two bodies, a current flashing between flesh, its two-dimensional mirror image, and a history.

That broad theme runs through all the chapters here. Ajeeb, sitting atop a mysterious closed box, joined the Turk, mechanics, skill at chess and checkers, the politics of immigration, leisure, magic, and the questions of movement and choice. Rosalie wove together mystical visions, multipersonated bodies, crucifixion, the spectacle of the Tuesday lectures, photography, psychiatry, gender, and the animal edges of the human. Juca Rosa combined in his extended person the issues of fetishism, spirits, sex, Africanness, race, truth and fraud, and the charisma and authority of a human possessed. All the nearhuman protagonists of this book were subjected to radical restraint—in space, in possibilities of motion, in choices about how to occupy time, in available relationships and forms of social capital. Yet act they did and presumably also in ways that far exceed the historical traces we have of them. We have no records of Juca Rosa during his six years of prison labor, for example. He must have found new, subtle ways to extend his personhood by proxy, even under duress and without the help of photography. We can easily imagine that, his reputation preceding him, he was able to create informal exchanges of power with his guards, many of whom probably knew him by name, were engaged with Afro-Brazilian religions, and shared parts of his history.

I imagine him surviving in terms set out in Lorna Rhodes's contemporary ethnography of prison life, in which incarceration becomes a microcosm of religion-like situations of agent ambiguity, a hardened but nevertheless riven division between agents and automatons.[16] Prisoners' ability to act is tightly circumscribed, so screwed down that the drama of agency collapses into a very small orbit of things and possible moves: the meal tray and whether one passes it back through the slot, or retains it (leading to the inevitable violent restraint), or gives it back with reluctant pressure (a middle degree of resistance). Agency can be realized only in and through the thin repertories that are available, with the result that juxtapositions between the automatic and will are negotiated with the simplest of moves and the smallest set of props. Through this compression, each single material exchange generates a radical surplus of power that Rhodes calls *uncanny*, much like the Lieutenant turning before an ancient, possibly magic mirror or, to return to examples used by Jentsch and Freud, the uncertainty of whether the beloved is a person or an automaton.

Machado's story opens out to a new engagement with an enduring problem. *Agency* as an analytic has long been saddled with a stilted version of the individual. Erving Goffman called this imagined individual a *sacred object*, a discrete, autonomous god. Charles Taylor's polemical *A Secular Age* linked the rise of agency to nothing less than the death of that god and the rise of a newborn savior, the buffered self, the individual that members of political society now must serve. "Free agency," Taylor writes, "is central to their self-understanding [referring to the proponents of this society]. The emphasis on rights, and the primacy of freedom among them . . . reflects the holders' sense of their own agency, and of the situation which that agency demands in the world, viz. freedom."[17] Individual agency is tied, for Taylor, to a "closed-world system" emptied of lively mirrors, photographs, drawings, animals, and automatons.

Agency's emphasis on the individual serves certain projects and groups well but pushes others out of view. That is why Talal Asad and Walter Johnson each noted a hint of self-congratulatory praise, even paternalism, attached to the idea. Johnson likened it to a Trojan horse that smuggles in emphases on free will, choice, independence, and autonomy. But these rarely fit the history of most people in history, especially slaves. Slaves did and do many things—love, suffer, plant, nurse, dance, wash, talk—but mostly these fit the rubric of agency awkwardly. Agency, Johnson accused, blinds scholars to collectively made forms of solidarity or thriving. Worse still, it can serve as an attempt at self-positioning in relation to slave history. Yes, I may be a privileged person studying people with few opportunities, but at least I am restoring or giving them agency. That makes it look like a new version of the seigneurial will depicted by Machado: agency as a gift given, a concession to the barely deserving.[18]

One reason I have tried to unhinge agency from the individual is that, as I have shown, agency is always hybrid, built of interactions between humans, nearhumans, and nonhuman things. Another reason is that, if the notion is that the individual is a god, its own religion-like thing, so to speak, religious persons seem awfully devoted to projects of denying and undoing that notion of solitary individual power. Instead, they are engaged in doing things that gods, spirits, and ancestors tell them to and narrating their everyday lives in those terms. Think of spirit possession, spirit writing, revival jerking, speaking in tongues, ritual demonstrations of extraordinary resistance to pain, or even being inspired by an unexpected voice, stricken by a muse that set your painting or your writing on its way. All of us have witnessed and some may have experienced being at times and in part managed by nonhuman beings or, put differently, attuning the experience of the body to the question of the other, an impinging external force. Its most familiar and paradigmatic cipher, the possessed body, pushes back against assumptions that the quests for voice, status, autonomy, or power are universal.

Yet, whether asserted or effaced, the individual remains part of the game of agency, however dubious and opaque. We know this to be a mistake but too easily forget how suspect the individual already was in the time of Juca Rosa, the two Rosalies, and Jean-Martin Charcot. Edward B. Tylor, writing in 1871, already mused on involuntary dreams and how they motivated theories of the soul.[19] At around the same time, Marx described man as "infused" by the spirit of the state; a bit later, Durkheim wrote of one who "even feels possessed by a moral force greater than he," society; and Freud used possession by spirits as an image of personality's multiple composition by the conscious and unconscious, manifest and latent selves.[20] We are born into a language we did not choose and vulnerable to the address of others in ways beyond our control. The "I" is always "dispossessed by the very social conditions of its emergence."[21]

Religion-like events help correct the mistaken dependency on the individual. That is one of the reasons the founders of the social sciences like Marx, Freud, and Simmel, not otherwise especially inclined toward religion, gave it their full attention. Religion-like situations come into being when agency is ambiguous—when the "I" is dispossessed—and they also craft the conditions for that to happen. But never fully. Too much individual will, too obvious an agent and source of agency, and a religion-like situation collapses into something else, a tragic or triumphant kind of event. Too little, too much sheer violence, and automaticity overwhelms and overdetermines agent ambiguity. Only think of Franz Kafka's 1914 short story "In the Penal Colony," which describes a punitive stabbing machine named "The Harrow," used for ritual applications. The machine is supposed to penetrate a captive slowly, inspiring religious ecstasy after six hours of pain and transfiguration after twelve hours, just prior to death. In Kafka's telling, the machine goes haywire, and the Officer who sought transfiguration via his own beatific suicide suffers a banal industrial execution, the harrow misfiring and stabbing him without mercy so that he bleeds to death without ecstasy or epiphany and dies like a butchered pig. No machine magic here, only brute force. No agent ambiguity. No religion.

Religion-like scenes grow from the soil caked between assertions of and uncertainties about who and what is acting. To be sure, there are other versions of agent ambiguity besides that of the mediated self. There is, for example, automaton agency, when nature acts of its own accord in fate-changing ways, as Aristotle posed it. When humans seem close to machines, or animals, or both at once, in Descartes's frame. When custom or habit or tradition acts through bodies, for Pascal or, much later, Bourdieu. When the state acts in us, as Hobbes and then Marx pointed out in their very different ways. In the agency of fate, as Simmel described: "Because of its externality, all 'fate' contains something that is not comprehensible to us, and in this it acquires the religious cachet."[22] When bodies are hidden in other bodies, one possessing or encompassing the other, or when multiple persons act in one body, as we saw at the Salpêtrière and the Hospício Pedro II. When larger-than-life heroes take on godlike silhouettes in the darkened cinema or on the field and become models to mimic. These are religion-like scenes, situations, and events all. The elementary forms of religion are made present whenever automatic action and willed action together welter, placing each into doubt and debate.

That things like the Lieutenant's mirror and uniform also act is by now a familiar track in the analysis of agency.[23] And it is likewise a familiar move to observe that, in religion-like situations, agency is often deferred, mediated, and renounced.[24] In "The Mirror," however, Machado points to an issue crosscutting even theories of agency that problematize the individual. If the self and the agentive act are always hybrid transactions, *intra-actions*, to take Barad's phrase, what exactly is this avowed self that is or is not present? Even deferred or renounced agency would seem to require a strong notion of an individual that can then be renounced or amplified, deferred or distributed. But what does it even mean for a self to be present in an action or not?[25]

In terms of the twentieth-century scholarly activation of this modern individual, so far as I have been able to discern it was Talcott Parsons who founded the contemporary uses of *agency* and led us down this path.[26] Here is the example he provided. When we say that a man has an IQ of 120, we describe a quality called *intelligence*. However: "When . . . we say, 'he gave the right answer to the question' we describe a performance, which is thus a process of change in his relation to a situational object, the questioner, which can be ascribed to his 'agency.'"[27] Unlike structural functionalism, which emphasized closed systems or so-called great man histories starring heroic individuals, agency called attention to the tension between constraint and action. Clifford Geertz, who was Parsons's student, began to apply the analytic of *agency* by the 1960s—certainly by the 1966 "Religion as a Cultural System"—and it is roughly this opposition between structure and agency that Pierre Bourdieu deployed with enormous influence in the 1977 *Outline of a Theory of Practice*.[28] Those were perhaps the two books that most crossed disciplines, read by historians, anthropologists, and religionists of all stripes, and dragged *agency* into standard currency.

Between theories of practice, gender studies, and the postcolonial age, everything was turned toward agency and for important reasons and to good effect: to give voice to historical and anthropological subjects who had mostly been lost or unheard. Within the discipline of history, meanwhile, agency rode the new wave of microhistory. Religionists eagerly devoured texts like Le Roy Ladurie's *Montaillou* (1975), which gave a window into religious nonconformity in a medieval village and showed how weak allegedly hegemonic Christendom actually was on the ground, and Carlo Ginzburg's *The Cheese and the Worms* (1976), which pulled a poor dissident miller named Mennochio out from the inquisitorial records.[29] The attention to everyday, lived experience and lived religion was born out of this investment. When Ginzburg's book first appeared, the term *microhistory* did not yet exist; neither did *lived religion* (other than in, e.g., the French *la religion vécue*). Microhistory, together with agency, was still shiny and new. As Ginzburg wrote in the preface to the 2013 edition of *The Cheese and the Worms*: "The persecuted and the vanquished, whom many historians dismissed as marginal and usually altogether ignored, were here the focus."[30]

The challenge arises, however, in that the individual and her agency remain pivotal to the historical project in narrowly human ways, so to speak. Historians remain challenged by the idea of expanding agency beyond the flesh to the nearhuman. Listen to Constantin Fasolt: "To study history in order to produce an adequate account of the past is in and of itself to take a stand in favor of individual autonomy against all other possibilities, including, but by no means limited to, providence and custom."[31] Dipesh Chakrabarty famously described the conundrum that historians want to give agency to their subjects, an agency that those subjects refuse in the name of gods, spirits, kinship, and custom.[32] Loosening the bounds of the individual agent seeking to shift the conditions of life—a hard-won victory of social history—seems an anxiety-inducing concession. It may, nevertheless, be necessary. For where are these individuals, these buffered selves? The anthropologist Stephan Palmié considers this figure of the autonomous individual agent a North Atlantic fiction, part of Occidental mythology.[33] The division of the world between so-called agents and automatons seems above all a device for building centers walled off from peripheries. Given its substantial liabilities, it is tempting to give up on *agency* in favor of simply *agents* as a more capacious category that includes the near- and the nonhuman. After all, *agency* does not really exist in either Portuguese or French, other than as a secondary import from Anglophone social sciences.[34] But there are ways to move forward other than jettisoning worn-out terms, as though we had the power to do so.

To that end, let me offer some modest suggestions. To begin, we should think of religion-like situations as shifters of agency but not in any unidirectional way. Religion-like situations do not always diffuse individual agency, but they are always playing across the question of the agent. For example, David Mosse juxtaposed the ritual idioms of *confession* and *possession* as enacted in the same Indian town. Jesuit confessions draw people toward declarations of personal morality, the need for a clear conscience, and individual accountability. In the same site, however, through events in which people are possessed by an array of Hindu demons, gods, and goddesses, their bodies are temporarily made into public spaces into which individual action disappears. Personal problems become group afflictions, the very opposite of Jesuit confessional practice. Confession, on the one hand; possession, on the other.[35] In both cases, attributions of agency are being moved, allocated, questioned, divided, or consolidated. The juxtaposition between these modes and the movement across them generates religion-like experience.

Religion-like scenes and situations like those presented in chapters 1–5 above all put agency in motion by crafting scenes of transformation and uncertainty. Religion has to do with playing across differences in the forms of presence perceived to act. In other words, it is less about the individual self or its lack than it is about the movement *between* agency and automaticity that causes presence—whether an infilling of self or of an outside power—to become discernible. Then, too, the narration of agency and its lack is part and parcel of its constitution in a given event. As Kristina Wirtz explored in the Cuban context, it is the very ambiguity of deciding what happened in a given ritual event—its "discursive wake" and "interpretive ferment"—that constitutes much of religious speech.[36] Machado's story points to the techniques of making and unmaking agency and automaticity in discourse. Jacobina is persuasive because he rarely speaks, because it is the middle of the night, because he insists on being taken seriously, because he is sincere, because he moves from anecdotes to an uncanny inflection point from his own life. He creates the moment in part with the content of the story and in part through his performance.[37]

Second, if religion-like situations put agency in motion, they do so in very different ways. We should see agency as a comparative question, not as an answer. How do people allocate causality or responsibility? What do those allocations say about the sources, places, and directions of power? We should pay attention to all the varieties of action that exist between the myth of individual agency and sheer automatism. Put differently, we can investigate the varieties of agency instead of assuming we know what it is. The study of religion seems uniquely equipped to do this, to explore hybrid forms of acting. We can compare how different traditions achieve and perform agent ambiguity, the kinds of spaces, materials, and modes of action it employs, and how it is authorized or rejected. By now, scholarship on agency has fragmented into many foci: on political agency, constitutional agency, aesthetic agency, the agency of things, the agency of a mode of production, animal agency, delegated agency, corporate agency, state agency, divine agency, etc. Surely the forms of renounced agency, nonagency and agent ambiguity are as varied. Many are the tools applied in religion-like situations to generate agent ambiguity: dreams, spirit possession, concealment that announces possible revelation (the door on the closed compartment, the third eye painted on the forehead), or the voice distancing that communicates, "It is not me who speaks" but a god.[38]

Third, we need to make a clear distinction between agency as a feature or quality of all human action and agency as something one has to a greater or lesser degree. In the first sense, *agency* is an analytic feature of every event. In the second sense, it refers to the relative amount of control exerted over one's own or a group's life circumstances. We should be cautious, however, comparing slaves' or concentration camp victims' agency in the same terms as we do Norwegian graduate students' agency. We can ask of any person or act what its agency is and where it is. At the same time, the fact that agency is always present as a dimension of an event does not mean that agency in the second sense is equally present everywhere. Rather, it is present in varying degrees. Moreover, distinct forms of agency can offset or even work against one another. The assertion of one's individual will and autonomy can diminish the capacity to act in concert with others. The assumption of a position of agency in one scenario requires a departure from previous conditions that had offered a different capacity to act.[39] Agency deployed to reproduce familiar schemata is pitted against agency applied to effect change or transformation. There are multiple agencies—sets of schemata linked to a set of resources—in play at any given time. This is true even within a single multiperson, as Rosalie, Juca Rosa, Anastácia, Ajeeb, and Chico have each after their own fashion helped us see.

* * *

If we want to study lived religion, *la religion vécue*, in the world rather than only in its familiar institutions and most familiar channels—church, mosque, prayer, belief, gods, *churinga*, mana, *ashe, wakan*—we need to widen the aperture to take in the religion-like features of life, all of life, including nearhuman beings like Ajeeb, the two Rosalies, and Slave Anastácia. Religion-like figures and situations are constructive, a moment of regaining humanness, as in the story of the mirror. Think again about the paintings of Bispo do Rosário or Hilma af Klint, with which this long tour began. Beginning in 1896, Hilma painted fluently and automatically in response to the instruction of her spirit guides. When Rudolf Steiner told her in 1908 to forget the otherworldly and follow her own intuition, calling on an individual self, she lost her ability for four years. She forfeited her "automatic freedom," to borrow William James's phrase. The weight of individual agency left her as paralyzed as Rosalie Leroux on her cross. Only an ambiguous agency, an unwilled, automatic interface with spirits, gave her license to create. Perhaps the capacity to craft such scenes is part of our necessary human equipment or the equipment that makes us human at all. That is, to be human is to be able to imagine and model non- and nearhumanness, to play at being another. Such play allows a shift of frame, even healing: *I was no longer an automaton, I was a living being*. Seeing the human refracted—as a photograph, a drawing, or an icon, as a chess-playing machine, as a spirit writer, as a legal document, as a mirror image—transforms. It can disfigure, but it can also cure. It can be a source of creation. Playing at not being oneself becomes, paradoxically, a path to identity.[40] Humans even devise games for playing out *other* beings' agency. That is, humanness includes, among other things, the capacity to play at other beings playing at being other. In *The Expression of the Emotions*, Darwin describes showing a monkey a fake human—a dressed-up doll—to see what would happen.[41] Children in Brazil sometimes play at being possessed by *orixás*.[42] This can then work recursively, as when terms of agency play infiltrate ritual practice. Thus Rita Laura Segato points to the arrival of a *santo* in Afro-Brazilian spirit possession that evokes a sense of one's own body as a nearhuman doll, even as Juca Rosa's clients experienced him at once as a spirit and as a photograph. In this scenario, humans imagine gods playing with humans as though they were toys (figure c.1).[43]

But there is also risk. I cannot quite do without the agentive individual, and, now that I am pressed here, I do not think we should try. The peril of bringing the religious prestige of automaticity into sites requiring autonomous individual agents appeared in chapter 5, when legal outcomes were suffused with the automatically transcribed voices of the dead. Possibility becomes danger in situations that require a different threshold of reliable personhood, when only an individual will do. Hannah Arendt warned against the loss of that kind of personhood, after which all that would remain would be "sheer automatic functioning," the last stage of the laboring society.[44] "Dazed, 'tranquilized,' functional," a sad remainder consisting of nothing but citational agency or the lateral agency of bare survival.[45] Even more ominous is the figure of the automaton not as self-acting mechanism but as a body directed by an outside force. Think of Dostoevsky's Grand Inquisitor as inscribed in the character Ivan proclaiming that what people most desire is to be relieved of their unbearable freedom.[46] A plague of leaders only too happy to oblige now spans the globe—in Brazil, Hungary, Poland, Israel, the United States, Great Britain, Venezuela, Russia, Zimbabwe, China, Turkey, the Philippines. Politicians offer to relieve citizens of their freedoms by claiming special dispensation, privilege, and divine right. Charismatic political and religious leaders urge their jumped-up followers to "step over to the next plane"[47] or burn it all down. An automatic writer ventriloquizes a corpse to promote a certain legal verdict. One reason to pay close attention to religion-like scenes and situations is to patrol the boundary between scenes of healing and inspiration, on the one hand, and scenes

FIGURE C.1. A human plays at being a soothsaying automaton named Zoltan, New Orleans, Mardi Gras, February 2018. Photograph by Emily Floyd.

of authoritarianism and the evasion of accountability, on the other.[48] The trick is to recognize the difference and to be able to calibrate needed thresholds of reliable personhood to a given context. Law and politics require a different version of humanness than do music, graphic arts, and religion. Academe probably falls somewhere in between.

Machado took a normative position on automaticity in its creative and malign modes. He was more sympathetic to curandeiros like Afro-Brazilian priest-healers than he was to elite spiritists.[49] For the latter's stagey mediations of Nostradamus and Napoléon he had only scorn. The former, figures like Juca Rosa, he saw as potential cells of medical knowledge. I share his perspective. We should beware of those in power who claim special knowledge, god-men (and it is almost always men) prosthetically extending their power. On the other hand, we should be receptive to and ready to learn from subaltern ritual crafts of automatism that seek to shift the conditions of life, however temporarily or tenuously, and see what those visions hold.

The distinction between automatic and intentional actors is historically *made* by differences in power, a distinction that then seduces and attracts. Anastácia was a collectively imagined slave-woman made into an automaton. Ajeeb condensed figurations of Ottoman Empire immigrants and their place in Brazil. Juca Rosa's photograph exerted automatic force on the margins of medicine, in secret ritual gatherings. Monkey Rosalie and Rosalie Leroux were both cast out of the former lives and contained by walls, made into pets that amused and inspired through their near-humanness. They were converted into automatic actors, bent under the scrutiny of captors who then, in comparison, imagined themselves autonomous and free. "History makes the history-makers [agents]," Marshall Sahlins wrote.[50] They never simply exist. History also makes the automatons. Such visions of divisions endure and take on a life of their own, producing the very conditions they claim merely to describe.

And it is not as though the classifications *the human, the nearhuman,* and *the nonhuman* are going away. If the late nineteenth century and the early twentieth announced one age of automaticity, we are now fully embarked on another, and the risks are even higher. Agency is increasingly unclear. A new virus has utterly enfolded the conditions of life, acting invisibly and transpersonally, a horrific new and frightening near- and interhuman agent. The global economy acts mostly on its own, announcing its next move in dazzling green-line tickers that, like a myth, descend from nowhere, documents with no author. Mass data processors anticipate the next clicks of your keyboard, guiding your fingers and views to anticipated destinations, and steering them from others. Amazon employees earning a pitiful hourly wage carrying out computer work now outsourced to humans are called *mechanical Turkers,* the new, live version of Ajeeb. (Apply today at MTurk.com!) A president just called his former assistant, an African American woman, a dog. A horse sued his owner for negligence—through a document drafted by the extended hand of a human scribe—but was denied legal standing on the grounds of insufficient legal personhood. An Afro-Brazilian soccer player on a field in Spain was harassed by thrown bananas and monkey hoots launched by fans hoping to render him nearhuman.[51] (He picked up the banana and ate it without a word, launching the international meme, "We are all monkeys.") Filmmakers fidget with the parameters of the uncanny valley, calibrating how humanish an animal or machine protagonist needs to be to attract viewers or how nonhuman a monster can become in order sufficiently to repulse and terrify; either will turn a profit if it is just human enough but not too human. The negotiations are not new, and they will never be done, at least not before the human adventure itself wheezes adieu.

Automatic nearhumans press close. They insist on your attention, press into your hand and ear, promise marvels. They will not stop, and the truth is that we need them as much as they need us. We love them because, as our photographic negatives, they make us into the agents we otherwise could never be. And, should they ever disappear or become too human, there are always more and other people available to convert into automatons. Students of the history of science and of religion should pay close attention, not because religion is in and of itself essential to humanness, as thinkers from Sepúlveda to Herder had it, but because religion-like scenes and situations are where the borders dividing humans from nearhumans and nonhumans are consequentially worried, played across, and affixed.

Notes

Introduction

1. Frederico Morais, *Arthur Bispo do Rosário: Arte além da loucura* (Rio de Janeiro: NAU Editora, 2013), 23–24. See also Hugo Denizart, dir., *O prisioneiro de passage* (Brasilia: Ministry of Health, 1982); Dado Abreu, "Arthur Bispo do Rosário: A arte contemporânia na delicada fronteira entre genialidade e a loucura," *Revista fator* 12 (2014): 6–9; and Kaira Marie Cabañas, "A contemporaneidade de Bispo," *ARS São Paulo* 16, no. 32 (2018): 47–80. Unless otherwise indicated, all translations from non-English sources are mine.

2. Quoted in Kate Kellaway, "Hilma af Klint: A Painter Possessed," *The Guardian*, February 26, 2016, https://www.theguardian.com/artanddesign/ 2016/feb/21/hilma-af-klint-occult-spiritualism-abstract-serpentine -gallery.

3. Pascal Rousseau, "Premonitory Abstraction: Mediumism, Automatic Writing, and Anticipation in the Work of Hilma af Klint," in Iris Müller Westermann with Jo Widoff, eds., *Hilma af Klint: A Pioneer of Abstraction, Exhibition Catalogue* (Stockholm: Moderna Museet, 2013), 161–75.

4. For example, Hobbes writes: "For he is free to do a thing, that may do it if he have the will to do it, and may forbear, if he have the will to forbear." Thomas Hobbes, *The English Works of Thomas Hobbes of Malmesbury*, vol. 5, *The Questions concerning Liberty, Necessity, and Chance*, ed. Sir William Molesworth (London: John Bohn, 1841), 38. John Locke described agents' liberty in similar terms: "*Liberty* . . . is the power a Man has to do or forbear doing any particular Action, according as its doing or forbearance has the actual preference in the Mind, which is the same thing as to say, according as he himself *wills* it." John Locke, *The Works of John Locke, Esq.*, vol. 1, bk. 2, *An Essay concerning Human Understanding* (London: A. Churchill, A. Manship, 1722), 101. Leibniz's *Theodicy* (1710) described human morality as dependent on free will. Free will includes three features: the *spontaneity* of action, i.e., the assurance that action originates from the one who acts; the *contingency* of action, i.e., the fact that other courses not taken were possible; and the *rationality* of action, i.e., the guarantee that

the action follows from the deliberation of alternatives. The maintenance of these three qualities of action can ensure the maintenance of law. Gottfried Leibniz, *Theodicy: Essays on the Goodness of God, the Freedom of Man, and the Origin of Evil*, ed. with an introduction by Austin M. Farrer, trans. E. M. Huggard (Peru, IL: Open Court, 1985). At the end of the nineteenth century, will is conceptualized in medical terms in relation to automatism. For example, here is Daniel Hack Tuke: "An automaton is substituted for the true volitional self. The will is the slave of a dream or a suggestion." Daniel Hack Tuke, *Sleep-Walking and Hypnotism* (London: J. & A. Churchill, 1884), 4. Or see Pierre Janet, *Néuroses et idées fixes* (Paris: Félix Alcan, 1898), 390–91, where "l'acte volontaire" is juxtaposed with "phénomènes automotiques." The move toward the calculating of will in relation to the automatic is what this book explores.

5. David Graeber and Marshall Sahlins describe metahumans as parts of a "cosmic polity" in which humans are situated, a polity "populated by beings of human attributes and metahuman powers who govern people's fate. In the form of gods, ancestors, ghosts, demons, species-masters, and the animistic beings embodied in the creatures and features of nature, these metapersons are endowed with far-reaching powers of human life and death" and "control of the conditions of the cosmos" and are, therefore, "the all-round arbiters of human welfare and illfare." David Graeber and Marshall Sahlins, *On Kings* (Chicago: HAU, 2017), 2.

6. Possession is an *event*, wrote Michel de Certeau: "The possession rekindles former conflicts, but transposes them. . . . It reveals something that existed, but it also, and especially permits—makes possible—something that did not exist before. . . . Something happens that cannot be reduced to what was before. Thus what takes place becomes an event. It has its own rules, which displace previous divisions." Michel de Certeau, *The Possession at Loudun*, trans. Michael B. Smith (Chicago: University of Chicago Press, 2000), 22.

7. This is Mary Keller's argument with regard to spirit possession, echoing in certain respects David Hume's point of view on religious enthusiasm as a friend to civil liberty. See Mary Keller, *The Hammer and the Flute: Women, Power, and Spirit Possession* (Baltimore: Johns Hopkins University Press, 2002), 46; and David Hume, *Of Superstition and Enthusiasm* (1741), http://infomotions.com/etexts/philosophy/1700-1799/hume-of-738.htm.

8. Here I follow the pioneering work of Lucy A. Suchman, *Human-Machine Reconfigurations: Plans and Situated Actions*, 2nd ed. (Cambridge: Cambridge University Press, 2007).

9. Alfred Gell, *Art and Agency: An Anthropological Theory* (Oxford: Clarendon, 1998), 13–15. Here I am also indebted to the work of Ann Taves locating religion on a spectrum of "special things." See Ann Taves, *Religious Experience Reconsidered: A Building-Block Approach to the Study of Reli-*

gion and Other Special Things (Princeton, NJ: Princeton University Press, 2009).

10.   Gell, *Art and Agency*, 142, 148.

11.   Gell, *Art and Agency*, 132, 150–52. On the cognitive inevitability of anthropomorphism, see Stewart Elliott Guthrie, *Faces in the Clouds: A New Theory of Religion* (New York: Oxford University Press, 1993); and Pascal Boyer, *Religion Explained: The Evolutionary Origins of Religious Thought* (New York: Basic, 2001).

12.   *Assemblage* has become familiar above all through the work of Bruno Latour, but it has a longer history. In art, it was applied by Jean Dubuffet in 1953 to describe "assemblages d'empreintes," a juxtaposition in one work of multiple lithographs. He described *assemblage* as an aesthetic of accumulation that goes beyond mere collage. Jean Dubuffet, letter to William Seitz, April 21, 1961, Curatorial Exhibition Files, Exh. #695, Museum of Modern Art Archives, New York.

13.   Rüdiger Bilden, "Brazil, Laboratory of Civilization," *The Nation*, January 16, 1929, 73–74.

14.   Cited in Enylton de Sá Rego, preface to Machado de Assis, *The Posthumous Memoirs of Brás Cuba* (Oxford: Oxford University Press, 1997), clxx.

15.   Ruth Landes, *City of Women* (New York: Macmillan, 1947), 35. Landes's fieldwork began in 1938.

16.   "O tam-tam da Salpêtrière não teria maior eficacia para os hystericos de Charcot." Raimundo Nina Rodrigues, *O animismo fetichista dos negros baianos* (Rio de Janeiro: Fundação Biblioteca Nacional, 2006), 75.

17.   Michael Taussig, *Mimesis and Alterity: A Particular History of the Senses* (New York: Routledge, 1993), 213–14.

18.   Thomas Hobbes, *The Leviathan: Reprinted from the Edition of 1651* (Oxford: Clarendon, 1909), 83.

19.   To cite just one of many possible examples: "The Scotch banks ... were all obliged to employ constantly agents at London to collect money for them, at an expense which was seldom below one and a half or two percent." Adam Smith, *An Inquiry into the Nature and Causes of the Wealth of Nations* (Basil: J. J. Tourneisen & J. Legrand, 1791), 2:46.

20.   Herbert Spencer's *Social Statics* (London: John Chapman, 1851), e.g., used the familiar *joint-stock agency* and *state agency* but also proposed phrases like *personal agency, impersonal agency,* and *mental agency.* His *First Principles* (London: Williams & Norgate, 1863) expanded this repertory much further. In a revision of an earlier essay on social stratification, Talcott Parsons presented *agency* (with scare quotes, as though it had not been used in this way before) as one of three features of social systems, including qualities, performances, and possessions. *Agency* is a performance. Parsons contrasted it with *qualities,* or enduring structures. See Talcott Parsons, "A Revised Analytical Approach to the Theory of Social Strati-

fication," in *Class, Status and Power*, ed. Reinhard Bendix and Seymour Martin Lipset (Glencoe, IL: Free Press, 1953), 92–128, 95. The earlier essay is Talcott Parsons, "An Analytical Approach to the Theory of Social Stratification," *American Journal of Sociology* 45, no. 6 (1940): 841–62.

21. Classically, individual will requires spontaneity, contingency, and rationality. See n. 4.

22. Judith Butler, *Bodies That Matter: On the Discursive Limits of Sex* (New York: Routledge, 1993), 220.

23. Gayatri Spivak, "Subaltern Talk," in *The Spivak Reader*, ed. Donna Landry and Gerald Maclean (New York: Routledge, 1996), 287–96, 294.

24. William H. Sewell, "A Theory of Structure: Duality, Agency, and Transformation," *American Journal of Sociology* 98, no. 1 (1992): 1–29, 2, 18, 20.

25. Among many other possible examples, Walter Johnson, "On Agency," *Journal of Social History* 37, no. 1 (2003): 113–24; Talal Asad, *Genealogies of Religion: Discipline and Reasons of Power in Christianity and Islam* (Baltimore: Johns Hopkins University Press, 1993), 19; Constantin Fasolt, *The Limits of History* (Chicago: University of Chicago Press, 2004); Dipesh Chakrabarty, *Provincializing Europe: Postcolonial Thought and Historical Difference* (Princeton, NJ: Princeton University Press, 2000), 103; and Bruno Latour, *An Inquiry into the Modes of Existence* (Cambridge, MA: Harvard University Press, 2013), 229. In a similar vein, Ian Baucom considers agency "melancholy cosmopolitanism": using history "as a way of making ourselves happen within the space of the traumatic." See Ian Baucom, *Specters of the Atlantic: Finance Capital, Slavery, and the Philosophy of History* (Durham, NC: Duke University Press, 2005), 248. Meanwhile, Jean Baudrillard proposes that there cannot be anything like spontaneous action or choice because there is longer a real world in which to act. (Baudrillard does not use *agency* as such because there is no direct parallel in French; he often uses *instance* [akin to Marshall Sahlins's use of *event*], as in "une *instance* psychique," translated in the English version as *psychic agency*.) See Jean Baudrillard, *L'echange symbolique et la mort* (Paris: Gallimard, 1976), 211 (translated by Iain Hamilton Grant as *Symbolic Exchange and Death* [London: Sage, 2017], 157).

26. Saba Mahmood, *The Politics of Piety: The Islamic Revival and the Feminist Subject* (Princeton, NJ: Princeton University Press, 2005), 15–16. Samuli Schielke chides Mahmood that these women are not quite "antiliberal" insofar as they still seem devoted to the goal of self-realization. See Samuli Schielke, *Egypt in the Future Tense: Hope, Frustration and Ambivalence Before and After 2011* (Bloomington: Indiana University Press, 2015). Thanks to Roxana-Maria Aras for pointing this out.

27. Pierre Bourdieu, *Pascalian Meditations* (Stanford, CA: Stanford University Press, 2000), 146; Judith Butler, *Notes toward a Performative Theory of Assembly* (Cambridge, MA: Harvard University Press, 2015), 230. This notwithstanding Durkheim's claim that members of religious communi-

ties are far less likely to commit suicide. See Émile Durkheim, *Le suicide* (Paris: Félix Alcan, 1897). Specifically, Durkheim pointed out that Jews and Catholics were unlikely to commit suicide; Protestants gain no such immunity. In *The Elementary Forms of Religious Life*, however, he describes "religious suicide" as a particularly radical form of "mystical asceticism" and, in that sense, a possible form of agency. See Émile Durkheim, *The Elementary Forms of Religious Life*, trans. Joseph Swain (London: Dover, 2008), 40.

28. On how the précising of the boundary defines religious communities, see esp. Webb Keane, *Christian Moderns* (Berkeley and Los Angeles: University of California Press, 2007). John Lardas Modern and Eduardo Kohn have each, in important ways, troubled agency as a uniquely human property. Modern shows how it is an intersectional domain or couplet, the jointed "springs and motives" of human action. See John Lardas Modern, *Secularism in Antebellum America* (Chicago: University of Chicago Press, 2011), 279. Eduardo Kohn analyzes it as a composite product of human and nonhuman ways of thinking. See Eduardo Kohn, *How Forests Think: Anthropology beyond the Human* (Berkeley and Los Angeles: University of California Press, 2013), 42.

29. Veena Das, "Of Mistakes, Errors, and Superstition," in *The Mythology in Our Language: Remarks on Frazer's Golden Bough*, by Ludwig Wittgenstein, trans. Stephan Palmié, ed. Giovanni da Col (Chicago: HAU, 2018), 157–82, 172.

30. Charles Taylor, *A Secular Age* (Cambridge, MA: Harvard University Press, 2007), 37–41. Taylor juxtaposes the modern buffered self from the "porous self" of an earlier enchanted age when people understood themselves as permeated by gods, spirits, and similar metahuman beings. But there are other ways of thinking about permeability that do not presuppose metahuman agents, like Charles Sanders Peirce's idea of "continuity of being." Peirce wrote: "When I communicate my thought and my sentiments to a friend with whom I am in full sympathy, so that my feelings pass into him and I am conscious of what he feels, do I not live in his brain as well as in my own—most literally?" This "continuity of being," as "a sort of loosely compacted person, in some respects is of higher rank than the person of an individual organism." C. Hartshorne, P. Weiss, and A. Burks, eds., *Collected Papers of Charles Sanders Peirce*, 8 vols. (Cambridge, MA: Belknap Press of Harvard University Press, 1931–60), 7:591, 5:421.

31. Sewell, "A Theory of Structure," 21.

32. William James, *The Varieties of Religious Experience* (New York: Modern Library, 1902), 372. Marcel Mauss also emphasized the dialectic between bodily techniques and mystical states: "Technical action, physical action, and magico-religious action are confused for the actor." Marcel Mauss, "The Techniques of the Body" (1935), trans. Ben Brewster, *Economy and Society* 2 (1973): 70–88, 75.

33. Deirdre de la Cruz, *Mother Figured: Marian Apparitions and the Making of a Filipino Universal* (Chicago: University of Chicago Press, 2015), 224. Asad is also especially subtle on the ways in which agency can be articulated in relation to the renunciation of will. He describes how much of professional life entails the capacity of successfully acting out scripts. Thus, e.g., a good stage or film actor learns to be taken over by a text or a character persuasively: "Actors' ability to disavow or *empty* themselves articulates their agency in relation to a particular acting tradition." Talal Asad, *Formations of the Secular: Christianity, Islam, Modernity* (Stanford, CA: Stanford University Press, 2003), 76.

34. Suchman, *Human-Machine Reconfigurations.* See also Debbora Battaglia, "Toward an Ethics of the Open Subject: Writing Culture in Good Conscience," in *Anthropological Theory Today*, ed. Henrietta Moore (London: Polity, 2000), 137–39.

35. Stanley Cavell, *The World Viewed: Reflections on the Ontology of Film* (Cambridge, MA: Harvard University Press, 1971), 16, 107–8.

36. Walter Benjamin, *The Arcades Project* (Cambridge, MA: Belknap Press of Harvard University Press, 2003), 396 (J80, 1).

37. Dan Sperber, *Explaining Culture: A Naturalistic Approach* (Oxford: Wiley-Blackwell, 1996), 108.

38. See, e.g., Jerome M. Segal, *Agency and Alienation: A Theory of Human Presence* (London: Rowan & Littlefield, 1991), 9: "An action occurs when there is some event with respect to which a person is the agent, and that this relationship between the person and the event, which is called agency, is a direct causing of the event by the person. Agency, on this view, is not a matter of some state of the person or some event within the person causing some other event, but is something different, unique and extra." On the other hand: "A person is an agent of his actions when and only when his self is present in them." Ibid., 50. The question that religious acts would seem to problematize is what it means to have a self that is present in action.

39. The example is inspired by G. E. M. Anscombe, *Intention* (Cambridge, MA: Harvard University Press, 2000). To oversimplify, Anscombe argues that *intent* is a subclass of actions about which one can reasonably ask the question, Why? This excludes perhaps the majority of human acts, including some that can be construed as agency.

40. The observation of bodily acts without will has catalyzed religious crises, doctrines, and revelatory techniques. For example, Augustine was stricken by his own involuntary sexual arousal. If sex was necessary to reproduction, why was it at least in part outside will? The problem led to his doctrine of original sin. See Stephen Greenblatt, "How St. Augustine Invented Sex," *New Yorker*, June 12, 2017. The automatic can serve not only as a subversive, ambiguating trickster to the category *religion* but also as its resource, catalyst, and defense. Chapter 5 below considers the work of Chico Xavier, a spiritist automatic writer and the best-selling author in Brazilian history.

Chico was hardly anomalous. William James supposed that, much like Chico, almost all religious leaders had experiences of automatism. James, *The Varieties of Religious Experience*, 467.

41. Shoshana Zuboff, *The Age of Surveillance Capitalism: The Fight for a Human Future at the New Frontier of Power* (New York: Public Affairs, 2019).

42. Lauren Berlant, "Slow Death (Sovereignty, Obesity, Lateral Agency)," *Critical Inquiry* 33, no. 4 (2007): 754–80.

43. Thomas Hobbes, *Hobbes's Leviathan, Reprinted from the Edition of 1651* (Oxford: Clarendon, 1909), 8.

44. René Descartes, *Meditations and Other Metaphysical Writings* (London: Penguin, 2003), 29. Centuries later, Wittgenstein expressed much the same idea: "But can't I imagine that the people around me are automatons, lack consciousness, even though they behave in the same way as usual? If I imagine it now—alone in my room—I see people with fixed looks (as in a trance) going about their business—the idea is perhaps a little uncanny." Ludwig Wittgenstein, *Philosophical Investigations* (Hoboken, NJ: John Wiley & Sons, 2010), 23.

45. Descartes also argued that an observer would not be able to tell a mechanical monkey from a biological one since both are automatic actors. René Descartes, *Discourse on Method and Meditations on First Philosophy* (4th ed.), trans. Donald A. Cress (Indianapolis: Hackett, 1999), 31–32.

46. Here I follow Eugene Marshall, *The Spiritual Automaton: Spinoza's Science of the Mind* (Oxford: Oxford University Press, 2013). "Spiritual automaton" appears in Spinoza's *Treatise on the Emendation of the Intellect* (1677).

47. Blaise Pascal, *Pensées*, trans. W. F. Trotter (Mineola, NY: Dover, 2003), 74.

48. Gaby Wood, *Living Dolls: A Magical History of the Quest for Mechanical Life* (London: Faber & Faber, 2002), 1–5.

49. Descartes, *The Passions of the Soul*, in *The Philosophical Writings of Descartes* (Cambridge: Cambridge University Press, 1985), 325–404. See also Marshall, *The Spiritual Automaton*, 4.

50. George L. Hersey, *Falling in Love with Statues: Artificial Humans from Pygmalion to the Present* (Chicago: University of Chicago Press, 2009), 11–12. On the classical period in general and the ways its uses of automatons foreshadow certain contemporary uses of androids, see Adrienne Mayor, *Gods and Robots: Myths, Machines, and Ancient Dreams of Technology* (Princeton, NJ: Princeton University Press, 2018).

51. Gershom Gerhard Scholem, *On the Kabbalah and Its Symbolism* (London: Routledge, 1965), 198–99. For the comparisons with automata, see ibid., 164, 195, 202. For links between the golem and androids, see Eric G. Wilson, *The Melancholy Android: On the Psychology of Sacred Machines* (Albany: State University of New York Press, 2006), 63–94.

52. Roger Caillois, "La mante religieuse: Recherches sur la nature et la signification du mythe," *Mesures* 3, no. 2 (1937): 110.

53. Ismail Al-Jazari, *The Book of Ingenious Devices*, trans. Donald R. Hill (Dordrecht: D. Reidel, 1979), 19–23.

54. Joachim Sighart, *Albert the Great: His Life and Scholastic Labours from Original Documents*, trans. T. A. Dixon (London: R. Washbourne, 1876), 143.

55. Arthur Edward Waite, *Lives of Alchemystical Philosophers: Based on Materials Collected in 1815* (London: George Redway, 1888), 58–59. Waite cites the sixteenth-century writer Michael Maier as the source.

56. Jessica Riskin, "Introduction: The Sistine Gap," in *Genesis Redux: Essays in the History and Philosophy of Artificial Life*, ed. Jessica Riskin (Chicago: University of Chicago Press, 2007), 1–35, 27, 23 (quote).

57. Elizabeth King, "Perpetual Devotion: A Sixteenth-Century Machine That Prays," in Riskin, ed., *Genesis Redux*, 263–90.

58. Scott Maisano, "Descartes avec Milton: The Automata in the Garden," in *The Automaton in English Renaissance Literature*, ed. Wendy Beth Hyman (London: Routledge, 2011), 21–44.

59. Sir John Mandeville, *The Travels of Sir John Mandeville* (London: Penguin, 1983), 171.

60. The homunculus, Paracelsus clarified, resembles humans but has no soul and is akin to a slave. See Anthony Grafton, *Natural Particulars: Nature and the Disciplines in Renaissance Europe* (Cambridge, MA: MIT Press, 1999), 328–29.

61. Henry Cornelius Agrippa, *Three Books of Occult Philosophy*, ed. Donald Tyson, trans. James Freake (Saint Paul, MN: Llewellyn, 2004), 109.

62. According to the report of Karl Windisch: "One old lady, in particular, who had not forgot the tales she had been told in her youth, crossed herself, and sighing out a pious ejaculation, went and hid herself in a window seat, as distant as she could from the vile spirit, which she firmly believed possessed the machine" ("Eine alte Dame aber, die vielleicht die ersten Eindrücke von guten und bösen Geistern durch ihre Umma erhalten hatte, schlug ein Kreuz mit einem andächtigen Seufzer vor sich, und schlich an ein etwas entferntes Fenster, um dem—Gott sei mit uns! den sie unfehlbar um, oder in der Machine vemuthete, nicht zu nahe zu sein"). See Karl Windisch, "Letter I, Sept. 7, 1783," in *Inanimate Reason; or, A Circumstantial Account of That Astonishing Piece of Mechanism, M. de Kempelen's Chess-Player; Now Exhibiting at No. 8 Saville-Row, Burlington Gardens* (London, 1784), 15. I first learned of Windisch's text from Kara Reilly, *Automatons and Mimesis on the Stage of Theatre History* (New York: Palgrave Macmillan, 2011). Such experiences recall Rudolph Otto's description of religious experience as *mysterium tremendum et fascinans*, a horrified fascination or a simultaneous repulsion and pull. See Rudolf Otto, *The Idea of the Holy* (1917; New York: Oxford University Press, 1958), 8.

63. On the impact of Bertillon's photographic identification and Francis Galton's fingerprint system, see, e.g., Giorgio Agamben, "Identity without the

Person," in *Nudities* (Stanford, CA: Stanford University Press, 2011), 46–54. Galton also pursued "automatic thought" and automatic sketching. See Francis Galton, *Inquiries into the Human Faculty and Its Development* (New York: Macmillan, 1883), 205.

64. *Jornal do comércio*, January 17, 1840. The full passage in Portuguese reads: "É preciso ter visto a cousa com os seus próprios olhos para se fazer ideía da rapidez e do resultado da operação. Em menos de nove minutos, o chafariz do largo de Paço, a praça do Peixe, o mosteiro de São Bento e todos os outros objetos circunstantes se acharam reproduzidos com tal fidelidade, preçisao e minuciosidade, que bem se via que a cousa tinha sido feita pela própria mão de natureza, e quase sem intervenção do artista."

65. A few years later, Martin made a popular automaton monkey, a template already established in the late nineteenth century. We find, e.g., "le singe fumeur habillé en Incroyable" by Léopold Lambert (1890) and "le singe savant" by Martin (1908). Inventory 43867, Musée des Arts et Métiers, Paris. Lambert's company, Maison Lambert, also manufactured an automaton called the "Turc fumeur" in 1905, thus juxtaposing the monkey and the Turk and setting them in comparison.

66. Lisa Gitelman, *Scripts, Grooves and Writing Machines: Representing Technology in the Edison Era* (Stanford, CA: Stanford University Press, 1999), 172–81.

67. *Jornal do Brasil*, April 14, 1897: "Ajeeb, o afamado automato jogador de damas, que ainda continua a exciter a curiosidade do povo fluminense." Parenthetically, it is worth noting how the Orientalism of makers of automatons in Europe appears to have continued in force in Brazil. Machado de Assis made reference to the same automaton in his column of June 7, 1896, in the *Gazeta de notícias*: "Não leverão daqui a nossa vasta baía, as grandezas naturais e industriais, a nossa Rua do Ouvidor, com o seu autômato jogador de damas, nem as próprias damas."

68. "L'automate disparaît en tant que modèle et objet solitaires pour qualifier la forme du travail en milieu industriel." Jean-Claude Beaune, *L'automate et ses mobiles* (Paris: Flammarion, 1980), 256.

69. Jules Verne, *Around the World in Eighty Days*, trans. Frederick Paul Walter (Albany: State University of New York Press, 2013), 8.

70. E.T.A. Hoffman, *Tales of Hoffman* (London: Penguin, 1982), 106.

71. Machado de Assis, "The Mirror" ("O espelho"), in *The Collected Stories of Machado de Assis*, trans. Margaret Jull Costa and Robin Patterson (New York: Liveright, 2018), 452.

72. Euclides da Cunha, *Rebellion in the Backlands*, trans. Samuel Putnam (Chicago: University of Chicago Press, 1944), 394. Here, *automaton* also flirts with the idea of the primitive. That flirtation extends at least to the work of Claude Lévi-Strauss. Lévi-Strauss described primitive societies as automata, mechanical machines that could go on operating indefinitely with the same energy they started with, as distinct from modern societies,

which are like thermodynamic machines: "Our modern societies are not only societies which make extensive use of the steam-engine; structurally, they resemble the steam-engine in that they work on the basis of a difference in potential." *Conversations with Claude Lévi-Strauss*, ed. Georges Charbonnier, trans. John Weightman and Doreen Weightman (London: Jonathan Cape, 1969), 32–33.

73. I say *refurbished* rather than *invented* because the trope of the autonomous, discrete individual is a recurring myth. As Bakhtin put it: "This distinctive correspondence of an identity with a particular self is the organizing center of the human image in the Greek romance." M. M. Bakhtin, "Forms of Time and of the Chronotope in the Novel," in *The Dialogic Imagination*, trans. Caryl Emerson and Michael Holquist (Austin: University of Texas Press, 1981), 84–258, 105.

74. Marx wrote further: "An organised system of machines, to which motion is communicated by the transmitting mechanism from a central automaton, is the most developed form of production by machinery. Here we have, in the place of the isolated machine, a mechanical monster whose body fills whole factories, and whose demon power, at first veiled under the slow and measured motions of his giant limbs, at length breaks out into the fast and furious whirl of his countless working organs." Karl Marx, *Capital* (London: Charles H. Kerr, 1912), 1:416–17. The automaton is animate, but its consciousness, Marx argued, resides elsewhere, namely, in the person of the capitalist who wields the mysterious power of "the master." Ibid., 440, 462. If Marx proffered an epic of man against machine, he also demonstrated how humans were transmuted into hybrid machines: "To work at a machine, the workman should be taught from childhood, in order that he may learn to adapt his own movements to the uniform and unceasing motion of an automaton." Young boys become machine-human hybrids, "live chimney-sweeping machines." Ibid., 433. Marx was first disseminated in Brazil by the Recife law professor Tobias Barreto, who taught himself German and was citing *Das Kapital* by 1885, less than two years after its first publication.

75. Durkheim, *Le suicide*, 29.

76. "Vivia machinalmente: era um perfeito automato o infeliz operario," *Jornal do Brasil*, May 6, 1898.

77. Max Weber, *Economy and Society: An Outline of Interpretive Sociology*, ed. Guenther Roth and Claus Wittich (1922; Berkeley and Los Angeles: University of California Press, 1978), 978.

78. Steven Levingston, *Little Demon in the City of Light* (New York: Anchor, 2014).

79. Dain Borges, "Healing and Mischief: Witchcraft in Brazilian Law and Literature, 1890–1922," in *Crime and Punishment in Latin America*, ed. Ricardo D. Salvatore, Carlos Aguirre, and Gilbert M. Joseph (Durham, NC: Duke University Press, 2001), 181–210, 198, 207.

80. Gustave Le Bon, *Psychologie des foules* (Paris: Félix Alcan, 1895), 20: "Il n'est plus lui-mème, il est devenu un automate que sa volonté ne guide plus." Around the same time, Friedrich Engels noted the dubious influence of the crowd over individual agency, describing what he called *false consciousness*: "Ideology is a process accomplished by the so-called thinker consciously, it is true, but with a false consciousness. The real motive forces impelling him remain unknown to him." Friedrich Engels, letter to Franz Mehring, July 14, 1893, in *Marx and Engels Correspondence*, trans. Donna Torr (New York: International, 1968), https://www.marxists.org/archive/marx/works/1893/letters/93_07_14.htm. Well before Le Bon's treatise, the crowd and "the religion of the masses" feature in, among others, William Robertson Smith, *Lectures on the Religion of the Semites* (Edinburgh: A. & C. Black, 1889), 14.

81. "Não ser um titere das multidões, nem um automato das facções em que os paixões tumultuam em convulses ——, confuses e desordenadas." *Jornal do Brasil*, October 25, 1897.

82. Gustave Le Bon, *Les monuments de l'Inde* (Paris: Firmin-Didot, 1893).

83. *Gazeta da tarde*, January 28, 1884: "O crime da criança foi tentar oppor-se ao castigo de uma escrava, que apesar de reduzida à posição de authomato [*sic*], todavia possuia ainda o pudor, para não deixar saciar os desejos lebidinosos [*sic*] de seu tyranno."

84. "Além da educação do espirito, recebem os dignos moços a educação oral e civica, a educação do character que faz com que o caixeiro deixe de ser um automato, brutalmente inconsciente, para ser um cidadão convencido do papel que deve representar na sociedade." *Jornal do Brasil*, June 24, 1897.

85. "Com efeito, o homem primitivo não é bom, nem é mau naturalmente, é um mero autômato." José Bonifácio cited in Lourenço Dantas Mota, *Introdução ao Brasil: Um banquete no trópico* (Rio de Janeiro: Editora SENAC, 1999), 84.

86. Harriet Beecher Stowe, *Uncle Tom's Cabin* (1852; New York: Race Point, 2016), 12. See also Perdigão Malheiro, *A escravidão no Brasil: Ensaio historico-juridico-social*, 3 vols. (Rio de Janeiro, 1866), 3:14–15. Further: "Autômato com o pretext de o julgarem indefinidamente incapaz de se reger." Ibid., 2:28. On slaves as machines or things, see, among others, Carl Degler, *Neither Black nor White* (New York: Macmillan, 1971), 31.

87. John Rogers Commons, *Races and Immigrants in America* (New York: Macmillan, 1920), 131. Paradoxically, these human automatons were trapped within systems of encompassing mechanization that rendered their automatic labor obsolete. As Sidney Mintz noted, one way of framing the expansion of sugar production was as a shift from an agricultural form of cultivation to an industrial one, a slow machining of human labor of which slaves were surely more keenly aware than anyone. See Sydney W. Mintz, *Sweetness and Power: The Place of Sugar in Modern History* (New York: Penguin, 1985), 47.

88. J.-M. Charcot and Paul Richer, *Les démoniaques dans l'art* (Paris: Adrien Delahaye & Émile Lecrosnier, 1887); Jeanne de Belcier, *Soeur Jeanne des Anges: Autobiographie d'une hystérique possédée*, ed. Gabriel Legué and Gilles de la Tourette, with a preface by Jean-Martin Charcot (Paris: Aux Bureaux du Progrès Médical, 1886). In another example, Charcot tracked spiritist mediumship as a form of hysteric "contagion" as it traversed the members of one family. See Roger Luckhurst, *The Invention of Telepathy* (Oxford: Oxford University Press, 2002), 96; and Jean-Martin Charcot, "Seizième leçon: Spiritisme et hystérie," in *Oeuvres complètes*, 9 vols. (Paris: Aux Bureaux du Progrès Médical/Lecrosnier & Babé, 1890), 3:71. Similarly, by the 1890s, Freud had taken up the medieval notion of possession as "identical with our theory of a foreign body and the splitting of consciousness." Sigmund Freud, "Hysteria and Witches" (letter 56, January 17, 1897), in *Abstracts of the Standard Edition of the Psychological Works of Sigmund Freud*, vol. 1, *Pre-Psycho-Analytic Publications and Unpublished Drafts (1886–1899)*, ed. Carrie Lee Rothgeb (Washington, DC: US Department of Health, Education and Welfare, 1971), 10.

Perhaps we should take caution when thinking of Charcot as always translating religion into psychofunctional terms. At his summer house in Neuilly, a series of totems guarded the site: one sign read "On ne me touché pas avec impunité," another (from Dante's *Inferno*) "Les ennemis, on les regarde, ils passent." Finally, above the entrance Charcot hung a portrait of Franz Anton Mesmer. The objects hint at his own practices of magic, automatic religion, or fetishism, albeit potentially in a mode of irony or play. See Catherine Bouchara, *Charcot: Une vie avec l'image* (Paris: Philippe Rey, 2013), 217.

89. Psychiatry appears to have arrived in South America mostly through the influence of France and not only in Brazil. In Argentina, Freud was first mentioned, via French commentary, only in 1910, by which time Pierre Janet was much better known. See Mariano Ben Plotkin, *Freud in the Pampas* (Stanford, CA: Stanford University Press, 2001), 13–14. Plotkin proposes that psychiatry was taken up more rapidly in Brazil than in Argentina, "in the hope of applying it to their concerns about subduing the exotic and 'savage' components of their culture." Ibid., 14.

90. Pierre Janet, *L'automatisme psychologique* (Paris: Félix Alcan, 1889). Janet ultimately developed an entire theory of religion from his study of automatism and dissociation. (He moved from using *dissociation* to using *automatism* in 1889.) In a style that Durkheim later mimicked or unknowingly replicated, he began his *L'automatisme psychologique* by proposing a reduction to the most simple and "*elementary.*" While most scholars are engaged with the most elevated human actions, namely, questions of deliberation and free will, Janet proposed attending to the most basic, rudimentary, and simple: the automatic. He presented his ideas at Harvard in 1906, and they were published in English in multiple editions through at

least 1920. See Pierre Marie Felix Janet, *The Major Symptoms of Hysteria; Fifteen Lectures Given in the Medical School of Harvard University*, 2nd ed. (New York: Macmillan, 1920).

91. Minsoo Kang persuasively argues for the eighteenth century as the golden age of the automaton. See Minsoo Kang, *Sublime Dreams of Living Machines: The Automaton in the European Imagination* (Cambridge, MA: Harvard University Press, 2011).

92. There were many eighteenth-century around-the-world descriptions published as well, the most famous being James Cook's. See George Forster, *A Voyage round the World in His Britannic Majesty's Sloop Resolution, Commanded by Capt. James Cook, during the Years, 1772, 3, 4, and 5*, 2 vols. (London, 1777). Noteworthy in the rash of late nineteenth-century around-the-world narratives is the emphasis on speed and technologies of mobility.

93. Jacques Arago, *Narrative of a Voyage round the World, in the Uranie and Physicienne Corvettes, Commanded by Captain Freycinet, during the Years 1817, 1818, 1819, and 1820* (London: T. Davison, Whitefriars; Howlett & Brimmer, 1823).

94. Ralph Watts Leyland, *Round the World in 124 Days* (Liverpool: Gilbert G. Walmsley, 1880), 1.

95. Ida Pfeifer, *A Lady's Travels round the World*, trans. W. Hazlitt (New York: G. Routledge, 1852); David F. Dorr, *A Colored Man around the World* (Cleveland, OH: David Dorr, 1858); Thomas Stevens, *Around the World on a Bicycle* (New York: Scribner's & Sons, 1889). Pfeifer spent extensive time in Brazil. In Rio de Janeiro, she found, not "real religion," which was "quite wanting," but only prayers, processions, and festivals that serve for "amusement." Pfeifer, *A Lady's Travels round the World*, 32.

96. Stevens, *Around the World on a Bicycle*, 459.

97. James, *The Varieties of Religious Experience*, 236, 467. See also Ann Taves, "Religious Experience and the Divisible Self: William James (and Frederic Myers) as Theorist(s) of Religion," *Journal of the American Academy of Religion* 71, no. 2 (2003): 303–26.

98. Alfred Russell Wallace, *The World of Life* (New York: Moffat, Yard, 1911), 93, 425–26.

99. Toby Gelfand, ed. and trans., *Charcot in Morocco* (Ottawa, ON: University of Ottawa Press, 2012), 71, 117. Charcot cross-mapped racial types and hysteria. For example, he commented on "the extent to which that race [i.e., the Jews] displays to an unmatched frequency nervous manifestations of all kinds," but he was more subtle on black vs. white Muslims of Morocco, arguing that intermarriage is part of what causes nervous diseases. Ibid., 21. See also William James, *Brazil through the Eyes of William James: Letters, Diaries, and Drawings, 1865–1866*, ed. Maria Helena P. T. Machado, trans. John M. Monteiro (Cambridge, MA: Harvard University Press, 2006), 23.

100. Bourdieu, *Pascalian Meditations*, 185–86.

101.   The animals described in relation to personhood or mimicry and questions of authentic will were most often parrots or monkeys, animals that attracted attention for their human-like qualities. Descartes described talented monkeys and parrots as equal in certain capacities to human children, though with very different souls. See Descartes, *Discourse on Method*, 32–33. Locke calls on a parrot in Brazil in his exploration of individual personhood. See John Locke, *An Essay concerning Human Understanding* (1689), 4th ed. (1700; New York: Dover, 1975), 446–47. Spinoza invokes a parrot and a robot as beings that speak "without mind and sense." See Benedict de Spinoza, *Theological-Political Treatise* (1670), ed. Jonathan Israel (New York: Cambridge University Press, 2007), 174. David Hume invoked a parrot from the world of slavery: "In Jamaica, indeed, they talk of one Negro as a man of parts and learning; but it is likely he is admired for slender accomplishments, like a parrot who speaks a few words plainly." See David Hume, *Essays and Treatises on Several Subjects in Two Volumes*, vol. 1, *Essays, Moral, Political, and Literary* (London, 1784), 551. William James's and Jean Martin Charcot's closest companions were monkeys, as the next chapter explains.

102.   "At this point we leave Africa, not to mention it again. For it is no historical part of the world; it has no development or movement to exhibit." Georg Wilhelm Hegel, *Philosophy of History* (Mineola, NY: Dover, 1956), 99. Hegel blamed Brazil's lack of progress less on its Africanness than on its Catholicity. In North America, by contrast: "From the Protestant religion sprang the principle of the mutual confidence of *individuals*." Ibid., 84 (emphasis added).

103.   Gustave Le Bon, *The Crowd: A Study of the Popular Mind* (New York: Macmillan, 1897), 34, 114. Le Bon also attended Charcot's lectures at the Salpêtrière. See Jaap van Ginneken, *Crowds, Psychology, and Politics* (New York: Cambridge University Press, 1992), 143. Le Bon's writings on the automatism of crowds were informed by the putative automatism of hysteria and other psychic maladies.

104.   David Hume first made this connection in 1741, linking the directness of religious enthusiasm to the possibility of political resistance. While he placed superstition and enthusiasm as opposed forces, only superstition led to political tyranny: "My third observation on this head is, that superstition is an enemy to civil liberty, and enthusiasm a friend to it." Hume, *Of Superstition and Enthusiasm*. More recently, as Jeremy Stolow describes, "the automatic" helped instate a colonial/racial divide but also helped bridge it. Spiritism, e.g., summoned racially diverse spirits into segregated salons. See Jeremy Stolow, "Techno-Religious Imaginaries: On the Spiritual Telegraph and the Atlantic World of the Nineteenth Century," *Globalization Working Papers* 6, no. 1 (2006): 1–32, 8.

105.   Many local techniques of worlding do not require physical transport. For example, one of David Brown's Afro-Cuban informants reported on world

making through a ritual object called a *prenda* that is built in an iron pot: "The prenda is like the whole world, there is something of everything, wherever you are, you have to put something in it: if I go to New York to establish a point, I have to take something back from there and put it in the prenda. You see, we are like warriors. When an army conquers a country, they leave an occupying army. I live in Union City; if I go to New York to 'work' I will have to leave scouts or guards, build a perimeter, a fortress." David H. Brown, "Garden in the Machine: Afro-Cuban Sacred Art and Performance in New Jersey and New York" (PhD diss., Yale University, 1989), 389.

106.   James George Frazer, *Totemism and Exogamy* (New York: Cosimo, 2010), 1:281; Durkheim, *The Elementary Forms of Religious Life*, 363.

Automatisms have often been cast as illegitimate, and for reasons similar to the aspersions cast on magic. Stanley Tambiah summarized: "Magic is ritual action that is held to be automatically effective, and ritual action that dabbles with forces and objects that are outside the scope, or independent, of the gods. Magical acts in their ideal forms are thought to have an intrinsic and automatic efficacy." Stanley Jeyaraja Tambiah, *Magic, Science, Religion, and the Scope of Rationality* (Cambridge: Cambridge University Press, 1990), 7. Durkheim described rites (i.e., Vedic sacrifice) that "work by themselves": "Their efficacy depends upon no divine power; they mechanically produce the effects which are the reason for their existence. They do not consist either in prayers or offerings addressed to a being upon whose goodwill the expected result depends; this result is obtained by the automatic operation of the ritual." Durkheim, *The Elementary Forms of Religious Life*, 34. Every religion, he argued, includes "practices which act by themselves, by a virtue which is their own, without the intervention of any god between the individual who practices the rite and the end sought after": "It was believed that the desired phenomenon would result automatically from the rite." Ibid., 35. Compare Marcel Mauss, *A General Theory of Magic*, trans. Robert Brain (London: Routledge, 2005), 144: "We feel justified in concluding that a concept, encompassing the idea of magical power, was once found everywhere. It involves the notion of automatic efficacy." Elsewhere on automatic ritual: "Magic derives from errors of perception, illusions and hallucinations, as well as acute, emotive and subconscious states of expectation, prepossession and excitability: all range from psychological automatism to hypnosis." And: "Even the most run-of-the-mill rites, which work automatically, are never devoid of emotions." Ibid., 159–60. Mary Douglas, likewise, defined *magic* as ritual practice with an anticipated "automatic effect." Mary Douglas, *Purity and Danger* (London: Routledge & Kegan Paul, 1966), 18.

Clifford Geertz, to take another example, famously asserted that automatic action is by definition *not* genuinely religious because it does not summon the (for him) required "symbolic fusion of ethos and worldview."

"However, though any religious ritual, no matter how apparently automatic or conventional (if it is truly automatic or merely conventional it is not religious), involves this symbolic fusion of ethos and world-view, it is mainly certain more elaborate and usually more public ones, ones in which a broad range of moods and motivations on the one hand and of metaphysical conceptions on the other are caught up, which shape the spiritual consciousness of a people." Clifford Geertz, *The Interpretation of Cultures* (New York: Basic, 1973), 113. With this juxtaposition of the automatic and the genuinely religious, Geertz mirrored overtly theological writers of the turn of the nineteenth century like Frederick Morgan Davenport, who dismissed revival-meeting automatisms as inauthentic religion: "So far as their relation to a genuine religious experience is concerned, the most that can be said of them is that they may sometimes be the concomitants of such experience but ought never to be mistaken for it." Frederick Morgan Davenport, *Primitive Traits in Religious Revivals: A Study in Mental and Social Evolution* (New York: Macmillan, 1905), 244.

107. *Mark Twain's Own Autobiography* (Madison: University of Wisconsin Press, 1990), 174. The autobiography was composed in fragments between 1870 and 1910. Twain elaborated: "[Automatic religion] betrayed Susy into an injustice toward me. It had to be automatic, for she would have been far from doing me an injustice when in her right mind." Ibid., 174. The incident motivating Twain's neologism is not important here. But note his juxtaposition of the automatic, the "right mind," and the questions of justice and injustice. Twain had been reading William James, who was also fascinated by automatisms, and the two had become personally acquainted in Florence in 1896. See Jason Horn, *Mark Twain and William James: Crafting a Free Self* (Columbia: University of Missouri Press, 1996). The two men's interest in the automatic converged in spiritism and psychic phenomena. Twain was recruited into the Society for Psychic Research, chaired by James, and was deeply convinced of the research's merit. We read of his own experiences of an uncanny automatic: "Letters often act like that. Instead of the thought coming to you in an instant . . . the (apparently) unsentient letter imparts it to you as it glides invisibly past your elbow in the mail-bag." Mark Twain, "Mental Telepathy Again" (1895), In *The Writings of Mark Twain* (New York: Harper & Bros., 1897), 22:131–49, 135. Or: "I am now not able to believe that I often originate ideas in my mind but get almost all of them out of somebody else's by unconscious and uninvited thought-transference." Mark Twain, "Mental Telepathy?," in *The Bible according to Mark Twain: Writings on Heaven, Eden, and the Flood*, ed. Howard G. Baetzhold and Joseph B. McCullough (Athens: University of Georgia Press, 1995), 203–12, 206.

Hegel invoked the automatic in relation to religion in Germany: "The Church was no longer a spiritual power, but an ecclesiastical one; and the relation which the secular world maintained with it was unspiritual, automatic, and destitute of independent insight and conviction." The other instance of invoking *automatic* in the text was in relation to the dialectical progress of history, "the automatic self-mirroring activity of consciousness." Hegel, *Philosophy of History*, 381, 77.

108. William James, *The Principles of Psychology*, 2 vols. (1890; Cambridge, MA: Harvard University Press, 1981), 1:126. See also Edmund Gurney, Frederic W. H. Myers, and Frank Podmore, *Phantasms of the Living* (London: Society for Psychical Research, 1886), vol. 1. As Frederick Myers dramatically wrote in his introduction to that text: "We have at length got hold of a handle which turns the mechanism of our being . . . an eclipse of the normal consciousness which can be repeated at will." Gurney, Myers, and Podmore, *Phantasms of the Living*, xlii–xliii. The theologian James Freeman Clarke argued roughly the same thing as James with his discussion of "automatic morality." See James Freeman Clarke, *Every-Day Religion* (Boston: Ticknor, 1886).

109. "The impulses may take the direction of automatic speech or writing, the meaning of which the subject himself may not understand even while he utters it; and generalizing this phenomenon, Mr. Myers has given the name of automatism, sensory or motor, emotional or intellectual, to this whole sphere of effects, due to 'uprushes' into the ordinary consciousness of energies originating in the subliminal parts of the mind." James, *The Varieties of Religious Experience*, 234, 244.

110. James, *The Varieties of Religious Experience*, 293–94.

111. Friedrich Schleiermacher, *On Religion: Speeches to Its Cultured Despisers* (Cambridge: Cambridge University Press, 1996), 33. Perhaps the organic terms should not surprise: the economic historian Werner Sombart once described the eighteenth century as *wooden*—not only in its dependence on wood but also in its culture, in its "material and sensual aspect." Werner Sombart, *Der moderne Kapitalismus* (Munich, 1902), 2:1138.

112. Johan G. Herder, *Against Pure Reason* (Eugene, OR: Wipf & Stock, 2005), 85.

113. Ludwig Feuerbach, *Essence of Christianity* (New York: Calvin Blanchard, 1855), 168.

114. Compare Schleiermacher and Feuerbach's uses of the word *heart*. First Schleiermacher: "for everyone who has a feeling for all that issues from the depths of the heart." Schleiermacher, *On Religion*, 13. Now Feuerbach: "As the action of arteries drives the blood into the extremities, and the action of the veins brings it back again, the life in general consists in a perpetual systole and diastole; so is it in religion." Feuerbach, *Essence of Christianity*, 54. Religion, like the human, had been mechanized before, in Descartes's rereading of Hermeticism and Rosicrucianism. See Frances Yates, *The Rosicrucian Enlightenment* (London: Routledge & Kegan Paul, 1972), 152ff.

But this was automatic in a different sense, not least in that the mechanical forfeited its holy patina. Descartes's automaton reflected the natural order of God. The new automatic created both God and his demonic other.

115. See Jeremy Stolow, ed., *Deus in Machina: Religion, Technology, and the Things in Between* (New York: Fordham University Press, 2013); and Ian Hacking, *Rewriting the Soul: Multiple Personality and the Sciences of Memory* (Princeton, NJ: Princeton University Press, 1995), and *Mad Travelers: Reflections on the Reality of Transient Mental Illnesses* (Cambridge, MA: Harvard University Press, 2002).

116. Dr. E. Thwing (President of the New York Academy of Anthropology), "The Involuntary Life," *Phrenological Journal and Science of Health* 80, no. 5 (May 1885): 307–8: "The completeness with which the voluntary life is abrogated measures the thoroughness of the control exhibited in the involuntary life. Then again, if the soul of man can be so completely enthralled by his fellow that the verities of life, even his own identity, are contradicted, no one can doubt the possibility of the possession of a soul by demoniacal influences, now as in earlier days. . . . In the vividness, accuracy, and intensity of the soul's involuntary life we have, if not a parallel, a prophetic hint of the immortal supremacy of the spiritual life over the earthly, transitory life of the body. Processes of automatic computation of time—called by Dr. Carpenter 'unconscious chronometry'—are illustrations of this superior accuracy of involuntary action. Indeed, as Francis Galton says, 'consciousness appears to be a helpless spectator of but a minute fraction of a huge amount of automatic brain-work.'"

117. Studies of what is known as both *mediumship* and *possession* have mostly adhered to this strict geographic divide. *Mediumship* is used in Euro-American traditions of spiritism, with their attendant problematics of technology, incipient neurology and psychiatry, and the reification of the autonomous individual. *Possession* has been used to describe ritual contexts from further afield, either temporally or geographically—in the safely distant medieval Christian past, or in contemporary South Asia or Trinidad; but especially and above all where spirits are rendered present in African, Afro-American, and Afro-inspired ritual events. What is important is to account both for the uses of these terms by practitioners themselves as a form of boundary work and for the genealogies and itineraries into which different traditions are plotted.

118. "Senti uma dor agudíssima no alto do crânio; corpo estranho penetrou até o interior do cérebro. Não sei de mais nada. Creio que desmaiei." Machado de Assis, "Capitão Mendonça," in *Contos fantásticos de Machado de Assis*, ed. Raimundo Magalhães Jr. (Rio de Janeiro: Edições Bloch, 1973), 182–202, 202.

119. Schelling first describes "a condition that was still free from religious terror and all those uncanny feelings by which later humanity was harried." Next he comes to "personifications and concepts of nature that, comparable at

the most to the games of a childish wit, were hardly able for a moment to seriously engage their creators, even in comparison to the games of a childish joke," and then "the dark and uncanny power of the belief in gods." Then we find: "The thoughtless dread before something uncanny and unseen in nature will not be foreign to the savages who roam about the wide plains of La Plata, a dread that we believe to perceive even in some animals." And finally: "To the degree that the unity still has a greater power, the representations of the Indian and Egyptian system of the gods still appear with much more doctrinal content, but to the same extent also more uncanny, excessive, in part even monstrous." F. W. J. Schelling, *Historical-Critical Introduction to the Philosophy of Mythology*, trans. Mason Richey and Markus Zisselsberger (Albany: State University of New York Press, 2007), 14, 45, 54, 65.

120. "The dark knowledge dawns on the unschooled observer that mechanical processes are taking place in that which he was previously used to regarding as a unified psyche." Ernst Jentsch, "On the Psychology of the Uncanny," trans. Roy Sellars, *Angelaki* 1 (1906): 7–16, 14.

121. Jentsch, "On the Psychology of the Uncanny," 13.

122. Freud's lack of regard for his reflections on the uncanny appears in his letters to Sándor Ferenczi, though it may be false modesty: "I had not only completed the draft of 'Beyond the Pleasure Principle,' which is being copied out for you, but I also took up the little thing about the 'uncanny' again." "I am very tired, what is more, ill-tempered, consumed by impotent rage. Have finished another—unnecessary—work on the 'uncanny' for Imago." *The Correspondence of Sigmund Freud and Sándor Ferenczi*, vol. 2, *1914–1919*, ed. Ernst Falzeder and Eva Brabant, trans. Peter T. Hoffer (Cambridge, MA: Belknap Press of Harvard University Press, 1996), 354 (May 12, 1919), 363 (July 10, 1919).

123. Nicholas Royle, *The Uncanny* (Manchester: Manchester University Press 2003), 13.

124. Sigmund Freud, *The Standard Edition of the Complete Psychological Works of Sigmund Freud*, trans. James Strachey, 24 vols. (1953–74; reprint, New York: Vintage, 1999), 17:232.

125. *The Letters of Sigmund Freud*, ed. Ernst Freud, trans. Tania and James Stern (New York: Basic, 1960), 187.

126. Roger Caillois even specified generic techniques applied to gaining such disorientation: *ilinx* (whirlpool or vertigo), masking, etc. See Roger Caillois, *Les jeux et les hommes* (Paris: Gallimard, 1958).

127. E. T. A. Hoffman, *Automata* (Lexington, KY: Objective Systems, 2006), 27–28.

128. Albert Binet preferred *double consciousness*, whereas Freud referred to *second consciousness*.

129. W. E. B. Du Bois, *The Souls of Black Folk* (New York: Barnes & Noble Classics, 2003), 9.

130. Leo Tolstoy, *Anna Karenina*, trans. Richard Pevear and Larissal Volokhonsky (London: Penguin, 2000), 288. The phrase *go double in her soul* is repeated twice more. See ibid., 290, 293.

131. Janet, *L'automatisme psychologique*, 478: "Les hommes ordinaires oscillent entre ces deux extremes, d'autant plus determinés et automates que leur force morale est plus faible, d'autant plus dignes d'ètre considérés comme des ètres libres et moraux."

132. See esp. Paul Ricoeur, *Oneself as Another*, trans. Kathleen Blamey (Chicago: University of Chicago Press, 1994). Nearhumanness conceptually engages with two key principles from the cognitive science of religion: first, anthropomorphism and, second, memorability as the slightly but not totally strange.

133. Juan Ginés de Sepúlveda, "Democrates Alter; or, On the Just Causes for War against the Indians," 1547, http://www.thelatinlibrary.com/imperialism/readings/sepulveda.html.

134. Oviedo cited in Claude Lévi-Strauss, *Tristes Tropiques* (London: Penguin, 1974), 76.

135. Herder, *Against Pure Reason*, 89.

136. Edmund B. Tylor, *Primitive Culture: Researches into the Development of Mythology, Philosophy, Religion, Art, and Custom*, 2 vols. (London: John Murray, 1871).

137. Jane Goodall, "Primate Spirituality," in *The Encyclopedia of Religion and Nature*, ed. Bron Taylor (New York: Continuum, 2005), 1303–6.

138. Christian MacLeod, Asheville, NC, cited in *New York Times*, February 21, 2017, B2.

139. The use of religion to distinguish animality from humanness and defend that boundary ideologically were beautifully sabotaged in Donovan O. Schaefer, *Religious Affects: Animality, Evolution, and Power* (Durham, NC: Duke University Press, 2015), 2, 217.

140. Henry Louis Gates, *The Signifying Monkey: A Theory of African-American Criticism* (New York: Oxford University Press, 1988).

141. James, *The Principles of Psychology*, 2:355.

142. Cecilia Veracini, "Nonhuman Primate Trade in the Age of Discoveries: European Importation and Its Consequences," in *Environmental History in the Making*, vol. 2, *Acting*, ed. Cristina Jonnaz de Melo, Estelita Vaz, and Lígia M. Costa Pinto (Basel: Springer International, 2017), 147–72, 159.

143. Hans Staden, *Hans Staden's True History: An Account of Cannibal Captivity in Brazil*, trans. Neil L. Whitehead and Michael Harbsmeier (Durham, NC: Duke University Press, 2008), 102.

144. Jean de Léry, *History of a Voyage to the Land of Brazil*, trans. Janet Whatley (Berkeley and Los Angeles: University of California Press, 1993), 84, 201.

145. Here and in the following paragraph I rely on Veracini, "Nonhuman Primate Trade," 147–72.

146. Louise E. Robbins, *Elephant Slaves and Pampered Parrots: Exotic Animals*

in Eighteenth-Century Paris (Baltimore: Johns Hopkins University Press, 2002), 130.

147. *Affiches de Paris*, February 23, 1788, 540, cited in Robbins, *Elephant Slaves*, 131.

148. Visitors who left written accounts include Thomas Ewbank, the Reverends James Fletcher and D. Kidder, William James, Charles Darwin, and the Frenchwoman Adèle Toussaint-Samon, among many others. Toussaint-Samson heard the cries of monkeys and parrots throughout. See her *A Parisian in Brazil* (1883), ed. June E. Hahner (Wilmington, DE: Scholarly Books, 2001), 14, 29, 53, 63. She also described the European habit of see-ing Brazilians as having "the manners of a savage or monkey," a pattern she hoped to break with her book. Ibid., 12.

149. Charles Darwin, *Charles Darwin's Beagle Diary* (Cambridge: Cambridge University Press, 1988), 52, 71.

150. James, *Brazil through the Eyes of William James*, 99–100.

151. Louis Agassiz, *A Journey in Brazil* (Boston: Houghton, Osgood, 1879), 180, 529.

152. Gobineau cited in Louis Agassiz, letter to A. Marie Dragoumis, July 21, 1869, in Georges Raeders, *Le comte de Gobineau au Brésil* (Paris: Fernand Sorlot, 1934), 44.

153. Thomas Ewbank, *Life in Brazil* (1856; New York: Elibron Classics, 2005), 95, 249.

154. Rev. James C. Fletcher and Rev. D. Kidder, *Brazil and the Brazilians* (Bos-ton: Little, Brown, 1868), 509, 522.

155. Mary McAuliffe, *Twilight of the Belle Epoque* (Lanham, MD: Rowman & Littlefield, 2014), 232.

156. Debra Charlton, "Sarah Bernhardt: Artist and Mythologist," in *Women in the Arts in the Belle Epoque*, ed. Paul Fryer (Jefferson, NC: McFarland, 2012), 13.

157. Nahum Capen, "Biography of Dr. Gall," in *On the Functions of the Brain and of Each of Its Parts* (Boston: Marsh, Capen & Lyon, 1835), 15.

158. Laura de Mello e Souza, *The Devil and the Land of the Holy Cross: Witchcraft, Slavery, and Popular Religion in Colonial Brazil*, trans. Diane Grosklaus Whittey (Austin: University of Texas Press, 2003), 157.

159. Sheridan Le Fanu, "Green Tea," in *Through a Glass Darkly*, 3 vols. (London: R. Bentley & Sons, 1872), 1:1–95.

160. Donna Haraway, "The Promises of Monsters: A Regenerative Politics for Inappropriate/d Others," in *Cultural Studies*, ed. Lawrence Grossberg, Cary Nelson, and Paula A. Treichler (New York: Routledge, 1992), 295–337; Bruno Latour, *Science in Action* (Cambridge, MA: Harvard University Press, 1987), 131. I leave aside Lacan's explication of *automaton* as a "net-work of signifiers" and "the return" as juxtaposed with "the real" and "en-counter" since Lacan largely sidesteps the questions of agency, will, and personhood that are central here. Jacques Lacan, *The Four Fundamental*

Concepts of Psycho-Analysis (1973), trans. Alan Sheridan (London: Routledge, 2018), 53–65.

161. Bruno Latour, *The Modern Cult of the Factish Gods* (Durham, NC: Duke University Press, 2010), 6.

162. A key recent exploration this issue is in Schaefer's *Religious Affects*.

163. Donna Haraway, *When Species Meet* (Minneapolis: University of Minnesota Press, 2008).

164. Donna Haraway, *Simians, Cyborgs and Women: The Reinvention of Nature* (New York: Routledge, 1991), 310.

165. Bénédicte Boisseron, *Afro-Dog: Blackness and the Animal Question* (New York: Columbia University Press, 2018), 35.

166. Frankenstein's man-machine is never called a *simian* but is frequently referred to as an *animal*. The best example of the drawing together of the mechanical automaton and apes is Ambrose Bierce's 1899 short story "Moxon's Master," discussed in chapter 4 below.

167. Giorgio Agamben, *The Open: Man and Animal* (Stanford, CA: Stanford University Press, 2004), 37.

Chapter 1

1. Freud visited Charcot and the Salpêtrière from October 1885 until February 28, 1886. Prior to leaving for Paris, he was working on the anesthetic properties of coca; in Paris, he became interested in hysteria and the use of hypnosis to get at its unconscious causes. On his return to Vienna, he used hypnosis himself, returning to Nancy to study with Bernheim in order to better master the technique and Bernheim's theory of suggestion, and bringing one of his best aristocratic female patients with him to practice on. He used hypnosis not only to "see" symptoms, as Charcot used it, but also to get patients to declare the reasons for their illness, which they could not do otherwise. He called this, *second consciousness*. From this, labeled until then *catharsis* from Joseph Breuer, he moved to *psychoanalysis* (ca. 1890), which entailed the longer work of sitting behind reclining patients while they talked.

2. Gilles de la Tourette, *Traité clinique et thérapeutique de l'hystérie d'après l'enseignement de la Salpêtrière* (Paris: Plon, 1891), 33.

3. This was the Saint Laure building, which had maintained the alienist Delasiauve's patients. See Christopher G. Goetz, Michel Bonduelle, and Toby Gelfand, *Charcot: Constructing Neurology* (New York: Oxford University Press, 1995), 180.

4. Georges Didi-Huberman, *Invention of Hysteria: Charcot and the Photographic Iconography of the Salpêtrière*, trans. Alisa Hartz (Cambridge, MA: MIT Press, 2003), 17. Didi-Huberman, citing J. Losserand, seems to have the addition wrong, counting a total tally of 4,383 people at the institution.

5. Joseph Jules Dejerine, "L'oeuvre scientifique de Charcot," *Paris médical* 21

(1925): 509–11; Edward Shorter, *A History of Psychiatry* (New York: John Wiley & Sons, 1997), 85.

6. Jan Goldstein, *Console and Classify: The French Psychiatric Profession in the Nineteenth Century* (1987; Chicago: University of Chicago Press, 2001), 328; Bouchara, *Charcot*, 110.

7. G. S. Rousseau and Roy Porter, introduction to *Hysteria beyond Freud*, by Sander L. Gilman, Helen King, Roy Porter, G. S. Rousseau, and Elaine Showalter (Berkeley and Los Angeles: University of California Press, 1993), vii–xxiv, ix.

8. See, among others, Hacking, *Rewriting the Soul*, and *Mad Travelers*; Elaine Showalter, *The Female Malady: Women, Madness, and English Culture, 1830–1980* (New York: Pantheon, 1985), and "Hysteria, Feminism, and Gender," in *Hysteria beyond Freud*, by Gilman, King, Porter, Rousseau, and Showalter, 286–344; Mark S. Micale, *Approaching Hysteria: Disease and Its Interpretations* (Princeton, NJ: Princeton University Press, 1995), and *Hysterical Men: The Hidden History of Male Nervous Illness* (Cambridge, MA: Harvard University Press, 2008); and Sander L. Gilman, "The Image of the Hysteric," in *Hysteria beyond Freud*, by Gilman, King, Porter, Rousseau, and Showalter, 345–452.

9. Such writing appeared in multiple genres. I find it, e.g., in Baudelaire's prose poems composed between 1855 and 1867: "I felt the terrible hand of hysteria grip my throat." Charles Baudelaire, *Paris Spleen, 1869*, trans. Louise Varèse (New York: New Directions, 1970), 26. A century earlier, Charles de Brosses described faked spirit possession as "hysterical vapours" in women otherwise under the control of men. Charles de Brosses, *Du culte des dieux fétiches; ou, Parallèle de l'ancienne religion de l'Egypte avec la religion actuelle de Nigritie* (1760;Westmead: Gregg International, 1970).

10. Ilza Veith, *Hysteria: The History of a Disease* (Chicago: University of Chicago Press, 1965), 232–33.

11. Goldstein, *Console and Classify*, 327–28.

12. Charcot cited in Helen King, "Once upon a Text: Hysteria from Hippocrates," in *Hysteria beyond Freud*, by Gilman, King, Porter, Rousseau, and Showalter, 3–90, 8 ("L'hystérie a toujours existé, en tous lieux et en tous temps").

13. Charcot and Richer, *Les démoniaques dans l'art*, v–vii, 28.

14. Cristina Mazzoni, *Saint Hysteria: Neurosis, Mysticism, and Gender in European Culture* (Ithaca, NY: Cornell University Press, 1996), 19.

15. Asti Hustvedt, *Medical Muses: Hysteria in Nineteenth-Century Paris* (London: Bloomsbury, 2011), 272, 289; Mazzoni, *Saint Hysteria*, 24–29; Charcot and Richer, *Les démoniaques dans l'art*, 91–109.

16. Désiré-Magloire Bourneville, preface to Jean-Martin Charcot, *La foi qui guérit* (Paris: FV Éditions, 2012), 2. See also Belcier, *Soeur Jeanne des Anges*.

17. See, e.g., Alain Boureau, *Satan the Heretic: The Birth of Demonology in the Medieval West*, trans. Teresa Lavender Fagan (Chicago: University of Chicago Press, 2006), 179–82. Stigmata as symptoms linking early modern demoniacs and late nineteenth-century hysterics feature prominently in, e.g., Tourette's *Traité clinique et thérapeutique de l'hystérie*. Steve Connor points out the strange psychiatric embrace of stigmata as symptom and the transformation from the terms of *stigmata* to *stigma*, far more common by the twentieth century, as indexical of a deliberate laicization, or at least relocation, of the term to medicine. See Steve Connor, *The Book of Skin* (London: Reaktion, 2004), 122–24. On the phrase *possessed hysteric*, see Belcier, *Soeur Jeanne des Anges*.

18. Charcot cited in Dianne F. Sadoff, *Sciences of the Flesh: Representing Body and Subject in Psychoanalysis* (Stanford, CA: Stanford University Press, 1998), 105.

19. Sigmund Freud, "Report on My Studies in Paris and Berlin (1886)—Carried Out with the Assistance of a Travelling Bursary Granted from the University Jubilee Fund (October, 1885—End of March, 1886)," *International Journal of Psycho-Analysis* 37 (1956): 2–7, 4 (emphasis added).

20. Didi-Huberman and Sander L. Gilman especially focus on the visual dimension of the Salpêtrière's fame. See Didi-Huberman, *Invention of Hysteria*; and Gilman, "The Image of the Hysteric."

21. Cited in Olivier Walusinski, "The Girls of La Salpêtrière," *Frontiers of Neurology and Neuroscience* 35 (2014): 65–77, 69. Compare Mazzoni, *Saint Hysteria*, 21–22. Bourneville's inclusion of detailed descriptions of "erotic delirium" in the publications of the *Iconographie* is noted in Goetz, Bonduelle, and Gelfand, *Charcot*, 185–86.

22. N. Y. Harold, "Hysteria: Two Peculiar Cases as Presented by Professor Charcot," *Kansas City Medical Index-Lancet* 10, no. 114 (June 1889): 210–11.

23. For example, from a text in Charcot's library: "An automaton is substituted for the true volitional self. The will is the slave of a dream or a suggestion." Tuke, *Sleep-Walking and Hypnotism*, 4. Or from Charcot's student Pierre Janet: "Ces sujets si disposes à l'habitude et a l'automatisme." Janet, *Névroses et idées fixes*, 266. Or from Charcot himself: "I will use the expression ambulatory automatism based on descriptions that I made in the past of patients who walk about automatically and do not show any external signs that their walking is unconscious." Cited in Hacking, *Mad Travelers*, 36. Léon Daudet's satirical novel about Charcot and the Salpêtrière also shows a doctor referring to patients as "les automates." See Léon Daudet, *Les morticoles* (Paris: Bibliothèque-Charpentier, 1894), 156.

24. Jean-Martin Charcot, "Episodes nouveaux de l'hystéro-épilepsie—Zoopsie—Catalepsie chez les animaux," in *Oeuvres complètes* (Paris: Lecrosnier & Babé, 1890), 9:289–97, 293.

25. In the year 1887, Wittman, together with Charcot, was rendered iconic in the painting *Une séance à la Salpêtrière*, by Brouillet, which today hangs in

the Musée de l'histoire de la médicine. A lithograph of it decorated Freud's office, first in Vienna, then in London. The image of Charcot and Wittman hovered over Freud for the length of his career. Wittman became further immortalized in the twentieth century, recast as the character Blanche in Tennessee Williams's *A Streetcar Named Desire.*

26. Hustvedt, *Medical Muses*, 68–70.

27. Hustvedt, *Medical Muses*, 70. While Charcot read his patients with reference to La Mettrie's machine-man, La Mettrie claimed to have discovered hysterical catalepsy back in 1737. See Jan Goldstein, *Hysteria Complicated by Ecstasy: The Case of Nanette Leroux* (Princeton, NJ: Princeton University Press, 2010), 49; and Julien Offray de La Mettrie, *L'homme machine* (Leiden: Elie Luzac, 1748).

28. Hustvedt, *Medical Muses*, 71.

29. Charles Féré cited in Andreas Mayer, *Sites of the Unconscious: Hypnosis and the Emergence of the Psychoanalytic Setting* (Chicago: University of Chicago Press, 2013), 48.

30. Thomas D. Savill, *Lectures on Hysteria* (New York: William Wood; London: Henry Glaishner, 1909), 18.

31. Pierre Janet, *The Mental State of Hystericals: A Study of Mental Stigmata and Mental Accidents*, trans. C. R. Carson (New York: Putnam & Sons, 1901), 150, 154.

32. Savill, *Lectures on Hysteria*, 18.

33. Jean-Martin Charcot, *Leçons sur les maladies du système nerveux* (Paris: Delahaye, 1872–73), 301.

34. Désiré-Magloire Bourneville, *Science et miracle: Louise Lateau; ou, La stigmatisée belge* (Paris: Delahaye, 1878), 43.

35. See John Forrester, "If *p*, Then What? Thinking in Cases," *History of the Human Sciences* 9, no. 3 (1996): 1–25, 14.

36. This was, of course, Freud's point in the 1907 essay "Obsessive Actions and Religious Practices," translated into English in 1924. See Sigmund Freud, "Obsessive Actions and Religious Practices," in Strachey, trans., *Standard Edition*, 9:115–28.

37. Charcot, *Leçons sur les maladies du système nerveux*, 301; Désiré-Magloire Bourneville and Paul Regnard, *Iconographie photographique de la Salpêtrière* (Paris: Aux Bureau de Progrès Médical, 1876–77), 15–19.

38. Charcot, *Leçons sur les maladies du système nerveux*, 301; Goetz, Bonduelle, and Gelfand, *Charcot*, 193.

39. The case is summarized in Goetz, Bonduelle, and Gelfand, *Charcot*, 192–96.

40. Harold, "Hysteria," 210.

41. Charcot, "Episodes nouveaux de l'hystéro-épilepsie," 292.

42. Joseph Breuer and Sigmund Freud, *Studies in Hysteria* (1895; New York: Basic, 2009), 48–105.

43. The syndrome of believing one had transformed into an animal or being accused of such in a witch trial is called *lycanthropy*, after the Greek Lycaon,

who was turned into a wolf by Zeus. Later, it was given a more specifically medical cast with the diagnostic phrase *zoophilic metamorphosis*. Salman Akhtar and Jodi Brown, "Animals in Psychiatric Symptomatology," in *Mental Zoo: Animals in the Human Mind and Its Pathology*, ed. Salman Akhtar and Vamik Volkan (Madison, CT: International Universities Press, 2005), 3–40, 8.

44.   See Désiré-Magloire Bourneville, *Compte-rendu des observations recueillies á la Salpêtrière, concernant l'épilepsie et l'hystérie* (Paris: Aux Bureaux du Progrès Médical/Delahaye, 1875), 142. (The English translation is taken from Goetz, Bonduelle, and Gelfand, *Charcot*, 195.) Bourneville also described the events in his *Science and miracle: Louis Lateau; ou, La stigmatisée belge* (Paris: A. Delahaye, 1875), 43–46.

45.   Bourneville, *Compte-rendu des observations recueillies á la Salpêtrière*, 143.

46.   Paula M. Kane, *Sister Thorn and Catholic Mysticism in Modern America* (Chapel Hill: University of North Carolina Press, 2013), 169.

47.   Charcot, *Leçons sur les maladies du système nerveux*, 300. See also Hustvedt, *Medical Muses*, 216, 273.

48.   In his book on Lateau, Bourneville detoured repeatedly to explain her case in relation to Rosalie Leroux's. See Bourneville, *Science et miracle*, 40–47, 56.

49.   Hustvedt, *Medical Muses*, 277–78. See also Mazzoni, *Saint Hysteria*, 32; and Kane, *Sister Thorn and Catholic Mysticism*, 169.

50.   Bernard Taithe, *Defeated Flesh: Welfare, Warfare, and the Making of Modern France* (Manchester: Manchester University Press, 2010).

51.   Alexandre-Achille Souques and Henri Meige, "Jean-Martin Charcot," *Les biographies médicales* 13, no. 5 (1939): 337–52, 341.

52.   "Cette haute distinction, Sire, dont je me sens bien fier, me semble d'autant plus precieuse qu'elle me ratache par un lien nouveau au souverain liberal que, depuis longtemps j'admire comme savant et que j'ais appris recemment a aimer respecteusement d'une affection vive et sincère. De votre confrére à l'Institut de France, Charcot." Maço 145-Doc. 7074, Correspondence Charcot, Arquivo histórico, Museu Imperial, Petrópolis.

53.   Mary del Priore, *Condessa do Barral: A paixão do imperador* (Rio de Janeiro: Editora Objetiva, 2008).

54.   Letters from Dom Pedro II to Brown-Séquard, February 24, 1876, and June 29, 1876 (from Philadelphia), London: Archives of the Royal College of Physicians: "Ma femme souffre depuis longtemps avec des interruptions plus ou mois longues d'horribles douleurs neuralgiques à la jambe, et tous dernièrement, pour la première fois, du corps et à la tête, dans le cuir chevelu. Deux points sur l'épine dorsale se ressentent plus ou moins à la pression. Son état general est bon." "Je veux y consulter aussi le Dr. Charcot et c'est bon que vous deux puissant s'entendre aux meme temps avec mon médicin qui a soigné ma femme, et vous donnera tous les renseigments nécessaires."

55. Cited in Rose Brown, *American Emperor: Dom Pedro II of Brazil* (New York: Viking, 1945), 240.

56. "La politique n'est, pour moi, que la dur accomplissement d'un devoir . . . je porte ma croix." Letter from Dom Pedro II to Gobineau, July 23, 1873, Rio de Janeiro, Biblioteca Nacional, Caderno 64.02.002, No. 003.

57. Jean Thuillier, *Monsieur Charcot de la Salpêtrière* (Paris: Robert Laffont, 1993), 185.

58. Cited in José Murilo de Carvalho, *Dom Pedro II: Ser ou não ser* (São Paulo: Editora Schwarcz, 2007), 223.

59. A letter from Ferdinand Denis, writing from Paris on March 9, 1875, declares the emperor's nomination "the news of Paris." See Georges Raeders, *Dom Pedro II e os sábios franceses* (Rio de Janeiro: Atlantica Editora, 1944), 172.

60. "Sire, La science a un peu chômé! . . ." 24.01.1890 Maço 202-Doc. 9168, Correspondence Charcot, Museu do Império, Petrópolis.

61. "Dans le categorie de la medicine l'evènement a eté la communication de Ms. Pasteur relative à la vaccination anticholerique du Dr. Gamalei d' Oduje. Malheureusement il ne s'agit —— que d'experiences faites sur les animaux et il faudrait faire la prevue chez l'homme." 1.09.1888. I-D MM-1887/92-Ch. 1–19, Museu do Império, Petrópolis.

62. "Elle est place au beau milieu des sections françaises qui semblent l'acuellir comme hôté [?] preferé." Maço 28-988-Cat. B, Arquivo histórico, Museu do Império, Petrópolis.

63. ". . . et S. M. don Pedro, empereur du Brésil, très lié d'amitié avec Charcot et hôte assidu de la maison." Georges Guinon, "Charcot intime," *Paris médical* 1 (1925): 511–16, 511.

64. "23 de outubro de 1887 (domingo) . . . 7h 10' da noite. Fui à Salpêtrière. Assisti a experiências de Charcot de hipnotismo sobre pessoas nervosas. Dão-se fatos notáveis que não se podem atribuir a fingimento." Maço 36, Doc. 1056 Cad. 27, Museu do Imperio, Petrópolis. Charcot wrote a letter to Motta Maia on the same day, describing the emperor's keen memory and attention during his visits to Salpêtrière and to Charcot's home. Charcot, letter to Motta Maia, October 23, 1887, 63.05.006, No. 36, Biblioteca Nacional, Rio de Janeiro.

65. "10h ½ Vi meus netos grandes. Estive com o Charcot a quem falei sobre os trabalhos da Academia das Ciências o qual parte hoje para Paris onde encarreguei-o de lembranças para os meus confrades mais conhecidos dizendo a de Quatrefages que me deixou lendo seu artigo sobre 'Théories transformistes' no *Journal des Savants* de março." Maço 36, Doc. 1056 Cad. 27, Museu do Imperio, Petrópolis.

66. "10h 50' Jantei bem em companhia de Charcot com quem conversei sobre suas experiências de hipnotismo sobretudo." Maço 36, Doc. 1056 Cad. 27, Museu do Imperio, Petrópolis.

67. "Visitei Charcot em sua casa no Faubourg St. Germain nº 237. É como um

museu e não poderia de pronto falar do que aí vi de artístico e interessante. A casa tem jardim bonito. Esteve toda a família Charcot, retirando-se o filho antes de eu sair por ter seguir um curso. Vou agora falar a uma senhora." Maço 36, Doc. 1056 Cad. 27, Museu do Imperio, Petrópolis.

68. Though, on one occasion after he went into permanent exile, he did transcribe in his journal an article from the *New York Herald* on the "unrest" in Rio de Janeiro and the provisional government established since his departure. March 27, 1890. Maço 37-Doc. 1057 caderno 31, Museu do Império, Petrópolis.

69. Diary entry of May 23, 1890, Maço 36-Doc. 1056 Cad. 27, Muséu do Império, Petrópolis.

70. The letter is translated in Raeders, *Dom Pedro II*, 137.

71. The book he studied was Paul Bourget's *Essai de psychologie contemporaine* (Paris: A. Lemerre, 1883). The emperor's annotated text is found in the Arquivo Hélio Viana DL1446/11, Instituto Histórico e Geográfico Brasileiro.

72. "Jantei com appetite. Depois assisti a experiencias d'hypnotismo feitos por Pickman. Parece-me um grande charlatan, mas divertiram-me bastante porque fizeram-me rire." 25. Novembro, 1887, Maço 36, Cad. 27, 126–244, Museu do Império, Petrópolis.

73. Letter of July 29, 1888 from Aix les Bains. I-DMM-1887/92-Cha. C1-19. Museu do Imperio, Petrópolis. Additional long letters from Pedro's personal court physician, Motta Maia, to Pedro's son-in-law, the Conde d'Eu, from June 28, 1887, and July 4, 1888, detail Charcot's several trips from Paris to Milan to attend to the emperor. Instituto Histórico e Geográfico Brasileiro Lata 490, caderno 41, cartas 8–9.

74. In a sense, these terms reprised Pinel's older category *melancholia*, one of four major classes of illness described in the *Traité*. See Philippe Pinel, *A Treatise on Insanity* (1801), trans. D. D. Davis (Sheffield: W. Todd, 1806), 136–49.

75. On the initial recommendation of another consulting physician, Dr. Mariano Semmola, of Naples.

76. Thousands of men allegedly tried the therapy in the wake of Brown-Séquard's announcement. Charles-Édouard Brown-Séquard, "The Effects Produced on Man by Subcutaneous Injection of a Liquid Obtained from the Testicles of Animals," *The Lancet* 134 (1889): 105–7.

77. Louis Pasteur, letter to Dom Pedro, September 22, 1884, and Dom Pedro, letter to Pasteur, October 10, 1884, in Raeders, *Dom Pedro II*, 145–48.

78. Hustvedt, *Medical Muses*, 10.

79. Goetz, Bonduelle, and Gelfand, *Charcot*, 275.

80. Marthe Emmanuel, *Tel fut Charcot* (Paris: Beauchesne, 1967), 12–13; Hustvedt, *Medical Muses*, 17. Emmanuel described the larger dog as a mastiff, not a Great Dane. In her memoir, Marie-Louise Pailleron, who in childhood had lived for a decade (from about 1875 to 1884) next door to the Charcots, recalled the dog breeds differently: Carlo was not a Labrador but a grey-

hound, and Sigurd was in fact a Great Dane. She also reported that Rosalie was a "grande guenon," black with a vest of white, and a gift of Dom Pedro and that the smaller monkey was an *oustiti* (marmoset) named Gustave. Marie-Louise Pailleron, *Le paradis perdu: Souvenirs d'enfance* (Paris: Éditions Albin Michel, 1947), 35. Guinon recorded that the second monkey was gone by 1884, when he began working for Charcot, though he heard stories about it. By 1884 there was only Rosalie, a "petite guenon à queue prenante de l'Amérique du Sud, vive comme la poudre, futée comme . . . un singe, câline comme un chatte, propre comme un sou. Le patron l'aimait beaucoup." Guinon, "Charcot intime," 515–16. See also Marthe Emmanuel, *Charcot, navigateur polaire* (Paris: Éditions des Loisirs, 1945), 33–34.

81. Thuillier, *Monsieur Charcot*, 187.

82. Guinon, "Charcot intime," 515.

83. For example, the Grammont Law of 1850, so-called after Jacques Delmas de Grammont, the congressional deputy who drafted it.

84. Sadoff, *Sciences of the Flesh*, 84.

85. Sadoff, *Sciences of the Flesh*, 85.

86. For example, Charcot, *Leçons sur les maladies du système nerveux*, 171.

87. Jean-Martin Charcot, *Nouvelle iconographie de la Salpêtrière* (Paris: Lecrosnier & Babé, 1890), 3:273.

88. Cited in Goetz, Bonduelle, and Gelfand, *Charcot*, 71.

89. Act 4, scene 1, cited in Thuillier, *Monsieur Charcot*, 188. Léon Daudet also recalled Charcot's predilection for that passage. León Daudet, *Les oeuvres dans les hommes* (Paris: Nouvelle Librairie Nationale, 1922), 242.

90. Thuillier, *Monsieur Charcot*, 188.

91. Pailleron, *Paradis perdu*, 36.

92. Daudet, *Les oeuvres dans les hommes*, 236.

93. Thuillier, *Monsieur Charcot*, 188.

94. Marthe Ouliér, *Jean Charcot* (Paris: Gallimard, 1937), 35.

95. Pailleron, *Paradis perdu*, 35–36.

96. George Guillain, *J.-M. Charcot, 1825–1893: Sa vie, son oeuvre* (Paris: Masson, 1955), 30; Emmanuel, *Tel fut Charcot*, 12 (based on personal communication from Jean Charcot fils). The same story, based on personal communication from Charcot's granddaughter, was recounted in Goetz, Bonduelle, and Gelfand, *Charcot*, 271–72. There is some confusion between the accounts whether the monkey involved was Rosalie, Zoë, or Zibidie (and whether two of those names referred to the same being).

97. Thuillier, *Monsieur Charcot*, 187.

98. "Figurez vous que le grand singe noir (une guenon) que vous avez envoyé a Mlle Charcot est une creature delicieuse, douce, intelligente, faite a elever et que nous esperons bien, en raison de tres —— au'on lui predignon. Un peu plus elle parlerait—Elle mange tous les jours avec nous à table, assise dans une chaise d'enfant!!" January 24, 1890, I-DMM 1887/92 c.1.19d.11, Museu do Império, Petrópolis.

99.   Guinon, "Charcot intime," 516.

100. Ouliér, *Jean Charcot*, 35. On Charcot's voyage, see Gelfand, ed. and trans., *Charcot in Morocco*.

101. Roland Bonaparte, "Les Somalis au Jardin d'Acclimatation de Paris," *La nature* 903 (1890): 247–50; Robert Aldrich, *Vestiges of Colonial Empire in France* (London: Palgrave 2005), 61.

102. Sadoff, *Sciences of the Flesh*, 102–4.

103. "Cette sensibilité, qu'il tenait à garder secrète, éclatait sans retenue à propos des bêtes." Souques and Meige, "Jean-Martin Charcot," 341.

104. Guinon, "Charcot intime," 516.

105. Sigmund Freud, *Group Psychology and the Analysis of the Ego*, trans. James Strachey (London: International Psycho-Analytical Press, 1922), 10–12, 61–64.

106. Henry David Thoreau, *Walden; or, Life in the Woods* (Boston: Houghton, Mifflin, 1882), 1:42.

107. François Jouin, "Une visite a l'asile de Pédro II," *Annales médico-psychologiques* 3 (1880): 237–49, 244–45. See also Philippe-Marius Rey, "L'hospice Pedro II et les alienés au Brésil," *Annales médico-psychologiques* 98 (1875): 75–98.

108. Rey, "L'hospice Pedro II," 94.

109. Her first-class accommodations were not sustained, however. In 1894 she was downgraded to "second class" and in 1897 to "third class." Presumably, her parents or patron died or lost interest in her fate. Case file DC 17, 01, Fundo Hospício de Pedro II, Centro de Documentação e Memória Instituto Municipal Nise da Silveira.

110. I found 217 registered as "slave," 3 as "captive," 146 as "liberto," 2 as "alforriado," 4 as "forro," and 1,389 as "free." The status of the rest was not indicated.

111. Case file DC 13, 43a, Fundo Hospício de Pedro II, Centro de Documentação e Memória Instituto Municipal Nise da Silveira.

112. Anne Harrington, *Mind Fixers: Psychiatry's Troubled Search for the Biology of Mental Illness* (Cambridge, MA: Harvard University Press, 2019), 6.

113. During this period, 3,741 were registered as "white," 1,475 as "brown" (*parda*), and 1,362 as "black" (*preta*), not to mention an array of other categories.

114. *Observações clínicas de 25 de junho a 1 setembro*, 1914, 315; *Observações clínicas de 26 de novembro a 30 de dezembro*, 1919, 389. See also Lilia Moritz Schwarcz, "O homen da ficha antropométrica e do uniforme pandemônio: Lima Barreto e a internação de 1914," *Sociologia e antropologia* 1, no. 1 (2011): 119–49, 142.

115. Machado de Assis, *The Alienist* (1881), in *The Collected Stories of Machado de Assis*, trans. Margaret Jull Costa and Robin Patterson (New York: Liveright, 2018), 315–62, 320.

116. Pinel, *A Treatise on Insanity*, 78, 82. One of the most fascinating parts of

Pinel's book is his description of the French Revolutionary purge of religion from the asylum. How to remove the icons of saints and crosses from the chapel, given the devotion of many of the patients? The solution was to enlist other patients to do the work, amplifying their devotion to "the revolution," and then destroy the images and objects by fragmenting them into many pieces, apparently to render them less available to identify with.

117. Examples of doctors' secularizing efforts are abundant. In his doctoral thesis on the insanity of the crowd, one Dr. João Pacifico was direct: "Religions should not be considered the causes of insanity, but rather their effect. Medicine is the one true religion." João Pacifico, "A Loucura das multidões" (PhD thesis, Clinical Psychiatry, Rio de Janeiro, 1915), 83.

118. See Pacifico, "A Loucura das multidões," xxii.

119. Machado de Assis, *O alienista e outras histórias* (Rio de Janeiro: EDIOURO, 1996), 21.

120. Monique de Siqueira Gonçalves, "Mente sã, corpo são (disputas, debates e discursos medicos na busca pela cura das 'nevroses' a da loucura na Corte Imperial, 1850–1880)" (PhD thesis, Casa de Oswaldo Cruz/Fiocruz, 2011), 75. Certainly the Hospício Pedro II did not always follow the rules of the Salpêtrière. Magali Gouveia Engel reports, e.g., that, in its 1852 bylaws (Art. 25), the Rio de Janeiro institution prohibited the use of treatment baths on the grounds that they too easily veered into a form of punishment. See Magali Gouveia Engel, *Os delírios da razão: Medicos, loucos e hospícios, Rio de Janeiro, 1830–1930* (Rio de Janeiro: Editora FIOCRUZ, 2001), 212. Perhaps in theory. In practice, the admission documents and treatment protocols make it clear that baths were widely applied in Rio, as in Paris.

121. "O medico alienista pouco receita; observa porém as condições higiênicas do doentes, consola-o, anima-o e procura por todos os meios ao seu alcance a restituir-lhe a calma do espírito." Manoel José Barbosa cited in Gonçalves, "Mente sã, corpo são," 63.

122. *Observações clínicas de 20 abril a 17 de julho*, 1897, vol. 7, 156, 160.

123. Schwarcz, "O homen da ficha antropométrica," 137.

124. Afonso Henriques de Lima Barreto, *Diário do hospício e c cemitério dos vivos* (Rio de Janeiro: Biblioteca Carioca, 1993), 66.

125. Lima Barreto cited in Schwarcz, "O homen da ficha antropométrica," 142.

126. Maria Vanessa Andrade, Aluísio Ferreira de Lima, and Maria Elisalene Alves dos Santos, "A razão e a loucura na literatura: Um estudo sobre o alienista, de Machado de Assis," *Revista psicologia e saúde* 6, no. 1 (2014): 37–48, 40.

127. On the new school for training nurses, see Arquivo Nacional, Série Saúde IS3 21, ofícios e relatórios 1900–1901, 6. "Fetish" of university degrees, in Lima Barreto, *Diário*, 60.

128. Lima Barreto, *Diário*, 83.

129. The first case where it appears is that of "Margarida," described as black, fifty years old, and suffering from alcoholism and alcohol-related delirium. Margarida entered observation on May 25, 1897. *Observações clínicas de*

20 abril a 17 de julho, 1897, vol. 7, 117. *Zoopsia* is a clear loan word imported from abroad. In other cases, however, it is equally obvious that psychiatric terms had independent origins on both sides of the Atlantic. For example, *oceanic feeling*, commonly attributed to Romain Rolland in a 1927 letter to Freud, had already appeared in January 1897 in the observation records of a Brazilian institution situated, in fact, right on the sea. *Observações clínicas de 4 de janeiro a 22 de março*, vol. 6, 1897, 17.

130.   *Observações clínicas de 20 abril a 17 de julho*, 1897, vol. 7, 157.

131.   *Observações clínicas de 15 janeiro a 27 abril*, 1898, vol. 10, 20–25.

132.   *Observações clínicas de 2 novembero a 12 de outubro*, vol. 19, 1899, 73.

133.   *Observações clínicas de 18 de julho a 16 de outubro*, vol. 8, 1898, 25.

134.   *Observações clínicas de 18 de julho a 16 de outubro*, vol. 8, 1898, 71.

135.   *Observações clínicas de 23 de setembro a 15 de dezembro*, vol. 5, 1896, 36.

136.   *Observações clínicas de 2 novembro a 12 de dezembro*, vol. 19, 1899, 66.

137.   *Observações clínicas de 23 de setembro a 15 de dezembro*, vol. 5, 1896, 105.

138.   *Observações clínicas de 21 de abril a 24 de maio*, 1899, 146.

139.   *Observações clínicas de 18 de julho a 16 de outubro*, vol. 8, 1898, 36.

140.   *Observações clínicas de 18 de julho a 16 de outubro*, vol. 8, 1898, 135.

141.   Erving Goffman described this as characteristic of the asylum. Adults would be administered punishments typically reserved for animals and children; this would be part of the necessary "embarrassment to one's autonomy." See Erving Goffman, *Asylums: Essays on the Social Situation of Mental Patients and Other Inmates* (New York: Anchor, 1961), 44, 51.

142.   *Observações clínicas de 20 de junho a 28 de setembro*, 1896, vol. 4, 30. See also these other cases: Angelo Paulo Fudomenico, admitted June 20, 1896 (*Observações clínicas de 26 de maio a 19 de junho*, vol. 3, 72), Pedro Gonzaga da Costa (*Observações clínicas de 23 de setembro a 15 de dezembro*, 1896, vol. 5, 26–27); unnamed patient (*Observações clínicas de 20 de junho a 28 de setembro*, 1896, vol. 4, 22). "Movimentos automaticos" as a symptom appears in *Observações clínicas de 21 de abril a 24 de maio*, 1899, 36.

143.   *Observações clínicas de 2 de novembro a 12 de dezembro*, vol. 19, 1899, 27.

144.   *Observações clínicas de 26 de maio à 19 de julho*, 1896, vol. 3, p. 26.

145.   *Observações clínicas de 20 de julho à 28 de setembro*, 1896, vol. 4, p. 30.

146.   Harold Garfinkel, "Conditions of Successful Degradation Ceremonies," *American Journal of Sociology* 61, no. 5 (1956): 420–24.

147.   Evaluation of October 8, 1896. *Observações clínicas 23 de setembro à 15 de dezembro*, 1896, vol. 5, 6–7. *Confesses* does not appear frequently other than in relation to participation in spiritism. One additional topic it appears in relation to is onanism, as in, "Confesses to onanism" ("Confessa que foi onanista"). *Observações clínicas de 21 de abril a 24 de maio*, 1899, 35.

148.   *Observações clínicas de 20 de julho a 28 de setembro*, 1896, vol. 4, 112.

149.   *Observações clínicas de 21 de abril a 24 de maio*, 1899, 139.

150.   *Observações clínicas de 2 novembro a 12 de dezembro*, vol. 19, 1899, 48.

151.   *Observações clínicas 23 de setembro à 15 de dezembro*, 1896, vol. 5, 89.

152. *Observações clínicas de 17 outubro a 14 janeiro, 1898*, vol. 9, 172.

153. *Observações clínicas de 15 janeiro a 27 abril*, 1898, vol. 10, 39.

154. *Observações clínicas de 15 janeiro a 27 abril*, 1898, vol. 10, 186.

155. Pinel, *A Treatise on Insanity*, 66.

156. Nina Rodrigues, *O animismo fetichista*, 51.

157. Raymundo Nina Rodrigues, *L'animisme fétichiste des nègres de Bahia* (Bahia: Reis, 1900), 1.

158. Nina Rodrigues, *O animismo fetichista*, 77–82.

159. This happens in Cuba too, where, Fernando Ortiz reported, he was easily able to discover simulated possession. See Fernando Ortiz, *Los negros brujos* (1906; Miami: Ediciones Universal, 1973), 84.

160. de Certeau, *The Possession at Loudun*, 22.

161. Zora Neale Hurston, "Race Cannot Become Great Until It Recognizes Its Talent," *Washington Tribune*, December 29, 1934. Charcot and Janet each recorded similar instances of failed hypnotism. Charcot failed to hypnotize Louise Augustine Gleizes, who escaped the Salpêtrière in 1880, disguised in men's clothing. See Hustvedt, *Medical Muses*, 297. Janet tried and failed to hypnotize Achilles. See Janet, *Néuroses et idées fixes*, 379–86. He even tried to call in the chaplain "to teach him how to distinguish between true religion and diabolical superstition," but the priest was unable to attend. Ibid., 386.

162. Nina Rodrigues, *O animismo fetichista*, 75, 87; Henri Meige, *Les possédées noires* (Paris: Imprimerie Schiller, 1894). See also Plotkin, *Freud in the Pampas*, 14. Plotkin writes that psychoanalysis was rapidly appropriated in Brazil for different reasons than it was in Argentina, "in the hope of applying it to . . . concerns about subduing the exotic and 'savage' components of their culture." Ibid. Evidence for this is abundant in the writing of both Nina Rodrigues and his student Arthur Ramos. Ramos sent his manuscripts to Freud, including his "Primitivo e loucura" (Insanity and the primitive) (PhD thesis, Faculdade da Medicina da Bahia, 1926). Freud thanked him for the texts in cards sent from Vienna on November 3, 1928, January 6, 1932, and February 1, 1932. Arquivo Ramos, I-35, 29, 1303; I-35, 29, 1306, Biblioteca Nacional, Rio de Janeiro.

163. The other signatories were Pedro's longtime physician in Brazil, Mota Maia, and the French doctor Bouchard, though the emperor had also consulted with Pasteur and others. See Carvalho, *Dom Pedro II*, 200, 238.

164. See, e.g., Francisco Cândido Xavier, *Parnaso de Além Túmulo: Poesias mediumnicas psychographadas* (Rio de Janeiro: Livraria da Federação Espírita Brasileira, 1932).

165. "Vers les quatre heures du matin, au petit jour, je me révellai dans ma chamber d'hôtel, donnant sur le parc, plein de chants d'oiseaux. Je perçus une présence, et, sans que la porte se fût ouverte, le professeur Charcot m'apparut, telle une forme grave et pesante, très reconnaissable, traversant la pièce dans sa largeur. Sa chemise, d'une blancheur mystique, était

ouverte sur son cou puissant et il portait la main à son coeur. Il disparut, il s'évapora dans les trilles du petit people ailé, lui qui aimait tant la belle musique. J'eus immédiatement l'intuition qu'il était arrivé malheur." Daudet, *Les oeuvres dans les hommes*, 238.

166. Hacking, *Mad Travelers*, 31.

167. Goldstein, *Console and Classify*, 330.

168. A. Baudouin, "Quelques souvenirs de la Salpêtrière," *Paris médical* 21 (1925): 517–20.

169. *Neuromimésie*: "cette propriété qu'on les affections sine material de simuler les maladies organiques." Jean-Martin Charcot, "Clinique des maladie nerveuses," *Paris médical* 58 (1925): 465–78, 468. In this inaugural lesson, Charcot was direct about the possibilities of fakery in hysteria: "Il s'agit de la catalepsie produite par hypnotization chez certaines hystériques. La question est celle-ci: cet état peut-il être simulé de façon à tromper le médecin?" He described tests he devised to compare simulators and real cataleptics. The former, he noted, begin to have trembling limbs, whereas the latter never tire of holding an arm outstretched. Ibid., 469. See also Charcot, *Leçons sur les maladies du système nerveux*, 248. Here, Charcot noted: "Les supercheries de tout genre dont les hystériques se rendent coupables."

170. Léon Daudet, the son of Charcot's close friend Alphonse Daudet and a frequent visitor to the Charcots' home in his childhood and early adulthood, was especially brutal in his satirical *Les morticoles*, among other writings. In the present period, Edward Shorter is particularly sharp in his critique. See Shorter, *A History of Psychiatry*.

171. Josef Babinski, *Hysteria or Pithiatism*, trans. by J. D. Rolleston (London: University of London Press, 1918), 17.

172. Souques and Meige, "Jean-Martin Charcot," 345. The report that, nearing death, Charcot acknowledged the need to rethink his model was reported by his last personal secretary. See Guillain, *Charcot*, 176.

173. Guy de Maupassant, "Une femme," *Gil Blas*, August 16, 1882, 355. The invention of psychiatric illness is a figure that has lived at least nine lives. Frantz Fanon, e.g., proposed that Europeans' colonial imposition of psychiatry on continental Africans produced new psychoses. See Frantz Fanon, *Peau noire, masques blancs* (Paris: Editions du Seuil, 1952). Thanks to Nana Quarshie for drawing my attention to Fanon in this context.

174. Didi-Huberman, *Invention of Hysteria*, 229. In a similar vein, the anthropologist I. M. Lewis describes Charcot as inducing the "grand hysteria" he then cured. See I. M. Lewis, *Ecstatic Religion* (Harmondsworth: Penguin, 1971), 45.

175. Veith, *Hysteria*, 228. In terms of Charcot's loss of status in Brazil, consider just one major Rio de Janeiro newspaper as representative, the *Gazeta de notícias*. There Charcot appears in print 1 time in the 1870s, 95 times in the 1880s, 119 times in the 1890s, 328 times from 1900 to 1919, 28 times in the 1920s, and 12 times in the 1930s. The diagnosis *hysterica* follows a similar

arc in the Brazilian press, though it lingers longer, with 50 citations in the 1940s before a swift descent.

176. Hacking, *Mad Travelers*, 1–2.
177. Malcolm Macmillan, *Freud Evaluated* (Cambridge, MA: MIT Press, 1997), 66–67.
178. This had implications for law, among other domains. Charcot was called as an expert witness on the most famous homicide case of the time, "l'affaire Gouffé" (1889), in which, as we have seen, an accomplice in the strangulation of Toussaint-Augustin Gouffé, Gabrielle Bompard, claimed to have been hypnotized by her partner, Michel Eyraud, and to have acted automatically, beyond will. To the police, she said: "This man . . . he stole my free will." Eyraud was guillotined. Bompard served a much lesser sentence of fourteen years of labor in prison. Bompard cited in Levingston, *Little Demon in the City of Light*, 20.
179. James, *Brazil through the Eyes of William James*, 99–100.
180. Perhaps it should not come as a surprise that André Breton was a psychiatry intern prior to launching surrealism. It's possible to imagine the techniques of automatic writing used by spiritists and surrealists involving actual diffusion out from the sanitarium, since Breton studied psychiatric medicine, including hysteria, from 1913 to 1920. He worked at La Pitié Hospital next to the Salpêtrière, under the direction of Charcot's former pupil Joseph Babinski. His First Manifesto of Surrealism appeared just after he left medicine, in 1924. See Joost Haan, Peter J. Koehler, and Julien Bogousslavsky, "Neurology and Surrealism: André Breton and Joseph Babinski," *Brain* 135, no. 12 (2012): 3830–38.
181. Henrique de Brito Belford Roxo, *Manual de psiquiatria* (1921; Rio de Janeiro: Françisco Alves, 1938), 743.
182. Paulo Barreto (João do Rio), *As religões no Rio* (1906; Rio de Janeiro: Edição da Organização Simões, 1951), 51.

Chapter 2

1. For example: "Pedem-se providencias para um Segundo Juca Rosa existente na rua do Principe, de nome Laurentino, chefe de feitiçaria, tendo por companheiro um tal Alfa, pretos minas que têm em seu poder filhas-familia, e nesse zungú encontram-se diversos objectos proprios da feitiçaria." *Gazeta de notícias*, March 19, 1880, 3. And: "Não havia meio de descobrir se o medico seria ou não algum Juca Rosa." *Gazeta da tarde*, July 6, 1882, 2. And: "Existe nas proximidades d'aquella villa um celebre preto, conhecido por Pai Cabinda, o qual é um verdadeiro Juca Rosa d'aquellas paragens." *Gazeta de notícias*, February 3, 1881, 1. And: "Na fatal epidemia da questão Juca Rosa." *A nação*, October 14, 1872, 1.
2. Débora Michels Mattos, "Saúde e escravidão na Ilha de Santa Catarina, 1850–1888" (PhD diss., Universidade de São Paulo, 2015), 122–24.

3. As for the accusation of the theft of Catholicism, the lead inspector, Miguel José Tavares, wrote in the opening pages of the case file: "The audacity and perversity of these criminals goes to the point of involving our Holy Religion in its infamous practices, succeeding in substituting it with the most crude and abject superstition." ("A audacia e perversidade d'estes criminosos chega ao ponto de involver a nossa Santa Religião em suas practices infames, consequindo substituila pela mais grosseira e abjecta superstição.") A few pages further on: "Rosa dares to make use of the images and names of the saints of the Catholic Church, in order to take advantage of even the religiosity of his victims, which he transforms into the crudest and vilest superstition." ("Rosa atreve-se a servir-se de imagens e do nome de Santos da Igreja Catholica, afim de aproveitar-se até da religiosidade de suas victimas . . . religiosidade que elle transforma na mais grosseira e vil superstição.") Supremo Tribunal de Justiça BR AN RIO BV.O.RCR.0470, 1870.3, Maço 196, No. 1081, Arquivo Nacional, Rio de Janeiro, 12b. Not incidental in these discourses is the debate over what constitutes religion. The defense lawyer, Fillipe Jansen de Castro Albuquerque Jr., rejected the notion that Rosa could be declared guilty on the basis of a dubious opposition between sorcery and religion: "This fame, this power, these wonders, when tolerated and not suppressed by the police, repeated over many years, will elevate these 'sorceries' to a 'belief' or 'religion.'" Ibid., 214b.

4. "O feiticeiro . . . para tudo tem poder, porque o seu santo tudo sabe, tudo ouve e tudo conta. . . . O feiticeiro diz-se inspirado por um poder invisível que não é Deus, nem santo do nosso conhecimento." *Diário de notícias,* October 2, 1870, cited in Gabriela dos Reis Sampaio, *Juca Rosa: Um pai-de-santo na Corte Imperial* (Rio de Janeiro: Prêmio Arquivo Nacional 2007), 40.

5. Sampaio, *Juca Rosa,* 99. One of these "weak spirits" was Leopoldina Fernandes Cabral, who told Tavares that even when she wanted to break free from Rosa's influence, she could not because he had threatened her, "telling her that if she does (leave), he, with the spirit that he ruled for good as for harm, would disgrace her and make her end up in at Mercy Hospital." In the case record, see Supremo Tribunal de Justiça BR AN RIO BV.O.RCR.0470, 1870.3, Maço 196, No. 1081, Arquivo Nacional, Rio de Janeiro, 12b.

6. See, e.g., "Cronica da semana," *Gazeta de notícias,* September 23, 1888, 1.

7. My thinking on religion, photography, and the visual has been informed by, among others, Colleen McDannell, *Material Christianity: Religion and Popular Culture in America* (New Haven, CT: Yale University Press, 1995); Birgit Meyer, "'There Is a Spirit in That Image': Mass-Produced Jesus Pictures and Protestant-Pentecostal Animation in Ghana," *Comparative Studies in Society and History* 52, no. 1 (2010): 100–130; David Morgan, *Visual Piety: A History and Theory of Popular Religious Images* (Chicago: Univer-

sity of Chicago Press, 1999), and *The Sacred Gaze: Religious Visual Culture in Theory and Practice* (Berkeley and Los Angeles: University of California Press, 2005); W. J. T. Mitchell, *What Do Pictures Want? The Lives and Loves of Images* (Chicago: University of Chicago Press, 2005); Daniel Miller, ed., *Materiality* (Durham, NC: Duke University Press, 2005); Christopher Pinney, *Photos of the Gods: The Printed Image and Political Struggle in India* (London: Reaktion, 2004); Sally Promey, ed., *Sensational Religion: Sensory Cultures in Material Practice* (New Haven, CT: Yale University Press, 2014); Webb Keane, "The Evidence of the Senses and the Materiality of Religion," *Journal of the Royal Anthropological Institute* 14 (2008): 110–27; and Geneviève Zubrzycki, *Beheading the Saint: Nationalism, Religion, and Secularism in Quebec* (Chicago: University of Chicago Press, 2016). Sally Promey has been especially important as an interlocutor and mentor on all things visual.

8. Beatriz Jaguaribe and Maurício Lissovsky, "The Visible and the Invisibles: Photography and Social Imaginaries in Brazil," *Public Culture* 21, no. 1 (2009): 175–209, 177.

9. If Marcel Gauchet is right, disenchantment cannot ever be fully or at least so easily achieved, not least because we do not even yet have the tools to know how an autonomous individual might really work, apart from in relation to a state that automatically guarantees a degree of social cohesion, economic structure, and many other functions, a backdrop without which the individual is hard to conceive. Marcel Gauchet, *The Disenchantment of the World: A Political History of Religion*, trans. Oscar Burge (Princeton, NJ: Princeton University Press, 1997), 188.

10. On photography and materializing spirits, see Fritz Kramer, *The Red Fez: Art and Spirit Possession in Africa* (London: Verso, 1987), 257. On spirits and phonography, see Stephan Palmié, "The Ejamba of North Fairmont Avenue, the Wizard of Menlo Park, and the Dialectics of Ensoniment: An Episode in the History of an Acoustic Mask," in *Spirited Things: The Work of "Possession" in Black Atlantic Religions*, ed. Paul Christopher Johnson (Chicago: University of Chicago Press, 2013), 47–78.

11. Giordana Charuty, "La 'boîte aux ancêtres': Photographie et science de l'invisible," *Terrain* 33 (1999): 57–80.

12. Lorraine Daston and Peter Galison, *Objectivity* (New York: Zone, 2007), 120–21. And: "The automatism of the photographic process promised images free of human interpretation." Ibid., 130–31.

13. See Gilberto Ferrez and Weston J. Naef, *Pioneer Photographers of Brazil, 1840–1920* (New York: Center for Inter-American Relations, 1976), 14. Almost simultaneously with Daguerre, and wholly independently of him, a French émigré named Antoine Hercules Romauld Florence who arrived in Brazil in 1824 appears to have also invented what he called *photographie*, in the town of Vila São Paulo (now called Campinas) in the state of São Paulo. See Robert Levine, *Images of History: Nineteenth and Early Twen-*

tieth Century Latin American Photographs as Documents (Durham, NC: Duke University Press, 1989), 7–9; and Ana Maria Mauad, "Imagem e auto-imagem do Segundo Reinado," in *História da vida privada no Brasil*, vol. 2, *Império: A corte e a modernidade nacional*, ed. Luiz Felipe de Alencastro and Fernando A. Novais (São Paulo: Editora Schwarcz, 1997), 187.

14. Photography revealed what the naked eye cannot see, presenting an *agenda of the invisible*, as Lissovsky put it: "The history of nineteenth-century photography was marked by this agenda of the invisible: spirit portraits, the dissection of movement by Muybridge and Marey, the iconographies of the insane and the sickness of the soul (Hugh Diamond and the assistants of Jean Charcot), the inventories of criminal types, ethnographic photography. . . ." Maurício Lissovsky, "Guia prático das fotografias sem pressa," in *Retratos modernos*, ed. Cláudia Beatriz Heynemann and Maria do Carmo Teixeira Rainho (Rio de Janeiro: Arquivo Nacional, 2005), 2. See also Hacking, *Rewriting the Soul*, 5.

15. *Jornal do comércio*, January 17, 1840. "É preciso ter visto a cousa com os seus próprios olhos para se fazer ideía da rapidez e do resultado da operação. Em menos de nove minutos, o chafariz do largo de Paço, a praça do Peixe, o mosteiro de São Bento e todos os outros objetos circunstantes se acharam reproduzidos com tal fidelidade, preçisao e minuciosidade, que bem se via que a cousa tinha sido feita pela própria mão de natureza, e quase sem intervenção do artista."

16. *New York Observer*, April 20, 1839, 62.

17. *O país*, March 31, 1889.

18. Stieglitz cited in Diamuid Costello, *On Photography: A Philosophical Inquiry* (New York: Routledge, 2017), 6.

19. Costello, *On Photography*, 6.

20. André Bazin, *What Is Cinema?*, trans. Hugh Gray (Berkeley and Los Angeles: University of California Press, 1967), 1:10–14.

21. Susan Sontag, *On Photography* (New York: Farrar, Strauss & Giroux, 1977), 3, 8, 10, 12.

22. Roland Barthes, *Camera Lucida: Reflections on Photography*, trans. Richard Howard (New York: Farrar, Strauss & Giroux, 1981), 9.

23. Charuty, "La 'boîte aux ancêtres.'"

24. For the idea of the photograph as "the advent of myself as other," see Barthes, *Camera Lucida*, 12. For "photographic ecstasy," see ibid., 119. *Poiesis* gestures here especially toward Heidegger's idea of ecstasies as a breaking forth from one state into another and Plato's idea in the "Symposium" of making as a quest for immortality. The term is used in Michael Lambek, "The Sakalava Poiesis of History: Realizing the Past through Spirit Possession in Madagascar," *American Ethnologist* 25, no. 2 (1998): 106–27. John Collins also refers to Heidegger and poiesis in his exploration of the work of "heritage" in Bahia. See John F. Collins, *The Revolt of the Saints: Memory*

and Redemption in the Twilight of Brazilian Racial Democracy (Durham, NC: Duke University Press, 2015), 32.

25. João Vasconcelos, "Homeless Spirits: Modern Spiritualism, Psychical Research and the Anthropology of Religion in the Late Nineteenth and Early Twentieth Centuries," in *On the Margins of Religion*, ed. Frances Pine and João de Pina-Cabral (New York: Berghahn, 2007), 13–38.

26. Alfred Russell Wallace, *Perspectives in Psychical Research*, 3rd ed. (1896; New York: Arno, 1975), xiv; Cesare Lombroso, *After Death—What? Spiritistic Phenomena and Their Interpretation*, trans. William Sloane Kennedy (Boston: Small, Maynard, 1909), 167; Arthur Conan Doyle, *History of Spiritualism* (Cambridge: Cambridge University Press, 2011). Lombroso explained in detail how spirit photography worked: "Here, as in other tests, it is evident that we are dealing with a substance invisible to the eye, and one that is self-luminous, and which reflects upon photographic plates rays of light to the action of which our retina is insensible, and which is formed in the presence of certain mediums, or psychics, and has such photochemical energy as to enforce the development of its own image before other images, and also has a progressive development." Lombroso, *After Death—What?*, 261.

27. Sontag, *On Photography*, 9. Sontag echoes Bazin's reference to the death mask, though without acknowledging it.

28. James George Frazer, *The Golden Bough: A Study in Magic and Religion*, vol. 3, pt. 2, *Taboo and the Perils of the Soul*, 3rd ed. (London: Macmillan, 1911), 96–99. Frazer's examples were drawn mostly from Amerindians and Africans, but included a few Southeast Asian cases, and ended with the margins of Europe: an old woman on the Greek island of Carpathius, a 110-year-old Albanian, and a "gypsy girl" in England.

29. James, *Brazil through the Eyes of William James*, 22–23. The mid-twentieth century found North Americans seeking out Brazilian photographs for examples of racial integration, apparently absent in the North. Arthur Ramos wrote a letter to a Brazilian military commander stating that the writer and journalist Dr. George S. Schuyler desired to take photographs of harmonious racial integration in the Brazilian army and navy. Arquivo Ramos, "Cara ao comandante do Corpo de Fuzileiros Navais," Rio de Janeiro, July 13, 1948, Document 114, Biblioteca Nacional, Rio de Janeiro. In another example, Mr. Joseph Birdsell wrote to Ralph L. Beals, who in turn wrote to Ramos requesting a photograph of a Brazilian crowd with "as much mixture of racial types as possible." Arquivo Ramos, Document 90, January 11, 1948, Biblioteca Nacional, Rio de Janeiro.

30. The anecdote is related in Tuke, *Sleepwalking and Hypnotism*, 64. Tuke presents it as a personal communication from Richer. I first encountered Tuke's *Sleepwalking and Hypnotism* in Charcot's library.

31. Letter to Bastide from Bernard Beisenberger, October 20, 1961, Bastide

Archives, IMEC (Institut Mémoires de l'Édition Contemporaine), Fonds Roger Bastide, Fonds Roger Bastide, BST2.N1-02.05.

32. Exod. 20:4; Deut. 5:8. The idea is that creating a likeness of God's creation is an extension of the violation of the Second Commandment against creating a likeness of God.

33. See *United States v. Slabaugh*, 852 F.2d 1081 (1988).

34. Georges Bataille, *L'erotisme* (Paris: Editions de Minuit, 1957); Karen McCarthy Brown, *Mama Lola: A Vodou Priestess in Brooklyn* (Berkeley and Los Angeles: University of California Press, 1991), 7.

35. Jean-Martin Charcot, "The Faith-Cure," *New Review* 8, no. 44 (1893): 18–31.

36. Arquivo Tobias Monteiro 63,04,004, No. 26, 1288, Biblioteca Nacional, Rio de Janeiro.

37. On the tension between aesthetic and scientific photography, see Daston and Galison, *Objectivity*, 120–30.

38. Nancy Leys Stepan, "Portraits of a Possible Nation: Photographing Medicine in Brazil," *Bulletin of the History of Medicine* 68, no. 1 (1994): 137.

39. The small, 2.5- by 4-inch *carte de visite* photographs and the much cheaper wet-plate process used to make them were patented in Paris in 1854 by André Adolphe E. Disdéri and popularized after Napoléon III had a *carte de visite* photograph produced in 1859. Eight shots would be printed from a single plate, making these portraits much cheaper to reproduce than earlier kinds. *Carte de visite* photographs took both Europe and the Americas by storm in the 1860s, becoming standard currency of social exchange, and inspiring an early culture of celebrity with the circulation of photographs of royalty. See Levine, *Images of History*, 24. Cabinet cards, which eclipsed *cartes de visite* by the 1880s, were produced by the same process but were larger, 6.5 by 4.5 inches.

40. Jaguaribe and Lissovsky, "The Visible and the Invisible," 178.

41. Mattijs Van de Port, *Ecstatic Encounters: Bahian Candomblé and the Quest for the Really Real* (Amsterdam: Amsterdam University Press, 2011), 85.

42. In London, there were 284 studios in operation. On Rio's data, see Mauad, "Imagen e auto-imagem do Segundo Reinado," 199. The data comparing London and Rio appear in Pedro Karp Vasquez, *Dom Pedro II e a fotografia no Brasil* (Rio de Janeiro: Fundação Roberto Marinho, 1985), 20.

43. Lisa Earl Castillo, "Icons of Memory: Photography and Its Uses in Bahian Candomblé," *Stockholm Review of Latin American Studies* 4 (2009): 11–23, 12.

44. On the comaking of anthropology and photography, see Elizabeth Edwards, ed., *Anthropology and Photography* (London: Royal Anthropological Institute, 1992); and esp. Christopher Pinney, "The Parallel Histories of Anthropology and Photography," in ibid., 74–95. Spiritism, too, claimed a positivist stance: "As a means of elaboration, Spiritism proceeds in exactly the same course as the positive sciences; that is to say, it ap-

plies the experimental method." Allan Kardec, *Genesis: The Miracles and the Predictions According to Spiritism* (1868; New York: Spiritist Alliance, 2003), 18.

45. Stepan, "Portraits of a Possible Nation," 138. The issue of national evolution and progress appears in the choice of subject matter among nineteenth-century photographers in Brazil, who often favored shots of technological progress (a coffee plantation, a mine, a locomotive, a new tunnel, a modern city block) and national types (the slave, the Indian, the European immigrant family).

46. Jens Andermann, "Espetáculos da diferença: A Exposição Antropológica Brasileira de 1882," *Topoi—Revista de história* 5, no. 9 (2004): 128–70. Noteworthy in the exposition was the absolute absence of persons of African descent.

47. Sontag, *On Photography*, 3.

48. Sontag, *On Photography*, 7. Disdéri took portraits of the dead in their coffins. With up to forty thousand killed, spirit photography surged as an attempt to revive and retain the dead, just as it did in the wake of World War I.

49. Patricia Lavelle, *O espelho distorcido: Imagens do individuo no Brasil oitocentista* (Belo Horizonte: UFMG, 2003), 24–25.

50. Charcot, "The Faith-Cure," 24.

51. Van de Port, *Ecstatic Encounters*, 87.

52. Edison Carneiro, *Candomblés da Bahia* (Salvador: Museu do Estado, 1948).

53. Van de Port, *Ecstatic Encounters*, 85. On the dressing of deceased babies as *anjos*, see Dain Borges, *The Family in Bahia, 1870–1945* (Stanford, CA: Stanford University Press, 1985), 156.

54. Borges, *The Family in Bahia*, 155.

55. Roger Sansi, "Images and Persons in Candomblé," *Material Religion* 7, no. 3 (2011): 374–93, 385. See also Castillo, "Icons of Memory," 19–20; Van de Port, *Ecstatic Encounters*, 80; and Olívia Maria Gomes da Cunha, "Do ponto do visto de quem? Diálogos, olhares e etnografias dos/nos arquivos," *Estudos históricos* 36 (2005): 7–32. Olivia Gomes da Cunha describes how contemporary Candomblé adepts view photographs taken in 1938 in terms of their own spatial maps, genealogies, and present-day politics even as she adopts the same images into a project of finding alternative histories—"ethnographic time"—from the events documented in published texts.

56. One reason for spiritism's success in Brazil is that communication with spirits was and is a familiar phenomenon, even part of the social fabric. See Gilbert Velho, "Unidade e fragmentação em sociedades complexas," in *Duas conferências*, ed. Gilberto Velho and Otávio Velho (Rio de Janeiro: UFRJ Editora, 1992), 13–46, 27, 34, 41: "Identificamos a crença em espíritos e em possessão como um forte fator aglutinador de um universo so-

ciologicamente heterogêneo . . . da metrópole brasileira contemporânea."
Ibid., 27.

57. Marion Aubrée and François Laplantine, *La table, le livre et les esprits: Naissance, evolution et actualité du mouvement social spirite entre France et Brésil* (Paris: J. C. Lattès, 1990), 110.

58. Aubrée and Laplantine, *La table, le livre et les esprits*, 112–14; Emerson Giumbelli, *O cuidado dos mortos: Uma história da condenação e legitimação do Espiritismo* (Rio de Janeiro: Arquivo Nacional, 1997), 56, 61; David J. Hess, *Spirits and Scientists: Ideology, Spiritism, and Brazilian Culture* (University Park: Pennsylvania State University Press, 1991), 86.

59. Crista Cloutier, "Mumler's Ghosts," in *The Perfect Medium: Photography and the Occult*, ed. Clément Chéroux, Andreas Fischer, Pierre Apraxine, Denis Canguilhem, and Sophie Schmit (New Haven, CT: Yale University Press, 2005), 20–28.

60. Janet, *L'automatisme psychologique*, 385.

61. For details on Buguet's arrest, see Charuty, "La 'boîte aux ancêtres.'" His studio was located at 5, Montmartre Blvd. As Charuty described, his legitimacy had been consecrated by the spirit of Kardec himself, writing through the hand of his widow.

62. Militão's *Portrait with Spirit* (1880) is reproduced in Ferrez and Naef, *Pioneer Photographers of Brazil*, 69. Like Mumler in the United States, Buguet was accused of fraud for posing as a medium and pretending to produce spirits in his portraits. On interrogation, he immediately confessed, explained how he had achieved the illusion, and, once freed, reopened his studio as an antispirit portrait shop, offering portraits of clients with the overtly declared illusion of any spirit desired. His business card of 1875 read: "Photographie Anti-Spirite: Manipulation invisible. Le Spectre choisi est garanti. Illusion compléte. . . ." Clément Chéroux, "Ghost Dialectics: Spirit Photography in Entertainment and Belief," in Chéroux, Fischer, Apraxine, Canguilhem, and Schmit, eds., *The Perfect Medium*, 50. See also Cathy Gutierrez, *Plato's Ghost: Spiritualism in the American Renaissance* (New York: Oxford University Press, 2009), 69–71.

63. Despite the ample photographic documentation in João Reis's magisterial work on Domingos Sodré, a Ladino African priest in Bahia, no comparable sort of incriminating photograph—one used in the forensic process of unraveling secret ritual procedures—is present, nor am I aware of any other comparable photograph. See João José Reis, *Domingos Sodré, um sacerdote Africano: Escravidão, liberdade e Candomblé na Bahia do século XIX* (São Paulo: Companhia das Letras, 2008).

64. Sampaio, *Juca Rosa*, 185, 189. The term *macumba* appears multiple times in the case file as the name of an instrument and its music as well as of a class of people, *macumbeiros*, who frequent events where the *macumba* is played. See Supremo Tribunal de Justiça BR AN RIO BV.O.RCR.0470,

1870.3, Maço 196, No. 1081, Arquivo Nacional, Rio de Janeiro, 12b, 104, 138b.

65. Supremo Tribunal de Justiça BR AN RIO BV.O.RCR.0470, 1870.3, Maço 196, No. 1081, Arquivo Nacional, Rio de Janeiro, 35.

66. According to Michel-Rolph Trouillot, "silences enter the process of historical production at . . . the moment of fact making (the making of the *sources*)," not to mention in their assembly in an archive, their retrieval, and their narration. Michel-Rolph Trouillot, *Silencing the Past: Power and the Production of History* (Boston: Beacon, 1995), 26.

67. Supremo Tribunal de Justiça BR AN RIO BV.O.RCR.0470, 1870.3, Maço 196, No. 1081, Arquivo Nacional, Rio de Janeiro, 16, 20.

68. Mozart Dias Teixeira, also referred to as "Professor." See *Jornal do Brasil*, March 3, 1925, 16; *Jornal do Brasil*, January 22, 1925, 14; and *Jornal do Brasil*, September 9, 1930, 14. See also the case file of Dr. Mozart, 1930–36, 158. The presence or absence of photographs and other physical objects was key to investigators' decisions about whether a given ritual practice was *macumba* or so-called high spiritism, black magic, white magic, etc., and definitions of these classes of spiritism were integral to decisions about whether to prosecute, whether something was legitimately a religion or not, and so forth. See, e.g., the case file of Bento José Pereira, of 1928, 11–13b.

69. Supremo Tribunal de Justiça BR AN RIO BV.O.RCR.0470. 1870.3, Maço 196, No. 1081, Arquivo Nacional, Rio de Janeiro, 11.

70. Jonathan Crary, *Techniques of the Observer: On Vision and Modernity in the Nineteenth Century* (Cambridge, MA: MIT Press, 1992), 13.

71. Supremo Tribunal de Justiça BR AN RIO BV.O.RCR.0470, 1870.3, Maço 196, No. 1081, Arquivo Nacional, Rio de Janeiro, 67b, Deposition of November 23, 1870, 104, 129b, 132b.

72. Supremo Tribunal de Justiça BR AN RIO BV.O.RCR.0470, 1870.3, Maço 196, No. 1081, Arquivo Nacional, Rio de Janeiro, 67b, Deposition of November 23, 1870, 86b, 14b: "Fica considerado Pai da filiada e já senhor da alma, pela superstição torna-se senhor do corpo . . . prefere gosar das mulheres de um modo antenatural!"

73. Holloway finds that Afro-Brazilian religions were rarely directly policed in Rio during the nineteenth century, except when they intruded on "what the white elite considered a necessary level of social peace and public calm." Thomas H. Holloway, "'A Healthy Terror': Police Repression of Capoeiras in Nineteenth-Century Rio de Janeiro," *Hispanic American Historical Review* 69, no. 4 (1989): 645. I would argue that the Juca Rosa case marked the beginning of the problematizing of Afro-Brazilian religions as emancipation neared and those religions would become part of national life.

74. Sampaio, *Juca Rosa*, 186.

75. As we saw in chapter 1, even two decades later, when Nina Rodrigues, the psychiatrist and first anthropologist of Afro-Brazilian religions, brought one young woman into his office during the 1890s and, first inducing hypnosis, caused her to be possessed by a god, no photographic record was kept. Given the effort he took to control and document trance states, Nina Rodrigues almost certainly would have photographed her if he could have, but his documents are accompanied only by still-life photographs of statues and ritual implements, never ritual action. Photographs of trance in ritual action began to be taken only after 1930, enabled by higher-speed film, new repeating cameras made by Leica and Rolleiflex, and the flash bulb, a set of advances that generated the birth of photojournalism. See Castillo, "Icons of Memory," 17. To my knowledge, the first spontaneous photograph of spirit possession occurring in ritual action appeared in an ethnographic study by Michel Leiris. The photograph was taken in Ethiopia on September 27, 1932, and published in L'Afrique fantôme. See Michel Leiris, L'Afrique fantôme (1934; Paris: Gallimard, 1981), 388, plate 26.

76. Roger Bastide, "Cavalos dos santos: Esbôço de uma sociologia do transe místico," in Estudos afro-brasileiros, 3.a serie (São Paulo: Universidade de São Paulo, 1953), 29–60, 36–37 (redacted).

77. See Stephan Palmié, The Cooking of History: How Not to Study Afro-Cuban Religion (Chicago: University of Chicago Press, 2013), 307–8.

78. On transduction, see Webb Keane, "On Spirit Writing: Materialities of Language and the Religious Work of Transduction," Journal of the Royal Anthropological Institute 19 (2012): 1–17.

79. See, among others, Stefania Capone, Searching for Africa in Brazil: Power and Tradition in Candomblé, trans. Lucy Lyall Grant (Durham, NC: Duke University Press, 2010); Stefania Capone and Kali Argyriadis, La religion des orisha: Un champ social transnational en pleine recomposition (Paris: Editions Hermann, 2011); Chakrabarty, Provincializing Europe; Paul Christopher Johnson, Diaspora Conversions: Black Carib Religion and the Recovery of Africa (Berkeley and Los Angeles: University of California Press, 2007); Michael Lambek, The Weight of the Past: Living with History in Mahajanga, Madagascar (New York: Palgrave Macmillan, 2002); Stephan Palmié, Wizards and Scientists: Explorations in Afro-Cuban Modernity and Tradition (Durham, NC: Duke University Press, 2002); Richard Price, Travels with Tooy: History, Memory and the African American Imagination (Chicago: University of Chicago Press, 2007); Rosalind Shaw, Memories of the Slave Trade: Ritual and the Historical Imagination in Sierra Leone (Chicago: University of Chicago Press, 2002); and Paul Stoller, Embodying Colonial Memories: Spirit Possession, Power, and the Hauka in West Africa (New York: Routledge, 1995).

80. Roger Sansi, Fetishes and Monuments: Afro-Brazilian Art and Culture in the 20th Century (London: Berghahn, 2007), 22.

81. "—— escuros, mas você sabe que o pessoal não pode dansar fora do bar-

racão." Letter from Carneiro to Ramos, April 23, 1936, Coleção Ramos, Doc. 60, Rio de Janeiro, Biblioteca Nacional.

82. As Lisa Earl Castillo suggests, the role of photographs is conflicted even in present-day Afro-Brazilian religion. Contemporary Candomblé participants often seem to understand photographs not merely as representing or copying their subject but as retaining that person's substance. See Castillo, "Icons of Memory."

83. "Burning in effigy. Kissing a picture of a loved one. This is *obviously not* based on a belief that it will have a direct effect on the object that the picture represents. It aims at some satisfaction, and does achieve it, too. Or rather, it does not aim at anything; we act in this way and then feel satisfied." See Ludwig Wittgenstein, "Remarks on Frazer's *Golden Bough*," in Palmié, trans., and da Col, ed., *The Mythology in Our Language*, 29–54, 33. Wittgenstein's notes were also recounted and analyzed in Tambiah, *Magic, Science, Religion*, 59.

84. On the deeply ambivalent aspects of the use of Candomblé in Afro-Brazilian patrimonialization projects, see, among others, Collins, *Revolt of the Saints*; and Patrícia Pinho, *Mama Africa: Reinventing Blackness in Bahia* (Durham, NC: Duke University Press, 2010).

85. "No domingo passado, tirei umas fotografias que iam fazer furor, se prestassem. 'Assento' de Irôko, apetrechos dos orixás (carabina de Oxóssi, espada de Ogún, etc.), instrumentos musicais, tabaques, coisa muita. Mas o film estava velho e machucado. Perdi tudo. Pra semana vou tirar novamente." Letter of Carneiro to Ramos, February 21, 1936, Coleção Ramos, Doc. 58 (I-35, 25, 869), Rio de Janeiro, Biblioteca Nacional.

86. Roger Bastide's classic 1953 essay on possession in Candomblé, e.g., uses Verger's possession photographs as evidence of the "complete modification" of the person, narrating the appearance of the gods (*orixás*), "as the photographs show": "When an individual is possessed by Ogum, it matters little whether male or female, their face immediately takes on a terrifying look, *as the photographs show*; the person incarnates brute force, the genius of war and the magic of domination." Bastide, "Cavalos dos santos," 50–51 (emphasis added). What is striking here is that the photographs are claimed to show the complete and authentic transformation of the human being by virtue of the terrifying expression that appears on the face; the captions name only the god present, not the human carrier. It is as though no human subject or agent is present at all. The camera verifies the inner condition. Possession shots became the favored subject by around 1950 and continued to be applied as visual evidence of an internal state. They remain the most-desired target of camera-toting tourists visiting temples of Candomblé in Bahia today, setting up nearly routine confrontations between initiates and visitors based on contrasting notions of what photographs are and are for, a conflict over putative intent played out for probably the first time with Rosa's image in the police file.

87. Not only in ritual practice. In the mid-twentieth century, foreigners traveled to Brazil to study the country's race relations, taken as a global model. The ability to find what they sought was aided and abetted by photography, a techne for causing a desired truth to appear. For example, the North American journalist and writer George S. Schuyler traveled in Brazil in 1948, hoping to document the degree to which different "racial elements" were integrated in the Brazilian navy and army. The anthropologist Arthur Ramos therefore wrote on his behalf to the commander of naval gunners, asking him to facilitate Schuyler's photographs. Arquivo Coleção Ramos, Document 114, letter of July 13, 1948. The specific feature of the Brazilian crowd—racial integration—was routinely sought and made in photographs. Here is another example: "Mr. Joseph Birdsell of my department writes me . . . that he very much needs a glossy print of a photograph of a Brazilian crowd, front face view, which shows as much mixture of racial types as possible, as an illustration for a chapter he is writing in a book." Letter of Ralph L. Beals to Arthur Ramos, November 1, 1948, Coleção Ramos, Doc. 90.

88. Both citations are taken from Chéroux, "Ghost Dialectics," 48.

89. Leiris, L'Afrique fantôme, 499. Compare: "Once I feel myself observed by the lens, everything changes: I constitute myself in the process of 'posing,' I instantaneously make another body for myself." Barthes, Camera Lucida, 10.

90. Michel Leiris, La possession et ses aspects théâtraux chez les Éthiopiens de Gondar (Paris: Librairie Plon, 1958), 64.

91. Clara Saraiva, "Afro-Brazilian Religions in Portugal: Bruxos, Priests and Pais de Santo," Etnográfica 14, no. 2 (2010): 275 (emphasis added). Aisha M. Beliso–De Jesús shows the effects of digital mediations of the spirits and how spirits are rendered present via television and computer screens in Cuban and transnational Santería. The key issue for my purposes is how spirits, orichas, gain new qualities in what Beliso–De Jesús calls techno-ritual interspaces. See Aisha M. Beliso–De Jesús, Electric Santería: Racial and Sexual Assemblages of Transnational Religion (New York: Columbia University Press, 2015), 65.

92. Pierre Verger, Notas sobre o culto aos orixás e voduns (São Paulo: Editora USP, 1998), 83.

93. "Je l'avais prises en pleine hypnose; l'éclatement du magnesium, à deux mètres de ses yeux, n'avait pas amené le moindre tressaillement." Henri-Georges Clouzot, Le cheval des dieux (Paris: Julliard, 1951), 218.

94. Meyer, "'There Is a Spirit in That Image.'"

95. Tanya M. Luhrmann, "How Do You Learn to Know That It Is God Who Speaks?," in Learning Religion: Anthropological Approaches, ed. David Berliner and Ramon Sarró (New York: Berghahn, 2007), 92.

96. Edward Clarke, Visions: A Study of False Sight (Boston: Houghton, Osgood, 1878), 300.

97. Crary, *Techniques of the Observer*, 5; Daston and Galison, *Objectivity*, 143.

98. Katherine J. Hagedorn, *Divine Utterances: The Performance of Afro-Cuban Santería* (Washington, DC: Smithsonian Books, 2001), 11.

99. Mauad, "Imagem e auto-imagem do Segundo Reinado," 191.

100. "Order and progress" was derived from "L'Amour pour principe; l'Ordre pour base; le Progrès pour but," which appeared as the epigraph of Auguste Comte's *Système de politique positive; ou, Traité de sociologie, instituant le religion de l'humanité* (Paris: Larousse, 1851). Robert Levine notes that, even through the 1890s, photography continued to be understood in Latin America as a "compiler of facts." Levine, *Images of History*, 60. In Europe and the United States, by contrast, its use had shifted dramatically to take on the role of social critic in addition to the role of harvester of the neutral document, though, as Susan Sontag noted, it is never wholly stripped of the authority it gained as the register of something that was really there, no matter how creative and interpretative it becomes. Sontag, *On Photography*, 11.

101. Cícero Antônio F. de Almeida, *Canudos: Imagens da guerra* (Rio de Janeiro: Lacerda, 1997).

102. *Jornal do Brasil*, January 29, 1898.

Chapter 3

1. David Brion Davis offers a solid entry point here by identifying three generally accepted characteristics of slaves: they are (i) the property of another man, (ii) subject to the will of his owner, and (iii) forced to provide free labor through coercion. However, he also notes that these traits may also apply to wives and children in certain patriarchal settings. See David Brion Davis, *The Problem of Slavery in Western Culture* (New York: Oxford University Press, 1966), 29–61. Miers and Kopytoff frown on the use of the term *slavery* to identify a universal typology. Instead, they advise using a taxonomy of *slaveries* to identify the specific context of servitude under examination precisely. They suggest, e.g., *lineage slavery, office slavery, palace slavery, individual slavery*, etc. See Igor Kopytoff and Suzanne Miers, "African 'Slavery' as an Institution of Marginality," in *Slavery in Africa: Historical and Anthropological Perspectives*, ed. Suzanne Miers and Igor Kopytoff (Madison: University of Wisconsin Press, 1977), 3–84, 77. Kopytoff later wrote: "Slavery is a matter of becoming rather than being." Igor Kopytoff, "Slavery," *Annual Review of Anthropology* 11, no. 1 (1982): 207–30, 221. Saints' power accrues from a loss of will analogous to that of the slave but accepted willingly, especially in death. As Robert Orsi writes: "In the hour of death there is 'the final holocaust of self-will.'" Saints are, in a sense, perpetually frozen in the hour of their death and the perfect abnegation of will. Robert A. Orsi, *History and Presence* (Cambridge, MA: Belknap Press of Harvard University Press, 2016), 169.

2. The concept of a slave as having no soul resonates with the contemporary idea of what Orlando Patterson terms the *secular excommunication* or *natal alienation* of slaves as a requisite trait for enslavement: "Not only was the slave denied all claims on, and obligations to, his parents and living blood relations but, by extension, all such claims and obligations on his more remote ancestors and on his descendants. He was truly a genealogical isolate." Orlando Patterson, *Slavery and Social Death* (Cambridge, MA: Harvard University Press 1982), 5.

3. *Object* is a better word here than *thing*. Bill Brown qualified a *thing* as a dangerous material that does not "work" for us and, thus, is emptied of presence or power. As I show below, the question of whether Slave Anastácia is, as image or icon, a *thing* or an *object* is contested. Brown cited in Matthew Engelke, *A Problem of Presence: Beyond Scripture in an African Church* (Berkeley and Los Angeles: University of California Press, 2007), 27.

4. Eric Santner, *The Weight of All Flesh: On the Subject Matter of Political Economy* (Chicago: University of Chicago Press, 2015), 244.

5. John Markham, *Selections from the Correspondence of Admiral John Markham*, ed. Sir Clements Markham (London: Navy Records Society, 1904), 81 (entry of May 8, 1796).

6. Martin Heidegger, *Being and Time*, trans. Joan Stambaugh (Albany: State University of New York Press, 2010), 132, 130, 325.

7. Walter Benjamin, "The Work of Art in the Age of Mechanical Reproduction," in *Illuminations*, ed. Hannah Arendt (New York: Schocken, 1968), 217–52, 237.

8. Clifford Geertz famously made much of the phrase *moods and motivations* in his seminal essay "Religion as a Cultural System," but he was, in fact, much more interested in the second term, *motivations*, than in the first. Moods, to him, were mostly visible in dispositions or liabilities toward kinds of action. Moods themselves "vary only as to intensity": "They go nowhere." Geertz, *The Interpretation of Cultures*, 97.

9. Hayden White, *Metahistory: The Historical Imagination in Nineteenth-Century Europe* (Baltimore: Johns Hopkins University Press, 1975), 196 (on Tocqueville as well as the "perverse" mood of Gobineau), 28 (on the optimism in Ranke), 27 (on the tragic in Spengler), 144 (on historical drama cast in an emotional "color"), 10 and 18 (on ideological implications, depending on what a given social drama is alleged to have been a revelation of), 253–54 (on Giotto's paintings of Saint Francis).

10. James Grehan, *Twilight of the Saints: Everyday Religion in Ottoman Syria and Palestine* (New York: Oxford University Press, 2016), 64. Grehan cites the nineteenth-century Muslim jurist Abd al-Ghani al-Nabulsi on this bifurcation.

11. June McDaniel, *The Madness of the Saints: Ecstatic Religion in Bengal* (Chicago: University of Chicago Press, 1989), 91, 97, 126, 261.

12. Peter Brown, *The Cult of the Saints: Its Rise and Function in Latin Christianity* (Chicago: University of Chicago Press, 1981), 44, 87, 92.

13. Wendy Doniger O'Flaherty, *Siva: The Erotic Ascetic* (Oxford: Oxford University Press, 1981), 252–53.

14. Luiz Mott, *Rosa Egipcíaca: Uma santa africana no Brasil* (Rio de Janeiro: Editora Bertrand Brasil, 1993). Per Mott, Rosa was perhaps the first African-born author in Brazil. She wrote at length about her visions in terms that eventually drew the attention of the authorities. In one such vision, she was flagellated by and then nursed Jesus. In 1765, she was accused by the Office of the Inquisition and sent to Lisbon for trial. Her fate thereafter is unknown. Still, in her words, sainthood gained a mood. As Jonathan Flatley argues, the fact that reading is in some way mimetic is part of what motivates writing: "Reading involves acting and therefore also feeling like others." Jonathan Flatley, "Reading for Mood," *Representations*, no. 140 (2017): 137–48, 140.

15. Eliane Tânia Martins Freitas, "Violência e sagrado: O que no criminoso anuncia o santo?," *Cienças sociales y religión/Ciências sociais e religião* 2, no. 2 (2000): 191–203, 198.

16. Philippe Descola, "Presence, Attachment, Origin: Ontologies of 'Incarnates,'" in *A Companion to the Anthropology of Religion*, ed. Janice Boddy and Michael Lambek (Oxford: Wiley Blackwell, 2013), 35–49, 37.

17. Kristina Wirtz, *Ritual Discourse and Community in Cuban Santería: Speaking a Sacred World* (Gainesville: University Press of Florida, 2007), 130–34.

18. Engelke, *A Problem of Presence*, 28.

19. Machado de Assis, *Iaiá Garcia*, trans. Albert I. Bagby Jr. (Lexington: University Press of Kentucky, 1977), 7.

20. Patrick Eisenlohr, "Mediality and Materiality in Religious Performance: Religion as Heritage in Mauritius," *Material Religion* 9, no. 3 (2013): 328–48.

21. Birgit Meyer, "Mediation and Immediacy: Sensational Forms, Semiotic Ideologies and the Question of the Medium," *Social Anthropology* 19, no. 1 (2011): 23–39, 32.

22. Johnson, *Diaspora Conversions*, 182.

23. Charles Hirschkind suggests that the idea that religion is *essentially* mediative may require Protestant-like theological presuppositions of inner essence then externalized in a reductive mode. But, he argues, the Quran is not mediative of the traditions of Islam, far less a reductive expression. Rather, it *is* the tradition; even as a soccer ball does not mediate the game of soccer, but is rather constitutive of it. Charles Hirschkind, "Media, Mediation, Religion," *Social Anthropology* 19, no. 1 (2011): 90–97, 93. See also Meyer, "Mediation and Immediacy"; and Maria José A. de Abreu, "Technological Indeterminacy: Medium, Threat, Temporality," *Anthropological Theory* 13, no. 3 (2013): 267–84, and "TV St. Claire," in Stolow, ed., *Deus in Machina*, 261–80.

24. De la Cruz, *Mother Figured*, 138. While saints and their shrines instantiate local identifications, certain saints become translocal and transtemporal powers, achieving even global reach. De la Cruz shows how in the Philippines, e.g., Mary and Marian*ism* are modes of joining local apparitions to global circuits. Mother Mary is not only a product of mass media; she helped create mass mediation as a form and conduit of communications both local and global.

25. *Sanctorum mater* (Rome 2007), pt. 1 ("Causes of Beatification and Canonization"), title 2, article 4, http://www.vatican.va/roman_curia/congregations/csaints/documents/rc_con_csaints_doc_20070517_sanctorum-mater_en.html#Reputation_of_Holiness_or_of_Martyrdom_and_of_Intercessory_Power.

26. What is unusual about the incarnate, the saint called Slave Anastácia, is that she is a figuration that was also a collective memory, a drawing that collated, condensed, and embodied the history of slavery in Brazil. On Anastácia as representative or a composite of actual histories of enslaved women, see Mary Karasch, "Anastácia and the Slave Women of Rio de Janeiro," in *Africans in Bondage*, ed. Paul Lovejoy (Madison: University of Wisconsin Press, 1986), 29–105.

27. John Burdick, *Blessed Anastácia: Women, Race, and Popular Christianity in Brazil* (New York: Routledge, 1998); Jerome S. Handler and Kelly E. Hayes, "Escrava Anastácia: The Iconographic History of a Brazilian Popular Saint," *African Diaspora* 2 (2009): 25–51; Karasch, "Anastácia and the Slave Women of Rio de Janeiro"; Andréa Lúcia da Silva de Paiva, "Quando os 'objetos' se tornam 'santos': Devoção e patrimônio em uma igreja no centro do Rio de Janeiro," *Textos escolhidos de cultura e arte populares* 11, no. 1 (2014): 53–70; Robin E. Sheriff, "The Muzzled Saint: Racism, Cultural Censorship and Religion in Urban Brazil," in *Silence: The Currency of Power*, ed. Maria-Luisa Achino-Loeb (New York: Berghahn, 1996), 113–40; Monica Dias de Souza, "Escrava Anastácia e Pretos-Velhos: A rebelião silenciosa da memoria popular," in *Imaginário, cotidiano e poder*, ed. Vagner Gonçalves da Silva (São Paulo: Edições Selo Negro, 2007), 15–42; Marcus Wood, "The Museu do Negro in Rio and the Cult of Anastácia as a New Model for the Memory of Slavery," *Representations*, no. 113 (2011): 111–49.

28. Jacques Étienne Victor Arago, *Souvenirs d'un aveugle: Voyage autour du monde: Ouvvrage enrichi de soixante dessins et de notes scientifiques* (Paris: Hortet & Ozanne, 1839), 1:119. The original reads: "Au Brésil seul les esclaves se taisent, immobiles, sous la noueuse chicote."

29. Arago, *Souvenirs d'un aveugle*, 119: "En attendant, voyez cet home qui passe là, avec un anneau de fer auquel est adaptée verticalement une épée du meme metal, le tout serrant assez fortement le cou."

30. Arago, *Souvenirs d'un aveugle*, 119: "En voici un autre dont le visage est entièrement couvert d'un masque de fer, où l'on a pratiqué deux trous pour

les yeux, et qui est fermé derrière la tête avec un fort cadenas. Le misérable se sentait trop malheureux, il mangeait de la terre et du gravier pour en finir avec le fouet; il expiera sous le fouet sa criminelle tentative de suicide."

31. We might also note that the textual description of a full iron mask with two eyeholes does not match the depicted mask, which merely prevents eating and, perhaps, speaking. Also, the two tools of torture that are separate events in Arago's text are joined in the image. Therefore, it might be a mistake to assume that Arago intended the written text to correspond to the drawing. He may have seen text and image as distinct didactic modes.

32. Arago, *Souvenirs d'un aveugle*, 120.

33. Arago, *Souvenirs d'un aveugle*, 135.

34. Thomas H. Holloway, *Policing Rio de Janeiro: Repression and Resistance in a 19th-Century City* (Stanford, CA: Stanford University Press, 1993), 201–5, and "'A Healthy Terror.'"

35. Though, by exercising the loophole of refusing the government indemnity payment for the child, slave owners could still maintain a child under their authority until age twenty-one. See Thomas E. Skidmore, *Black into White: Race and Nationality in Brazilian Thought* (Durham, NC: Duke University Press 1993), 16.

36. Sidney Chalhoub, *Visões da liberdade* (São Paulo: Editora Schwarcz, 1990), 199.

37. Paulina L. Alberto, *Terms of Inclusion: Black Intellectuals in Twentieth-Century Brazil* (Chapel Hill: University of North Carolina Press, 2011). As Alberto shows, the movement built on decades of important earlier, if less visible, movements like the 1930s Black Front (Frente Negra).

38. The petition and letters requesting canonization as well as the archbishop's rejection are archived at the Museu do Negro. Thanks to Ricardo Passos, the museum director, for his help in locating them.

39. "A Arquidiocese do Rio de Janeiro não deixará, em conjunto com a Irmandade de Nossa Senhora do Rosário e São Benedito dos Homens Pretos e o Capelão da Igreja, de alertar os féis para a observância das normas eclesiasticas."

40. "Para isso espera também contar com a cooperação inteligente de ambos os signatários."

41. "Outrossim, informo ser inadequada a utilização do termo, 'agente de pastoral social.'"

42. Dias de Souza, "Escrava Anastácia e Pretos-Velhos," 39. According to Dias de Souza, the announcement was drafted by Dom Romeu Brigenti. The legitimacy of souls of slaves is one reason Slave Anastácia is presented as a member of that class in the Church of the Rosary in Bahia. This allows her a tolerated presence on the margins of the church site.

43. The conclusion was summarized in a press editorial: "Assim, devemos chegar à conclusão de que, por mais justo que seja compadecer-se com o sofrimento dos escravos negros, não podemos aceitar o culto litúrgico

duma figura que não existiu, baseando-nos numa gravura que não apresenta uma mulher, mas um homen (melhor: dois homens). Um movimento popular surgiu pela fantasia inventora do sr. Yolando Guerra. Esta fantasia pode server para um romance, um filme se quiser. Se a Umbanda aceita isso, não sabemos. A Igreja Católica não aceita." *Jornal do Brasil*, September 9, 1987, 11.

44.   *Jornal do Brasil*, March 25, 1988, Caderno B, p. 2

45.   Paiva, "Quando os 'objetos' se tornam 'santos,'" 68.

46.   Dias de Souza, "Escrava Anastácia e Pretos-Velhos," 39.

47.   See, among many examples, the issue of *O jornal* for May 13, 1973, to my knowledge the first such mainstream publication on Anastácia.

48.   Along Rua General Caldwell, just off Avenida Presidente Vargas near the city center.

49.   Examples include Bangu during the period of Marinho (Mário dos José dos Reis Emiliano) in 1987 and the player Maurício (de Oliveira Anastácio) of America and then Botafogo, reported as declaring: "In any case, I get out of bed with my right foot first and pray a lot to Saint Judas Tadeu, Nossa Senhora Aparecida, and Escrava Anastácia." *Jornal do Brasil*, October 14, 1989, 21.

50.   Dias de Souza, "Escrava Anastácia e Pretos-Velhos," 15.

51.   Andrea Paiva reports that the sculpture of the Unknown Slave was created by an Argentine, Humberto Cozzo, in 1970. Visitors whisper in the slave's ear, touch his face, and leave offerings ranging from cigarette butts (*giumba*), to bullets, to notes. Paiva, "Quando os 'objetos' se tornam 'santos,'" 56.

52.   Ricardo Santos, "Escrava Anastácia," in *Encyclopedia of the African Diaspora* (Denver, CO: ABC-CLIO, 2008), 85–86.

53.   Her presence and its modes are, we should insist, not fixed. No one I spoke with has seen her incorporated as a spirit possession in a living body, though one informant went into detail about the ways in which possession is relative. Some saints, after all, do not "possess" but do "lean against" living bodies (*encostar*). Possession as incorporation is a matter of degree, of coming near (*chegando perto*) to a human body. This person suggested that Anastácia may "come near."

54.   Burdick, *Blessed Anastácia*, 159.

55.   Burdick, *Blessed Anastácia*, 154; Wood, "The Museu do Negro," 133.

56.   As someone like Georges Bataille taught, such acts in no way contravene genuinely sacred impulses. Quite the contrary. See Georges Bataille, *Erotism: Death and Sensuality*, trans. Mary Dalwood (San Francisco: City Lights, 1986), 90.

57.   No case is a pure, full-blown manifestation of one of these modes. The types (and there are no doubt more) are variously combined in any actual empirical figuration of Anastácia. Yet any given site or situation incarnating her will hew closer to one or another as the dominant attractor position.

58. The National Day of Black Consciousness was instituted as a school holiday in 2003 and a national holiday in 2011. The estimates of visitors are from Ricardo Passos. Personal interview, May 28, 2016.

59. "Deusa-escrava, escrava-princesa, princesa-deusa . . . dai-nos tua força para lutarmos e nunca sermos escravas." Noteworthy is the informal and intimate mode of address (*tua força*), unusual in petitions addressed to other saints.

60. I invoke the problematic term *syncretism* with reluctance for obvious reasons: its imprecision and vague implications of pure vs. mixed traditions. It may prove more productive to speak of layered affiliations, multireligious practices, shifting arenas, and the strategic cultivating of parallelisms and double participation within larger, heterogeneous religious ecologies. On shifting arenas, see James Hoke Sweet, *Recreating Africa: Culture, Kinship, and Religion in the African-Portuguese World, 1441–1770* (Chapel Hill: University of North Carolina Press, 2003), 114. On strategic parallelisms and double participation, see Luis Nicolau Parés, *The Formation of Candomblé: Vodun History and Ritual in Brazil*, trans. Richard Vernon (Chapel Hill: University of North Carolina Press, 2013), 76–77. On the genealogies and different formulations of so-called syncretism, see Paul Christopher Johnson, "Syncretism and Hybridisation," in *Oxford Handbook of the Study of Religion*, ed. Steven Engler and Michael Stausberg (New York: Oxford University Press, 2016), 754–72.

61. Statement prepared by the Venerável Ordem Terceira do Rosário de Nossa Senhora às Portas do Carmo, the Brotherhood of Blacks (Irmandade dos Homens Pretos).

62. Here I adapt the phrase *politics of serenity*. See Burdick, *Blessed Anastácia*, 162.

63. The Brazilian Catholic Church was founded by a dissident Roman Catholic priest, Carlos Duarte Costa, who opposed the close relationship between the dictatorial regime of President Getúlio Vargas and the Roman Catholic Church. Costa accused the church of harboring Nazi sympathies and also opposed papal infallibility and the celibacy of the priesthood, among other things. Priests of the (independent) Brazilian Catholic Church have long supported popular syncretic ritual events, including those of Umbanda, so it is no surprise that they have likewise been supportive of devotion to Slave Anastácia. According to Roger Bastide: "Since 1945 [the Brazilian Catholic Church's] priests have been visiting Umbanda spiritism séances, blessing statues of the Virgin identified with Yemanjá, saying mass in macumba sanctuaries, and buying land where Negroes can celebrate their 'national Brazilian' festivals, regardless of the fact that these are proscribed by the Roman church." Roger Bastide, *The African Religions of Brazil: Towards a Sociology of the Interpenetration of Civilizations*, trans. Helen Sebba (Baltimore: Johns Hopkins University Press, 1978), 233.

64. Burdick, *Blessed Anastácia*, 162, 149.

65. https://www.facebook.com/CentroDeUmbandaPaiJoaoDeAngola.
66. The description of Anastácia in the show is taken from Wood, "The Museu do Negro," 129–34.
67. The text was self-published and circulated as a folio. It is reprinted in Burdick, *Blessed Anastácia*, 68–70.
68. "A nova superprodução da Manchete," *Correio braziliense*, May 15, 1990, sec. 2.
69. "O que mais me fascinou foi a possibilidade da reconstrução histórica de um dos períodos mais instigantes de nosso passado."
70. *O estado de Minas Gerais*, May 18, 1990.
71. *O correio*, May 22, 1990.
72. Wood, "The Museu do Negro," 137.
73. Wood, "The Museu do Negro," 125, 141.
74. http://www.lilianpacce.com.br/desfile/adriana-degreas-primavera-verao -201213.
75. "Adriana Degreas Racist Potrayal [*sic*] of Black Slaves in Her Runway Fashion Show," https://www.change.org/p/adriana-degreas-adriana-degreas -racist-potrayal-of-black-slaves-in-her-runway-fashion-show.
76. "RESPONSE—Adriana Degreas Racist Potrayal [*sic*] of Black Slaves in Her Runway Fashion Show," https://www.change.org/p/adriana-degreas -adriana-degreas-racist-potrayal-of-black-slaves-in-her-runway-fashion -show/u/13617560.
77. Wood, "The Museu do Negro," 143.
78. Paiva, "Quando os 'objetos' se tornam 'santos,'" 61.
79. Sheriff, "The Muzzled Saint."

Chapter 4

1. Two years prior to conceiving and writing *Frankenstein*, Mary Shelley had passed through Neuchâtel and witnessed Pierre Jaquet-Droz's automatons—one a draftsman, the other a "Musical Lady" that played a harpsichord. The visit likely played a role in her later musing on the machine-man that made her famous. See Wood, *Living Dolls*, xiv.
2. Wood, *Living Dolls*, 162.
3. Mary Shelley, *Frankenstein* (Mineola, NY: Dover, 1994), 35, 93, 150, 141.
4. Shelley, *Frankenstein*, 104, 122, 164.
5. Otto, *The Idea of the Holy*, 18.
6. Rudolf Otto, *Das Heilige* (1917; Munich: Beck, 2014), passim. The proximity of Otto's mysterium and monstrous is addressed in Timothy K. Beals, *Religion and Monsters* (New York: Routledge, 2002).
7. Shelley, *Frankenstein*, 163, 152.
8. "The strange resemblance to Drosselmeier which had struck her at first setting her eyes on the manikin, came again into her mind." Clara later insists that the Nutcracker is Herr Drosselmeier's young nephew from Nurem-

berg. E. T. A. Hoffman, *Nutcracker and Mouse King; and The Educated Cat* (New York: T. Fisher Unwin, 1892), 28, 163.

9. Shelley, *Frankenstein*, 105.

10. Karel Čapek, *R.U.R. (Rossum's Universal Robots)* (New York: Penguin, 2004), 17–20, 26–27, 32.

11. Čapek, *R.U.R.*, 75, 80.

12. Anonymous, "The Metaphysics of an Automaton," *The Spectator*, no. 1881 (July 16, 1864): 816–17.

13. Charles Dickens, "Mediums under Other Names," *All the Year Round* 7, no. 156 (April 19, 1862): 130–37, 135.

14. Nahum F. Bryant, "Magic and Mystery," *Household Monthly* 2, no. 5 (August 1859): 411–18, 414.

15. See n. 62 of the introduction and the text at that point.

16. George Allen, "The History of the Automaton Chess-Player in America: A Letter Addressed to William Lewis, London," in *The Book of the First American Chess Congress*, ed. Willard Fiske (New York: Rudd & Carleton, 1859), 430.

17. Brad Leithauser, "The Space of One Breath," *New Yorker*, March 9, 1987, 14–73, 46.

18. Allen, "The History of the Automaton Chess-Player," 466. Smyth himself denied the report.

19. Allen, "The History of the Automaton Chess-Player," 448.

20. Allen, "The History of the Automaton Chess-Player," 464. See also Eduardo González, *Cuba and the Tempest: Literature and Cinema in the Time of Diaspora* (Chapel Hill: University of North Carolina Press, 2006), 149–50.

21. Allen, "The History of the Automaton Chess-Player," 468–74.

22. Allen, "The History of the Automaton Chess-Player," 478, 483.

23. Cited in James W. Cook, *The Arts of Deception: Playing with Fraud in the Age of Barnum* (Cambridge, MA: Harvard University Press, 2001), 72.

24. Cook, *The Arts of Deception*, 71.

25. Edgar Allan Poe, "Maelzel's Chess-Player," in *The Complete Works of Edgar Allan Poe* (1836; Akron, OH: Werner, 1908), 138–74, 138, 164.

26. Masahiro Mori, "The Uncanny Valley" (1970), trans. K. F. MacDorman and Norri Kageki, *IEEE: Robotics and Automation* 19, no. 2 (2012): 98–100.

27. Citation of "modern Prometheus," making the link with Mary Shelley's title, is from Mark Sussman, "Performing the Intelligent Machine: Deception and Enchantment in the Life of the Automaton Chess Player," in *Puppets, Masks, and Performing Objects*, ed. John Bell (Cambridge, MA: MIT Press, 2001), 78.

28. John Kobler, "The Pride of the Eden Musée," *New Yorker*, November 20, 1943, 34.

29. See esp. Richard King, *Orientalism and Religion: Post-Colonial Theory, India and "The Mystic East"* (London: Routledge, 1999). The joining of rationality to the question of permeability is from Taylor, *A Secular Age*.

30. "Ajeeb, the Chess Player," in *Eden Musée Catalogue* (Brooklyn, NY: Eden Bureau, 1899), 30.

31. Kobler, "The Pride of the Eden Musée."

32. Trade card from the Eden Museé, New York, 1896, National Museum of American History.

33. *The World* cited in Stephen Davies, *Samuel Lipschutz: A Life in Chess* (Jefferson, NC: McFarland 2014), 259.

34. Kobler, "The Pride of the Eden Musée." 36–38.

35. The *Laredo Times* for May 13, 1890, printed his registration at the Wilson Hotel.

36. His passport application of 1893 stated that he planned to return to the United States within two years. The passport was sent to the residence of A. Rosenberg, 14th Street, New York. Rosenberg also served as his witness. NARA M1372, images of handwritten letters and application forms for US passports, 1795–1905, National Archives, https://www.fold3.com/document/71613041.

37. Ricardo Cravo Albin, *Dicionário Houaiss ilustrado música popular brasileira* (Rio de Janeiro: Editora Paracatu, 2006); Humberto M. Franceschi, *Registro sonoro por meios mecânicos no Brasil* (Rio de Janeiro: Studio HMF, 1984). According to Franceschi, Figner paid $175 for a Pacific Phonograph, powered by a battery. Ibid., 17.

38. As cited in Flora Süssekind, *Cinematograph of Words: Literature, Technique, and Modernization in Brazil*, trans. Paulo Henriques Britto (Stanford, CA: Stanford University Press, 1997), 34.

39. Figner is listed as arriving in Rio on April 8, 1892, after traveling for two and half days from Bahia. *Jornal do comércio*, April 9, 1892, 6. For an announcement of his demonstration of the phonograph, see *Jornal do comércio*, June 3, 1892, 2.

40. *Jornal do comércio*, June 9, 1892, 2.

41. "O maravilhoso apparelho que nos permitte ver e ouvir ao mesmo tempo, sera hoje mesmo posto em experiencia publica." *O paiz*, October 8, 1895, 2.

42. Capellaro quotes the Montevideo newspaper *El dia* stating that Figner's Ajeeb arrived from Europe on November 20, 1895, but he seems not to be aware of the existence of multiple Ajeeb automatons in the United States just then or of Figner's trip to New York, posted in the passenger logs in the Rio de Janeiro newspapers. See Jorge Capellaro, *Verdades sobre o início do cinema no Brasil* (Rio de Janeiro: FUNARTE, 1996), 102.

43. Capellaro, *Verdades sobre o início do cinema no Brasil*, 102.

44. Figner's name appears on a list of passengers embarking for New York. See *Jornal do Brasil*, August 9, 1895.

45. "Sou muito estimado na Rua do Ouvidor; mas quem não o é aí?" Lima Barreto, *Diário*, 78.

46. On the history of lighting on Ouvidor Street, see Joaquim Manuel de Macedo, *Memórias da Rua do Ouvidor* (Brasília: Senado Federal, 2005).

47. "Tivemos occasião de apreciar ontem o engenhoso automato que joga damas com a mais rematada perícia, batendo todos os adversarios que se lhe apresentão. É um apparelho [*sic*] mecánico, representando um Turco, ricamente vestido, com largo turbante de seda, sentado á oriental, de pernas cruzadas, tendo ao collo um taboleiro de damas. A expressão da figura é magnifica, e a sua attitude physionomica é a de um indivíduo que medita ... seu jogo é perfeita, como todo o seu aparelho. ... Qual o segredo do apparelho, qual a alma do automato? Esta reside em um homunculo, emerito jogador, que se insinua dentro das grandes cavidades do automato. Isso, porem, não diminue a curiosidade do apparelho, que merece bem uma visita." *Jornal do comércio*, May 19, 1896, 3.

48. *Jornal do Brasil*, May 17, 1896, 2.

49. Alexandre Haas, "O jogo de damas: Ajeeb, o autômato," *Jornal do Brasil*, November 20, 1949, 2, 4.

50. "Ontem, porém, ficou completamente desmoralisado ... merecendo o seu emprezario a attenção e providencias da policia. ... A partida logo no seu inicio tornou-se interessante: no fim de um quarto de hora o Ajeeb invencivel via-se seriamente atrapalhado; 20 minutos passavam e, ó glorias de Ajeeb! Todos os espectadores tremiam de emoção; só restavam ao boneco duas jogadas e qualquer dellas trazia-lhe a derrota mais vergonhosa possivel. A victoria estava já conquistada visivelmente pelo Sr. Castilho. Ajeeb só não suava porque era de gesso. O emprezario, porém, esse, em colicas, parecia um fogo de artificio: de verde passava a amarelo, a roxo, a azul, ao diabo. O automato hesitava, a mão suspense, como se fosse de carne e as pedras do taboleiro fossem brazes." *O paiz*, June 5, 1896, 2.

51. Haas, "O jogo de damas," 7.

52. "O automato Ajeeb, que de si deixou tão triste lembrança entre nós, está sendo exhibido no Rosario de Santa Fé, na República Argentina." *O paiz*, January 8, 1897, 2.

53. "É um aparelho curiossissimo e que merece ser visto, pois é dificil fazer-se idea da precisão com que é feito o movimento das pedras pelo inconsciente jogador. A concurrencia de curiosos foi hontem extraordinaria, e todos sahiram sem explicar o maravilhoso companheiro do sr. Fred Figner, seu digno proprietario." *Minas Geraes*, February 11, 1897, 7.

54. *Jornal do Brasil*, May 8, 1897, 2.

55. Machado de Assis, "A semana," *Gazeta de notícias*, June 7, 1896, 1: "Não leverão daqui a nossa vasta baía, as grandezas naturais e industriais, a nossa Rua do Ouvidor, com o seu autômato jogador de damas, nem as próprias damas." Machado also likely read about the history of Ajeeb. At least Magalhães de Azeredo reported sending him a work of fiction. See "Ajeeb, O Turco." Magalhães de Azeredo, letter to Machado de Assis, December 23, 1895, in *Correspondência de Machado de Assis*, vol. 3, *1890–1900*, ed. Serigo Paulo Rouane (Rio de Janeiro: Biblioteca da Academica Brasileira de Letras, 2011), 134.

56. *Jornal do comércio*, May 19, 1896, 3.

57. "A alma do automato é um anão que está dentro do Turco." *Jornal do comércio*, May 24, 1896, 3.

58. Wittgenstein gestured toward this idea: "P. 179. (The Malays conceive the human soul as a little man . . . who corresponds exactly in shape, proportion, and even in complexion to the man in whose body he resides . . .) How much more truth in granting the soul the same multiplicity as the body than in a watered-down modern theory." See Wittgenstein, "Remarks on Frazer's *Golden Bough*," 44.

59. Poe, "Maelzel's Chess-Player," 165.

60. Cited in Sussman, "Performing the Intelligent Machine," 80.

61. Erving Goffman, *The Presentation of Self in Everyday Life* (New York: Anchor, 1959). In later work, Goffman broke the apparent individual speaker down further. Any speech act is inhabited by three different parts: an animator, who performs or presents a message; an author, who actually generates the message, and a principal, who is responsible for the message. See Erving Goffman, *Frame Analysis* (New York: Harper & Row, 1974).

62. Edan Dekel and David Gantt Gurley, "How the Golem Came to Prague," *Jewish Quarterly Review* 103, no. 2 (2013): 241–58.

63. See also Paul Christopher Johnson, "Objects of Possession: Spirits, Photography and the Entangled Arts of Appearance," in Promey, ed., *Sensational Religion*, 25–46.

64. The term *aparelho* came into use through spiritism, in the writings of Kardec himself, who used the term to refer at once to electric devices and to the human body: "We have an image of life and death still more exact in the electric battery. The battery, like all natural bodies, contains electricity in a latent state: but the electrical phenomena are only manifested when the fluid is set in motion by a special cause. When this movement is superinduced, the battery may be said to become alive; but when the cause of the electrical activity ceases, the phenomena cease to occur, and the battery relapses into a state of inertia. Organic bodies may thus be said to be a sort of electric battery, in which the movement of the fluid produces the phenomena of life, and in which the cessation of that movement produces death." Allan Kardec, *The Spirits' Book* (New York: Cosimo, 1996), 85. And elsewhere: "Incarnation has another aim . . . of fitting the spirit to perform his share in the work of creation; for which purpose he is made to assume a corporeal apparatus [*appareil*] in harmony with the material state of each world into which he is sent." Ibid., 107. The original reads: "Nous avons une image plus exacte de la vie et de la mort dans un appareil électrique. Cet appareil recèle l'électricité comme tous les corps de la nature à l'état latent. Les phénomènes électriques ne se manifestent que lorsque le fluide est mis en activité par une cause special: alors on pourrait dire que l'appareil est vivant. La cause d'activité venant à cesser, le phénomène cesse: l'appareil rentre dans l'état d'inertie. Les corpes organiques seraient

ainsi des sortes de piles ou appareils électriques dans lesquels l'activité du fluide produit le phénomène de la vie: la cessation de cette activité produit la mort." Allan Kardec, *Le livre des esprits*, 6th ed. (Paris: Didier, 1869), 29.

65. Walter Benjamin, "The Doll, the Automaton," in *Arcades Project*, 694 (Z1, 5). Here, Benjamin cites Paul Lindau, *Der Abend* (Berlin, 1896), 17.

66. *Jornal do Brasil*, July 1, 1897.

67. Jeffrey Lesser, "'Jews are Turks who sell on credit': Elite Images of Arabs and Jews in Brazil," *Immigrants and Minorities* 16, nos. 1–2 (1997): 38–56, 40; Jamil Safady, *O café e o mascate* (São Paulo: Editora Safady, 1973).

68. Cited in Jeffrey Lesser, *Negotiating National Identity: Immigrants, Minorities, and the Struggle for Ethnicity in Brazil* (Durham, NC: Duke University Press, 1999), 49.

69. João do Rio, *Religions in Rio*, trans. Anna Lessa Schmidt (Hanover, CT: New London Librarian, 2015), 123.

70. Lesser, "'Jews are Turks who sell on credit,'" 51.

71. Lesser, *Negotiating National Identity*, 53; Lesser, "'Jews are Turks who sell on credit,'" 43.

72. Lesser, "'Jews are Turks who sell on credit,'" 44.

73. *Jornal do Brasil*, November 21, 1891, 1.

74. Dain Borges, "'Puffy, Ugly, Slothful and Inert': Degeneration in Brazilian Social Thought, 1880–1940," *Journal of Latin American Studies* 25, no. 2 (1993): 235–56.

75. *Jornal do Brasil*, September 13, 1891, 3; *Jornal do Brasil*, August 12, 1895, 1 ("swarm").

76. Cited in Lesser, *Negotiating National Identity*, 51.

77. Ambrose Bierce, *The Collected Works of Ambrose Bierce*, vol. 3, *Can Such Things Be?* (New York: Neale, 1910), 88–105, 100.

78. Seth Leacock and Ruth Leacock, *Spirits of the Deep: A Study of an Afro-Brazilian Cult* (Garden City, NY: Anchor, 1975), 55.

79. Mundicarmo M. R. Ferretti, "The Presence of Non-African Spirits in an Afro-Brazilian Religion," in *Reinventing Religions: Syncretism and Transformation in Africa and the Americas*, ed. Sidney M. Greenfield and A. F. Droogers (Oxford: Rowman & Littlefield, 2001), 99–112, and "Repensando o Turco no Tambor de Mina," *Afro-Asia* 15 (1992): 56–70. On Pajé, see also Ana Stela de Almeida Cunha, "João da Mata Family: Pajé Dreams, Chants, and Social Life," in *The Social Life of Spirits*, ed. Ruy Blanes and Diana Espírito Santo (Chicago: University of Chicago Press, 2014), 157–78.

80. Ferretti, "The Presence of Non-African Spirits," 70.

81. Leacock and Leacock, *Spirits of the Deep*, 133. As the Leacocks describe, there are still other possible sources of the *turco* spirits. While some spirit entities emerge from long-term human experience—in the north of Brazil the dolphins (*bôtos*) or wise African slaves (*pretos velhos*)—others joined the repertory through very specific historical encounters. One such spirit, Dom Luiz, embodies King Louis XVI of France. Another, Father Thomas,

is named for Harriet Beecher Stowe's Uncle Tom; he too must have arrived in the pantheon after a specific leader encountered the character in the book. The located and traceable births of new entities open hermeneutic space to consider other sources for the Turks than the Portuguese sagas of the Christians and Moors. See ibid., 155–60.

82. Alejandro Frigerio, *Cultura negra en el Cono Sur: Representaciones en conflicto* (Buenos Aires: Ediciones de la Universidad Católica Argentina 2000), 134.

83. Diana Brown, *Umbanda: Religion and Politics in Urban Brazil* (New York: Columbia University Press, 1994), 88; Cristina Rocha, *Zen in Brazil: The Quest for Cosmopolitan Modernity* (Honolulu: University of Hawaii Press, 2006), 99.

84. Ferretti, "The Presence of Non-African Spirits," 62.

85. Marcos Moraes de Sá, *A Mansão Figner: O eclectismo e a casa burguesa no início do século XX* (Rio de Janeiro: Senac, 2002), 28–34.

86. Leacock and Leacock, *Spirits of the Deep*, 133.

87. Ferretti, "The Presence of Non-African Spirits," 66–68.

88. Leacock and Leacock, *Spirits of the Deep*, 130–31.

89. Leacock and Leacock, *Spirits of the Deep*, 55–57, 130.

90. Kardec, *The Spirits' Book*, 85, 107.

91. Aubrée and Laplantine, *La table, le livre et les esprits*, 110.

92. Bruno Latour, *Pandora's Hope: Essays on the Reality of Science Studies* (Cambridge, MA: Harvard University Press, 1999).

93. Palmié, "The Ejamba of North Fairmount Avenue," 47–78, 48, 50. The broader notion of how divine presences appear in and through technologies is programmatically articulated in Stolow, ed., *Deus in Machina*.

94. Palmié, "The Ejamba of North Fairmount Avenue," 50. Palmié goes further, showing how Edison's research in audiology was itself something of a sorcerous contrivance including research on ears taken from cadavers, but that story is beyond the ken of this chapter.

95. Moraes de Sá, *A Mansão Figner*, 20.

96. "Chronica espírita," *Correio da Manhã*, April 9, 1931, 5. Among other things, Lima Drummond questioned the defense of crimes of passion, arguing that *passion* was not a unique category, that, following Enrico Ferri, crimes of passion were indistinguishable from crimes of emotion and should be closely scrutinized in terms of their premeditation. See Lima Drummond, "Responsabilidade dos criminosos passionais," *A epoca* 48 (May 1913): 1–6.

97. Francisco Cândido Xavier and Brother Jacob (spirit), *Voltei* (1949; Rio de Janeiro: Federação Espírita Brasileira Editora, 2017), 120–24.

Chapter 5

1. *Revista da semana*, September 28, 1935, 29.

2. Celestino Silveira, "O espirito de Emanuel," *Revista da semana*, July 22,

1944 (interview with Chico Xavier): "É como si aplicassem no meu coto-velo direito um aparêlho electric com dispositivo automatic. Não sou eu quem escreve. Obedeço à força superior."

3. André Breton, *Manifestoes of Surrealism*, trans. Richard Seaver and Helen R. Lane (Ann Arbor: University of Michigan Press, 1969), ix ("Preface for a Reprint of the Manifesto [1929]"). Recall that, from 1915 to 1922, Breton worked as a psychiatric medical student under several of Charcot's former colleagues and students: first Raoul-Achille Leroy, at Saint-Dizier, and then Joseph Babinski, at the Neurological Center of La Pitié, adjoining the Salpêtrière. See Jacques Philippon and Jacques Poirier, *Joseph Babinski: A Biography* (New York: Oxford University Press, 2009), 45–46.

4. Gertrude Stein, "Cultivated Motor Automatism: A Study of Character in Relation to Attention," *Psychological Review* 5 (1898): 295–306, 296. See also Steven Meyer, *Irresistible Dictation: Gertrude Stein and the Correlations of Writing and Science* (Stanford, CA: Stanford University Press, 2003), 47, 226. Stein denied that her writing was truly automatic, calling it, rather, *dissociative*.

5. Henry Olcott, *Isis Unveiled* (1877), cited in Hugh B. Urban, *Secrecy: The Adornment of Silence, the Vestment of Power* (Chicago: University of Chicago Press), in press.

6. Anne W. Lane and Harriet Blaine Beale, *To Walk with God: An Experience in Automatic Writing* (New York: Dodd, Mead, 1920), v.

7. Here are the titles (and rough translations): *Crônicas de além-túmulo* (Chronicles from beyond the grave); *Brasil, coração do mundo, pátria do evangelho* (Brazil, heart of the world, fatherland of the good news); *Novas mensagens* (New messages); *Boa nova* (Good news); and *Reportagens de além-túmulo* (Reports from beyond the grave).

8. Humberto de Campos, "Os 'Reddis,'" in *A serpente de bronze* (Rio de Janeiro: Editora Leite Ribeiro, 1921), 194–96, 194.

9. Cited in *Revista da semana*, December 15, 1934, 1 (Humberto's obituary).

10. The suit against Francisco Cândido Xavier (Chico Xavier) and his publisher, Federação Espirita Brasileira, was filed in civil court in 1944. The case was heard by Judge João Frederico Mourão Russel of Federal District 8. I follow the case summary in Miguel Timponi, *Psicografia ante os tribunais: O caso de Humberto Campos* (Brasília: Federação Espirita Brasileira, 1959).

11. Renata Soltanovich, *Direitos autorais e a tutel de urgência na proteção da obra psicografada* (São Paulo: Leud, 2012), 192.

12. On transduction as the means by which spirits are able to become present, see Keane, "On Spirit Writing." On revealing moments of transgression, witness the concern when a report and a photograph surfaced of the then vice presidential candidate Sarah Palin consulting with a Kenyan pastor to exorcise her "bad spirits" or the House of Representatives stenographer Dianne Reidy making headlines on October 16, 2013, when she abruptly

grabbed the microphone in Congress while possessed by the Holy Spirit and had to be dragged off the floor by security. In both cases, this kind of hyperagency—the excess of persons in a given body acting in political or judicial space—seemed dangerously opaque.

13. They are *irrational* in Weber's sense of residing mostly outside or adjacent to systems of governance or knowledge that are bureaucratically organized with the goal of maximum efficiency.

14. João Pedro Pitombo, "Cantora Karina Buhr acusa babalorixá de extorsão e estupro," *Folha de São Paulo*, December 24, 2019, https://www1.folha .uol.com.br/cotidiano/2019/12/cantora-karina-buhr-acusa-babalorixa-de -extorsao-e-estupro.shtml.

15. Velho, "Unidade e fragmentação em sociedades complexas."

16. "It came in my head to ask him an idle question, because I thought it not very likely for me to see him again, and I had a mind to know from his own mouth, the account of a common, but much credited Story, that I had heard so often from many others, of an old Parrot he had in *Brasil*, during his Government there, that spoke, and ask'd, and answer'd common questions like a reasonable creature; so that those of his Train there, generally concluded it to be Witchery or Possession; and one of his Chaplains, who liv'd long afterwards in *Holland*, would never from that time endure a Parrot, but said, They all had a Devil in them." Locke, *An Essay concerning Human Understanding* (1700), 446–47. Locke quotes the story at length from William Temple, *Memoirs of What Past in Christendum, from the War Begun 1672 to the Peace Concluded 1679* (London: Chiswell, 1692), 76–77. See also Peter Walmsley, "Prince Maurice's Rational Parrot: Civil Discourse in Locke's Essay," *Eighteenth-Century Studies* 28, no. 4 (1995): 413–25.

17. Leibniz's *New Essays on Human Understanding* (1704) refuted Locke's thought experiment with his own experiment in metempsychosis. Say that you become the king of China, in the process losing all your present memories. Would you as a person continue to exist? Contra Locke, Leibniz's answer was no; personhood is inseparable from the perceiving body. Future rewards and punishments could not have meaning or any systematic character without the preservation of memory and personal identity; thus, any idea of justice depends on the firm union of consciousness and body. See Franklin Perkins, *Leibniz: A Guide for the Perplexed* (London: Bloomsbury, 2007), 145.

18. Immanuel Kant, *Dreams of a Spirit Seer* (1766; West Chester, PA: Swedenborg Foundation, 2002).

19. Immanuel Kant, *Religion within the Limits of Reason Alone* (1791; New York: Harper & Row, 1960), 189.

20. William James, "Person and Personality: From Johnson's Universal Cyclopaedia," in *Essays in Psychology* (Cambridge, MA: Harvard University Press, 1983), 315–21, 317.

21. William James, "Notes on Automatic Writing (1889)," in *Essays in Psychical Research* (Cambridge, MA: Harvard University Press, 1986), 37–56, 44.

22. James, "Notes on Automatic Writing," 45.

23. Ortiz, *Los negros brujos*, 1, vii, 55, 21.

24. Nina Rodrigues notes that this is unfortunately said by others but nevertheless lamentably true (*aliás bem fundado*). Nina Rodrigues, *O animismo fetichista*, 29.

25. Nina Rodrigues, *O animismo fetichista*, 18, 112, 15, 28, 99, 99, 116, 101–3, 130, 123–26.

26. Here, and in the following paragraph, I am relying on Yvonne Maggie, *Medo do feitiço: Relações entre magia e poder no Brasil* (Rio de Janeiro: Arquivo Nacional, 1992), 22–23, 43.

27. Spiritism spread rapidly among European cosmopolitans as well. It appears, e.g., in Tolstoy's *Anna Karenina*, first published from 1873 to 1877, where at a high-society party "the conversation moved on to table-turning and spirits, and Countess Nordston, who believed in spiritualism, began telling about the wonders she had seen." A debate follows about electricity and spiritism, in the wake of which a cluster of people in the drawing room gather to "try the tables." Leo Tolstoy, *Anna Karenina* (New York: Dover, 2012), 47–49.

28. Hess, *Spirits and Scientists*, 218.

29. Matthew Hull, *A Government of Paper* (Berkeley and Los Angeles: University of California Press, 2012), 18, 25–26.

30. For example, documents are used in spiritist practice to certify one's training as a spirit writer or psychographer, a practice that is itself the production of mediated documents. For one example, see http://www.aluzdoespiritismo.com/espiritismo-mensagens-historico.htm.

31. Xavier and Jacob, *Voltei*, 16–19.

32. Goffman, *Frame Analysis*, 517ff.

33. Judith T. Irvine, "Shadow Conversations: The Indeterminacy of Participant Roles," in *Natural Histories of Discourse*, ed. Michael Silverstein and Greg Urban (Chicago: University of Chicago Press, 1996), 131–59.

34. Irvine, "Shadow Conversations," 137.

35. Goffman, *Frame Analysis*, 573.

36. Irvine, "Shadow Conversations," 134.

37. Irvine, "Shadow Conversations," 156.

38. Irvine, "Shadow Conversations," 157.

39. There are also interesting variations, such as the Fernanda Lages case, initially ruled a suicide. A spirit-written letter from Fernanda herself declared that she did not kill herself. It helped motivate social pressure to continue the investigation, which was still ongoing but with some indications that the death was, in fact, a homicide.

40. The case details are recounted in Nemer da Silva Ahmad, *Psicografia: O novo olhar da justiça* (Rio de Janeiro: Aliança, 2008). See also Orimar de

Bastos, *O justo juiz: História de uma sentence* (Goiânia: Editora Kelps, 2010); and Francisco Cândido Xavier and Maurício Garcez Henrique (spirit), *Lealdade* (São Paulo: Instituto de difusão espírita, 1982). The former is the judge's own story of the case; the latter tells the story from the perspective of the deceased as mediated by Chico.

41. Ahmad, *Psicografia*, 173.

42. Ahmad, *Psicografia*, 175: "Os motivos determinados constituem, no direito penal moderno, a pedra de toque do crime. Não há crime gratuito ou sem motivo, e é no motivo que reside à significação mesma do crime."

43. Ahmad, *Psicografia*, 175.

44. Chico appeared before and was honored by the Goiâs State Legislature on May 7, 1974.

45. The deceased wrote again (on May 12, 1979), this time to his mother (presented to the father on television, Programa Flávio Cavalcanti): "Ask Father to accept the version that I gave of this event (that my physical body had suppressed). Don't look for a guilty party. Everything ended in peace, because the accident really was an accident, and father must reflect on this, based on my own words." See Xavier and Henrique, *Lealdade*, 19. Chico Xavier died in 2002.

46. Léo Gerchmann, "Carta psicografada ajuda a inocentar ré por homicídio no RS," *Folha de São Paulo*, May 30, 2006, http://www1.folha.uol.com.br/folha/cotidiano/ult95u122179.shtml..

47. Rio Grande do Sul, Apelação Crimes contra pessoa, Câmara criminal 70016184012, data de distribuição 24.7.2006.

48. Maria Helena Gozzer Benjamin, "Mantida a absolvição de acusada que apresentou carta psicografada ao Júri," *Âmbito Jurídico*, November 11, 2010, https://ambito-juridico.jusbrasil.com.br/noticias/2017790/mantida-a-absolvicao-de-acusada-que-apresentou-carta-psicografada-ao-juri?ref=amp.

49. The numbers are from "Editorial," *Revista de ABRAME*, no. 16 (2015): 4, http://abrame.org.br/wp-content/uploads/2014/08/Revista-ABRAME-n.16f-Definitivo.pdf.

50. See http://www.ajesaopaulo.com.br.

51. Vinícius Queiroz Galvão, "Associação quer espiritualizar o Judiciário," *Folha de São Paulo*, May 19, 2008, http://www1.folha.uol.com.br/fsp/cotidian/ff1905200801.htm. "Não enxergaria nenhuma diferença entre uma declaração feita por mim ou por você e uma declaração mediúnica, que foi psicografada por alguém."

52. I note here that the legal notion of a *testimonial individual* (a witness) is much less narrowly circumscribed than is that of the *authorial individual*. This is because legal defenses allow greater latitude than do legal claims or accusations.

53. Alejandro Frigerio, "Levels of Possession Awareness in Afro-Brazilian Religions," *Association for the Anthropological Study of Consciousness Quarterly*

5, no. 2 (1989): 5–11. Frigerio also points out the ritual value of discursive claims of full possession, or "incorporation," that confirm and reinforce the basic ontological premises of spirits' being authentically rendered present and available to humans.

54. I take these categories from Fredie Didier and Paula Sarno Braga, "Carta psicografada como fonte de prova no processo civil," *Revista da Programa de Pós-Graduação em Direito da Universidade Federal da Bahia* 25 (2013): 190–228, 200.

55. Hull, *A Government of Paper*, 131, 139.

56. Didier and Braga, "Carta psicografada," 202.

57. Georg Wilhelm Hegel, *The Logic of Hegel*, trans. William Wallace (London: Oxford University Press, 1892), 274. Chimpanzees were championed as legal persons by, among others, the Nonhuman Rights Project, which filed suit against Stony Brook University in 2013. See Julie Turkewitz, "Corporations Have Rights; Why Shouldn't Rivers?" *New York Times*, September 26, 2017.

58. Juan Obarrio, *The Spirit of the Laws in Mozambique* (Chicago: University of Chicago Press, 2014), 26; Matthew Hull, "Incorporations: Capitalism and Collective Life" (typescript, University of Michigan, Ann Arbor, 2018).

59. Otto von Gierke, *Political Theories of the Middle Ages*, trans. Frederic William Maitland (Cambridge: Cambridge University Press, 1900). Pierre Legendre described the numinous inhabitations of the "law of persons" by returning, like Mauss, to the Latin etymology of *persona* as coming from *mask*: "In all institutional systems the political subject is reproduced through masks." Or: "The great ravings of power, those which make the body walk with the soul . . . can only be stated poetically, because power is organized fictively." Pierre Legendre, *Law and the Unconscious*, ed. Peter Goodrich, trans. Peter Goodrich with Alain Pottage and Anton Schütz (London: Macmillan, 1997), 13, 19.

60. Legendre, *Law and the Unconscious*, 142.

61. Edward Mussawir, *Jurisdiction in Deleuze: The Expression and Representation of Law* (Oxford: Taylor & Francis, 2011), 23.

62. Annemarie Mol, *The Body Multiple: Ontology in Medical Practice* (Durham, NC: Duke University Press, 2002), vii.

63. "Administrative acts, decisions, and rules are formulated and recorded in writing, even in cases where oral discussion is the rule or is even mandatory. This applies at least to preliminary discussions and proposals, to final decisions, and to all sorts of orders and rules. The combination of written documents and a continuous operation by officials constitutes the 'office' (*Bureau*) which is the central focus of all types of modern organized action." Weber, *Economy and Society*, 219.

64. "When we see in every sick man someone whose being has been augmented or diminished, we are somewhat reassured, for what a man has lost can be restored to him, and what has entered him can also leave. We

can hope to conquer disease even if it is the result of a spell, or magic, or possession. . . . Disease enters and leaves man as through a door." Georges Canguilhem, *The Normal and the Pathological* (New York: Zone, 2007), 39.

65. Ismar Estulano Garcia, *Psicografia como prova jurídica* (Goiânia: Editora AB, 2010), 183–84.

66. In Brazil's 1890 penal code, offenders "under a state of total perturbation of the senses and intelligence at the time of the crime were not criminally responsible." "Honor crimes" are regarded as "temporary insanity." The 1940 code introduced *semi-imputable* as a category of mental status—the partial impairment of cognitive or volitive elements—and this feature was continued in article 121 of the 1984 code: "Se o agente comete o crime impelido por motivo de relevante valor social ou moral, ou sob o domínio de violenta emoção, logo em seguida a injusta provocação da vítima, ou juiz pode reduzir a pena de um sexto a um terço. Aumento de penal—se o crime é praticado por motivo egoístico."

67. Borges, "Healing and Mischief," 198, 207.

68. See Taylor, *A Secular Age*, 37–41.

69. Susanna L. Blumenthal, "The Default Legal Person," *UCLA Law Review* 54, no. 5 (2007): 1135–1267.

70. Here is Marriott's inaugural formulation of the *dividual*: "Single actors are not thought in South Asia to be 'individual', that is, indivisible, bounded units, as they are in much of Western social and psychological theory, as well as in common sense. Instead, it appears that persons are generally thought by South Asians to be 'dividual' or divisible. To exist, dividual persons absorb heterogeneous material influences." McKim Marriott, *Hindu Transactions: Diversity without Dualism* (Chicago: University of Chicago Press, 1976), 109.

71. Judith Butler, *The Psychic Life of Power: Theories in Subjection* (Stanford, CA: Stanford University Press, 2006), 1–2.

72. Butler clarifies the power of law over subjecthood: "When a woman who is raped goes before the law in order to have the crime against her prosecuted, she has to comply with the very idea of the reliable narrator and legitimate subject inscribed in the law. As a result, if the law finds that she is not a legitimate subject, that what she claims has no value, and that her speech in general is without value, then she is actually deconstituted as a subject by the law in question." Judith Butler and Athena Athanasiou, *Dispossession: The Performative in the Political* (Cambridge: Polity, 2013), 77.

73. Colin Dayan, *The Law Is a White Dog: How Legal Rituals Make and Unmake Persons* (Princeton, NJ: Princeton University Press, 2011), xii.

74. Here I am drawing on Rihan Yeh's argument about the performance of the "fully documented person" required at the border of Mexico and the United States and subjects' partial ability to protect and maintain a sovereign reserve through jokes. Rihan Yeh, "Visas, Jokes, and Contraband:

Citizenship and Sovereignty at the U.S.-Mexico Border," *Comparative Studies in Society and History* 59, no. 1 (2017): 154–82.

75. Machado de Assis, "Encerrando o primeiro anno academico," December 7, 1897, in Humberto de Campos, ed., *Anthologia da Academia Brasileira de Letras: Trinta annos de discursos academicos, 1897–1927* (Rio de Janeiro: Editora Leite Ribeiro, 1928), 6.

Conclusion

1. Machado de Assis, "The Mirror," 444–45.

2. Machado de Assis, "The Mirror," 450, 452.

3. Roberto Schwarz, *A Master on the Periphery of Capitalism*, trans. John Gledson (Durham, NC: Duke University Press, 2001), 73.

4. Sidney Chalhoub, "Dependents Play Chess: Political Dialogues in Machado de Assis," in *Machado de Assis: Reflections on a Master Writer*, ed. Richard Graham (Austin: University of Texas Press, 1999), 51–84, 53–54; Roberto Schwarz, *Ao vencedor as batatas* (São Paulo: Editora 34, 1977), 83–94.

5. To put this in context, in the 1876 census almost 80 percent of the population was revealed to be illiterate, quite a shock to the intelligentsia. Elaine Cristina Maldonado, *Machado de Assis e o espiritismo* (Jundiaí: Paco Editorial, 2015), 25–27.

6. One of his poems described a convulsive dog in ways that seem in part autobiographical, argues Cláudio Murilo Leal: "Arfava, espumava e ria, De um riso espúrio e bufão, Ventre e pernas sacudia, Na convulsão." Cláudio Murilo Leal, *O círculo virtuoso: A poesia de Machado de Assis* (Rio de Janeiro: Biblioteca Nacional, 2008), 146.

7. Machado describes reading about the death of Léon Gambetta in a letter to his friend Joaquim Nabuco of April 14, 1883. Machado de Assis and Joaquim Nabuco, *Correspondência*, ed. Graça Aranha (Rio de Janeiro: Topbooks, 2003), 94.

8. Kenneth David Jackson, *Machado de Assis: A Literary Life* (New Haven, CT: Yale University Press, 2015), 181.

9. Jackson, *Machado de Assis*, 25.

10. Machado de Assis, "Bons dias!," *Gazeta de notícias*, June 7, 1888, August 29, 1888.

11. Machado de Assis, "Bons dias!," *Gazeta de notícias*, August 29, 1889, in *Bons dias!*, ed. John Gledson (São Paulo: Editora da Unicamp, 1990), 204.

12. For example, the story "A Felicidade" was published in 1871 under the name "X" in the *Jornal das famílias*. See Patrícia Lessa Flores da Cunha, *Machado de Assis: Um escritor na capital dos trópicos* (Porto Allegre: Editora Unisinos, 1998), 218. During the 1880s, Machado also sometimes wrote comic satire under the pseudonym "Malvólio." Leal, *O círculo virtuoso*, 165–73.

13. As to animals that speak, I have been especially influenced by Machado's

story "A Canary's Ideas." For an English translation, see Jack Schmitt and Lorie Chieko Ishimatsu, trans., *The Devil's Church and Other Stories* (Austin: University of Texas Press, 1977), 125–29. Here, Machado uses a caged, loquacious canary to think through Hegel's parable of the master and the slave in the context of Brazil. At least that is how I read it.

14. Charles Darwin, *The Expression of the Emotions in Man and Animals* (London: John Murray, 1872); Jacques Lacan, "The Mirror Stage as Formative of the *I* Function as Revealed in Psychoanalytic Experience" (1949), in *Écrits: The First Complete Edition in English*, trans. Bruce Fink (New York: Norton, 2006), 75–81.

15. Latour, *On the Modern Cult of the Factish Gods*, 62–63. On self-making and initiation in Candomblé, see also Sansi, *Fetishes and Monuments*, 22: "Candomblé people 'construct' their saints as autonomous agents, at the same time that they build themselves as persons. 'Making the saint' is a dialectical process of continuously constructing the person, in relation to the spirits that she embodies and to the 'other body' of these spirits, the shrines."

16. Lorna A. Rhodes, *Total Confinement: Madness and Reason in the Maximum Security Prison* (Berkeley and Los Angeles: University of California Press, 2004), 39–44. Thanks to Cyrus O'Brien for calling my attention to this example.

17. Taylor, *A Secular Age*, 171, 565–66; Erving Goffman, *Interaction Ritual* (1967; New Brunswick, NJ: Transaction, 2005), 95.

18. Responding to such a top-down view, John Collins shows how Afro-Brazilians in the *gueto* of Pelourinho work their agency through unregulated media like the neighborhood's soundscape or the board of a dominos game. John F. Collins, "The Sounds of Tradition: Arbitrariness and Agency in a Brazilian Cultural Center," *Ethnos* 72, no. 3 (2007): 383–407.

19. Tylor, *Primitive Culture*, 1:108–11.

20. Robert C. Tucker, ed., *The Marx and Engels Reader* (New York: Norton, 1978), 34–35; Durkheim, *The Elementary Forms of Religious Life*, 212; Sigmund Freud, *Totem and Taboo*, trans James Strachey (New York: Norton, 1950), 116–18. Durkheim was right to locate religion in the collective experience of social assemblies. That is one site of the production of automaticity and agent ambiguity. Is it I who is acting or the crowd in me? Durkheim described the roots of the religious life as a collective affect gathered around sacred things. From the point of view adopted in this book, collective feeling around a sacred thing is generated, in part, by that thing's agent-ambiguous quality. There is, if I am right, a missing phenomenology in Durkheim's idea of collective affect and the problem of what *kinds* of things such experiences, sanctions and taboos tend to accrue around.

21. Judith Butler, *Giving an Account of Oneself* (New York: Fordham University Press, 2005), 8. Paradoxically, that very "I" keeps seeking human-like agency in the world. Cognitive scientists of religion inform us that the

attempt to find human-like agency in the world is part of our brain's evo-
lutionary hardwiring and constitutive of the human religious project. See,
among many other works, Guthrie, *Faces in the Clouds*; Boyer, *Religion
Explained*; Harvey Whitehouse, *Icons and Arguments: Divergent Modes of
Religiosity* (New York: Oxford University Press, 2000); and Emma Cohen,
*The Mind Possessed: The Cognition of Spirit Possession in an Afro-Brazilian
Religion* (New York: Oxford University Press, 2007).

22.   Georg Simmel, *Essays on Religion* (New Haven, CT: Yale University Press,
       1997), 148. The 1959 Rosenthal translation uses the English *through the
       agency of* for the German *die Entwicklung des Menschen durch das, was
       nicht er selbst ist, erfährt*, roughly, "that through which human development
       passes that is not himself." See Georg Simmel, *Sociology of Religion*, trans.
       Curt Rosenthal (New York: Philosophical Library, 1959), 9–10. The origi-
       nal text is from Georg Simmel, *Die Religion* (Frankfurt a.M.: Literarische
       Anstalt, 1906), 15. My use of *religion-like situations* is similar to Simmel's
       notion of the production of a "religious cachet."

23.   It reminds of Lucy Suchman's "subject-objects," in which agents are nei-
       ther unqualified humans nor unqualified things. See Suchman, *Human-
       Machine Reconfigurations*. It also reminds of Karen Barad's "intra-activity,"
       which describes how distinct agencies emerge out of and through intra-
       actions, with the result that distinct agencies are always relational, not ab-
       solute. Intra-action instead of interaction signals that there are no discrete
       agents prior to relation, that there is only relation. Karen Barad, *Meeting
       the Universe Halfway: Quantum Physics and the Entanglement of Matter
       and Meaning* (Durham, NC: Duke University Press, 2007). I encountered
       Barad's ideas in Stephan Palmié, "When Is a Thing? Transduction and Im-
       mediacy in Afro-Cuban Ritual; or, ANT in Matanzas, Cuba, Summer of
       1948," *Comparative Studies in Society and History* 60, no. 4 (2018): 786–809.
       See also the idea of the distributed person and "social agency" in Gell, *Art
       and Agency*, 96, and the distinctions between systemic and conjunctural
       agency in Marshall Sahlins, *Apologies to Thucydides: Understanding History
       as Culture and Vice Versa* (Chicago: University of Chicago Press, 2004),
       158–59. See as well even much earlier discussions like Husserl's descrip-
       tion of perception as "never present to actual consciousness as a finished
       datum": "It becomes 'clarified' only through explication of the given hori-
       zon and the new horizons continuously awakened [*der stetig neu geweckten
       Horizonte*]." Intention always includes a material and ontological horizon;
       intention is "intending-beyond-itself," "something more," which, however,
       usually remains implicit in consciousness. Edmund Husserl, *Cartesian
       Meditations*, trans. Dorion Cairns (The Hague: M. Nijhoff, 1960), 46.

24.   On deferred agency, see, among others, Keane, *Christian Moderns*, 193;
       and Janice Boddy, *Wombs and Alien Spirits* (Madison: University of Wis-
       consin Press, 1989). On renounced agency, see de la Cruz, *Mother Figured*,
       224–25. On the agency of a mode of production, see Harry Harootunian,

"Remembering the Historical Present," *Critical Inquiry* 33, no. 3 (2007): 471–94. On corporate agency and bureaucratic agency, see Matthew Hull, *A Government of Paper*, 129–30. On the agency of the commons, see Oana Mateescu, "Serial Anachronism: Re-Assembling Romanian Forest Commons" (PhD diss., University of Michigan, 2017), 107. The problem is that, even as a negation, the individual is in play and at stake in a way that scholars of religion might consider vaguely "Protestant."

25. Segal, *Agency and Alienation*. This was the question posed by Wittgenstein: "Let us not forget this: when 'I raise my arm,' my arm goes up. And the problem arises: what is leftover if I subtract the fact that my arm goes up from the fact that I raised my arm?" Cited in Segal, *Agency and Alienation*, 4.

26. See n. 20 of the introduction.

27. See Parsons, "An Analytical Approach to the Theory of Social Stratification," 848, and "A Revised Analytical Approach to the Theory of Social Stratification," 95. In "An Analytical Approach to the Theory of Social Stratification," Parsons linked the word *agency* to individual achievement within parameters of status and social stratification (kinship, personal qualities, achievements, possessions, authority, power). In other earlier works like *The Social System* (Glencoe, IL: Free Press, 1951), he still used it in more of a nominative sense than as a general analytic feature of any social situation.

28. Geertz, *The Interpretation of Cultures*, 87–125 ("Religion as a Cultural System"); Pierre Bourdieu, *Esquisse d'une théorie de la pratique, precede de trois études d'ethnologie kabyle* (Geneva: Librairie Droz, 1972) (translated by Richard Nice as *Outline of a Theory of Practice* [Cambridge: Cambridge University Press, 1977]). To be clear, Bourdieu is critical of Parsons's "objectivism" for showing neither the fluidity between different forms of structure nor the relations between them. *Agency* does not appear in Talal Asad's early 1970s work but is a key term in his 1993 *Genealogies of Religion*.

29. Emmanuel Le Roy Ladurie, *Montaillou: Village occitan de 1294 à 1324* (Paris: Gallimard, 1975); Carlo Ginzburg, *Il formaggio e i vermin: il cosmo di un mugnaio del '500* (Turin: G. Einaudi, 1976) (translated by John Tedeschi and Anne Tedeschi as *The Cheese and the Worms: The Cosmos of a Sixteenth-Century Miller* [London: Routledge & Kegan Paul, 1976]).

30. Ginzburg, *The Cheese and the Worms*, x–xi.

31. Constantin Fasolt, *Past Sense: Studies in Medieval and Early Modern European History* (Leiden: Brill, 2014), 514.

32. Chakrabarty, *Provincializing Europe*, 103.

33. Stephan Palmié, "Historicist Knowledge and Its Conditions of Impossibility," in *The Social Life of Spirits*, ed. Diana Espirito Santo and Ruy Blanes (Chicago: University of Chicago Press, 2013), 218–40.

34. On using the term *agents* instead of *agency*, I am echoing the argument of Michel Rolph-Trouillot. In his analysis, agents are occupants of structural

positions who are acting in interface with a context and wielding voices that are aware of their vocality. See Rolph-Trouillot, *Silencing the Past*, 23, 162. On *agency* as Anglophone, consider the example of Jean Baudrillard, who does not use *agency* as such because there is not really a direct parallel in French. Instead, he often uses *instance*, as in "une *instance* psychique," translated in the English version as *psychic agency*. See Baudrillard, *L'echange symbolique et la mort*, 211 (*Symbolic Exchange and Death*, 157). Deleuze and Guattari's *agencement* is not equivalent to *agency* and is usually translated as *assemblage*. See Gilles Deleuze and Félix Guattari, *Milles plateaux* (Paris: Minuit, 1980). *Agentivité* is a relatively recently developing Anglicism drawn from translations of *agency*.

35.   David Mosse, "Possession and Confession: Affliction and Sacred Power in Colonial and Contemporary South India," in *The Anthropology of Christianity*, ed. Fenella Cannell (Durham, NC: Duke University Press, 2006), 99–133.

36.   Wirtz, *Ritual, Discourse, and Community in Cuban Santería*.

37.   Webb Keane analyzed the representational regimes of the agentive individual, including that of sincerity and its import in, especially, Protestant speech. See Webb Keane, "Sincerity, 'Modernity,' and the Protestants," *Cultural Anthropology* 17, no. 1 (2002): 65–92. He argues that, while in one sense Protestants defer to the agency of God, that agency is a backdrop for the drama of individual human agency.

38.   On dreams generating new capacities for agency, see Amira Mittermaier, *Dreams That Matter: Egyptian Landscapes of the Imagination* (Berkeley and Los Angeles: University of California Press, 2011), 108, 242. On agentive potential, see Lara Deeb, *An Enchanted Modern: Gender and Public Piety in Shi'i Lebanon* (Princeton, NJ: Princeton University Press, 2011), 31. On implicit agency and creolization, see Aisha Khan, "Good to Think? Creolization, Optimism, and Agency," *Current Anthropology* 48, no. 5 (2007): 653–73, 654. Catherine Bell famously described the production of "ritualized agents" and how agency is acquired, and sentiments of affinity fortified, by incorporating norms and values into the body through ritual. In the context of ritual performance, norms and values are actually inscribed onto the participants' bodies to become automatic. They are transferred to new initiates through the bodily engagement with symbols, which in turn generates powerful sentiments of affinity and belonging. See Catherine Bell, *Ritual Theory, Ritual Practice* (New York: Oxford University Press, 1992), 94–117.

On voice-distancing, Cyrus O'Brien wrote: "When the man learned that his job had been changed, he immediately approached Robert to thank him. Robert, however, disavowed any role in the change. . . . 'It was all God,' he said. 'I was just the vessel.' In his statements to me and to the man he helped become an inmate facilitator, Robert not only worked to obscure of disavow his ability to effect change in the institution; by casting God as an omnipotent and animating force of human action and by insisting he was 'just a vessel,' he called into question the idea of human agency itself." Cyrus O'Brien, "Faith in Imprisonment: Religion and the Development of Mass Incarceration in Florida" (PhD diss., University of Michigan, 2018), 321.

39. On ways forms of agency can work against each other, see Eugene Genovese, *Roll, Jordan, Roll: The World the Slaves Made* (New York: Pantheon, 1974), 221ff. On the need to give up certain conditions of agency to open others, see Marilyn Strathern, *The Gender of the Gift* (Berkeley and Los Angeles: University of California Press, 1988), 301.

40. Jean-Claude Beaune, "The Classical Age of Automata: An Impressionistic Survey from the Sixteenth to the Nineteenth Century," *Fragments for a History of the Human Body* 1 (1989): 430–80, 437: "the paradoxical logic of the technological object which plays endlessly at not being itself in order to assert more effectively its own identity."

41. Darwin, *The Expression of the Emotions*, 144.

42. Children play at ritual as a way of learning it, including faking spirit possession, marking aspiration and their future trajectory, all over the African Americas. See Landes, *City of Women*, 174; Palmié, *The Cooking of History*, 296 n. 22; Karen Richman, "The Vodou State and the Protestant Nation: Haiti in the Long Twentieth Century," in *Obeah and Other Powers: The Politics of Caribbean Religion and Healing*, ed. Diana Paton and Maarit Forde (Durham, NC: Duke University Press, 2012), 268–87, 283; Rita Laura Segato, *Santos e daimones: O politeísmo afro-brasileiro e a tradição arquetipal* (Brasília: Editora Universidade de Brasília, 1995), 103; Carmen Opipari and Sylvie Timbert, dirs., *Barbara and Her Friends in Candomblé-land* (London: Royal Anthropological Institute, 1997); and Arnaud Halloy and Vlad Naumescu, "Learning Spirit Possession: An Introduction," *Ethnos* 77 (2012): 155–76. Likewise, children play at mass or masking. See, e.g., Roger Caillois, *Man, Play and Games*, trans. Meyer Barash (Glencoe, IL: Free Press, 1961), 62. At the same time, in sites that serve as centers of orthopraxy and traditional authority—for Candomblé, Salvador da Bahia and its surround—such possession play may be circumscribed or even outright prohibited. Thanks to John F. Collins for this cautionary note.

43. Segato, *Santos e daimones*, 218.

44. Hannah Arendt, *The Human Condition* (Chicago: University of Chicago Press, 1998), 322.

45. "Dazed, 'tranquilized,' functional" is from Arendt, *The Human Condition*, 322. The idea of citational agency is derived from Zuboff, *The Age of Surveillance Capitalism*. Lateral agency is from Berlant, "Slow Death," 754.

46. Ivan declares: "I tell thee that man is tormented by no greater anxiety than to find someone quickly to whom he can hand over that gift of freedom with which the ill-fated creature is born." Fyodor Dostoevsky, *The Brothers Karamazov* (1880; London: Dover, 2005), 230. I take the example of Dos-

toevsky's Grand Inquisitor from Michael Meng, "On Authoritarianism," *Comparative Studies in Society and History* 59, no. 4 (2017): 1008–20.

47. From Jim Jones's exhortations to his flock in Jonestown just prior to the November 18, 1978, mass suicide. See "Q042 Transcript, FBI Transcription," November 18, 1978, Alternative Considerations of Jonestown & Peoples Temple, https://jonestown.sdsu.edu/?page_id=29081.

48. The most extreme example of how differences in power can produce an automaton who is viewed as a conduit of the sacred by virtue of his or her lack of will is the case of "Little Audrey Santo." Left in a coma at age three following a swimming-pool accident in 1987, Audrey became an object of Catholic pilgrimage, on one occasion in 1998 attracting eight thousand pilgrims, who gathered in the College of the Holy Cross football stadium to be near her silent body. She died in 2007. See Mathew Schmalz, "The Silent Body of Audrey Santo," *History of Religions* 42, no. 2 (2002): 116–42.

49. Maldonado, *Machado de Assis e o espiritismo*, 109–32.

50. Sahlins, *Apologies to Thucydides*, 155.

51. The player was the Brazilian striker Dani Alves, playing for Barcelona against Villareal in Villareal, Spain, April 2014.

Bibliography

Archives Consulted

Arquivo do Museu Imperial, Petrópolis
Arquivo Nacional do Brasil, Rio de Janeiro
Arquivo Público do Estado do Rio de Janeiro, Rio de Janeiro
Arquivo Ramos, Biblioteca Nacional, Rio de Janeiro
Arquivo Tobias Montero, Biblioteca Nacional, Rio de Janeiro
Bibliothèque de Neurosciences Jean-Martin Charcot, Salpêtrière, Paris
Centro de Documentação e Memória, Instituto Municipal de Assistência à Saúde Nise da Silveira (IMASNS), Rio de Janeiro
Collection Charcot, Jubilothèque, Paris
Conservatoire Numérique des Arts et Métiers (CNUM), Paris
Fonds Lacassagne, Bibliothèque Municipale de Lyon, Lyon
Fundação Casa de Rui Barbosa, Rio de Janeiro
Institut Mémoires de l'Édition Contemporaine (IMEC), Ardennes
Instituto Histórica e Geografica do Brasil (IHGB), Rio de Janeiro
Museu do Folclore Edison Carneiro, Rio de Janeiro
Museu do Negro, Igreja da Nossa Senhora do Rosário dos Homens Pretos do Rio de Janeiro, Rio de Janeiro
Museu Histórico Nacional, Rio de Janeiro
Núcleo de Memória, Instituto de Psiquiatria da Universidade Federal do Rio de Janeiro (UFRJ), Rio de Janeiro

Archival Sources

Arquivo Hélio Viana, DL1446/11. Instituto Histórico e Geográfico Brasileiro, Rio de Janeiro, Brazil.

Beisenberger, Bernard. Letter to Roger Bastide, October 20, 1961. Fonds Roger Bastide, BST2.N1-02.05. Bastide Archives, IMEC (Institut Mémoires de l'Édition Contemporaine), Saint-Germain-la-Blanche-Herbe, France.

Câmara criminal 70016184012, data de distributição 24/7/2006. Apelação Crimes contra pessoa, Rio Grande do Sul.

Case file DC 13, 43a. Fundo Hospício de Pedro II. Centro de Documentação e Memória Instituto Municipal Nise da Silveira, Rio de Janeiro, Brazil.

Charcot, Jean-Martin. I-DMM-1887/92. Museu do Imperio, Petrópolis, Brazil.

———. Letter to Motta Maia, October 23, 1887. 63.05.006. No. 36. Biblioteca Nacional, Rio de Janeiro.

———. Maço 28-988-Cat. B. Arquivo histórico, Museu do Império, Petrópolis, Brazil.

Correspondence Charcot. Museu do Império, Petrópolis, Brazil.

Documentation on Slave Anastácia. Museu do Negro. Rio de Janeiro, Brazil.

Dubuffet, Jean. Letter to William Seitz, April 21, 1961. Curatorial Exhibition Files, Exh. #695. Museum of Modern Art Archives, New York.

Maia, Motta. Letters to the Conde d'Eu, June 28, 1887, July 4, 1888. Caderno 41, cartas 8-9. Instituto Histórico e Geográfico Brasileiro, Rio de Janeiro, Brazil.

NARA M1372. Images of handwritten letters and application forms for US passports, 1795-1905. The US National Archives.

Observações clínicas. Fundo Hospício de Pedro II. Centro de Documentação e Memória Instituto Municipal Nise da Silveira, Rio de Janeiro, Brazil.

Pacifico, João. "A loucura das multidões." PhD diss., Clinical Psychiatry, Rio de Janeiro, 1915. Archived at Núcleo da memória, T-01, 001, 005.

Pedro II. Dom. Doc. 1056. Maço 36, Cad. 27. Museu do Imperio, Petrópolis, Brazil.

———. Dom. Doc. 1057. Maço 37, Cad. 31. Museu do Império, Petrópolis, Brazil.

———. Dom. Letters to Brown-Séquard. Archives of the Royal College of Physicians London.

———. Dom. Letter to Gobineau, July 23, 1873. Caderno 64.02.002, No. 003. Biblioteca Nacional, Rio de Janeiro, Brazil.

———. Dom. Letter to Princess Augusta Victoria of Germany, 1881. 63,04,004, No. 26, 1288. Arquivo Tobias Monteiro, Biblioteca Nacional, Rio de Janeiro, Brazil.

Série Saúde IS3 21, ofícios e relatórios 1900-1901. Arquivo Nacional, Rio de Janeiro, Brazil.

Supremo Tribunal de Justiça. BR AN RIO BV.O.RCR.0470. 1870.3, Maço 196, No. 1081. Arquivo Nacional, Rio de Janeiro.

Trade card advertising Ajeeb the Wonderful from the Eden Museé, New York, 1896. National Museum of American History, Washington, DC.

Published Works

Abreu, Dado. "Arthur Bispo do Rosário: A arte contemporânia na delicada fronteira entre genialidade e a loucur." *Revista fator* 12 (2014): 6-9.

Abreu, Maria José A. de. "TV St. Claire." In *Deus in Machina: Religion, Technol-*

ogy, and the Things in Between, ed. Jeremy Stolow, 261–80. New York: Fordham University Press, 2013.

———. "Technological Indeterminacy: Medium, Threat, Temporality." *Anthropological Theory* 13, no. 3 (2013): 267–84.

Agamben, Giorgio. *The Open: Man and Animal*. Stanford, CA: Stanford University Press, 2004.

———. "Identity without the Person." In *Nudities*, 46–54. Stanford, CA: Stanford University Press, 2011.

Agassiz, Louis. *A Journey in Brazil*. Boston: Houghton, Osgood, 1879.

Agrippa, Henry Cornelius. *Three Books of Occult Philosophy*. Edited by Donald Tyson. Translated by James Freake. Saint Paul, MN: Llewellyn, 2004.

Ahmad, Nemer da Silva. *Psicografia: O novo olhar da justiça*. Rio de Janeiro: Aliança, 2008.

"Ajeeb, the Chess Player." In *Eden Musée Catalogue*, 30. Brooklyn: Eden Bureau, 1899.

Akhtar, Salman, and Jodi Brown. "Animals in Psychiatric Symptomatology." In *Mental Zoo: Animals in the Human Mind and Its Pathology*, ed. Salman Akhtar and Vamik Volkan, 3–40. Madison, CT: International Universities Press, 2005.

Alberto, Paulina L. *Terms of Inclusion: Black Intellectuals in Twentieth-Century Brazil*. Chapel Hill: University of North Carolina Press, 2011.

Albin, Ricardo Cravo. *Dicionário Houaiss ilustrado música popular brasileira*. Rio de Janeiro: Editora Paracatu, 2006.

Aldrich, Robert. *Vestiges of Colonial Empire in France*. London: Palgrave, 2005.

Al-Jazari, Ismail. *The Book of Ingenious Devices*. Translated by Donald R. Hill. Dordrecht: D. Reidel, 1979.

Allen, George. "The History of the Automaton Chess-Player in America: A Letter Addressed to William Lewis, London." In *The Book of the First American Chess Congress*, ed. Willard Fiske, 420–84. New York: Rudd & Carleton, 1859.

Almeida, Cícero Antônio F. de. *Canudos: Imagens da guerra*. Rio de Janeiro: Lacerda, 1997.

Andermann, Jens. "Espetáculos da diferença: A Exposição Antropológica Brasileira de 1882." *Topoi—Revista de história* 5, no. 9 (2004): 128–70.

Andrade, Maria Vanessa, Aluísio Ferreira de Lima, and Maria Elisalene Alves dos Santos. "A razão e a loucura na literatura: Um estudo sobre o alienista, de Machado de Assis." *Revista psicologia e saúde* 6, no. 1 (2014): 37–48.

Anonymous. "The Metaphysics of an Automaton." *The Spectator*, no. 1881 (July 16, 1864): 816–17.

Anscombe, G. E. M. *Intention*. Cambridge, MA: Harvard University Press, 2000.

Arago, Jacques Étienne Victor. *Narrative of a Voyage round the World, in the Uranie and Physicienne Corvettes, Commanded by Captain Freycinet, during the Years 1817, 1818, 1819, and 1820*. London: T. Davison, Whitefriars; Howlett & Brimmer, 1823.

———. *Souvenirs d'un aveugle: Voyage autour du monde: Ouvvrage enrichi de soixante dessins et de notes scientifiques*. Vol. 1. Paris: Hortet & Ozanne, 1839.

Arendt, Hannah. *The Human Condition*. Chicago: University of Chicago Press, 1998.

Armstrong, Tim. *The Logic of Slavery: Debt, Technology, and Pain in American Literature*. Cambridge: Cambridge University Press, 2012.

Asad, Talal. *Genealogies of Religion: Discipline and Reasons of Power in Christianity and Islam*. Baltimore: Johns Hopkins University Press, 1993.

———. *Formations of the Secular: Christianity, Islam, Modernity*. Stanford, CA: Stanford University Press, 2003.

Assis, Machado de. "Captain Mendonça." In *Contos fantásticos de Machado de Assis*, ed. Raimundo Magalhães Júnior, 182–202. Rio de Janeiro: Edições Bloch, 1973.

———. "A Canary's Ideas." Translated by Jack Schmitt and Lorie Chieko Ishimatsu. In *The Devil's Church and Other Stories*, 125–29. Austin: University of Texas Press, 1977.

———. *Iaiá Garcia*. Translated by Albert I. Bagby Jr. Lexington: University Press of Kentucky, 1977.

———. *Bons dias!* Edited by John Gledson. São Paulo: Editora da Unicamp, 1990.

———. *O alienista e outras histórias*. Rio de Janeiro: EDIOURO, 1996.

———. "The Mirror" ("O espelho"). In *The Collected Stories of Machado de Assis*, trans. Margaret Jull Costa and Robin Patterson, 444–52. New York: Liveright, 2018.

———. *The Collected Stories of Machado de Assis*. Translated by Margaret Jull Costa and Robin Patterson. New York: Liveright, 2018.

Assis, Machado de, and Joaquim Nabuco. *Correspondência*. Edited by Graça Aranha. Rio de Janeiro: Topbooks, 2003.

Aubrée, Marion, and François Laplantine. *La table, le livre et les esprits: Naissance, evolution et actualité du mouvement social spirite entre France et Brésil*. Paris: J. C. Lattès, 1990.

Aukeman, Anastacia. *Welcome to Painterland: Bruce Connor and the Rat Bastard Protective Association*. Berkeley and Los Angeles: University of California Press, 2016.

Babinski, Josef. *Hysteria or Pithiatism*. Translated by J. D. Rolleston. London: University of London Press, 1918.

Bakhtin, M. M. "Forms of Time and of the Chronotope in the Novel." In *The Dialogic Imagination*, trans. Caryl Emerson and Michael Holquist, 84–258. Austin: University of Texas Press, 1981.

Barad, Karen. *Meeting the Universe Halfway: Quantum Physics and the Entanglement of Matter and Meaning*. Durham, NC: Duke University Press, 2007.

Barreto, Paulo (João do Rio). *As religões no Rio*. 1906. Rio de Janeiro: Edição da Organização Simões, 1951.

Barthes, Roland. *Camera Lucida: Reflections on Photography*. Translated by Richard Howard. New York: Farrar, Strauss & Giroux, 1981.

Bastide, Roger. *Estudos afro-brasileiros*. 3rd ser. São Paulo: Universidade de São Paulo, 1953.

———. *The African Religions of Brazil: Towards a Sociology of the Interpenetration of Civilizations*. Translated by Helen Sebba. Baltimore: Johns Hopkins University Press, 1978.

Bastos, Orimar de. *O justo juiz: História de uma sentence*. Goiânia: Editora Kelps, 2010.

Bataille, Georges. *L'erotisme*. Paris: Editions de Minuit, 1957.

———. *Erotism: Death and Sensuality*. Translated by Mary Dalwood. San Francisco: City Lights, 1986.

Battaglia, Debbora. "Toward an Ethics of the Open Subject: Writing Culture in Good Conscience." In *Anthropological Theory Today*, ed. Henrietta Moore, 114–50. London: Polity, 2000.

Baucom, Ian. *Specters of the Atlantic: Finance Capital, Slavery, and the Philosophy of History*. Durham, NC: Duke University Press, 2005.

Baudelaire, Charles. *Paris Spleen, 1869*. Translated by Louise Varèse. New York: New Directions, 1970.

Baudouin, A. "Quelques souvenirs de la Salpêtrière." *Paris médical* 21 (1925): 517–20.

Baudrillard, Jean. *L'echange symbolique et la mort*. Paris: Gallimard, 1976. Translated as *Symbolic Exchange and Death* by Iain Hamilton Grant (London: Sage, 2017).

Bazin, André. *What Is Cinema?* Vol. 1. Translated by Hugh Gray. Berkeley and Los Angeles: University of California Press, 1967.

Beals, Timothy K. *Religion and Monsters*. New York: Routledge, 2002.

Beaune, Jean-Claude. *L'automate et ses mobiles*. Paris: Flammarion, 1980.

———. "The Classical Age of Automata: An Impressionistic Survey from the Sixteenth to the Nineteenth Century." *Fragments for a History of the Human Body* 1 (1989): 430–80.

Belcier, Jeanne de. *Soeur Jeanne des Anges: Autobiographie d'une hystérique possédée*. Edited by Gabriel Legué and Gilles de la Tourette. With a preface by Jean-Martin Charcot. Paris: Aux Bureaux du Progrès Médical, 1886.

Beliso–De Jesús, Aisha M. *Electric Santería: Racial and Sexual Assemblages of Transnational Religion*. New York: Columbia University Press, 2015.

Bell, Catherine. *Ritual Theory, Ritual Practice*. New York: Oxford University Press, 1992.

Benjamin, Walter. "The Work of Art in the Age of Mechanical Reproduction." In *Illuminations*, ed. Hannah Arendt, 217–52. New York: Schocken, 1968.

———. *The Arcades Project*. Cambridge, MA: Belknap Press of Harvard University Press, 2003.

Berlant, Lauren. "Slow Death (Sovereignty, Obesity, Lateral Agency)." *Critical Inquiry* 33, no. 4 (2007): 754–80.

Bierce, Ambrose. "Moxon's Master." In *The Collected Works of Ambrose Bierce*, vol. 3, *Can Such Things Be?*, 88–105. New York: Neale, 1910.

Blavatsky, H. P. *Isis Unveiled: A Master-Key to the Mysteries of Ancient and Modern Science and Theology*. Cambridge: Cambridge University Press, 1877.

Blumenthal, Susanna L. "The Default Legal Person." *UCLA Law Review* 54, no. 5 (2007): 1135–1267.

Boddy, Janice. *Wombs and Alien Spirits: Women, Men, and the Zār Cult in Northern Sudan*. Madison: University of Wisconsin Press, 1989.

Boisseron, Bénédicte. *Afro-Dog: Blackness and the Animal Question*. New York: Columbia University Press, 2018.

Bonaparte, Roland. *La nature* 903 (1890): 247–50.

Bonifácio, José. *José Bonifácio de Andrada e Silva*. Edited by Jorge Caldeira. Rio de Janeiro: Catalogação na Fonte do Departamento Nacional de Livro, 2002.

Borges, Dain. *The Family in Bahia, 1870–1945*. Stanford, CA: Stanford University Press, 1985.

———. "'Puffy, Ugly, Slothful and Inert': Degeneration in Brazilian Social Thought, 1880–1940." *Journal of Latin American Studies* 25, no. 2 (1993): 235–56.

———. "Healing and Mischief: Witchcraft in Brazilian Law and Literature, 1890–1922." In *Crime and Punishment in Latin America*, ed. Ricardo D. Salvatore, Carlos Aguirre, and Gilbert M. Joseph, 181–210. Durham, NC: Duke University Press, 2001.

Bouchara, Catherine. *Charcot: Une vie avec l'image*. Paris: Philippe Rey, 2013.

Bourdieu, Pierre. *Esquisse d'une théorie de la pratique, precede de trois études d'ethnologie kabyle*. Geneva: Librairie Droz, 1972. Translated as *Outline of a Theory of Practice* by Richard Nice (Cambridge: Cambridge University Press, 1977).

———. *Pascalian Meditations*. Stanford, CA: Stanford University Press, 2000.

Boureau, Alain. *Satan the Heretic: The Birth of Demonology in the Medieval West*. Translated by Teresa Lavender Fagan. Chicago: University of Chicago Press, 2006.

Bourget, Paul. *Essai de psychologie contemporaine*. Paris: A. Lemerre, 1883.

Bourneville, Désiré-Magloire. *Compte-rendu des observations recueillies á la Salpêtrière, concernant l'épilepsie et l'hystérie*. Paris: Aux Bureaux du Progrès Médical/Delahaye, 1875.

———. *Science et miracle: Louise Lateau; ou, La stigmatisée belge*. Paris: Delahaye, 1875.

———. Preface to *La foi qui guérit*, by Jean-Martin Charcot, 2–4. Paris: FV Éditions, 2012.

Bourneville, Désiré-Magloire, and Paul Regnard. *Iconographie photographique de la Salpêtrière*. Paris: Aux Bureau de Progrès Médical, 1876–77.

Boyer, Pascal. *Religion Explained: The Evolutionary Origins of Religious Thought*. New York: Basic, 2001.

Breton, André. *Manifestoes of Surrealism*. Translated by Richard Seaver and Helen R. Lane. Ann Arbor: University of Michigan Press, 1969.

Brosses, Charles de. *Du culte des dieux fétiches: ou, Parallèle de l'ancienne religion de l'Egypte avec la religion actuelle de Nigritie*. 1760. Westmead: Gregg International, 1970.

Brown, Bill. "Thing Theory." *Critical Inquiry* 28, no. 1 (2001): 1–22.

Brown, David H. "Garden in the Machine: Afro-Cuban Sacred Art and Performance in New Jersey and New York." PhD diss., Yale University, 1989.

Brown, Diana. *Umbanda: Religion and Politics in Urban Brazil.* New York: Columbia University Press, 1994.

Brown, Karen McCarthy. *Mama Lola: A Vodou Priestess in Brooklyn.* Berkeley and Los Angeles: University of California Press, 1991.

Brown, Peter. *The Cult of the Saints: Its Rise and Function in Latin Christianity.* Chicago: University of Chicago Press, 1981.

Brown, Rose. *American Emperor: Dom Pedro II of Brazil.* New York: Viking, 1945.

Brown-Séquard, Charles-Édouard. "The Effects Produced on Man by Subcutaneous Injection of a Liquid Obtained from the Testicles of Animals." *The Lancet* 134 (1889): 105–7.

Bryant, Nahum F. "Magic and Mystery." *Household Monthly* 2, no. 5 (August 1859): 411–18.

Burdick, John. *Blessed Anastácia: Women, Race, and Popular Christianity in Brazil.* New York: Routledge, 1998.

Butler, Judith. *Bodies That Matter: On the Discursive Limits of Sex.* New York: Routledge, 1993.

———. *Giving an Account of Oneself.* New York: Fordham University Press, 2005.

———. *The Psychic Life of Power: Theories in Subjection.* Stanford, CA: Stanford University Press, 2006.

———. *Notes toward a Performative Theory of Assembly.* Cambridge, MA: Harvard University Press, 2015.

Butler, Judith, and Athena Athanasiou. *Dispossession: The Performative in the Political.* Cambridge: Polity, 2013.

Cabañas, Kaira Marie. "A contemporaneidade de Bispo." *ARS São Paulo* 16, no. 32 (2018): 47–80.

Caillois, Roger. "La mante religieuse: Recherches sur la nature et la signification du mythe." *Mesures* 3, no. 2 (1937): 87–119.

———. *Les jeux et les hommes.* Paris: Gallimard, 1958.

———. *Man, Play and Games.* Translated by Meyer Barash. Glencoe, IL: Free Press, 1961.

Campos, Humberto de, ed. *Anthologia da Academia Brasileira de Letras: Trinta annos de discursos academicos, 1897–1927.* Rio de Janeiro: Editora Leite Ribeiro, 1928.

———. "Os 'Reddis.'" In *A serpente de bronze*, 194–96. Rio de Janeiro: Editora Leite Ribeiro, 1921.

Canguilhem, Georges. *The Normal and the Pathological.* New York: Zone, 2007.

Čapek, Karel. *R.U.R. (Rossum's Universal Robots).* New York: Penguin, 2004.

Capellaro, Jorge. *Verdades sobre o início do cinema no Brasil.* Rio de Janeiro: FUNARTE, 1996.

Capen, Nahum. "Biography of Dr. Gall." In Franz Joseph Gall, *On the Functions of the Brain and of Each of Its Parts*, 13–54. Boston: Marsh, Capen & Lyon, 1835.

Capone, Stefania. *Searching for Africa in Brazil: Power and Tradition in Candomblé.* Translated by Lucy Lyall Grant. Durham, NC: Duke University Press, 2010.

Capone, Stefania, and Kali Argyriadis. *La religion des orisha: Un champ social transnational en pleine recomposition.* Paris: Editions Hermann, 2011.

Carneiro, Edison. *Candomblés da Bahia.* Salvador: Museu do Estado, 1948.

Carvalho, José Murilo de. *Dom Pedro II: Ser ou não ser.* São Paulo: Companhia das Letras, 2007.

Castillo, Lisa Earl. "Icons of Memory: Photography and Its Uses in Bahian Candomblé." *Stockholm Review of Latin American Studies,* no. 4 (2009): 11–23.

Cavell, Stanley. *The World Viewed: Reflections on the Ontology of Film.* Cambridge, MA: Harvard University Press, 1971.

Certeau, Michel de. *The Possession at Loudun.* Translated by Michael B. Smith. Chicago: University of Chicago Press, 2000.

Chakrabarty, Dipesh. *Provincializing Europe: Postcolonial Thought and Historical Difference.* Princeton, NJ: Princeton University Press, 2000.

Chalhoub, Sidney. *Visões da liberdade.* São Paulo: Editora Schwarcz, 1990.

———. "Dependents Play Chess: Political Dialogues in Machado de Assis." In *Machado de Assis: Reflections on a Master Writer,* ed. Richard Graham, 51–84. Austin: University of Texas Press, 1999.

Charcot, Jean-Martin. *Leçons sur les maladies du système nerveux.* Paris: Delahaye, 1872–73.

———. "Episodes nouveaux de l'hystéro-épilepsie—Zoopsie—Catalepsie chez les animaux." In *Oeuvres complètes* (9 vols.), 9:289–97. Paris: Aux Bureaux du Progrès Médical/Lecrosnier & Babé, 1890.

———. "Seizième leçon: Spiritisme et hystèrie." In *Oeuvres complètes* (9 vols.), 3:229–37. Paris: Aux Bureaux du Progrès Médical/Lecrosnier & Babé, 1890.

———. *Nouvelle iconographie de la Salpêtrière.* Vol. 3. Paris: Lecrosnier & Babé, 1890.

———. "The Faith-Cure." *New Review* 8, no. 44 (1893): 18–31.

———. "Clinique des maladie nerveuses." *Paris médical* 58 (1925): 465–78.

———. *Charcot in Morocco.* Edited and translated by Toby Gelfand. Ottawa, ON: University of Ottawa Press, 2012.

Charcot, J.-M., and Paul Richer. *Les démoniaques dans l'art.* Paris: Adrien Delahaye & Émile Lecrosnier, 1887.

Charlton, Debra. "Sarah Bernhardt: Artist and Mythologist." In *Women in the Arts in the Belle Epoque,* ed. Paul Fryer, 12–27. Jefferson, NC: McFarland, 2012.

Charuty, Giordana. "La 'boîte aux ancêtres': Photographie et science de l'invisible." *Terrain* 33 (1999): 57–80.

Chéroux, Clément. "Ghost Dialectics: Spirit Photography in Entertainment and Belief." In *The Perfect Medium: Photography and the Occult,* ed. Clément Chéroux, Andreas Fischer, Pierre Apraxine, Denis Canguilhem, and Sophie Schmit, 45–71. New Haven, CT: Yale University Press, 2005.

Clarke, Edward. *Visions: A Study of False Sight.* Boston: Houghton, Osgood, 1878.

Clarke, James Freeman. *Every-Day Religion*. Boston: Ticknor, 1886.

Cloutier, Crista. "Mumler's Ghosts." In *The Perfect Medium: Photography and the Occult*, ed. Clément Chéroux, Andreas Fischer, Pierre Apraxine, Denis Canguilhem, and Sophie Schmit, 20–28. New Haven, CT: Yale University Press, 2005.

Clouzot, Henri-Georges. *Le cheval des dieux*. Paris: Julliard, 1951.

Cohen, Emma. *The Mind Possessed: The Cognition of Spirit Possession in an Afro-Brazilian Religion*. New York: Oxford University Press, 2007.

Collins, John F. "The Sounds of Tradition: Arbitrariness and Agency in a Brazilian Cultural Center." *Ethnos* 72, no. 3 (2007): 383–407.

———. *The Revolt of the Saints: Memory and Redemption in the Twilight of Brazilian Racial Democracy*. Durham, NC: Duke University Press, 2015.

Commons, John Rogers. *Races and Immigrants in America*. New York: Macmillan, 1920.

Connor, Steve. *The Book of Skin*. London: Reaktion, 2004.

Cook, James W. *The Arts of Deception: Playing with Fraud in the Age of Barnum*. Cambridge, MA: Harvard University Press, 2001.

Costello, Diamuid. *On Photography: A Philosophical Inquiry*. New York: Routledge, 2017.

Crary, Jonathan. *Techniques of the Observer: On Vision and Modernity in the Nineteenth Century*. Cambridge, MA: MIT Press, 1992.

Cunha, Ana Stela de Almeida. "João da Mata Family: Pajé Dreams, Chants, and Social Life." In *The Social Life of Spirits*, ed. Ruy Blanes and Diana Espírito Santo, 157–78. Chicago: University of Chicago Press, 2014.

Cunha, Euclides da. *Rebellion in the Backlands*. Translated by Samuel Putnam. Chicago: University of Chicago Press, 1944.

Cunha, Olívia Maria Gomes da. "Do ponto do visto de quem? Diálogos, olhares e etnografias dos/nos arquivos." *Estudos históricos* 36 (2005): 7–32.

Cunha, Patrícia Lessa Flores da. *Machado de Assis: Um escritor na capital dos trópicos*. Porto Allegre: Editora Unisinos, 1998.

Darwin, Charles. *The Expression of the Emotions in Man and Animals*. London: John Murray, 1872.

———. *Charles Darwin's Beagle Diary*. Cambridge: Cambridge University Press, 1988.

Das, Veena. "Of Mistakes, Errors, and Superstition." In *The Mythology in Our Language: Remarks on Frazer's Golden Bough*, by Ludwig Wittgenstein, trans. Stephan Palmié, ed. Giovanni da Col, 157–82. Chicago: HAU, 2018.

Daston, Lorraine, and Peter Galison. *Objectivity*. New York: Zone, 2007.

Daudet, Léon. *Les morticoles*. Paris: Bibliothèque-Charpentier, 1894.

———. *Les oeuvres dans les hommes*. Paris: Nouvelle Librairie Nationale, 1922.

Davenport, Frederick Morgan. *Primitive Traits in Religious Revivals: A Study in Mental and Social Evolution*. New York: Macmillan, 1905.

Davies, Stephen. *Samuel Lipschutz: A Life in Chess*. Jefferson, NC: McFarland, 2014.

Davis, David Brion. *The Problem of Slavery in Western Culture*. New York: Oxford University Press, 1966.

Dayan, Colin. *The Law Is a White Dog: How Legal Rituals Make and Unmake Persons*. Princeton, NJ: Princeton University Press, 2011.

Deeb, Lara. *An Enchanted Modern: Gender and Public Piety in Shi'i Lebanon*. Princeton, NJ: Princeton University Press, 2011.

Degler, Carl. *Neither Black nor White*. New York: Macmillan, 1971.

Dejerine, Joseph Jules. "L'oeuvre scientifique de Charcot." *Paris médical* 21 (1925): 509–11.

Dekel, Edan, and David Gantt Gurley. "How the Golem Came to Prague." *Jewish Quarterly Review* 103, no. 2 (2013): 241–58.

De la Cruz, Deirdre. *Mother Figured: Marian Apparitions and the Making of a Filipino Universal*. Chicago: University of Chicago Press, 2015.

de Mello e Souza, Laura. *The Devil and the Land of the Holy Cross: Witchcraft, Slavery, and Popular Religion in Colonial Brazil*. Translated by Diane Grosklaus Whittey. Austin: University of Texas Press, 2003.

Denizart, Hugo, dir. *O prisioneiro de passage*. Brasilia: Ministry of Health, 1982.

Descartes, René. *The Passions of the Soul*. In *The Philosophical Writings of Descartes*, 325–404. Cambridge: Cambridge University Press, 1985.

———. *Meditations and Other Metaphysical Writings*. London: Penguin, 2003.

———. *Discourse on Method and Meditations on First Philosophy*. 4th ed. Translated by Donald A. Cress. Indianapolis: Hackett, 1999.

Descola, Philippe. "Presence, Attachment, Origin: Ontologies of 'Incarnates.'" In *A Companion to the Anthropology of Religion*, ed. Janice Boddy and Michael Lambek, 35–49. Oxford: Wiley Blackwell, 2013.

Dias de Souza, Monica. "Escrava Anastácia e Pretos-Velhos: A rebelião silenciosa da memoria popular." In *Imaginário, cotidiano e poder*, ed. Vagner Gonçalves da Silva, 15–42. São Paulo: Edições Selo Negro, 2007.

Dickens, Charles. "Mediums under Other Names." *All the Year Round* 7, no. 156 (April 19, 1862): 130–37.

Didier, Fredie, and Paula Sarno Braga. "Carta psicografada como fonte de prova no processo civil." *Revista da Programa de Pós-Graduação em Direito da Universidade Federal da Bahia* 25 (2013): 190–228.

Didi-Huberman, Georges. *Invention of Hysteria: Charcot and the Photographic Iconography of the Salpêtrière*. Translated by Alisa Hartz. Cambridge, MA: MIT Press, 2003.

Douglas, Mary. *Purity and Danger*. London: Routledge & Kegan Paul, 1966.

Dorr, David F. *A Colored Man around the World*. Cleveland: David Dorr, 1858.

Dostoevsky, Fyodor. *The Brothers Karamazov*. 1880. London: Dover, 2005.

Doyle, Arthur Conan. *History of Spiritualism*. Cambridge: Cambridge University Press, 2011.

Du Bois, W. E. B. *The Souls of Black Folk*. New York: Barnes & Noble Classics, 2003.

Durkheim, Émile. *Le suicide*. Paris: Félix Alcan, 1897.

———. *The Elementary Forms of Religious Life*. Translated by Joseph Swain. London: Dover, 2008.

Edwards, Elizabeth, ed. *Anthropology and Photography*. London: Royal Anthropological Institute, 1992.

Eisenlohr, Patrick. "Mediality and Materiality in Religious Performance: Religion as Heritage in Mauritius." *Material Religion* 9, no. 3 (2013): 328–48.

Emmanuel, Marthe. *Charcot, navigateur polaire*. Paris: Éditions des Loisirs, 1945.

———. *Tel fut Charcot*. Paris: Beauchesne, 1967.

Engel, Magali Gouveia. *Os delírios da razão: Medicos, loucos e hospícios, Rio de Janeiro, 1830–1930*. Rio de Janeiro: Editora FIOCRUZ, 2001.

Engelke, Matthew. *A Problem of Presence: Beyond Scripture in an African Church*. Berkeley and Los Angeles: University of California Press, 2007.

Engels, Friedrich. Letter to Franz Mehring, July 14, 1893. In *Marx and Engels Correspondence*, trans. Donna Torr. New York: International, 1968. https://www.marxists.org/archive/marx/works/1893/letters/93_07_14.htm.

Ewbank, Thomas. *Life in Brazil*. 1856. New York: Elibron Classics, 2005.

Falzeder, Ernst, and Eva Brabant, eds. *The Correspondence of Sigmund Freud and Sándor Ferenczi*. Vol. 2, *1914–1919*. Translated by Peter T. Hoffer. Cambridge, MA: Belknap Press of Harvard University Press, 1996.

Fanon, Frantz. *Peau noire, masques blancs*. Paris: Editions du Seuil, 1952.

Fasolt, Constantin. *The Limits of History*. Chicago: University of Chicago Press, 2004.

———. *Past Sense: Studies in Medieval and Early Modern European History*. Leiden: Brill, 2014.

Ferretti, Mundicarmo. "Repensando o Turco no Tambor de Mina." *Afro-Asia* 15 (1992): 56–70.

———. "The Presence of Non-African Spirits in an Afro-Brazilian Religion." In *Reinventing Religions: Syncretism and Transformation in Africa and the Americas*, ed. Sidney M. Greenfield and A. F. Droogers, 99–112. Oxford: Rowman & Littlefield, 2001.

Ferrez, Gilberto, and Weston J. Naef. *Pioneer Photographers of Brazil, 1840–1920*. New York: Center for Inter-American Relations, 1976.

Feuerbach, Ludwig. *Essence of Christianity*. 1841. Translated by George Eliot. Amherst, NY: Prometheus 1989.

———. *Essence of Christianity*. New York: Calvin Blanchard, 1855.

Flatley, Jonathan. "Reading for Mood." *Representations*, no. 140 (2017): 137–48.

Fletcher, Rev. James C., and Rev. D. Kidder. *Brazil and the Brazilians*. Boston: Little, Brown, 1868.

Forrester, John. "If *p*, Then What? Thinking in Cases." *History of the Human Sciences* 9, no. 3 (1996): 1–25.

Forster, George. *A Voyage round the World in His Britannic Majesty's Sloop Resolution, Commanded by Capt. James Cook, during the Years, 1772, 3, 4, and 5*. 2 vols. London, 1777.

Franceschi, Humberto M. *Registro sonoro por meios mecânicos no Brasil*. Rio de Janeiro: Studio HMF, 1984.

Frazer, James George. *The Golden Bough: A Study in Magic and Religion*. Vol. 3, pt. 2, *Taboo and the Perils of the Soul*. 3rd ed. London: Macmillan, 1911.

———. *Totemism and Exogamy*. Vol. 1. New York: Cosimo, 2010.

Freitas, Eliane Tânia Martins. "Violência e sagrado: O que no criminoso anuncia o santo?" *Ciências sociales y religión/Ciências sociais e religião* 2, no. 2 (2000): 191–203.

Freud, Sigmund. "Hysteria and Witches" (letter 56, January 17, 1897). In *Abstracts of the Standard Edition of the Psychological Works of Sigmund Freud*, vol. 1, *Pre-Psycho-Analytic Publications and Unpublished Drafts (1886–1899)*, ed. Carrie Lee Rothgeb, 10. Washington, DC: US Department of Health, Education and Welfare, 1971.

———. *The Standard Edition of the Complete Psychological Works of Sigmund Freud*. Translated by James Strachey. 24 vols. 1953–74. New York: Vintage, 1999.

———. *Group Psychology and the Analysis of the Ego*. Translated by James Strachey. London: International Psycho-Analytical Press, 1922.

———. *Totem and Taboo*. Translated by James Strachey. New York: Norton, 1950.

———. "Report on My Studies in Paris and Berlin (1886)—Carried Out with the Assistance of a Travelling Bursary Granted from the University Jubilee Fund (October, 1885–End of March, 1886)." *International Journal of Psycho-Analysis* 37 (1956): 2–7.

———. "Obsessive Actions and Religious Practices." In *The Standard Edition of the Complete Psychological Works of Sigmund Freud* (24 vols.), trans. James Strachey, 9:115–28. New York: Vintage, 1999.

Frigerio, Alejandro. "Levels of Possession Awareness in Afro-Brazilian Religion." *Association for the Anthropological Study of Consciousness Quarterly* 5, no. 2 (1989): 5–11.

———. *Cultura negra en el Cono Sur: Representaciones en conflicto*. Buenos Aires: Ediciones de la Universidad Católica Argentina, 2000.

Galton, Francis. *Inquiries into the Human Faculty and Its Development*. New York: Macmillan, 1883.

Garcia, Ismar Estulano. *Psicografia como prova jurídica*. Goiânia: Editora AB, 2010.

Garfinkel, Harold. "Conditions of Successful Degradation Ceremonies." *American Journal of Sociology* 61, no. 5 (1956): 420–24.

Gauchet, Marcel. *The Disenchantment of the World: A Political History of Religion*. Translated by Oscar Burge. Princeton, NJ: Princeton University Press, 1997.

Geertz, Clifford. *The Interpretation of Cultures: Selected Essays*. New York: Basic, 1973.

Gell, Alfred. *Art and Agency: An Anthropological Theory*. Oxford: Clarendon, 1998.

Genovese, Eugene. *Roll, Jordan, Roll: The World the Slaves Made*. New York: Pantheon, 1974.

Gierke, Otto von. *Political Theories of the Middle Ages*. Translated by Frederic William Maitland. Cambridge: Cambridge University Press, 1900.

Gilman, Sander L. "The Image of the Hysteric." In *Hysteria beyond Freud*, by Sander L. Gilman, Helen King, Roy Porter, G. S. Rousseau, and Elaine Showalter, 345–452. Berkeley and Los Angeles: University of California Press, 1993.

Ginzburg, Carlo. *Il formaggio e i vermin: Il cosmo di un mugnaio del '500*. Turin: G. Einaudi, 1976. Translated as *The Cheese and the Worms: The Cosmos of a Sixteenth-Century Miller* by John Tedeschi and Anne Tedeschi (London: Routledge & Kegan Paul, 1976).

Gitelman, Lisa. *Scripts, Grooves and Writing Machines: Representing Technology in the Edison Era*. Stanford, CA: Stanford University Press, 1999.

Giumbelli, Emerson. *O cuidado dos mortos: Uma história da condenação e legitimação do espiritismo*. Rio de Janeiro: Arquivo Nacional, 1997.

Goetz, Christopher G., Michel Bonduelle, and Toby Gelfand. *Charcot: Constructing Neurology*. New York: Oxford University Press, 1995.

Goffman, Erving. *The Presentation of Self in Everyday Life*. New York: Anchor, 1959.

———. *Asylums: Essays on the Social Situation of Mental Patients and Other Inmates*. New York: Anchor, 1961.

———. *Interaction Ritual*. 1967. New Brunswick, NJ: Transaction, 2005.

———. *Frame Analysis*. New York: Harper & Row, 1974.

Goldstein, Jan. *Console and Classify: The French Psychiatric Profession in the Nineteenth Century*. 1987. Chicago: University of Chicago Press, 2001.

———. *Hysteria Complicated by Ecstasy: The Case of Nanette Leroux*. Princeton, NJ: Princeton University Press, 2010.

Gonçalves, Monique de Siqueira. "Mente sã, corpo são (disputas, debates e discursos medicos na busca pela cura das 'nevroses' a da loucura na Corte Imperial, 1850–1880)." PhD diss., Casa de Oswaldo Cruz/Fiocruz, 2011.

González, Eduardo. *Cuba and the Tempest: Literature and Cinema in the Time of Diaspora*. Chapel Hill: University of North Carolina Press, 2006.

Goodall, Jane. "Primate Spirituality." In *The Encyclopedia of Religion and Nature*, ed. Bron Taylor, 1303–6. New York: Continuum, 2005.

Graeber, David, and Marshall Sahlins. *On Kings*. Chicago: HAU, 2017.

Grafton, Anthony. *Natural Particulars: Nature and the Disciplines in Renaissance Europe*. Cambridge, MA: MIT Press, 1999.

Grehan, James. *Twilight of the Saints: Everyday Religion in Ottoman Syria and Palestine*. New York: Oxford University Press, 2016.

Guillain, George. *J.-M. Charcot, 1825–1893: Sa vie, son oeuvre*. Paris: Masson, 1955.

Guinon, Georges. "Charcot intime." *Paris médical* 1 (1925): 511–16.

Gurney, Edmund, Frederic W. H. Myers, and Frank Podmore. *Phantasms of the Living*. Vol. 1. London: Society for Psychical Research, 1886.

Guthrie, Stewart Elliott. *Faces in the Clouds: A New Theory of Religion*. New York: Oxford University Press, 1993.

Gutierrez, Cathy. *Plato's Ghost: Spiritualism in the American Renaissance*. New York: Oxford University Press, 2009.

Haan, Joost, Peter J. Koehler, and Julien Bogousslavsky. "Neurology and Surrealism: André Breton and Joseph Babinski." *Brain* 13, no. 12 (2012): 3830–38.

Hacking, Ian. *Rewriting the Soul: Multiple Personality and the Sciences of Memory*. Princeton, NJ: Princeton University Press, 1995.

———. *Mad Travelers: Reflections on the Reality of Transient Mental Illnesses*. Cambridge, MA: Harvard University Press, 1998.

Hagedorn, Katherine J. *Divine Utterances: The Performance of Afro-Cuban Santería*. Washington, DC: Smithsonian Books, 2001.

Halloy, Arnaud, and Vlad Naumescu. "Learning Spirit Possession: An Introduction." *Ethnos* 77 (2012): 155–76.

Handler, Jerome S., and Kelly E. Hayes. "Escrava Anastácia: The Iconographic History of a Brazilian Popular Saint." *African Diaspora* 2 (2009): 25–51.

Haraway, Donna. *Simians, Cyborgs and Women: The Reinvention of Nature*. New York: Routledge, 1991.

———. "The Promises of Monsters: A Regenerative Politics for Inappropriate/d Others." In *Cultural Studies*, ed. Lawrence Grossberg, Cary Nelson, and Paula A. Treichler, 295–337. New York: Routledge, 1992.

———. *When Species Meet*. Minneapolis: University of Minnesota Press, 2008.

Harold, N. Y. "Hysteria: Two Peculiar Cases as Presented by Professor Charcot." *Kansas City Medical Index-Lancet* 10, no. 114 (June 1889): 210–11.

Harootunian, Harry. "Remembering the Historical Present." *Critical Inquiry* 33, no. 3 (2007): 471–94.

Harrington, Anne. *Mind Fixers: Psychiatry's Troubled Search for the Biology of Mental Illness*. Cambridge, MA: Harvard University Press, 2019.

Hartshorne, C., P. Weiss, and A. Burks, eds. *Collected Papers of Charles Sanders Peirce*. 8 vols. Cambridge, MA: Belknap Press of Harvard University Press, 1931–60.

Hegel, Georg Wilhelm. *The Logic of Hegel*. Translated by William Wallace. London: Oxford University Press, 1892.

———. *Philosophy of History*. Mineola, NY: Dover, 1956.

Heidegger, Martin. *Being and Time*. Translated by Joan Stambaugh. Albany: State University of New York Press, 2010.

Herder, Johan G. *Against Pure Reason*. Eugene, OR: Wipf & Stock, 2005.

Hersey, George L. *Falling in Love with Statues: Artificial Humans from Pygmalion to the Present*. Chicago: University of Chicago Press, 2009.

Hess, David J. *Spirits and Scientists: Ideology, Spiritism, and Brazilian Culture*. University Park: Pennsylvania State University Press, 1991.

Hirschkind, Charles. "Media, Mediation, Religion." *Social Anthropology* 19, no. 1 (2011): 90–97.

Hobbes, Thomas. *Hobbes's Leviathan*, Reprinted from the edition of 1651. Oxford: Clarendon, 1909.

———. *The English Works of Thomas Hobbes of Malmesbury*. Vol. 5, *The Questions*

Concerning Liberty, Necessity, and Chance. Edited by Sir William Molesworth. London: John Bohn, 1841.

Hoffman, E. T. A. *Nutcracker and Mouse King; and The Educated Cat*. New York: T. Fisher Unwin, 1892.

———. *Tales of Hoffman*. London: Penguin, 1982.

———. *Automata*. Lexington, KY: Objective Systems, 2006.

Holloway, Thomas H. "'A Healthy Terror': Police Repression of Capoeiras in Nineteenth-Century Rio de Janeiro." *Hispanic American Historical Review* 69, no. 4 (1989): 637–76.

———. *Policing Rio de Janeiro: Repression and Resistance in a 19th-Century City*. Stanford, CA: Stanford University Press, 1993.

Horn, Jason Gary. *Mark Twain and William James: Crafting a Free Self*. Columbia: University of Missouri Press, 1996.

Hull, Matthew. *A Government of Paper*. Berkeley and Los Angeles: University of California Press, 2012.

———. "Incorporations: Capitalism and Collective Life." Typescript, University of Michigan, Ann Arbor, 2018.

Hume, David. *Of Superstition and Enthusiasm*. 1741. http://infomotions.com/etexts/id/hume-of-738.

———. *Essays and Treatises on Several Subjects in Two Volumes*, vol. 1, *Essays, Moral, Political, and Literary*. London, 1784.

Hurston, Zora Neale. "Race Cannot Become Great until It Recognizes Its Talent." *Washington Tribune*, December 29, 1934.

Husserl, Edmund. *Cartesian Meditations*. Translated by Dorion Cairns. The Hague: M. Nijhoff, 1960.

Hustvedt, Asti. *Medical Muses: Hysteria in Nineteenth-Century Paris*. London: Bloomsbury, 2011.

Irvine, Judith T. "Shadow Conversations: The Indeterminacy of Participant Roles." In *Natural Histories of Discourse*, ed. Michael Silverstein and Greg Urban, 131–59. Chicago: University of Chicago Press, 1996.

Jackson, Kenneth David. *Machado de Assis: A Literary Life*. New Haven, CT: Yale University Press, 2015.

Jaguaribe, Beatriz, and Maurício Lissovsky. "The Visible and the Invisibles: Photography and Social Imaginaries in Brazil." *Public Culture* 21, no. 1 (2009): 175–209.

James, William. "Notes on Automatic Writing (1889)." In *Essays in Psychical Research*, 37–56. Cambridge, MA: Harvard University Press, 1986.

———. *The Principles of Psychology*. 2 vols. 1890. Cambridge, MA: Harvard University Press, 1981.

———. *The Varieties of Religious Experience*. New York: Modern Library, 1902.

———. "Person and Personality: From Johnson's Universal Cyclopaedia." In *Essays in Psychology*, 315–21. Cambridge, MA: Harvard University Press, 1983.

———. *Brazil through the Eyes of William James: Letters, Diaries, and Drawings, 1865–1866*. Edited by Maria Helena P. T. Machado. Translated by John M. Monteiro. Cambridge, MA: Harvard University Press, 2006.

Janet, Pierre. *L'automatisme psychologique*. Paris: Félix Alcan, 1889.

————. *Névroses et idées fixes*. Paris: Félix Alcan, 1898.

————. *The Mental State of Hystericals: A Study of Mental Stigmata and Mental Accidents*. Translated by C. R. Carson. New York: Putnam & Sons, 1901.

————. *The Major Symptoms of Hysteria; Fifteen Lectures Given in the Medical School of Harvard University*. 2nd ed. New York: Macmillan, 1920.

Jentsch, Ernst. "On the Psychology of the Uncanny." Translated by Roy Sellars. *Angelaki* 1 (1906): 7–16.

Johnson, Paul Christopher. *Diaspora Conversions: Black Carib Religion and the Recovery of Africa*. Berkeley and Los Angeles: University of California Press, 2007.

————. "Objects of Possession: Spirits, Photography and the Entangled Arts of Appearance." In *Sensational Religion: Sense and Contention in Material Practice*, ed. Sally Promey, 25–46. New Haven, CT: Yale University Press, 2014.

————. "Syncretism and Hybridisation." In *Oxford Handbook of the Study of Religion*, ed. Steven Engler and Michael Stausberg, 754–72. New York: Oxford University Press, 2016.

Johnson, Walter. "On Agency." *Journal of Social History* 37, no. 1 (2003): 113–24.

Jones, Jim. "Q042 Transcript, FBI Transcription." November 18, 1978. Alternative Considerations of Jonestown & Peoples Temple. https://jonestown.sdsu.edu/?page_id=29081.

Jouin, François. "Une visite a l'asile de Pédro II." *Annales médico-psychologiques* 3 (1880): 237–49.

Kane, Paula M. *Sister Thorn and Catholic Mysticism in Modern America*. Chapel Hill: University of North Carolina Press, 2013.

Kang, Minsoo. *Sublime Dreams of Living Machines: The Automaton in the European Imagination*. Cambridge, MA: Harvard University Press, 2011.

Kant, Immanuel. *Dreams of a Spirit Seer*. 1766. West Chester, PA: Swedenborg Foundation, 2002.

————. *Religion within the Limits of Reason Alone*. 1791. New York: Harper & Row, 1960.

Karasch, Mary. "Anastácia and the Slave Women of Rio de Janeiro." In *Africans in Bondage*, ed. Paul Lovejoy, 29–105. Madison: University of Wisconsin Press, 1986.

Kardec, Allan. 1868. *Genesis: The Miracles and the Predictions according to Spiritism*. New York: Spiritist Alliance, 2003.

————. *Le livre des esprits*. 6th ed. Paris: Didier, 1869.

————. *The Spirits' Book*. New York: Cosimo, 1996.

Keane, Webb. "Sincerity, 'Modernity,' and the Protestants." *Cultural Anthropology* 17, no. 1 (2002): 65–92.

————. *Christian Moderns*. Berkeley and Los Angeles: University of California Press, 2007.

————. "The Evidence of the Senses and the Materiality of Religion." *Journal of the Royal Anthropological Institute* 14 (2008): 110–27.

———. "On Spirit Writing: Materialities of Language and the Religious Work of Transduction." *Journal of the Royal Anthropological Institute* 19 (2012): 1–17.

Kellaway, Kate. "Hilma af Klint: A Painter Possessed." *The Guardian*, February 26, 2016. https://www.theguardian.com/artanddesign/2016/feb/21/hilma-af-klint-occult-spiritualism-abstract-serpentine-gallery.

Keller, Mary. *The Hammer and the Flute: Women, Power, and Spirit Possession.* Baltimore: Johns Hopkins University Press, 2002.

Khan, Aisha. "Good to Think? Creolization, Optimism, and Agency." *Current Anthropology* 48, no. 5 (2007): 653–73.

King, Elizabeth. "Perpetual Devotion: A Sixteenth-Century Machine That Prays." In *Genesis Redux: Essays in the History and Philosophy of Artificial Life*, ed. Jessica Riskin, 263–90. Chicago: University of Chicago Press, 2007.

King, Helen. "Once upon a Text: Hysteria from Hippocrates." In *Hysteria beyond Freud*, by Sander L. Gilman, Helen King, Roy Porter, G. S. Rousseau, and Elaine Showalter, 3–90. Berkeley and Los Angeles: University of California Press, 1993.

King, Richard. *Orientalism and Religion: Post-Colonial Theory, India and "The Mystic East."* London: Routledge, 1999.

Kohn, Eduardo. *How Forests Think: Toward an Anthropology beyond the Human.* Berkeley and Los Angeles: University of California Press, 2013.

Kopytoff, Igor. "Slavery." *Annual Review of Anthropology* 11, no. 1 (1982): 207–30.

Kopytoff, Igor, and Suzanne Miers. "African 'Slavery' as an Institution of Marginality." In *Slavery in Africa: Historical and Anthropological Perspectives*, ed. Suzanne Miers and Igor Kopytoff, 3–84. Madison: University of Wisconsin Press, 1977.

Kramer, Fritz. *The Red Fez: Art and Spirit Possession in Africa.* London: Verso, 1987.

Lacan, Jacques. "The Mirror Stage as Formative of the I Function as Revealed in Psychoanalytic Experience." In *Écrits: The First Complete Edition in English*, trans. Bruce Fink, 75–81. New York: Norton, 2006.

———. *The Four Fundamental Concepts of Psycho-Analysis.* 1973. Translated by Alan Sheridan. London: Routledge, 2018.

Ladurie, Emmanuel Le Roy. *Montaillou: Village occitan de 1294 à 1324.* Paris: Gallimard, 1975.

Lambek, Michael. "The Sakalava Poiesis of History: Realizing the Past through Spirit Possession in Madagascar." *American Ethnologist* 25, no. 2 (1998): 106–27.

———. *The Weight of the Past: Living with History in Mahajanga, Madagascar.* New York: Palgrave Macmillan, 2002.

La Mettrie, Julien Offray de. *L'homme machine.* Leiden: Elie Luzac, 1748.

Landes, Ruth. *City of Women.* New York: Macmillan, 1947.

Lane Anne W., and Harriet Blaine Beale. *To Walk with God: An Experience in Automatic Writing.* New York: Dodd, Mead, 1920.

Latour, Bruno. *Science in Action.* Cambridge, MA: Harvard University Press, 1987.

———. *We Have Never Been Modern.* 1991. Translated by Catherine Porter. Cambridge, MA: Harvard University Press, 1993.

———. *Pandora's Hope: Essays on the Reality of Science Studies.* Cambridge, MA: Harvard University Press, 1999.

———. *On the Modern Cult of the Factish Gods.* Durham, NC: Duke University Press, 2010.

———. *An Inquiry into the Modes of Existence.* Cambridge, MA: Harvard University Press, 2013.

Lavelle, Patricia. *O espelho distorcido: Imagens do individuo no Brasil oitocentista.* Belo Horizonte: UFMG, 2003.

Leacock, Seth, and Ruth Leacock. *Spirits of the Deep: A Study of an Afro-Brazilian Cult.* Garden City, NY: Anchor, 1975.

Leal, Cláudio Murilo. *O círculo virtuoso: A poesia de Machado de Assis.* Rio de Janeiro: Biblioteca Nacional, 2008.

Le Bon, Gustave. *Les monuments de l'Inde.* Paris: Firmin-Didot, 1893.

———. *Psychologie des foules.* Paris: Félix Alcan, 1895.

———. *The Crowd: A Study of the Popular Mind.* New York: Macmillan, 1897.

Le Fanu, Sheridan. "Green Tea." In *Through a Glass Darkly* (3 vols.), 1:1–95. London: R. Bentley & Sons, 1872.

Legendre, Pierre. *Law and the Unconscious.* Edited by Peter Goodrich. Translated by Peter Goodrich with Alain Pottage and Anton Schütz. London: Macmillan, 1997.

Leibniz, Gottfried. *New Essays on Human Understanding.* 1704. Translated and edited by Peter Remnant and Jonathan Bennett. Cambridge: Cambridge University Press, 1996.

———. *Theodicy: Essays on the Goodness of God, the Freedom of Man, and the Origin of Evil.* Edited with an introduction by Austin M. Farrer. Translated by E. M. Huggard. Peru, IL: Open Court, 1985.

Leiris, Michel. *L'Afrique fantôme.* 1934. Paris: Gallimard, 1981.

———. *La possession et ses aspects théâtraux chez les Éthiopiens de Gondar.* Paris: Librairie Plon, 1958.

Leithauser, Brad. "The Space of One Breath." *New Yorker*, March 9, 1987, 14–73.

Léry, Jean de. *History of a Voyage to the Land of Brazil.* Translated by Janet Whatley. Berkeley and Los Angeles: University of California Press, 1993.

Lesser, Jeffrey. "'Jews Are Turks Who Sell on Credit': Elite Images of Arabs and Jews in Brazil." *Immigrants and Minorities* 16, nos. 1–2 (1997): 38–56.

———. *Negotiating National Identity: Immigrants, Minorities, and the Struggle for Ethnicity in Brazil.* Durham, NC: Duke University Press, 1999.

Levine, Robert. *Images of History: Nineteenth and Early Twentieth Century Latin American Photographs as Documents.* Durham, NC: Duke University Press, 1989.

Levingston, Steven. *Little Demon in the City of Light.* New York: Anchor, 2014.

Lévi-Strauss, Claude. *Tristes Tropiques.* London: Penguin, 1974.

———. *Conversations with Claude Lévi-Strauss.* Edited by Georges Charbonnier.

Translated by John Weightman and Doreen Weightman. London: Jonathan Cape, 1969.

Lewis, I. M. *Ecstatic Religion*. Harmondsworth: Penguin, 1971.

Leyland, Ralph Watts. *Round the World in 124 Days*. Liverpool: Gilbert G. Walmsley, 1880.

Lima Barreto, Afonso Henriques de. *Diário do hospício e o cemitério dos vivos*. Rio de Janeiro: Biblioteca Carioca, 1993.

Lindau, Paul. *Der Abend*. Berlin, 1896.

Lissovsky, Maurício. "Guia prático das fotografias sem pressa." In *Retratos modernos*, ed. Cláudia Beatriz Heynemann and Maria do Carmo Teixeira Rainho. Rio de Janeiro: Arquivo Nacional, 2005.

Locke, John. *An Essay Concerning Human Understanding*. 1689. 4th ed. 1700. New York: Dover, 1975.

———. *The Works of John Locke, Esq*. Vol. 1, bk. 2, *An Essay concerning Human Understanding*. London: A. Churchill, A. Manship, 1722.

Lombroso, Cesare. *After Death—What? Spiritistic Phenomena and Their Interpretation*. Translated by William Sloane Kennedy. Boston: Small, Maynard, 1909.

Luckhurst, Roger. *The Invention of Telepathy*. Oxford: Oxford University Press, 2002.

Luhrmann, Tanya M. "How Do You Learn to Know That It Is God Who Speaks?" In *Learning Religion: Anthropological Approaches*, ed. David Berliner and Ramon Sarró, 83–102. New York: Berghahn, 2007.

Macmillan, Malcolm. *Freud Evaluated*. Cambridge, MA: MIT Press, 1997.

Maggie, Yvonne. *Medo do feitiço: Relações entre magia e poder no Brasil*. Rio de Janeiro: Arquivo Nacional, 1992.

Mahmood, Saba. *The Politics of Piety: The Islamic Revival and the Feminist Subject*. Princeton, NJ: Princeton University Press, 2005.

Maisano, Scott. "Descartes avec Milton: The Automata in the Garden." In *The Automaton in English Renaissance Literature*, ed. Wendy Beth Hyman, 21–44. London: Routledge, 2011.

Maldonado, Elaine Cristina. *Machado de Assis e o espiritismo*. Jundiaí: Paco Editorial, 2015.

Malheiro, Perdigão. *A escravidão no Brasil: Ensaio historico-juridico-social*. 3 vols. Rio de Janeiro, 1866.

Mandeville, Sir John. *The Travels of Sir John Mandeville*. London: Penguin, 1983.

Markham, John. *Selections from the Correspondence of Admiral John Markham*. Edited by Sir Clements Markham. London: Navy Records Society, 1904.

Marriott, McKim. *Hindu Transactions: Diversity without Dualism*. Chicago: University of Chicago Press, 1976.

Marshall, Eugene. *The Spiritual Automaton: Spinoza's Science of the Mind*. Oxford: Oxford University Press, 2013.

Marx, Karl. *Capital*. Vol. 1. London: Charles H. Kerr, 1912.

Mateescu, Oana. "Serial Anachronism: Re-Assembling Romanian Forest Commons." PhD diss., University of Michigan, 2017.

Mattos, Débora Michels. "Saúde e escravidão na Ilha de Santa Catarina, 1850–1888." PhD diss., Universidade de São Paulo, 2015.

Mauad, Ana Maria. "Imagem e auto-imagem do Segundo Reinado." In *História da vida privada no Brasil*, vol. 2, *Império: A corte e a modernidade nacional*, ed. Luiz Felipe de Alencastro and Fernando A. Novais, 181–232. São Paulo: Editora Schwarcz, 1997.

Maupassant, Guy de. "Une femme." *Gil Blas*, August 16, 1882, 355.

Mauss, Marcel. "The Techniques of the Body" (1935). Translated by Ben Brewster. *Economy and Society* 2 (1973) 70–88.

———. *A General Theory of Magic*. Translated by Robert Brain. London: Routledge, 2005.

Mayer, Andreas. *Sites of the Unconscious: Hypnosis and the Emergence of the Psychoanalytic Setting*. Chicago: University of Chicago Press, 2013.

Mayor, Adrienne. *Gods and Robots: Myths, Machines, and Ancient Dreams of Technology*. Princeton, NJ: Princeton University Press, 2018.

Mazzoni, Cristina. *Saint Hysteria: Neurosis, Mysticism, and Gender in European Culture*. Ithaca, NY: Cornell University Press, 1996.

McAuliffe, Mary. *Twilight of the Belle Epoque*. Lanham, MD: Rowman & Littlefield, 2014.

McDaniel, June. *The Madness of the Saints: Ecstatic Religion in Bengal*. Chicago: University of Chicago Press, 1989.

McDannell, Colleen. *Material Christianity: Religion and Popular Culture in America*. New Haven, CT: Yale University Press, 1995.

Meige, Henri. *Les possédées noires*. Paris: Imprimerie Schiller, 1894.

Meng, Michael. "On Authoritarianism." *Comparative Studies in Society and History* 59, no. 4 (2017): 1008–20.

Meyer, Birgit. "'There is a spirit in that image': Mass-Produced Jesus Pictures and Protestant-Pentecostal Animation in Ghana." *Comparative Studies in Society and History* 52, no. 1 (2010): 100–130.

———. "Mediation and Immediacy: Sensational Forms, Semiotic Ideologies and the Question of the Medium." *Social Anthropology* 19, no. 1 (2011): 23–39.

Meyer, Steven. *Irresistible Dictation: Gertrude Stein and the Correlations of Writing and Science*. Stanford, CA: Stanford University Press, 2003.

Micale, Mark S. *Approaching Hysteria: Disease and Its Interpretations*. Princeton, NJ: Princeton University Press, 1995.

———. *Hysterical Men: The Hidden History of Male Nervous Illness*. Cambridge, MA: Harvard University Press, 2008.

Miller, Daniel, ed. *Materiality*. Durham, NC: Duke University Press, 2005.

Mintz, Sydney W. *Sweetness and Power: The Place of Sugar in Modern History*. New York: Penguin, 1985.

Mitchell, W. J. T. *What Do Pictures Want? The Lives and Loves of Images*. Chicago: University of Chicago Press, 2005.

Mittermaier, Amira. *Dreams That Matter: Egyptian Landscapes of the Imagination*. Berkeley and Los Angeles: University of California Press, 2011.

Modern, John Lardas. *Secularism in Antebellum America*. Chicago: University of Chicago Press, 2011.

Mol, Annemarie. *The Body Multiple: Ontology in Medical Practice*. Durham, NC: Duke University Press, 2002.

Morais, Frederico. *Arthur Bispo do Rosário: Arte além da loucura*. Rio de Janeiro: NAU Editora, 2013.

Morgan, David. *Visual Piety: A History and Theory of Popular Religious Images*. Chicago: University of Chicago Press, 1999.

———. *The Sacred Gaze: Religious Visual Culture in Theory and Practice*. Berkeley and Los Angeles: University of California Press, 2005.

Mori, Masahiro. "The Uncanny Valley." Translated by K. F. MacDorman and Norri Kageki. *IEEE: Robotics and Automation* 19, no. 2 (2012): 98–100.

Mosse, David. "Possession and Confession: Affliction and Sacred Power in Colonial and Contemporary South India." In *The Anthropology of Christianity*, ed. Fenella Cannell, 99–133. Durham, NC: Duke University Press, 2006.

Mota, Lourenço Dantas. *Introdução ao Brasil: Um banquete no trópico*. Rio de Janeiro: Editora SENAC, 1999.

Mott, Luiz. *Rosa Egipcíaca: Uma santa africana no Brasil*. Rio de Janeiro: Editora Bertrand Brasil, 1993.

Mussawir, Edward. *Jurisdiction in Deleuze: The Expression and Representation of Law*. Oxford: Taylor & Francis, 2011.

Nina Rodrigues, Raymundo. *L'animisme fétichiste des nègres de Bahia*. Bahia: Reis, 1900.

———. *O animismo fetichista dos negros bahianos*. Rio de Janeiro: Civilização Brasileira, 1935.

———. *O animismo fetichista dos negros baianos*. Rio de Janeiro: Fundação Biblioteca Nacional, 2006.

Obarrio, Juan. *The Spirit of the Laws in Mozambique*. Chicago: University of Chicago Press, 2014.

O'Brien, Cyrus. "Faith in Imprisonment: Religion and the Development of Mass Incarceration in Florida." PhD diss., University of Michigan, 2018.

O'Flaherty, Wendy Doniger. *Siva: The Erotic Ascetic*. Oxford: Oxford University Press, 1981.

Opipari, Carmen, and Sylvie Timbert, dirs. *Barbara and Her Friends in Candombléland*. London: Royal Anthropological Institute, 1997.

Orsi, Robert A. *History and Presence*. Cambridge, MA: Belknap Press of Harvard University Press, 2016.

Ortiz, Fernando. *Los negros brujos*. 1906. Miami: Ediciones Universal, 1973.

Otto, Rudolf. *The Idea of the Holy*. 1917. New York: Oxford University Press, 1958.

———. *Das Heilige: Über das Irrationale in der Idee des Göttlichen und sein Verhältnis zum Rationalen*. 1917. Munich: Beck, 2014.

Ouliér, Marthe. *Jean Charcot*. Paris: Gallimard, 1937.

Pailleron, Marie-Louise. *Le paradis perdu: Souvenirs d'enfance*. Paris: Éditions Albin Michel, 1947.

Paiva, Andréa Lúcia da Silva de. "Quando os 'objetos' se tornam 'santos': Devoção e patrimônio em uma igreja no centro do Rio de Janeiro." *Textos escolhidos de cultura e arte populares* 11, no. 1 (2014): 53–70.

Palmié, Stephan. *Wizards and Scientists: Explorations in Afro-Cuban Modernity and Tradition*. Durham, NC: Duke University Press, 2002.

———. *The Cooking of History: How Not to Study Afro-Cuban Religion*. Chicago: University of Chicago Press, 2013.

———. "Historicist Knowledge and Its Conditions of Impossibility." In *The Social Life of Spirits*, ed. Diana Espirito Santo and Ruy Blanes, 218–40. Chicago: University of Chicago Press, 2013.

———. "The Ejamba of North Fairmount Avenue, the Wizard of Menlo Park, and the Dialectics of Ensoniment: An Episode in the History of an Acoustic Mask." In *Spirited Things: The Work of "Possession" in Afro-Atlantic Religions*, ed. Paul Christopher Johnson, 47–78. Chicago: University of Chicago Press, 2014.

———. "When Is a Thing? Transduction and Immediacy in Afro-Cuban Ritual; or, ANT in Matanzas, Cuba, Summer of 1948." *Comparative Studies in Society and History* 60, no. 4 (2018): 786–809.

Parés, Luis Nicolau. *The Formation of Candomblé: Vodun History and Ritual in Brazil*. Translated by Richard Vernon. Chapel Hill: University of North Carolina Press, 2013.

Parsons, Talcott. "An Analytical Approach to the Theory of Social Stratification." *American Journal of Sociology* 45, no. 6 (1940): 841–62.

———. *The Social System*. Glencoe, IL: Free Press, 1951.

———. "A Revised Analytical Approach to the Theory of Social Stratification." In *Class, Status and Power*, ed. Reinhard Bendix and Seymour Martin Lipset, 92–128. Glencoe, IL: Free Press, 1953.

———. *Working Papers in the Theory of Action*. Edited by Robert F. Bales and Edward A. Shils. New York: Free Press, 1953.

Pascal, Blaise. *Pensées*. Translated by W. F. Trotter. Mineola, NY: Dover, 2003.

Patterson, Orlando. *Slavery and Social Death*. Cambridge, MA: Harvard University Press, 1982.

Perkins, Franklin. *Leibniz: A Guide for the Perplexed*. London: Bloomsbury, 2007.

Pfeifer, Ida. *A Lady's Travels round the World*. Translated by W. Hazlitt. New York: G. Routledge, 1852.

Philippon, Jacques, and Jacques Poirier. *Joseph Babinski: A Biography*. New York: Oxford University Press, 2009.

Pinel, Philippe. *A Treatise on Insanity*. 1801. Translated by D. D. Davis. Sheffield: W. Todd, 1806.

Pinho, Patrícia. *Mama Africa: Reinventing Blackness in Bahia*. Durham, NC: Duke University Press, 2010.

Pinney, Christopher. "The Parallel Histories of Anthropology and Photography." In *Anthropology and Photography*, ed. Elizabeth Edwards, 74–95. London: Royal Anthropological Institute, 1992.

———. *Photos of the Gods: The Printed Image and Political Struggle in India*. London: Reaktion, 2004.

Plotkin, Mariano Ben. *Freud in the Pampas*. Stanford, CA: Stanford University Press, 2001.

Poe, Edgar Allan. "Maelzel's Chess-Player" (1836). In *The Complete Works of Edgar Allan Poe*, 10:138–74. Akron, OH: Werner, 1908.

Price, Richard. *Travels with Tooy: History, Memory and the African American Imagination*. Chicago: University of Chicago Press, 2007.

Priore, Mary del. *Condessa do Barral: A paixão do imperador*. Rio de Janeiro: Editora Objetiva, 2008.

Promey, Sally, ed. *Sensational Religion: Sensory Cultures in Material Practice*. New Haven, CT: Yale University Press, 2014.

Raeders, Georges. *Le comte de Gobineau au Brésil*. Paris: Fernand Sorlot, 1934.

———. *Dom Pedro II e os sábios franceses*. Rio de Janeiro: Atlantica Editora, 1944.

Rego, Enylton de Sá. Preface to *The Posthumous Memoirs of Brás Cuba*, by Machado de Assis, trans. Gregory Rabbassa, xi–xx. Oxford: Oxford University Press, 1997.

Reilly, Kara. *Automatons and Mimesis on the Stage of Theatre History*. New York: Palgrave Macmillan, 2011.

Reis, João José. *Domingos Sodré, um sacerdote africano: Escravidão, liberdade e Candomblé na Bahia do século XIX*. São Paulo: Companhia das Letras, 2008.

Rey, Philippe-Marius. "L'hospice Pedro II et les aliénés au Brésil." *Annales médico-psychologiques* 98 (1875): 75–98.

Rhodes, Lorna A. *Total Confinement: Madness and Reason in the Maximum Security Prison*. Berkeley and Los Angeles: University of California Press, 2004.

Richman, Karen. "The Vodou State and the Protestant Nation: Haiti in the Long Twentieth Century." In *Obeah and Other Powers: The Politics of Caribbean Religion and Healing*, ed. Diana Paton and Maarit Forde, 268–87. Durham, NC: Duke University Press, 2012.

Ricoeur, Paul. *Oneself as Another*. Translated by Kathleen Blamey. Chicago: University of Chicago Press, 1994.

Riesebrodt, Martin. *Pious Passion: The Emergence of Modern Fundamentalism in the United States and Iran*. Translated by Don Reneau. Berkeley and Los Angeles: University of California Press, 1993.

Rio, João do. *Religions in Rio*. Translated by Anna Lessa Schmidt. Hanover, CT: New London Librarian, 2015.

Riskin, Jessica. "Introduction: The Sistine Gap." In *Genesis Redux: Essays in the History and Philosophy of Artificial Life*, ed. Jessica Riskin, 1–35. Chicago: University of Chicago Press, 2007.

Robbins, Louise E. *Elephant Slaves and Pampered Parrots: Exotic Animals in Eighteenth-Century Paris*. Baltimore: Johns Hopkins University Press, 2002.

Rocha, Cristina. *Zen in Brazil: The Quest for Cosmopolitan Modernity*. Honolulu: University of Hawaii Press, 2006.

Rouane, Serigo Paulo, ed. *Correspondência de Machado de Assis*. Vol. 3, *1890–1900*. Rio de Janeiro: Biblioteca da Academica Brasileira de Letras, 2011.

Rousseau, G. S., and Roy Porter. Introduction to *Hysteria beyond Freud*, by Sander L. Gilman, Helen King, Roy Porter, G. S. Rousseau, and Elaine

Showalter, vii–xxiv. Berkeley and Los Angeles: University of California Press, 1993.

Rousseau, Pascal. "Premonitory Abstraction: Mediumism, Automatic Writing, and Anticipation in the Work of Hilma af Klint." In *Hilma af Klint: A Pioneer of Abstraction, Exhibition Catalogue*, ed. Iris Müller Westermann with Jo Widoff. eds., 161–75. Stockholm: Moderna Museet, 2013.

Roxo, Henrique de Brito Belford. *Manual de psiquiatria*. 1921. Rio de Janeiro: Françisco Alves, 1938.

Royle, Nicholas. *The Uncanny*. Manchester: Manchester University Press, 2003.

Sá, Marcos Moraes de. *A Mansão Figner: O eclectismo e a casa burguesa no início do século XX*. Rio de Janeiro: Senac, 2002.

Sadoff, Dianne F. *Sciences of the Flesh: Representing Body and Subject in Psychoanalysis*. Stanford, CA: Stanford University Press, 1998.

Safady, Jamil. *O café e o mascate*. São Paulo: Editora Safady, 1973.

Sahlins, Marshall. *Apologies to Thucydides: Understanding History as Culture and Vice Versa*. Chicago: University of Chicago Press, 2004.

Sampaio, Gabriela dos Reis. *Juca Rosa: Um pai-de-santo na Corte Imperial*. Rio de Janeiro: Prêmio Arquivo Nacional, 2007.

Sansi, Roger. *Fetishes and Monuments: Afro-Brazilian Art and Culture in the 20th Century*. London: Berghahn, 2007.

———. "Images and Persons in Candomblé." *Material Religion* 7, no. 3 (2011): 374–93.

Santner, Eric. *The Weight of All Flesh: On the Subject Matter of Political Economy*. Chicago: University of Chicago Press, 2015.

Santos, Ricardo. "Escrava Anastácia." In *Encyclopedia of the African Diaspora*, 85–86. Denver, CO: ABC-CLIO, 2008.

Saraiva, Clara. "Afro-Brazilian Religions in Portugal: Bruxos, Priests and Pais de Santo." *Etnográfica* 14, no. 2 (2010): 265–88.

Savill, Thomas D. *Lectures on Hysteria*. New York: William Wood; London: Henry Glaishner, 1909.

Schaefer, Donovan O. *Religious Affects: Animality, Evolution, and Power*. Durham, NC: Duke University Press, 2015.

Schelling, F. W. J. *Historical-Critical Introduction to the Philosophy of Mythology*. Translated by Mason Richey and Markus Zisselsberger. Albany: State University of New York Press, 2007.

Schielke, Samuli. *Egypt in the Future Tense: Hope, Frustration and Ambivalence Before and After 2011*. Bloomington: Indiana University Press, 2015.

Schleiermacher, Friedrich. *On Religion: Speeches to Its Cultured Despisers*. Cambridge: Cambridge University Press, 1996.

Schmalz, Mathew. "The Silent Body of Audrey Santo." *History of Religions* 42, no. 2 (2002): 116–42.

Scholem, Gershom Gerhard. *On the Kabbalah and Its Symbolism*. London: Routledge, 1965.

Schwarcz, Lilia Moritz. "O homen da ficha antropométrica e do uniforme pandemônio: Lima Barreto e a internação de 1914." *Sociologia e antropologia* 1, no. 1 (2011): 119–49.

Schwarz, Roberto. *Ao vencedor as batatas*. São Paulo: Editora 34, 1977.

———. *A Master on the Periphery of Capitalism*. Translated by John Gledson. Durham, NC: Duke University Press, 2001.

Segal, Jerome M. *Agency and Alienation: A Theory of Human Presence*. London: Rowan & Littlefield, 1991.

Segato, Rita Laura. *Santos e daimones: O politeísmo afro-brasileiro e a tradição arquetipal*. Brasília: Editora Universidade de Brasília, 1995.

Sepúlveda, Juan Ginés de. "Democrates Alter; or, On the Just Causes for War against the Indians." 1547. http://www.thelatinlibrary.com/imperialism/readings/sepulveda.html.

Sewell, William H. "A Theory of Structure: Duality, Agency, and Transformation." *American Journal of Sociology* 98, no. 1 (1992): 1–29.

Shaw, Rosalind. *Memories of the Slave Trade: Ritual and the Historical Imagination in Sierra Leone*. Chicago: University of Chicago Press, 2002.

Shelley, Mary. *Frankenstein*. Mineola, NY: Dover, 1994.

Sheriff, Robin E. "The Muzzled Saint: Racism, Cultural Censorship and Religion in Urban Brazil." In *Silence: The Currency of Power*, ed. Maria-Luisa Achino-Loeb, 113–40. New York: Berghahn, 1996.

Shorter, Edward. *A History of Psychiatry*. New York: John Wiley & Sons, 1997.

Showalter, Elaine. *The Female Malady: Women, Madness, and English Culture, 1830–1980*. New York: Pantheon, 1985.

———. "Hysteria, Feminism, and Gender." In *Hysteria beyond Freud*, by Sander L. Gilman, Helen King, Roy Porter, G. S. Rousseau, and Elaine Showalter, 286–344. Berkeley and Los Angeles: University of California Press, 1993.

Sighart, Joachim. *Albert the Great: His Life and Scholastic Labours from Original Documents*. Translated by T. A. Dixon. London: R. Washbourne, 1876.

Simmel, Georg. *Die Religion*. Frankfurt a.M.: Literarische Anstalt, 1906.

———. *Sociology of Religion*. Translated by Curt Rosenthal. New York: Philosophical Library, 1959.

———. *Essays on Religion*. New Haven, CT: Yale University Press, 1997.

Souques, Alexandre-Achille, and Henri Meige. "Jean-Martin Charcot." *Les biographies médicales* 13, no. 5 (1939): 337–52.

Skidmore, Thomas E. *Black into White: Race and Nationality in Brazilian Thought*. Durham, NC: Duke University Press 1993.

Smith, Adam. *An Inquiry into the Nature and Causes of the Wealth of Nations*. Vol. 2. Basil: J. J. Tourneisen & J. Legrand, 1791.

Smith, William Robertson. *Lectures on the Religion of the Semites*. Edinburgh: A. & C. Black, 1889.

Soltanovich, Renata. *Direitos autorais e a tutel de urgência na proteção da obra psicografada*. São Paulo: Leud, 2012.

Sombart, Werner. *Der moderne Kapitalismus*. Vol. 2. Munich, 1902.

Sontag, Susan. *On Photography*. New York: Farrar, Strauss & Giroux, 1977.

Spencer, Herbert. *Social Statics; or, The Conditions Essential to Happiness Specified, and the First of Them Developed*. London: John Chapman, 1851.

———. *First Principles*. London: Williams & Norgate, 1863.

Sperber, Dan. *Explaining Culture: A Naturalistic Approach*. Oxford: Wiley-Blackwell, 1996.

Spinoza, Benedict de. *Theological-Political Treatise*. 1670. Edited by Jonathan Israel. New York: Cambridge University Press, 2007.

Spivak, Gayatri. "Subaltern Talk: Interview With the Editors." In *The Spivak Reader*, ed. Donna Landry and Gerald Maclean, 287–308. New York: Routledge, 1996.

Staden, Hans. *Hans Staden's True History: An Account of Cannibal Captivity in Brazil*. Translated by Neil L. Whitehead and Michael Harbsmeier. Durham, NC: Duke University Press, 2008.

Stein, Gertrude. "Cultivated Motor Automatism: A Study of Character in Relation to Attention." *Psychological Review* 5 (1898): 295–306.

Stepan, Nancy Leys. "Portraits of a Possible Nation: Photographing Medicine in Brazil." *Bulletin of the History of Medicine* 68, no. 1 (1994): 136–49

Stevens, Thomas. *Around the World on a Bicycle*. New York: Charles Scribner's Sons, 1889.

Stoller, Paul. *Embodying Colonial Memories: Spirit Possession, Power, and the Hauka in West Africa*. New York: Routledge, 1995.

Stolow, Jeremy. "Techno-Religious Imaginaries: On the Spiritual Telegraph and the Atlantic World of the Nineteenth Century." *Globalization Working Papers* 6, no. 1 (2006): 1–32.

———, ed. *Deus in Machina: Religion, Technology, and the Things in Between*. New York: Fordham University Press, 2013.

Stowe, Harriet Beecher. *Uncle Tom's Cabin*. 1852. New York: Race Point, 2016.

Strathern, Marilyn. *The Gender of the Gift*. Berkeley and Los Angeles: University of California Press, 1988.

Suchman, Lucy A. *Human-Machine Reconfigurations: Plans and Situated Actions*. 2nd ed. Cambridge: Cambridge University Press, 2007.

Süssekind, Flora. *Cinematograph of Words: Literature, Technique, and Modernization in Brazil*. Translated by Paulo Henriques Britto. Stanford, CA: Stanford University Press, 1997.

Sussman, Mark. "Performing the Intelligent Machine: Deception and Enchantment in the Life of the Automaton Chess Player." In *Puppets, Masks, and Performing Objects*, ed. John Bell, 71–86. Cambridge, MA: MIT Press, 2001.

Sweet, James Hoke. *Recreating Africa: Culture, Kinship, and Religion in the African-Portuguese World, 1441–1770*. Chapel Hill: University of North Carolina Press, 2003.

Taithe, Bernard. *Defeated Flesh: Welfare, Warfare, and the Making of Modern France*. Manchester: Manchester University Press, 2010.

Tambiah, Stanley Jeyaraja. *Magic, Science, Religion, and the Scope of Rationality*. Cambridge: Cambridge University Press, 1990.

Taussig, Michael. *Mimesis and Alterity: A Particular History of the Senses.* New York: Routledge, 1993.

Taves, Ann. "Religious Experience and the Divisible Self: William James (and Frederic Myers) as Theorist(s) of Religion." *Journal of the American Academy of Religion* 71/2 (2003): 303–26.

———. *Religious Experience Reconsidered: A Building-Block Approach to the Study of Religion and Other Special Things.* Princeton, NJ: Princeton University Press, 2009.

Taylor, Charles. *A Secular Age.* Cambridge, MA: Harvard University Press, 2007.

Temple, William. *Memoirs of What Past in Christendum, from the War Begun 1672 to the Peace Concluded 1679.* London: Chiswell, 1692.

Thoreau, Henry David. *Walden; or, Life in the Woods.* Vol. 1. Boston: Houghton, Mifflin, 1882.

Thuillier, Jean. *Monsieur Charcot de la Salpêtrière.* Paris: Robert Laffont, 1993.

Thwing, E. "The Involuntary Life." *Phrenological Journal and Science of Health* 80, no. 5 (May 1885): 307–8.

Timponi, Miguel. *Psicografia ante os tribunais: O caso de Humberto Campos.* Brasília: Federação Espirita Brasileira, 1959.

Tolstoy, Leo. *Anna Karenina.* Translated by Richard Pevear and Larissal Volokhonsky. London: Penguin, 2000.

———. *Anna Karenina.* New York: Dover, 2012.

Tourette, Gilles de la. *Traité clinique et thérapeutique de l'hystérie d'après l'enseignement de la Salpêtrière.* Paris: Plon, 1891.

Toussaint-Samon, Adèle. *A Parisian in Brazil.* 1883. Edited by June E. Hahner. Wilmington, DE: Scholarly Books, 2001.

Trouillot, Michel-Rolph. *Silencing the Past: Power and the Production of History.* Boston: Beacon, 1995.

Tucker, Robert C., ed. *The Marx and Engels Reader.* New York: Norton, 1978.

Tuke, Daniel Hack. *Sleep-Walking and Hypnotism.* London: J. & A. Churchill, 1884.

Twain, Mark. "Mental Telepathy?" (1891). In *The Bible according to Mark Twain: Writings on Heaven, Eden, and the Flood,* ed. Howard G. Baetzhold and Joseph B. McCullough, 203–12. Athens: University of Georgia Press, 1995.

———. "Mental Telepathy Again" (1895). In *The Writings of Mark Twain,* 22:131–49. New York: Harper & Bros., 1897.

———. *Mark Twain's Own Autobiography.* Madison: University of Wisconsin Press, 1990.

Tylor, Edmund B. *Primitive Culture: Researches into the Development of Mythology, Philosophy, Religion, Art, and Custom.* 2 vols. London: John Murray, 1871.

Urban, Hugh B. *Secrecy: The Adornment of Silence, the Vestment of Power.* Chicago: University of Chicago Press, in press.

Van de Port, Mattijs. *Ecstatic Encounters: Bahian Candomblé and the Quest for the Really Real.* Amsterdam: Amsterdam University Press, 2011.

Van Ginneken, Jaap. *Crowds, Psychology, and Politics*. New York: Cambridge University Press, 1992.

Vasconcelos, João. "Homeless Spirits: Modern Spiritualism, Psychical Research and the Anthropology of Religion in the Late Nineteenth and Early Twentieth Centuries." In *On the Margins of Religion*, ed. Frances Pine and João de Pina-Cabral, 13–38. New York: Berghahn, 2007.

Vasquez, Pedro Karp. *Dom Pedro II e a fotografia no Brasil*. Rio de Janeiro: Fundação Roberto Marinho, 1985.

Veith, Ilza. *Hysteria: The History of a Disease*. Chicago: University of Chicago Press, 1965.

Velho, Gilberto. "Unidade e fragmentação em sociedades complexas." In *Duas conferências*, ed. Gilberto Velho and Otávio Velho, 13–46. Rio de Janeiro: UFRJ Editora, 1992.

Veracini, Cecilia. "Nonhuman Primate Trade in the Age of Discoveries: European Importation and Its Consequences." In *Environmental History in the Making*, vol. 2, *Acting*, ed. Cristina Jonnaz de Melo, Estelita Vaz, and Lígia M. Costa Pinto, 147–72. Basel: Springer International, 2017.

Verger, Pierre. *Notas sobre o culto aos orixás e voduns*. São Paulo: Editora USP, 1998.

Verne, Jules. *Around the World in Eighty Days*. Translated by Frederick Paul Walter. Albany: State University of New York Press, 2013.

Waite, Arthur Edward. *Lives of Alchemystical Philosophers: Based on Materials Collected in 1815*. London: George Redway, 1888.

Wallace, Alfred Russell. *Perspectives in Psychical Research*. 3rd ed. 1896. New York: Arno, 1975.

———. *The World of Life*. New York: Moffat, Yard, 1911.

Walmsley, Peter. "Prince Maurice's Rational Parrot: Civil Discourse in Locke's *Essay*." *Eighteenth-Century Studies* 28, no. 4 (1995): 413–25.

Walusinski, Olivier. "The Girls of La Salpêtrière." *Frontiers of Neurology and Neuroscience* 35 (2014): 65–77.

Weber, Max. *Economy and Society: An Outline of Interpretive Sociology*. 1922. Edited by Guenther Roth and Claus Wittich. Berkeley and Los Angeles: University of California Press, 1978.

White, Hayden. *Metahistory: The Historical Imagination in Nineteenth-Century Europe*. Baltimore: Johns Hopkins University Press, 1975.

Whitehouse, Harvey. *Icons and Arguments: Divergent Modes of Religiosity*. New York: Oxford University Press, 2000.

Wilson, Eric G. *The Melancholy Android: On the Psychology of Sacred Machines*. Albany: State University of New York Press, 2006.

Windisch, Karl. "Letter I, Sept. 7, 1783." In *Inanimate Reason; or, A Circumstantial Account of That Astonishing Piece of Mechanism, M. de Kempelen's Chess-Player; Now Exhibiting at No. 8 Saville-Row, Burlington Gardens*, 11–16. London, 1784.

Wirtz, Kristina. *Ritual Discourse and Community in Cuban Santería: Speaking a Sacred World*. Gainesville: University Press of Florida, 2007.

Wittgenstein, Ludwig. *Philosophical Investigations*. Hoboken, NJ: John Wiley & Sons, 2010.

———. "Remarks on Frazer's *The Golden Bough*: Ludwig Wittgenstein." Translated by Stephan Palmié. In *The Mythology in Our Language*, trans. Stephan Palmié, ed. Giovanni da Col, 29–54. Chicago: HAU, 2018.

Wood, Gaby. *Living Dolls: A Magical History of the Quest for Mechanical Life*. London: Faber and Faber, 2002.

Wood, Marcus. "The Museu do Negro in Rio and the Cult of Anastácia as a New Model for the Memory of Slavery." *Representations*, no. 113 (2011): 111–49.

Xavier, Francisco Cândido. *Parnaso de Além Túmulo: Poesias mediumnicas psychographadas*. Rio de Janeiro: Livraria da Federação Espírita Brasileira, 1932.

Xavier, Francisco Cândido, and Maurício Garcez Henrique (spirit). *Lealdade*. São Paulo: Instituto de difusão espírita, 1982.

Xavier, Francisco Cândido, and Brother Jacob (spirit). *Voltei*. 1949. Rio de Janeiro: Federação Espírita Brasileira Editora, 2017.

Yates, Frances. *The Rosicrucian Enlightenment*. London: Routledge & Kegan Paul, 1972.

Yeh, Rihan. "Visas, Jokes, and Contraband: Citizenship and Sovereignty at the U.S.-Mexico Border." *Comparative Studies in Society and History* 59, no. 1 (2017): 154–82.

Zuboff, Shoshana. *The Age of Surveillance Capitalism: The Fight for a Human Future at the New Frontier of Power*. New York: Public Affairs, 2019.

Zubrzycki, Geneviève. *Beheading the Saint: Nationalism, Religion, and Secularism in Quebec*. Chicago: University of Chicago Press, 2016.

Index

www.ingramcontent.com/pod-product-compliance
Lightning Source LLC
Chambersburg PA
CBHW060026030426
42334CB00019B/2192